The
Illustrated
Encyclopedia of Crafts
and
How to Master Them

The
Illustrated
Encyclopedia of Crafts
and
How to Master Them

GRACE BERNE ROSE

Drawings by Marta Cone

1978
Doubleday & Company, Inc.
Garden City, New York

Library of Congress Cataloging in Publication Data

Rose, Grace Berne.
The illustrated encyclopedia of crafts and how to
master them.

Includes index.
1. Handicraft—Dictionaries.   I. Title.
TT9.R68   702′.8
ISBN 0-385-02784-2
Library of Congress Catalog Card Number 74–12709

To Arthur, David, and Eric, who are ever helpful

and

To my brother, Eric Lennard Berne,

who aided me with a paradigm early in life

and

To our parents, who were very wise

Acknowledgments

To Mr. Nathan Cummings, whose exceptional art collection was so graciously made available to me.

To the Trustees of the British Museum, the Louvre, the Prado, the Vatican Museums, and the Tokyo National Museum, who responded so splendidly to my requests.

To Joan Silbert, who made countless sketches for me, and to Harumi Yoshizawa, who helped me to put the manuscript together.

To Robert Johnson, who, with utmost patience, shot and reshot innumerable *objets d'art* to achieve the best for every photograph.

To Thomas O'Conor Sloane III for his perspicacious editorial direction.

And above all to the many artists and craftspersons who over the years have so cheerfully shared with me their knowledge and their secrets.

My thanks.

GRACE BERNE ROSE

Contents

Halftone Illustrations

Preface

A small Moroccan child deftly and surely knotting an exquisite wool rug; an Israeli sabra collecting spent bullets and transforming them into tiny biblical figures, thus making silk purses out of sows' ears; a Puerto Rican boy on the beach in San Juan weaving an intricate hat from sea grasses, to be sold within the hour to a mainlander; a rock hound in Bavaria uncovering a magnificent streak of quartz with his little pick; in Russia, the children making papier-mâché animals; in Thailand, the women painting batik; in the market place in Mexico, the men blowing glass. In America's Middle West, I watched an aged Indian lady dig a chunk of black clay from the ground and form it into a perfect bowl with her bare hands, while her ancient husband held small turquoise beads between his toes and painstakingly drilled holes in them by rotating a long stick between his hands, forming prized *heishi* beads by simple friction.

In Japan, the incredibly thin waterleaves of handmade paper come out of the rice husks from the paddies; in Alaska, stone for the carvers is omnipresent; and alas, the world over, potters are dying of lead poisoning from holding their cigarettes in glaze-crusted fingers.

All artists are collectors. The actor collects motions and gestures; the poet collects words and images; the craftsman collects techniques and ideas. From North to South, from East to West, in many places, I have met and exchanged ideas with other craftsmen; even the barrier of language has been no deterrent. The dialogue of beautiful workmanship is everywhere, and the smile of recognition knows no bounds. I received much from those I observed, and I hoped that they would benefit as much from my experiences as I did from theirs.

All the fragments seen and heard in a lifetime are trifles in themselves. But stored away in the mind as a squirrel stores nuts, they have all come together in the writing of this book. Unfortunately I cannot, as I would like to, give credit to each and every teacher, colleague, and student who has added to my store of thoughts, but to each and every one I give my thanks for the time he spent with me, and for the interesting talks I have had the world over. My source for specific technical information has been encyclopedias in libraries, both public and private; I can offer no bibliography, because my sources have been universal. I have worked in every technique described here, sometimes with success, sometimes not, and I learned both the good and the bad from both the successes and the failures.

This book is about classic techniques. Everything that is made by hand is a craft, and over the ages these crafts have been practiced in the same manner to the same end: to produce a beautiful piece of work. It is intended to be a primer, to serve as an introduction to many crafts. It is for the beginner who would like to learn, for the professional who needs to learn, for the experienced craftsperson who desires to explore a different field, for the group leader, the teacher, the counselor.

Today, with new materials and new know-how, the work of the craftsperson is changing to keep up with modern inventions. But the old, timeworn methods are still the basis of every worthwhile endeavor, and while many books are being written on new techniques and new handling of materials, I offer this one so that the up-to-date young artisan can have a solid background for beginning work. Materials unheard of yesterday will be commonplace tomorrow, and as of today I have tried to include modern procedures. Primitive peoples turned their objects by hand, but eventually some bright soul invented the wheel, and today we have harnessed electricity to do the work. In the future—who knows what?

Modern materials require specific handling, and modern crafts sometimes seem to have no relation to the crafts learned in school. Don't be fooled: behind every abstract design is a solid foundation of basic knowledge, and without this foundation the new things could never have happened. Work done is work accomplished. Learn the basics well and they will stand you in good stead.

I suggest that in using this book you read a full chapter or section before buying materials or starting work. It is a book of alternatives and ideas, and sometimes you may find a process set forth later that looks more attractive to you than the one described earlier. For unfamiliar terms, consult the Glossary.

Have fun.

GRACE BERNE ROSE

Long Beach, California.

If I were to hear that the World

    was coming to an end to-morrow

I would still keep on planting

    my tulips today.

              Anon.

The
Illustrated
Encyclopedia of Crafts
and
How to Master Them

Tapa cloth. A crude but strong paper made by pounding bark into a thin sheet that is then decorated with natural vegetable dyes. Contemporary. South Sea Islands. Collection of the author.

1

Paper

PAPERMAKING

The making of paper has an interesting history. Back in ancient times in China it was made by pounding bark to a pulp, using sticks and stones. Then the Egyptians started using the long grass papyrus, and soon they were adding cotton and linen fibers to that to make it stronger and more durable. Then, until the early-nineteenth century, paper was made by hand out of fibers and rags, and about that time the first machine was invented to make paper in quantity, and soon the world was consuming so much paper that it ran out of rags. Much thought was given to the problem, and the remarkable discovery was made that paper could be commercially produced from bark and wood fibers! So the full circle was come, and today papers for magazines, newsprint, wrappings, and other purposes are made from the by-products of lumber mills and from forests planted expressly with pulpy trees for this purpose.

In the South Pacific, paper is still being made by hand by pulping the bark of trees. It is known as tapa cloth; we see it in wall hangings painted with archaic designs. Brushes made from the needles of the local pandanus pine are used. The tapa is pounded into thin, flat rectangles, and the dyes used by the artists are extracted from such exotic growing things as turmeric and the lipstick tree.

The best water-color papers are still made by hand. They are of 100 per cent rag content for strength to endure. A good water-color paper is one of the most durable materials known and will stay white and pristine for centuries. However, papers that are of interest to the craftsman can be made from other fibers mixed in with the rag.

Papermaking is not a mysterious craft when you realize the principle, which is really a very simple one: fibers are digested by boiling them in a caustic solution; the resultant pulp is beaten until smooth, then it is maneuvered into thin sheets, and when these are dry, lo! they are sheets of paper. Actually, a crude paper can be made by boiling cotton or linen rags in a solution of lye for several hours. This solution is strained through cheesecloth, and then the pulp is spread out on a board and pounded with a stick for ten to fifteen minutes. Then it is rolled as thin as possible with a rolling pin, and when it is dry it will be, if all goes well, a piece of handmade paper.

Let us set about making some paper, using a little more sophisticated procedure. The materials we will use in addition to cotton and linen scraps will be the fibers of all kinds of vegetation: grasses, woody plants, weeds, corn husks, stringy bean pods, hemp rope, cotton twine, dry twigs and leaves. (Figure 1.) Fleshy plants are not good, because the amount of fiber present in a succulent leaf does not warrant the amount of bulk it would demand: it takes a good deal of fibrous material to make one sheet of paper. Animal fibers such as wool and hair should never be used, because they will not digest to any good advantage. In the spring most plants are juicy, but in the fall they become tough and fibrous, like an old cabbage, and so autumn is a good time to make paper.

While you are working with the caustic solution, everything must be rustproof, so that the pulp will not become discolored. For that reason, the pot used for boiling the fibers should be stainless steel, copper, enamel, or perhaps Corning Ware. The sieve for washing the pulp can be made easily from copper screening by just bending it up to form a bowl shape; perhaps one of the new synthetic screenings would serve as well. A wooden spoon or dowel can be used for stirring, and rubber gloves should be worn to protect the hands. After the digested pulp is washed clean of all the caustic, any kind of container can be used, and the "sticks" for beating can be of wood, plastic, or hard rubber.

Figure 1

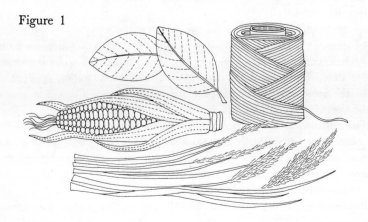

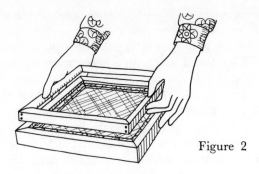

Figure 2

The sheets of paper are formed on a two-piece tray called a mould and deckle. This tray can be made from two wood picture frames the same size, or from 1×2-inch lumber cut to any size you wish your sheets to be, and joined to form a rectangle. The mould is made by attaching very-fine-gauge screening to one of these frames, and the deckle is the frame left empty. (Figure 2.) The deckle is laid on the screened side of the mould, and will act as the boundary to contain the pulp when the sheets of paper are being formed. The other things needed are a dishpan large enough to take the mould and deckle in a horizontal position, allowing room to move it around; several yards of white flannel with as little nap as possible; and caustic soda, which is sodium hydroxide, from the drugstore.

When you have collected all the plants and grasses and all the bits and pieces of material that you wish—about one quart chopped gives a yield of one cup of pulp—tear them and cut them into small pieces and set them in a pan with a small amount of water to allow the fibers to break down naturally. This is known as retting; you should allow them to ret for three days, stirring them occasionally to expose them to air and prevent them from rotting. After this retting period, drain off the excess water, place the mass in a large pot, and cover it with a solution of 5 per cent sodium hydroxide to complete the breaking-down process. The solution may be stronger; this will hasten the process but weaken the paper.

Bring the pot to a gentle boil and allow it to simmer for about three hours. Linen fibers are hard to digest, and if your solution has more than 25 per cent linen content, it should be boiled for five or six hours. However, threads of undigested colored materials will lend interest to the finished paper as long as they are not too large.

When the solution is pretty homogeneous, it is ready to be washed and beaten. Allow it to cool, and strain it through the copper sieve into a large can; throw the caustic water away outdoors where it cannot damage your drainpipes. If you must flush it away in the sink, dilute it well with running water. Now put the material in the sieve back into the pot, fill the pot with clean water, and strain it off again. Do this several times, and then hold the sieve under running water for a few minutes until all the caustic has surely been washed away from the material.

Now you are ready to beat it, literally, to a pulp. Place it in a shallow pan or on a wooden board, and with a heavy spoon or spatula or wood or rubber mallet beat at it for as long as you have the patience. You can use a large chopping knife to start this process, but as it is one of mashing rather than cutting, you must end up by using the blunt tool. The more the pulp is beaten, the finer the paper will be, although here again, bits and pieces that are not entirely beaten down may lend interest as bits of color on the sheet of paper—but they must be small enough not to cause lumps. If you allow the mixture to ret for a while again at this stage, it will make the later process of meshing the fibers together easier.

While the mixture is retting, prepare the flannel for the next stage, which is to form sheets from the beaten pulp. Cut the flannel into many pieces a little larger than the sheets of paper will be—that is, a little larger than the mould and deckle, which are what determine the size of the paper. Commercial houses use felt for this, and so these supports for each sheet of paper are known as felts. The procedure of laying a sheet of wet paper on a felt is called couching, and the purpose of couching is to keep the wet sheets of paper from sticking to each other.

When the mass is as finely beaten as you can get it, it is ready to be formed. Half fill the dishpan with warm water, add a few cupfuls of the pulp, to the consistency of heavy cream, and mix it thoroughly with your hands to be sure there are no lumps. Place the deckle on the screening of the mould, and dip mould and deckle well into the pan, holding them by the two sides. (Figure 3.) Lift them out horizontally, causing a layer of pulp to

Figure 3

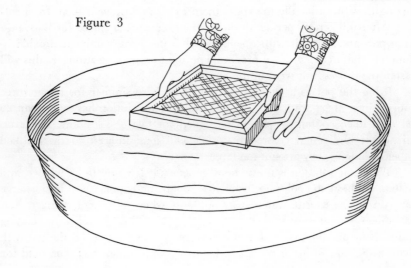

be deposited on the mould. Tilt it from side to side and back and forth a few times to mesh the fibers and level the pulp, and allow it to drain for a few moments. Then, when enough water has drained off so that the pulp is sufficiently firm to contain itself without spreading, remove the deckle and turn the mould upside down, allowing the pulp layer to drop off onto a felt. To do this, place one corner of the mould on one corner of the felt, and then, with a slow, firm, rolling motion, press the whole mould down so that the pulp releases from the mould and transfers to the felt. There must be a felt between each two adjacent sheets of paper, all piled one on top of the other neatly, to be ready for pressing later. Repeat this process of dipping and couching, adding a little pulp to the vessel each time. Each dipping uses up pulp but returns most of the water, and so the sheets of paper can be made only so long as there is enough pulp to form them.

The film of pulp that is picked up should be about one sixteenth of an inch thick, and is called a waterleaf. Sometimes it is interesting to laminate two waterleaves with a thin little something between them—a rose petal perhaps, or a bit of colored thread or silk. This must be done quickly, so that there is no spotty drying of the waterleaves to cause air pockets.

When you have a pile of sheets done, lay a felt on top of the pile, and a flat board on top of that, and apply pressure evenly to squeeze out the remaining water. If nothing better is available, put the pile on the floor and sit on it. When you have forced out all the water that you can (without disturbing them), the sheets are ready to be removed from the felts and set out to dry on lay sheets. Any white paper will serve as a lay sheet, which, again, is used to separate the waterleaves until they are completely dry. Pick up each felt by the corners of one end, turn it upside down on the lay sheet, and peel it away from the damp paper. (Figure 4.) The sheets should at this step

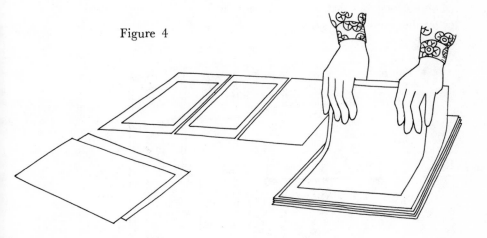

Figure 4

be spread out singly on a flat surface to allow air circulation, and when nearly dry they may be piled up neatly and put under a heavy weight to flatten them overnight. When they are completely dry, you can remove them from the lay sheets, and they are now full-fledged pieces of paper.

You can leave the paper as it is, with a matte finish, or for a slight gloss you can press it with a warm iron. The uneven edge is usually retained, because this deckle edge is the trademark of handmade paper; in fact, commercial papers are sometimes given an artificial deckle edge to make them look handmade. The watermark seen in many papers is formed by casting the words in very thin brass and then fusing the brass to the mesh of the mould, so that the design is pressed right into the wet pulp.

Sometimes the pulp is an interesting color, but other times it is muddy-looking and you might want to bleach it. This would be done to the washed material after the digestion in the caustic. You can add a cup of household bleach to two or three gallons of water, and the pulp can sit in this solution overnight or until it looks right. Then sieve it again and wash it thoroughly before you start the beating. Or you might marbleize the finished paper. In this technique you lay out several colors of artist's oil paints and mix each one with an equal quantity of mineral spirits. Pick up several little pools of the colors and lay them on the surface of a pan of water. Swirl them around with a matchstick, and then lay a sheet of paper gently on the water. Remove it immediately, and the swirled or marbled design will have transferred itself to the paper. It is necessary to add the mineral spirits because they influence the surface tension of the water, allowing the color to disperse instead of coagulating into blobs.

Handmade papers may be used for greeting cards, for a guest book perhaps, for end papers in a memory album, or for very elegant stationery for a very special occasion. Unfortunately, papers made by amateurs usually are not very strong, but they are a great satisfaction to the creative spirit, and a joy for the producer to behold.

Figure 5

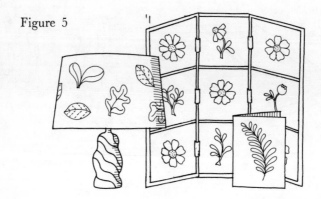

Figure 6

JAPANESE RICE PAPERS

Japanese rice papers, called *washi,* are some of the most beautiful decorative papers that we know. They are made from the fibrous husk of the rice plant and usually they are translucent, with leaves, flowers, et cetera imbedded into the waterleaves. (Figure 5.) The rice digests down to an almost transparent gelatinous mass, and this is what gives these papers their particular sheen.

It is quite easy to make a simulated rice paper by using a waxed freezer wrap and heating it so that the wax penetrates through to the uncoated side and the wrap becomes translucent and quite handsome with the imbedments that are added to it.

Not much is needed in the way of supplies. The freezer paper, a box of white facial tissues, a jar of Elmer's glue, a stiff stencil brush, and whatever you want to imbed—ferns, flower petals, pretty leaves, or perhaps some little cutouts of colored tissue paper. Suppose we make our paper with some delicate grasses picked in late summer, when they are most attractive.

Pour about an ounce of the glue into a small bowl and add about two ounces of water to make it quite thin. Cut a piece of freezer paper the size you want and lay it waxed side down on the table. Spread a thin coat of glue over it, and lay the grasses where you want them on the paper, scattered about pleasingly on the glued surface. (Figure 6.) Now separate a tissue into single sheets, and tear these into two or three strips. Lay a strip on top of each blade of grass, and then dab them down securely with the stencil brush dipped into the glue. The glue will penetrate the thin tissue, and the grass will be anchored and protected. Now tear more pieces of the tissue, and cover the whole piece of freezer paper with a single layer of them, but overlapping so that it is all covered. Add more glue if necessary.

Allow this sandwich to dry thoroughly, and then press both sides with a warm iron. (Figure 7.) This will send the wax through the paper, making it

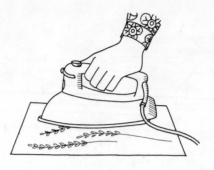

Figure 7

translucent, and it will smooth out the tissue side so as to make it really look bonded to its backing. Put it under a heavy weight of books for a day or so, and then it is ready to be used: mounted for a lampshade, or set into a screen for a shoji room divider, or perhaps added to a window for translucent privacy. Having the paper in a continuous roll is an advantage in that a large panel can be made with no seams; it could even be used like wallpaper to cover a whole problem area. Small pieces can be used for almost anything that calls for interesting paper—the backing for a beautiful oriental print, an insertion for an elegant greeting card, or perhaps a cover for a very special book.

Materials other than flat objects can be used—seed pods, dried flowers, ripened autumn fluff from the fields, bits of plastic, beads, feathers, anything you wish. If the imbedments are thick, then several layers of tissue will be needed to anchor them, and the ironing can be done on the waxed side only, placing it on a soft bed of terry toweling to keep from injuring the materials.

Painters use this same technique to make collages, mounting the material on any support—wood or wallboard, or scraps of canvas or water-color paper. The artist usually uses acrylic medium as the glue and might build up many layers of tissue on many layers of objects to lend an effect of depth to this "painting." The acrylic will give a hard, glassy finish, and this could make it a handsome assemblage of laminated materials, though a far cry from the delicate translucent paper that we started out with.

COLLAGE

Collage, which comes from the French word *coller,* meaning to paste or glue, first came into favor when the Cubists experimented with their paintings by adhering bits of newspaper to them for a new effect. Soon they found that there were many different things that could be glued to the canvas to add interest, and today artists will add anything that takes their fancy. Ferns, dried flowers, seaweed, seashells, pebbles, coins, bits of glass, bits of cloth—anything that can be adhered can become a collage. Modern artists often use hardware: tools, gears, metal junk, wooden junk; if the background is strong enough to support an object, epoxy cement is strong enough to keep it in place. If it can hang on the wall it is a collage; if it stands free it is a sculpture.

Matisse, in his last years, constructed whole "paintings" using bits of colored paper, and when cleansing tissue became readily available, artists started to use it to build semi bas-reliefs on canvas and on other background supports. This added a new dimension to painting, and tissue collage was born.

Suppose we concern ourselves with a tissue collage of a bouquet of flowers done on water-color paper. This is basic collage, and once you know the principle you can depart in any direction.

First of all, the paper background must be prepared so that it will not buckle under the onslaught of wet glue that is in store for it. Good water-color paper is very strong and can be handled like canvas. So choose a paper

"Winter Sands." A collage assembled from paper, cloth, foil, and seaweed. Mounted on burlap. Contemporary. American. Ina Frankel.

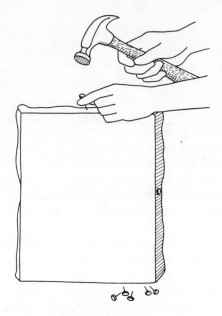

Figure 8

of high quality, soak it in cool water in the bathtub for twenty minutes, and then drain the excess water off. Tack it to canvas stretchers or to an empty wooden picture frame. (Figure 8.) Tack the paper in the same manner as you would stretch cotton or linen canvas: starting at the center of each side and working gradually out to the corners. If you don't want to go to all that trouble, then wet it thoroughly with a clean sponge, lay it to dry on a hard smooth surface such as glass or formica, and smooth it out from the center toward the edges to flatten it. Leave it in this position undisturbed, and by the time you have your materials assembled it should be stretched enough and flat enough to start work.

You will need a package of assorted-color tissue papers, a stippling brush—which is a short-bristled stiff artist's brush—and some Elmer's glue or acrylic medium mixed half and half with water in a small bowl or saucer.

If you wish, sketch out your design roughly so that you will have some idea of the color positions, but the charm of tissue collage is its spontaneity and surprise, so don't be too rigid in following a preconceived pattern. Tear and cut many pieces of paper into approximate shapes and sizes of the flower petals, leaves, stems, etc. Some should be torn for blending and some should be cut where you will want a clear definition. If you are using bright colors for the flowers, then you will want pale, soft colors for the background, and so don't forget to prepare for that too. The flowers will be built up from many layers, the background as you please.

Spread a thin coat of the diluted glue over the large sheet of paper, and lay down bits of tissue following the design you have in mind. You need not be concerned about exactly where they go, nor about whether they wrinkle, because this medium should be worked freely and casually. The pieces should overlap and the colors allowed to bleed one into the other to soften and blend the hues. When you have a semblance of a design, dip your stippling brush into the glue dish, and dab at the tissues to press them onto the paper and assure that they adhere properly. (Figure 9.) Now stand off and look at your picture, and decide where to start adding the second layer of tissue and whether it should be the same color as the first or perhaps a different shade to blend. The second and third and fourth layers could each vary slightly, or could each be identical, depending on the effect that you want. The background will also be filled in, but the flowers should be the more interesting: some flowers could be built up from many layers of petals, others left a little hazy as they recede into the background. Each layer of tissue is applied just like the first, but where you have many layers, thin out the glue a little more each time, so that the area doesn't become glue-heavy. When it is all finished, a thin coat of varnish or shellac or an acrylic spray will help preserve it, or it can be framed under glass to be enjoyed like any watercolor.

There are an infinite number of variables that can be used in collage. The support can be anything from paper through cardboard, canvas, plastic, plywood, metal—anything on which something can be glued: metal to lucite; fur to leather; colored cardboard cutouts to the cover of a shoe box; bits of yarn or material to burlap; metal foil to a heavy piece of rice paper. The combinations are endless.

The Japanese technique is to glue small bits of natural materials—grasses, ferns, blossoms, seashells—to a background and then cover them with very thin, gauze-like rice papers. This makes for a soft, misty effect, which might also be obtained by using single sheets of facial tissue. A hardedge pattern can be made by gluing small pieces of wood or plastic to make a relief design on a heavy piece of cardboard. Then the whole thing could

Figure 9

be coated with wallpaper paste, covered with brown paper, and smoothed down with a damp sponge. When dry, if it is rubbed over with an oil paint mixed with turpentine, a fine, "old" patina develops, and if a little gold powder is added to the oil paint a gilding results. This technique produces a soft monotone effect, with highlights that make it very attractive.

Collage also comes in mixed media. Acrylics, water colors, or oil paints can be used in combination with glued-on objects; also, the paints can be used to highlight the objects. Or vice versa, an object might be adhered onto a painting—a landscape with some real twigs where the trees are, or a floral with artificial flowers glued on for an unusual surprise.

Modern adhesives have expanded collage to the point where it is difficult to distinguish a wall hanging from a bas-relief sculpture. Cement is an adhesive, as is plaster, and acrylic or epoxy resins can bind and hold almost anything you might feel like tacking on. Areas can be cut out from a painted canvas and glued on elsewhere, just by using acrylic paint to adhere them; canvas or any cloth can be crumpled into a form, coated with resin to keep its shape, and then adhered to a background by any glue that comes to mind.

Collage could be made from Styrofoam, or foaming plastic, outlined with liquid metal for interest. A watch or a motor might be taken apart and reassembled flat on a sheet of clear plastic or stainless steel for background. (Figure 10.) All these constructions can be called assemblages, and an assemblage can be of anything the heart desires. Everything is possible, and with ingenuity and modern materials, you can make it happen.

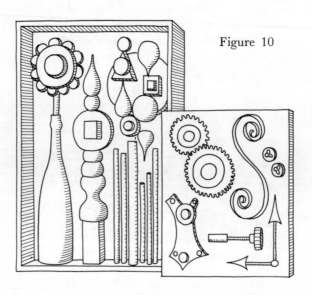

Figure 10

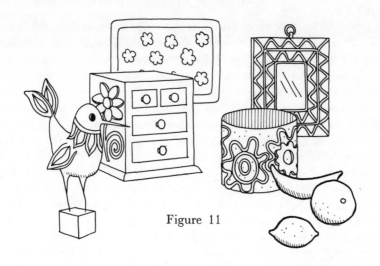

Figure 11

PAPIER MÂCHÉ

Papier mâché is just what the name implies: the term is French and means chewed paper. Soft, absorbent paper is soaked in a watery mixture of glue, and when it dries it becomes hard and durable. During the Renaissance period, delicately ornamented furniture came into vogue, and papier mâché was used for large pieces such as desks, chests of drawers, cabinets. Each piece was a work of art, and some pieces may still be seen in museums. The secret of their sturdiness is the care that was taken in their construction. The pieces were rococo, with lots of swirls and carvings and beadings, and in addition they were painted with intricate designs and then varnished many times with copal varnish. Copal, being natural resin, was able to penetrate the papier mâché enough to make a hard, glossy surface almost impervious to damage. Today there still are artisans who work with painstaking care, and beautiful pieces come to us from India and other Eastern countries. Mostly, they are small ornamental bibelots, trays, boxes, ashtrays—sometimes flashed with a thin layer of brass to make them actually usable. (Figure 11.)

For craft projects, papier-mâché pieces are made from narrow strips of newspaper soaked in a flour-and-water paste just long enough to saturate them. Single sheets of the newspaper are torn in half and then into strips about an inch wide. Torn pieces are preferable to cut ones, because a jagged edge will blend into the overlaps, whereas a straight-cut edge will tend to make a ridge. The paste is mixed to a thin, flowing consistency so that the piece will be made up of more paper than glue; too thick a paste will make the piece heavy but not strong, being made up, then, of more glue than paper. A thin liquid is enough to hold the strips together, and the crisscross layers of paper become surprisingly strong and durable. The medium of papier mâché is used by artists and sculptors today with little change in the old-time recipe. Some refinements have been made, mostly in the matter of glues, and Elmer's glue (or acrylic medium) diluted to half strength is perhaps the one most widely used. Not that the artist has any complaints about flour and water, but Elmer's seems handier in the studio.

In order to have a starting point on which to build, an armature is usually made. Milk cartons, plastic containers, stick figures fashioned from wire coat hangers, or even a balloon will form a base on which to start shaping the sculpture. Styrofoam carved to approximate the finished piece is good and so is chicken wire shaped into a rough form. Or to be true to the medium, crumpled newspaper can be loosely shaped, then dipped into the paste and allowed to harden overnight. The purpose of the armature is either to add necessary bulk—as in the case of a head, for instance—or to support an extended limb or the weight of the body of a standing animal figure. Any way that you can accomplish this is acceptable.

All the supplies that we need to make a papier-mâché sculpture are lots of newspaper, some kind of white glue, and an armature. Tear the newspaper into strips about five inches by one inch, and pour the glue into a large, shallow bowl or a dishpan. Add enough water to make it the consistency of light cream, and stir it often as you work. Set the armature on a

Figure 12

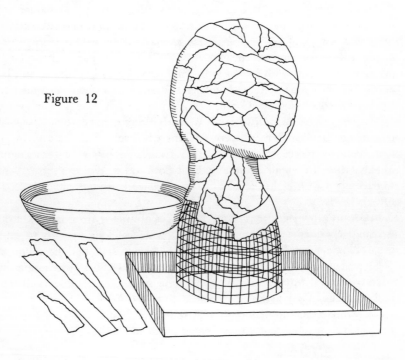

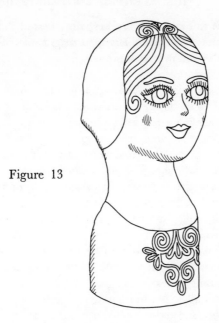

Figure 13

plastic tray or cardboard box to catch the drip, and you are ready to start work.

Dip the strips one at a time into the paste and apply them to the armature, overlapping them and covering the armature completely one layer thick. It is not good to apply them too regularly, because then there would be lines of demarcation, so crisscross them over the whole piece in a haphazard manner. (Figure 12.) When the armature is covered completely, put on another layer, having the strips go in different directions so that, again, there will be no ridges. Repeat this process until there are at least five layers, by which time the armature should be well padded and you should have created a strong enough form on which to add the textured surface layer. This is put on in blobs, with much the same technique used in ceramic sculpture. Put several handfuls of strips into the glue and let them soak until they become pulpy and start to disintegrate. There is no crucial point here— the paper can stay in the glue for a half hour or a half day. Pick up small blobs of this pulp and squeeze out most of the moisture, then apply them to the form all over to make an interesting surface texture. Model the details in with an orangewood stick or a pencil or knife, and add more pulp where needed, such as to form the nose on a head or the warts on a frog. The work can be put aside and picked up again at any stage.

Allow the piece to dry for several days, and when it is hard and firm it can be sanded or filed, and then painted with any kind of paint—water, oil, or synthetic. (Figure 13.) Artists working in oils usually keep a jar of turpentine handy in which to rinse their brushes; the dregs in this waste jar are good for making a patina: the consistency is just right, the color is softened, and a coat of this plus a rubdown with bronze powder gives a fine, aged appearance.

A flat piece such as a tray or a candy dish can be worked in a free design with no armature to guide it; if you want to duplicate an established design, then you can make it over a mold. You can use any existing bowl or box or what-have-you as the mold by covering it all over with a greasy separator such as soapy water or vaseline or hand lotion, and then applying the strips of paper in as many layers as you wish the piece to be thick. The strips can be put on over the outside or into the inside of the mold; perhaps the first layer should be Scotch-taped to the rim to keep it in place. As in all molding methods, you must be certain that there are no undercuts, which would interfere with the removal of the work when it is dry.

Papier-mâché sculpture is versatile, in that it can be worked into tiny, delicate objects that have an innate strength, or it can be worked on a massive scale with a bulk that belies its weight. Many of the old-time movies that were made indoors had rocks and boulders and whole mountains made of painted papier mâché, and today we see a lot of costume jewelry painted in brilliant colors with synthetic high-gloss paints. Papier mâché can be compressed into thin little petals that can then be manipulated into flowers and lacquered to resemble porcelain, or formed into balls and then painted to resemble Venetian glass beads. It can be shaped into little figures and animals to make a crèche at Christmastime, and could even be used to cover a store-bought desk or little table. So you, too, could have an heirloom piece in your home with no more investment than yesterday's newspaper, a basin of paste, and a little patience and ingenuity.

2

Wood

By reason of necessity, one of the first machines that man invented was the wood-turning lathe, and so he has been able to put trees to use for himself for a long, long time. Any object that is to be symmetrically round can be turned on a lathe—table legs, bowls, candleholders, pot handles; all are made in the same way: the wood is attached to the lathe in a horizontal position, and as the machine turns, the wood revolves and a sharp chisel is held against it, gradually cutting away until the desired shape is reached.

The essential parts of the lathe are the headstock and the tailstock. The headstock is stationary on the left, and to it a faceplate is attached. A block of wood is secured dead center to this faceplate, and the headstock is driven in a rotating motion by a motor. On the right is the movable tailstock, which anchors the work securely by means of a spindle, and along the front of the bed is a tool rest, which steadies the hand while working. (Figure 14.) The whole machine is long and narrow and can be either freestanding or bolted to the workbench; it is run by a variable-speed motor. Beginning the work on rough stock requires a speed of about 500 r.p.m., but as work progresses to the final stages of smoothing and polishing, the speed might be increased to perhaps 3,000 r.p.m. The motor is sometimes part of the lathe bed, and sometimes is rigged up separately to operate by means of a pulley.

The tools needed are just a few wood-turning chisels: a square-nose, a round-nose, a gouge, and a skew chisel (which has a diagonal cut for making decorative beadings on objects such as table legs or candlesticks). While you are working, goggles should be worn, sleeves and ties put out of the way, and precautions should constantly be observed to prevent the revolving piece of wood from flying off the lathe: the headstock and tailstock should be checked periodically to be sure they remain securely clamped. The chisel should never be held in place before the motor is turned on: if the piece is not accurately centered, it will knock the chisel out of your hand and could cause a serious accident. The motor should always be started at slow speed so that the alignment can be checked safely before you start work.

Tools should be kept sharp as you go along. Straight-edged tools can be ground on a wheel, and hollow ones such as the gouge can be honed with a slipstone. This is a small, arrowhead-shaped grindstone usually held in the left hand while the right hand moves the point of the tool back and forth to sharpen it, using water or thin oil as a lubricant. If designs are to be repeated, you need calipers, to check inside and outside measurements. They are also useful for checking the thickness of a wall when turning a hollow piece. Or if you prefer, a template can be made from heavy cardboard or thin wood or plastic to guide you as you shape.

Suppose you wish to turn a salad bowl six or seven inches in diameter. If you make it six inches deep, the first thing you will have to do is glue two or more pieces of wood together to achieve the depth you want. If you have access to a rare-wood dealer, you could have a choice, such as perhaps sandwiching a piece of rosewood between two slabs of ebony, but more probably you will get your wood from the local lumber yard, and any good grade of wood will do. Sugar pine is the easiest to work with; walnut or mahogany is good. Select enough to make an eight-inch cube, two pieces of four by eight for instance, and buy at the lumberyard or a hardware store

Figure 14

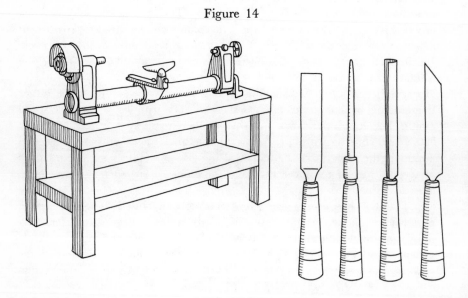

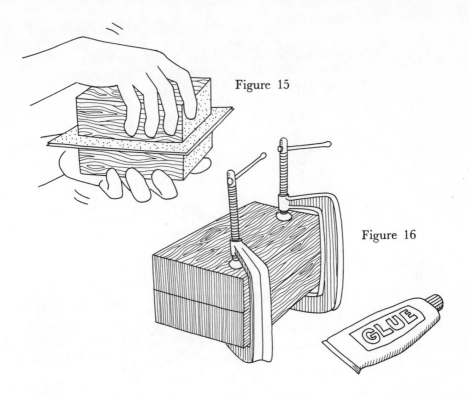

Figure 15

Figure 16

the best glue available—usually labeled *cabinet-maker's*—two or three large clamps, and some medium-coarse sandpaper in large sheets.

The joining of the pieces of wood must be a perfect bond: the two surfaces that are being glued together must be absolutely flat, to allow no air spaces anywhere. Lay the sandpaper on a hard surface such as a piece of glass or formica, and rub what will be the adjoining surfaces of both pieces of wood back and forth and around and around until you have removed every bump. Then glue two pieces of sandpaper together, grit side out, place this between the two sanded surfaces, and rub the wood around and around. (Figure 15.) This should end up in two even surfaces ready to be glued. Apply the glue according to directions, and clamp the pieces tightly together, leaving them undisturbed for at least three days to be sure they are firmly bonded. (Figure 16.)

Now we are ready to mount the block on the lathe. At this point, it would be helpful to have this cube of wood cut into a roughly circular shape. While it is possible to cut it into a round on the lathe, it is much easier to start with an approximation of a circle before mounting it. The people at the lumberyard might do this for you. Even better, have them cut the two original pieces into rounds before gluing them together.

With a ruler, measure off the flat ends of the wood, parallel to the join, to find the dead center as best you can. Line one up with the center of the faceplate, and screw it on securely. Attach the faceplate to the headstock,

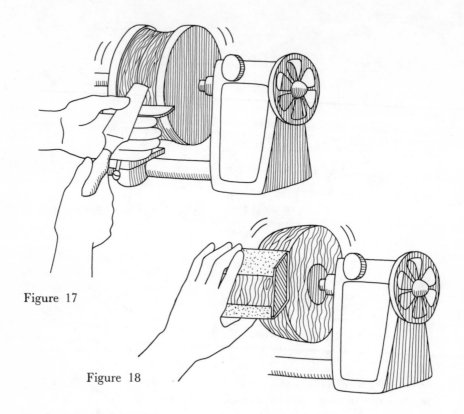

Figure 17

Figure 18

then attach the tailstock to the opposing surface of the wood, and you are ready to start turning the outside of the bowl. The bottom of the bowl is on the left—at the headstock.

Rest the chisel—a large square-nose to start with—on the tool rest, and rotating the wood by hand, find the point on it that is closest to you. Move the chisel back toward you about a quarter of an inch, so that it is completely clear of the block, and then turn on the motor at slow speed. Move the chisel into the work very gingerly; as the lathe rotates, the chisel will chip away bits of wood. It will be rough going at first, but as the work progresses, the wood block will become rounder and the chisel will have a smoother road to travel. It is especially important at this rough stage to check the anchoring screws often to be sure that nothing has been shaken loose. The wood can fly off the lathe, and that could be very dangerous.

Move the tool rest up and down the bed, left and right, as you work, so that the chisel is forming a cylinder of the whole block. (Figure 17.) Once you have the block rounded, you are ready to turn it to a shape. It could be bowl-shaped, that is, wide at the top and narrowing down toward the base. Or it could be hourglass-shaped, with one or two bulges down the side; or gently curved: in at the top, filling out softly toward the middle, and in again at the bottom. Start forming these contours with a round-nose or a skew chisel, which will cut away small areas and allow you to contemplate the shape as you go along. If you have a preconceived idea of what you want your finished bowl to be, then it is best to make a sketch of the bowl's actual size. Use calipers to check your work against this sketch.

When the outside is formed to the desired shape, wrap sandpaper around a small block of wood and hold it against the block while it is turning at slow speed. (Figure 18.) This will smooth it off, and then you are

Wooden pipe. Lathe turned, then hand carved and assembled. Contemporary. Mediterranean. Collection of the author.

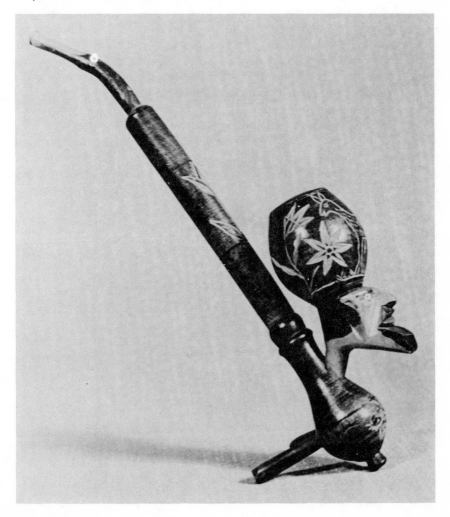

Figure 19

ready to begin shaping the interior of the bowl. Check the screws on the headstock and faceplate to be sure the wood is secure, and start hollowing out the inside of the bowl by holding the chisel against the surface anchored to the tailstock. Start near the center of the new surface, and work down toward the bottom of the bowl, which is attached to the headstock, but don't cut so deep that you might go right through the wood. (Figure 19.) Do the inside gradually along its depth, and check occasionally to be sure that the wall isn't getting too thin. The inside shape can match the outside, or it can just be smoothed out independently of the outside contours. Now remove the tailstock, and chisel away the thin post that has remained in the center.

When the inside is hollowed to your satisfaction, sand it, being very careful to keep your fingers out of the way, perhaps wearing heavy gloves, or holding the paper with a pair of pliers.

Remove the bowl from the faceplate and sand the bottom smooth. The screw marks on the bottom of a turned piece are not considered disfigurement. If they are offensive to you, they can be filled in with wood putty and then sanded flat.

Figure 20

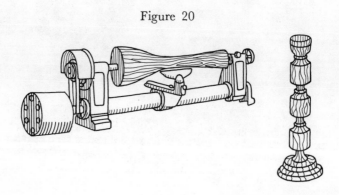

Now the bowl is ready to be oiled for preservation of the wood. Soak it liberally with boiled linseed oil for a period of three to four successive days, sanding it down with coarse steel wool between successive dousings. If you don't care for the odor that linseed oil leaves, I recommend using lemon oil instead, or salad oil with a little vinegar to cut it.

Turning a candlestick or a table leg is done in the same way. Here you would use a length of square stock, two by two or four by four, the length of the maximum distance between headstock and tailstock. (Figure 20.) Should you wish a very tall piece, such as a freestanding patio candleholder or posts for a four-poster bed, sections could be turned individually and then glued together end to end when the machining is all finished. If any piece is to be duplicated, then a template should be made and the calipers used often to check the work in progress. Finishing is always the same: oil and sanding, with lots of elbow grease.

Weed vase. Cut from a solid cube of walnut, then turned off center by holding it against a revolving sanding disk. Contemporary. American. Roger Sloan.

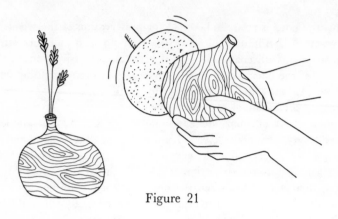

Figure 21

An interesting way to make a vase from a block of wood without using a lathe is to form the inside roughly with a drill press, then use a hand chisel to complete the gouging, and finally hold the block against a revolving sanding disk (Figure 21) to shape the outside. If you start with beautifully grained stock, you can turn it off center to take advantage of the swirls and burls. With this method, the vase need not be round; you can give it any shape you wish by changing its position against the disk. Small weed pots are particularly attractive when made this way, because the little neck that holds the plant stem can be placed anywhere you want it. You can use a drill press with a medium-sized bit to make a hole after each neck has been formed, and you can make as many of these little protuberances as you want to. A bowl made by this technique can be finished off smoothly or it can be left with rough contours to simulate chisel marks. It's a good conversation piece, for it's hard to understand a turned bowl that is off center.

VENEERING

Many beautiful pieces of veneered furniture that were made centuries ago are still in good condition today. The elegant furniture of the Louis XIV period was mostly veneered, in elaborate design, and pieces have withstood three hundred years of use. (Figure 22.)

Veneering is the application of a thin layer of wood to any other wood. Its purpose can be purely for ornament—to make the wood more attractive —or it can be used for a practical reason, as in the case of surfacing a soft wood with a hard one to make it more durable. Today many veneers used on furniture are synthetics such as formica and other plastic materials, and their application is strictly for convenience. A coffee table made with a walnut-grain formica top is obviously more resistant to wear and tear than one topped with a real walnut veneer. Sometimes it is hard to tell it from the

real thing, but we here will concern ourselves with true wood veneers, made
of real wood cut from real trees.

Veneers can be obtained in all sorts of unusual woods as well as in the
more commonly found grains, such as mahogany, walnut, rosewood. They
come in sheets and range in size from small precious scraps cut from a very
rare tree to full panels eight or ten feet long and perhaps two feet wide.
Sometimes they come stained with permanent dyes in unusual and beautiful
colors. All of them are cut to a standard thickness of one twenty-eighth of
an inch.

There is no great mystery to applying veneers. These thin sheets are
flexible and can be cut with a razor blade or utility knife, but they should be
handled with care to avoid cracking or splintering. They are applied to the
base with a special wood glue that is either a conventional strong binding
cement or the newer instant contact glue, which requires no pressure for
bonding. Veneering may be done on old furniture to restore damaged areas,
or on new or old painted or unpainted furniture that can be bought inexpensively and made very handsome by the application of a new facing.
When veneering is done in an intricate design composed of small pieces
fitted together, it is known as marquetry or inlay, and the pieces are laid in
such a way as to form the design. This is sometimes done with materials
other than wood, such as mother-of-pearl or ivory or tortoise shell glued to a
wood base.

Suppose you try your hand at applying a walnut veneer to an old
painted chest of drawers. First you must select your veneers with the same

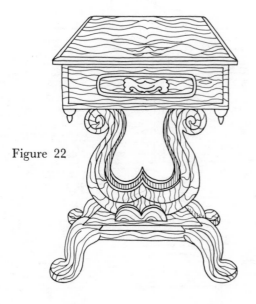

Figure 22

type of grain throughout, or with matching grains for the top and sides, and other matching grains for all the drawer fronts. (Figure 23.) There is no right or wrong side to a sheet of veneer, but one side may show more imperfections than the other. If you are fortunate, you may be able to buy a panel of veneer that is large enough not to require seams; however, the chances are that somewhere along the line you will have to make a join, and this is always done by butting the edges exactly, matching grain as nearly as possible. If you wish to make a symmetrical design at the center of the drawers by using the burls (knots) in the veneer, then you must keep in mind that they should be opposites (Figure 24) : one side of the veneer for the left half of each drawer and the reverse side for the right half. Using a burl requires accurate cutting, and these knots are difficult to cut without splintering, so your blade must be very sharp and the cutting done on a hard, smooth surface. (Figure 25.)

In addition to the veneers, your glue can be purchased from your fine-wood dealer, and for the chest of drawers you might use a contact cement. You will need varnish, lots of sandpaper, several small paintbrushes, a utility knife, a try square, shellac, steel wool, and linseed oil. Before you start work, the chest must be washed with a detergent such as Murphy's Oil Soap to remove all wax and grease, and then sanded to remove gloss and to be perfectly smooth. If there are any gouges or depressions in the wood, they should be filled in with a paste wood filler and then sanded level. An otherwise good job will be spoiled if this undersurface is not completely level.

Choose the best grain and/or the smoothest piece of veneer for the

Figure 23

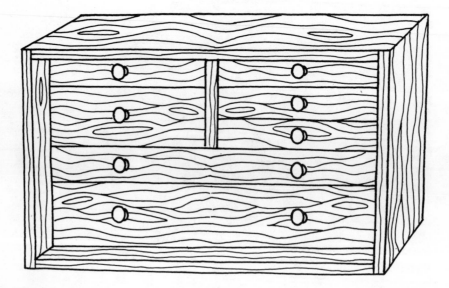

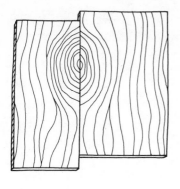

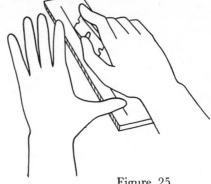

Figure 24   Figure 25

top. Try to avoid a seam here unless you want to match burls or otherwise form a marquetry design, in which case practice first on a less conspicuous area to get the feel of the materials. If you must make a seam, lay the veneer flat on the cutting table—a sheet of masonite or glass makes a good surface to cut on—and with the metal try square and sharp utility knife or a razor blade make a straight, clean cut along the edge to be joined or matched. You will not be cutting with the grain, and so you must make the first cut a clean, masterful one. Cut the second piece, which will adjoin the first, and lay the two pieces on the table face up to be sure they meet perfectly and look well together. When you are satisfied on both counts, butt them firmly together and carefully run a piece of masking tape the full length of the seam—on the face, where it will stay until the bonding is finished.

Now you are ready to cut all your panels roughly to the size of the area to be covered. Each panel should be a little larger all around and will be trimmed off later. Cut the most important panels first, using the best grains for the areas that show most. Usually the sides are the least obvious, and so any piecing or defects would be least obvious if used there. After you cut each piece, mark it lightly on the wrong side with a ball-point pen so you know just where it belongs. Then you are ready to start the bonding. With a conventional type of glue, you could manipulate your pieces until you got them into proper relation to each other, but, with the instant contact cement that you are using, there is no margin for error: as soon as the two glued surfaces meet, they are joined forever. So it is best that you work on one panel at a time, and you might start with the top.

Cover the floor with lots of newspaper and lay the cut veneer on it face down. Pour some glue into a pie tin and with an inexpensive small paintbrush apply a coat to the back of the veneer. Then apply a coat to the top of the chest. Allow it to dry for a half hour, and then apply another full coat to each surface. Allow this coat to dry until it stops feeling tacky to the touch—

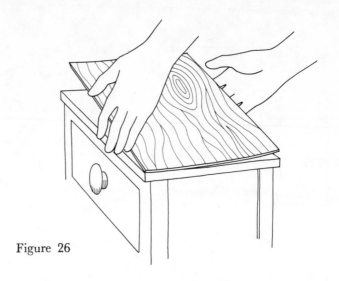

Figure 26

another half hour or longer. Lift the veneer up by the two corners of one end and allow the other two corners to barely touch the side edge of the chest. (Figure 26.) When you are sure the veneer is lined up true with the top of the chest, lower it into place slowly. (For this operation, try to find an extra pair of hands: it's tricky.) When the panel is in place, use a rolling pin or a round bottle or a piece of broomstick and roll the veneer from the center toward the edges to expel any bubbles that may have formed; roll the edges particularly well to be sure of a good bond. Remove the masking tape if any, and with your utility knife cut away the excess veneer around the edges. To avoid chipping away bits of the veneer when trimming, try resting your metal ruler along the top edge of the veneer and cutting from below against this metal. In this way you do not mar the surface, and you have a counterpressure to cut against. This cutting need not be too close: the sanding later will perfect it. Press the edges down tight by hand, and if convenient, put some weights such as books around the edges for assurance, and allow the glue to set overnight.

Next day, the side panels can be applied in the same manner, and then you are ready to finish off with the drawers.

Remove the drawers from the chest, take off the handles so that there is a flat surface to work on, and stand the drawers on the floor, face up. If you have a special pattern for each drawer, then apply these prepared panels in the same way, but if you do not wish a burled or matched design on them but, rather, a random grain, there is a way to veneer them collectively that is a great timesaver. (Figure 27.) Stand the drawers parallel, evenly lined up with a half inch of space between them. Then one piece of veneer can be used to cover them all at once. After the veneer is glued on, you can slice down between the drawers to separate them, and then trim each drawer till it's ready for sanding. (Figure 28.) The small areas on the chest between the

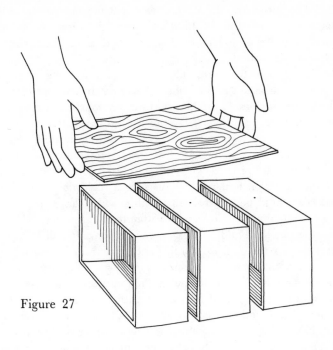

Figure 27

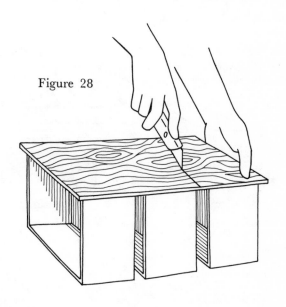

Figure 28

drawers might be faced by using an adhesive veneer tape, maybe using a contrasting color for interest.

Now that the veneering is all done, the sanding to a final finish is very important. The success of the whole piece will depend on the amount of work that you put into this finishing operation, the piece becoming as fine and as craftsmanlike as you make it. After sanding all the surfaces with a fine sandpaper and rounding the edges in the process, apply shellac or a liquid wood filler to seal the pores. Then sand again, dust the piece well, and apply a coat of varnish. Varnish should never be shaken, but stirred gently, to avoid making bubbles; if bubbles do form on your work, they might also have been caused by using yesterday's brush. So it is safest to use inexpensive brushes, just once. Repeat the process of sanding, dusting, and varnishing as many times as you can: at least three, preferably five, times. After the last coat, rub the piece down with steel wool moistened in linseed oil. Wipe off the excess oil and rub the piece to a high gloss. Or if you wish, your final coat could be an eggshell varnish, which has a soft finish, and your final rubbing down could be with rottenstone and water.

Now you put the handles back on the drawers. It will be necessary to drill new holes for them; these should be drilled from the outside in, so as not to put any counterpressure on the veneer.

When a piece is all done, if any swelling appears in the veneer, place a damp cloth over the spot and iron it out with a warm iron. If you have a bad swelling, it is sometimes necessary to inject glue into the area; your supply house has a glue injector, which is like a hypodermic syringe. (Figure 29.) Inject the glue, and apply heavy pressure on the spot for a few days. Sometimes it might be necessary to score a little X on the spot to allow gas to escape.

Figure 29

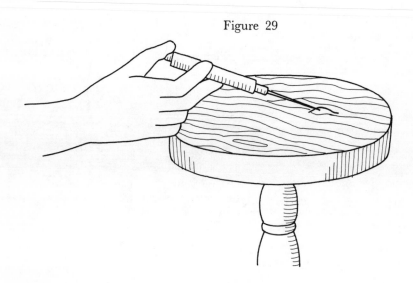

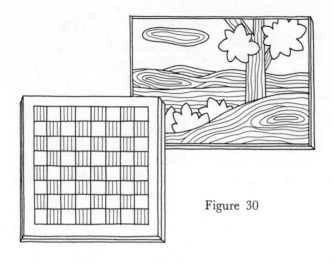

Figure 30

MARQUETRY

Small, intricately designed pieces of inlay or marquetry are done by using veneers of various colors and grains. They are fitted together to form a design that could be a simple geometric one such as a chessboard, or an elaborate picture such as a landscape, in which the grain of wood is used as well as the cut shape to form the various patterns. The Metropolitan Museum of Art in New York has a whole room called a *trompe l'oeil*—fooling the eye—which is simply four walls veneered in such a way as to give the impression that you are looking at a whole roomful of elaborate furniture.

In making a marquetry picture, draw the original sketch or cartoon on thin paper. Trace each section of this sketch with a very fine scriber onto a suitable veneer and cut out the veneers with a sharp X-acto knife. A more accurate method is to cut up the original cartoon into sections, paste each section onto a piece of veneer, and then cut the veneer with a very fine fret saw. In either method, the graining and burling of the wood is important, becoming part of the design in the marquetry work.

Glue these jigsaw pieces to a base such as plywood, itself a veneer: thin panels of wood glued together. If you were making a chessboard, you would use two kinds of wood in alternating squares. You might then cut strips of veneer to mitered corners to make a framing effect. (Figure 30.)

In the case of a "painting," you could use many different veneers or run the grainings in different directions to give varying effects. You then could glue quarter-round molding all around the edges to form the frame.

Inlay can be used on small boxes to hold trinkets or jewels, or it can be used as the jewelry itself. A small medallion of ebony veneer mounted on a silver disk would make a handsome cuff link. Or a thin sliver of mother-of-pearl outlined by veneer and glued onto a free-form copper shape for a pendant would be elegant.

INLAYS

Your supply house has inlays made up into designs to be used as decorations on handsome objects or for the repairing of antiques. In using an inlay to repair fine furniture, an area of the backing wood must be routed out to allow the new piece to be set in. This should be cut out carefully to exactly the size of the piece to be set in, and should be a little shallower than the thickness of the new veneer, to allow for sanding. Glue it into place, sand it level with the surrounding areas, and then varnish and sand it to match the rest.

Because fine veneers are sensitive to temperature changes, it is advisable to work on a temperate day at about 72° F and try to keep the object at a constant level of temperature and humidity. It should never be placed near a radiator, and if possible a dish of water should be hidden in it during the winter months, when the heating system dries the air. In repairing an inlay, you should gouge out the wood the same day that you set the new piece in; the next day, the space may be shrunken or swollen. Sometimes, in repairing large areas on antique furniture you can lift off the old veneers by applying hot compresses: the glue used in the old days was not waterproof, and the hot water will loosen the bond, allowing you to lift off the veneer in one piece. You then can flatten it with a warm iron and put it back in place with new glue. This is a difficult job on large surfaces, but not too hard for small areas; it is certainly worth a try. Many a fine piece has been saved by a little ingenuity and modern know-how.

Furniture made from veneers and that made from solid wood have equal value, providing they are well made and in good taste. Both should be treated well: kept clean and lasting with wax or oil; both will be a joy forever, especially if you have created them yourself.

POLYCHROMING

Polychromed sculpture is an old craft that has been allowed to die out, and unfortunately not many examples of this charming work remain to us. The *santos*, or religious figures, which are a particular heritage of the Spanish-speaking peoples, can be seen in museums, along with East Indian deities, American Indian braves, and a few of the figureheads that often decorated the bowsprits of Viking sailing vessels.

Polychroming is the art of painting on wood in many colors and in such a way that the colors become an integral part of the wood itself. To achieve this effect, weathered wood is used, so that the oily medium of the paints will be absorbed into the pores. The figures themselves are carved simply and crudely, and very little equipment is needed to turn out an interesting piece.

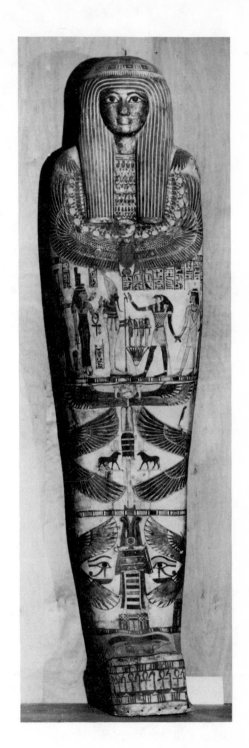

Sarcophagus. A wooden coffin
shaped to the figure and painted
elaborately with scenes of the
afterlife. Possibly it was a guide
for the soul on the road to
reincarnation. Sixth to seventh
century B.C. Egyptian. Courtesy
the Louvre, Paris. Cliché des
Musées Nationaux.

"Still Life." Bas-relief wall panel carved from white mahogany. Thirty-six inches long by two inches at its greatest depth. Contemporary. American. Stephen Werlick.

Because it is an old art form, the pieces remaining to us are crazed and cracked, and so, to do an "authentic" piece, we should start with wood that already shows the ravages of time and weather. Wherever buildings are being torn down, you can find newel posts, ceiling beams, barn sidings, wood paneling, or old piano legs, just waiting for the sculptor's tools. Old railroad ties, driftwood, or fallen tree limbs—all are aged and distressed enough to serve the purpose.

In addition to the wood, you will need lots of assorted colors in oil, some turpentine, rags, and newspaper to cover the work surface; it is a messy job, and rubber gloves would be advisable. Plastic or paper cups are good for mixing the paint in.

First trim the wood to the size and approximate shape that you would like the figure to be. Level off the base so that it stands well, and then, with a chisel or perhaps just a penknife, whittle the details in and sand lightly. (Figure 31.)

If the wood is very dry, add a teaspoon of linseed oil to half a cup of turpentine and brush it over the piece. This will penetrate and provide a vehicle to carry the color deep into the pores. And now you are ready to begin.

Squeeze out several dark colors into the cups and add turpentine to them until they are about the consistency of heavy cream. With a soft cloth, apply them at random all over the sculpture, and with a coarse cloth, rub them well into the depressions and crevices. Then apply lighter colors, the hues soft and earthy, to the high surfaces and rub the whole thing well to sink the colors into the pores of the wood. Now paint on the design of the figure: the face, clothing, hair, whatever is called for, still keeping the motif simple and naïve. You can feather these colors in with a clean, dry cloth so that they blend in with the background, or you can leave them dominant, to be blended in later by manipulating the glaze.

Allow the piece to dry until it is no longer tacky to the touch. This may be a week or more, and then it is ready to be glazed with soft, dark, "antique" colors. The old artisans used earth colors such as terre-verte, ocher, and cobalt, but if you want more depth and glow you can use one of the "bleeding" transparent colors such as alizarin crimson or ultramarine blue or violet. A good glazing medium is one part linseed oil, one part dammar varnish, and two parts turpentine. You can keep this in a tightly capped jar, and pour small amounts into a plastic dish as needed for each glazing color. Add very small quantities of colors to the glazing medium, then brush the glazes on, again in a random pattern. Polychrome means many-colored, and so the washes are applied not one on top of another but with each color adjacent to the next; so with soft, clean cloths, carefully rub over the whole piece to blend the colors gently. (Figure 32.) The whole idea of polychroming is to give the sculpture its birthright of looking weatherbeaten and timeworn; the way to achieve this is to keep the colors very subtle, warm, and understated.

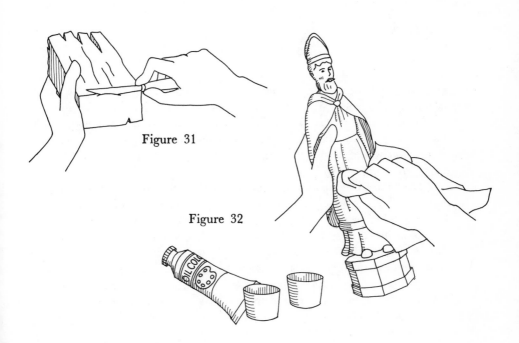

Figure 31

Figure 32

When the glaze is thoroughly dry, rub the whole piece over with fine steel wool until it glistens, and *voilà,* you have created a fine old artifact, ready to stand sentinel wherever you desire.

Tin or aluminum ware can be transformed, too, by treating it in the manner of old toleware. Tole was used widely in the eighteenth century to decorate objects of iron or tin; it was made by first brushing on a coat of varnish to resist rust, and then applying a base coat of enamel, which was sanded down to dull the gloss to a satiny finish. Then the decoration was painted on, using an equal mixture of artist's oils and varnish, and this was sealed in with two or three coats of the varnish. When dry, it was antiqued with burnt umber in turpentine, and was finished off with two or three more coats of varnish, each one sanded carefully with pumice.

Stenciling, on either metal or wood, was done in much the same way, but here gold and bronze powders were dusted onto tacky varnish, using a stencil cut from architect's linen, and a small dusting pad made from velvet or chamois. Each component of the design was cut individually, so that all could be assembled into various arrangements. In that way, several areas could be decorated with the same design, but with modifications made according to the space available.

These were all time-consuming labors of love, done with meticulous care and patience. But artists today use acrylics at the drop of a hat, and satisfactory results can probably be gotten by using muted colors and very thinned-down medium (or Elmer's glue) in place of varnish. Certainly in these hurried days the modern materials are great timesavers.

DÉCOUPAGE ON WOOD

The term découpage, which means literally "cutting out from," was originally reserved for the art of cutting designs into paper. The artist would sketch an intricate pattern and then, with a small manicure scissors, he would painstakingly cut away all the background so that the design would stand out in silhouette. Sometimes he would not even do a preliminary sketch, but would work out his design as he was cutting away. And the results were wondrous to behold.

Gradually, découpage has come to mean the mounting of a picture on a support. This can be done either by cutting the picture itself away from its background or by using a favorite print or child's drawing or a magazine illustration just as it comes on the paper. The designs can be pasted on cigarette boxes, lunch boxes, handbags, old trunks or sewing cabinets—on anything that asks for decoration. After being pasted down carefully so that no air bubbles remain trapped, they are varnished or shellacked many, many times, until the surface is completely smoothed and no ridge marks remain to mar it.

Figure 33   Figure 34

Suppose you were to take this one step further and make a wall plaque of "antique" wood. All the materials will be geared to making your découpage look genuinely old.

From the lumberyard, buy the widest shelving you can of common pine. If your picture is, say, 8×10 inches, the board should be 12×16 inches to allow sufficient border. The board will be aged by "distressing" it, and so any imperfections that are in the grain are so much to the good. Pictures may be inexpensive reproductions of any kind: old trains, automobiles, maps, portraits—all are suitable for découpage in an antique tradition. You will need Elmer's glue, wood stain, turpentine, antiquing color in oil paint— raw umber or burnt umber mixed with black and yellow—and varnish for the final finishing.

First, the wood must be made to look old and weather-beaten; with an ice pick or a can opener, hack at it to make dents, gouges, and pockmarks. (Figure 33.) But keep the center free of these distress marks so that the picture will lie flat. Now, with a whittling knife—a penknife or a sharp kitchen knife—round the edges of the board crudely by hacking away at an angle, so that the top surface is slightly beveled. Sand the piece lightly, apply stain to the whole board, and set it aside to dry.

With the tip of your finger, dampen the edges of the picture that you have chosen to mount, and then tear away a border on all sides so that you have a jagged torn edge all around the subject matter. Then apply glue to the back of the picture and glue it to the center of the board, smoothing it down well so that it is firmly in place, with no air pockets. (Figure 34.)

Mix the antiquing color with a little turpentine and apply it to the whole piece with a soft cloth. Wipe it off the picture immediately, let it settle for a few minutes on the ragged edges to blend, leave it a little longer on the bare wood, then wipe the entire surface off. Now the plaque should look mellowed and aged and right out of grandmother's attic.

Let it dry for a few days, then varnish it (which will further enhance it) and put screw eyes on the back for hanging.

The charm of an antiqued piece like this is its crudeness, so we do every operation with not too much attention to detail. You can varnish it as many times as you wish, with light sanding between successive coats, or you can leave it roughly finished with all the distress marks showing up in their pristine glory.

If you are lucky enough to find an old wooden kitchen table in a secondhand store, you can mount a handsome découpage on it. In the country, you can sometimes pick up old barn sidings, already distressed and very authentic; if you want a very large plaque, two or more pieces of wood can be glued together with epoxy cement and reinforced on the back with lattice stripping. A découpage piece can be as large or as small as you wish, and in this method of antique découpage, any bits and scraps are permissible. Tiny matchboxes can be stacked to make little drawers in a chest by binding them together with balsa wood, which can then be decorated. Even jewelry, such as earrings or pendants, can be made by applying découpage to tiny bits of wood, shingle, or slate.

Another method of distressing wood is to play a torch on it so that sections are lightly eaten away by burning. This is especially interesting when done on driftwood or fallen tree limbs, to which imaginative motifs can be applied by découpage. Interesting sculpture can be made by applying sections of pictures, such as a head or a pair of arms, to a piece of wood that is shaped so as to suggest the rest of the torso. An animal body might be glued on if the branch has its own appendages, conveying the idea of a four-legged creature, and additional interest can be gotten by painting in oil colors directly on the wood: first, stain the wood, then paint on the design, and when it is dry, antique the whole piece. You can add a drop of dammar varnish to the antiquing color to protect the piece from outdoor hazards; but, in general, this type of work is best if left more or less in its natural state, without too much spit and polish being added. Just have a good time and let your inspiration guide you.

3

Metal

SILVER JEWELRY

Jewelry today takes all manner of forms and is made from all sorts of materials. The new plastics are popular, as are bits of glass, slate, wood, cork, leather, yarn; anything that strikes your fancy is possible. Here, we will concern ourselves with methods of designing and working in metal.

All metals are worked in pretty much the same manner. Copper is inexpensive and might be used by the beginner for trial pieces. Gold is costly, and one should have experience before attempting that medium. We shall concentrate on sterling silver.

There are many tools and devices that are nice to have, but here we shall limit ourselves to the basic necessities. Jeweler's supplies should be obtained from a craft-supply house rather than a hardware or hobby shop, because they are precision-made for their purpose. There are, for instance, many different kinds of tweezers. (Figure 35.) There are round-end, pointy-end, flat-end; there are various kinds of files—round, half-round, flat. There are pliers, saw blades, and clamps, each one made of the finest material and for a particular purpose. They are priced far above hardware-store items, and it is up to you to decide where to buy them.

To begin with, you will need a small, fine-toothed file, a jeweler's saw or a hacksaw with a very fine blade, a pair of small, round pointy-nose pliers, and a propane or butane hand torch. The cleaning solution (pickle) and the liver of sulphur for oxidizing can be bought in a drugstore.

The oxidizing solution is made by simply dropping two or three lumps of the sulphur into a jar of warm water; after an hour or so, it is ready to use. The pickle is made from concentrated sulphuric acid diluted to 10 per

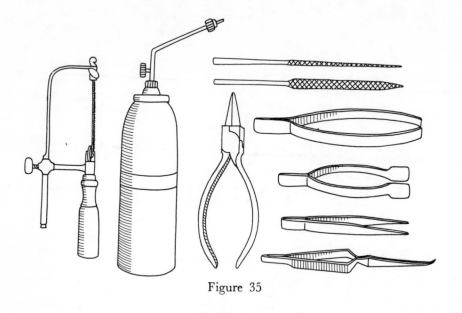

Figure 35

cent. To make it up, put nine volumes of water into a wide-mouthed jar and slowly add one volume of the concentrated acid. (Figure 36.) *Always add the acid to the water,* never vice versa, because then it would boil up and could cause a nasty burn. Keep it tightly stoppered and well labeled; it will keep indefinitely. (Your craft house has a cleaning solution called Sparex that can be used instead of the acid and is not so dangerous to keep around. For working, pour about an inch of the 10 per cent acid solution into an ovenproof glass bowl; it can be used over and over until it gets dirty.)

Ordinary household tongs will discolor in this acid pickle, and this discoloration would bleed onto your work. Copper, however, is safe, and so copper tongs are used for handling the objects in and out of the pickling solution. You can make these very simply by cutting a piece of copper sheeting into a narrow strip about twelve inches long and bending it in half. Make the ends meet closely. This will suffice to hold the object, avoiding injury to your fingers from contact with the acid.

Because you will be working with high temperatures, your work area should be protected with asbestos sheet or fireproof roofing shingle, and a thick asbestos block or a firebrick should be kept handy to rest hot pieces on. In addition, you will need a polishing grit such as powdered pumice, along with fine steel wool.

From the craft-supply house, buy your silver and findings, and solder and flux. The most practical silver solder to have on hand is known as "easy" solder. It melts and flows at about 1,325°. With it you use a flux, which is applied to minimize oxidation, or fire scale. "Findings" are accessories such as earring backs, pin catches, cuff-link packs, and clasps, and they come in nickel and in silver (Figure 37); use nickel, because it is the easier to work with. Materials are sheet metal, wire, circles, squares, beads, balls, stars, zodiac signs, et cetera. They are of silver and are sold by weight. The lower the gauge the thicker (and heavier) the metal, and you must decide on how heavy or how delicate your piece is going to be before you start, so that you can purchase the proper supplies.

One piece of equipment that you should have and that is simple to make is a "jeweler's bench pin," a piece of wood, about three inches by six inches, and a half inch thick, with a wedge-shaped triangle cut out of one end. It is clamped to the table by a C clamp with the wedge extending toward you. When you are sawing or filing, your piece will straddle this open wedge and allow for an up-and-down motion of the tool. If, for instance, you wanted a cutout design on a disk, you would first drill a small hole in the disk and slip your saw blade through it; then you would secure

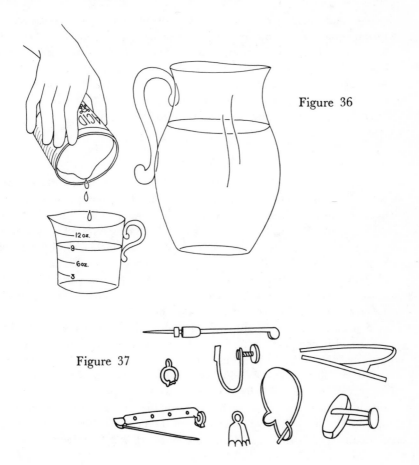

Figure 36

Figure 37

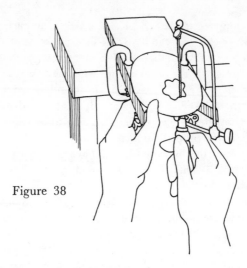

Figure 38

the saw blade in its frame, straddle the open triangle with the disk, and with an up-and-down motion cut out your design. (Figure 38.) Obviously, you could not do this operation if you did not have free access to the piece, and the open wedge gives you that freedom. A jeweler's bench also allows you to keep a clean box in your lap to collect the filings as you work. The silver dust from sawing will drop into the box, and when you have collected a few ounces, you can sell it back to your supplier.

Chains

Suppose you start off by making a link chain and pendant right from scratch. The chain will be medium heavy, made from wire, and the pendant will be made from sheet metal and will be ornamented with a bar and a couple of balls. You will need forty inches of 18-gauge round wire, and one square inch of 16-gauge silver sheet, and about five inches of 14-gauge wire, which can be round, half-round, or square, as you wish: the 14-gauge wire will form the decoration on the pendant. You will need a small amount of soft solder and flux and a large nail for forming the chain. No findings are necessary, because you are going to make your own clasp.

Saw off a length of about twelve inches of the 18-gauge wire and, holding one end in the pliers, wind it tightly around the nail to form a coil. Slip the coil off the nail, and place it on the jeweler's bench, and saw through it lengthwise. (Figure 39.) As you saw, small open circles of wire will detach themselves, and you will have made a whole lot of links. Slip one link through another, and close each gap with the pliers. Continue doing this until you have made enough links to form the necklace. Now take about one inch of the straight wire and form this into an S shape. Attach one loop of the S to the last link of the chain, and close it with the pliers. Leave the other loop open to form the clasp, which will be hooked into the last link on the other end of the chain. If your saw blade is not fine enough, it will have left rough edges on the coils; these should be filed smooth with the file and then with steel wool.

Now that you have a chain, you next can make a pendant to hang on it. You might make it a flat free form with the bar and two balls soldered on for decoration. Draw the design on a small piece of tracing paper, cut out the outline, and glue it to the piece of silver sheet metal. Straddle the open triangle of the jeweler's bench with it, firmly holding it flat with your left hand. Hold the saw perpendicular to it in your right hand, being sure that the blade is taut and the teeth face down, and start sawing with an easy up-and-down motion. Once you have made your initial cut, you will find that the blade does the work, and if you use force you will only end up with a broken blade. So go gently around corners: sharp corners, too, will break your blades. Don't get discouraged; this is difficult at first, but it gets easier with practice. Saw out the rough shape, and then lay it on the edge of the bench and start filing to perfect the shape and to smooth the rough edges. The finer the file the smoother will be the end result. (Jeweler's tools are fine instruments, and that is why they are so expensive. With care, they will last a lifetime.) Polish the edges with fine steel wool, and polish the surface too, so that it will be scrupulously clean and ready for soldering.

Figure 39

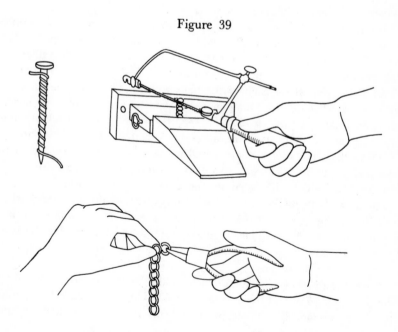

For the bar ornament, saw off a small piece of the 14-gauge wire. File the ends down to a bevel—or slant—so that it will "belong" and not just be stuck onto the base, and try it at different angles, to see which one pleases you. Then smooth it with steel wool to remove any roughness and set it aside while you make the balls.

Take a piece of wire about one inch long, or a small, thin piece of sheet silver. Lay it on the asbestos board and, using the propane torch with the narrow-flame attachment to concentrate the heat, apply the torch up and down the length of the wire. As the metal heats, it starts to melt, and when it melts it will crawl up on itself and form a ball. Remove the heat as soon as the ball is formed, otherwise you will burn craters in it. In applying intense heat to the metal, always play your torch along the full length so that there will not be too sudden a change in temperature from one part to another, which would weaken the metal. While it is still hot, pick up the ball with copper tongs and plunge it into the pickling solution. The pickle will clean the metal and remove the oxidation caused by the heat. Pick it out of the acid with the tongs and drop it into plain water to wash it off. (The sulphuric acid must be treated with caution. It will burn holes in your clothes and stain your sink, and it is dangerous if it spatters.) You will need two balls for this particular design; make one a little larger for interest, starting with a larger scrap. The balls will not by any means be perfect spheres; if you want them perfect, it is better to buy them ready-made and just assemble the parts. This is a matter of taste.

All the parts are now ready for soldering. Soldering is a ticklish job but will become easier as you gain experience.

Having everything scrupulously clean, lay the free-form base face up on the asbestos sheet and apply flux with a very small, soft, pointed artist's brush. The flux is applied to both parts that are to be soldered together, but this is not an exact operation; just put a line of flux down where the bar will go and a drop on where each of the balls will go. This flux will allow the solder to "flow." Cut very small pieces of solder—the size of a pinhead— with an ordinary pair of scissors, and keep them on a piece of white paper, where you can see them. Pick up one piece with the wet flux brush and lay it down in the flux exactly where a ball will go. Lay the ball on top of the solder and apply heat. (Figure 40.) Play the torch around and around the silver; keep it moving, to distribute the heat evenly and so as not to burn any one area: both pieces to be soldered must be brought simultaneously to pink heat. At the moment the solder melts, you will see the ball give a little jump and then settle into place. Remove the flame immediately. Occasionally, it is necessary to press on the ball with a long instrument such as an ice pick or a dentist's probe.

Repeat the process with the other ball, and for the bar use two pieces of solder, one near each end. As long as the soldering is done on a flat surface, those objects previously soldered on should stay in place. Should they jump

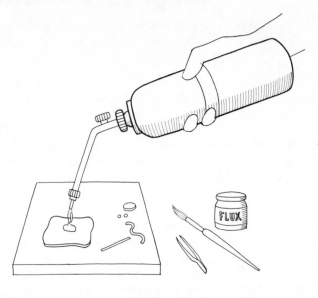

Figure 40

around, you can anchor them in place by wrapping the whole thing with iron binding wire, like a package. Or you can apply powdered rouge or ocher (from the supply house) to those parts previously soldered. The iron binding wire will reject the solder, but it must be removed before pickling. The ocher or rouge will prevent the soldered areas from melting again, so things will not move from a set position, but ocher and rouge are a bit of a nuisance to polish away. After pickling, drill a small hole in the pendant and hang it by a link attached to the chain. Scrub the whole thing with a toothbrush to clean it, polish it with fine pumice or toothpaste or a rouge cloth, and boil it in a little detergent for a brighter finish if this is desired. And you are all finished.

Earrings and pins are made the same way as the pendant but with the addition of findings on the back. Cuff links must be cleaned in the pickle before soldering on the backs, because the spring is not made from sterling silver and would discolor. Suppose you make a pair of earrings to match the pendant. Use ordinary soft lead solder with its own flux, for the back of the piece will not be seen, and this solder, having a much lower flowing point than silver solder, is easier to use and requires less heat. When the design on the front is finished, turn it over so that it is face down; make sure that it lies flat so that the ornaments will not fall off when the heat is applied. A small sheet of soft asbestos is good for this purpose: in addition to asbestos being fireproof, your piece can be embedded in it so that it is supported at all points.

Soft Soldering

Put a drop of soft-solder flux on the spot where the finding is to go, and cut a very small piece of solder and lay it on the flux. Play the torch on the piece until the solder melts, immediately put your finding on top of the melted solder, and play your torch over the whole thing. The finding is small and delicate and will melt sooner than the piece, so make sure everything is heating up at the same time by playing more heat on the larger surface to equalize. When the temperature of the two parts is the same, and high enough, the solder will join the pieces. If the soldering does not hold, it is probably because both pieces were not brought up to temperature simultaneously.

Soft lead solder has to be allowed to cool while setting. If you are in a hurry, you can put a drop of cold water on the joint to hurry it along. Otherwise, leave it undisturbed for about five minutes. Silver solder, on the other hand, may be plunged right into the pickle, which will clean it beautifully while it is hot. Soft solder and its flux are purchased in a hardware store, but silver solder and its flux must be purchased from your craft-supply dealer.

After the final soldering, pickle the whole piece, wash it off, and polish it with very fine steel wool. If the piece is cold, warm it slightly or else warm the pickling solution: it does a better job when warm. If you want to, you can now oxidize it in some areas, for interest. Mix a few sulphur lumps in a glass of warm water and then apply the liquid with a cotton swab around the ornaments, or wherever you want a darker finish. Allow it to stand for a few minutes, until it turns black, and then wash it off and polish it with a soft damp cloth and pumice, leaving the oxidized parts dark. Toothpaste makes a good final polishing agent, because it has just enough grit to remove fine scratches and will leave some of the oxidation on.

Figure 41

Bangle Bracelets

Bangle bracelets are easy to make in many styles. The simplest is made from a seven-inch length of very heavy—12- or 10-gauge—half-round wire, which is almost as thick as a pencil. Mark lines in pairs across or diagonally across the width of the rounded surface, and with a very small round or triangular file, notch the design in by simply filing back and forth until the lines are etched in as deep as you want them; then file the ends of the wire to a smooth, tapered finish. (Figure 41.) To form the bracelet, place the piece

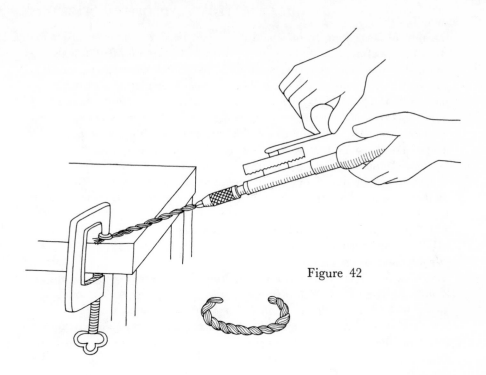

Figure 42

across a thick, round surface such as a chair leg or a rolling pin, and bend it gradually into an oval shape to fit the wrist. This type of bracelet may be left as wide open at the ends as you wish, providing that it is closed enough to stay on the wrist. If the bending is too difficult to do, then you must anneal your silver. Annealing is a process used to soften the metal, because the more it is worked, the stiffer and harder it becomes. To do this, lay the piece on the asbestos sheet and heat it to a red heat, then plunge it into cold water, using tongs, of course; it will become quite malleable and easy to bend. Sometimes frequent annealings are necessary to keep the metal workable.

Another type of bangle is made by twisting two or three lengths of thin wire together and then forming this "rope" into an oval or circle. Round and/or square wire may be used for these. Take two or three 10-inch lengths of 18-gauge wire and place the ends together in a hand drill. Hold the other ends rigid and taut by clamping them in a vise or by holding them in a pair of flat-nosed pliers or a clamp fixed to the table. (Figure 42.) (Wrapping the ends in a piece of soft leather will protect the silver from scratch marks.) Now turn the handle of the drill slowly; a spiral will form as the wires twist around each other. Keep turning until you have a fairly tight twist. When the design looks good, clean and file the ends, and apply silver solder just at the tips, to keep them from separating. Then bend the bracelet around a chair leg as before, and your bangle is formed. If you wish a continuous circle, make your ends meet perfectly and neatly and solder them together. The coils of the twisted wire might be hammered flat on a very hard surface, such as a steel block, before shaping; this gives an interesting effect of interlacing or macramé. These bangles are handsome when oxidized: cover the whole bracelet with sulphur solution and then polish it with pumice, the oxidation will remain in the crevices where the polish does not reach.

A coil bracelet that rides up the arm may be made by winding a two- or three-foot length of heavy silver wire around a small tin can. Use a can smaller than the wrist, for the wire coil will spring open a little when it is removed. Annealing the wire first will help it to keep its shape. Hammer the ends flat and file them smooth, or ball them by applying heat with the torch as a finishing touch. The coils may be worn tight together, or spread apart to cover more of the arm.

With imagination, you can design from wire many pieces that do not require soldering at all. You may form a piece of 18-gauge wire into a spiral and then hammer it flat to form a pin: curl one end under and file the other end to a sharp point to form the pin back and catch. You can cut flat pieces of silver sheet into interesting shapes and hang them on a chain by drilling a hole in each and inserting a link by which to hang it from the chain. Handsome Mexican- and Peruvian-type necklaces are often made this easily.

Fine woods may be used in combination with silver. An interesting way to join them is with a rivet or a peg. Drill a hole through a small oblong of highly polished rosewood or ebony. Insert a piece of round silver wire slightly longer than the thickness of the wood, and then hammer the ends of the silver wire on a steel block to flatten them. This will form a decorative little circle of silver on the wood, and the hammering will have spread the metal to make it secure. If you drill a hole in one end of the wood, you can hang it from a chain or a leather thong or looped earring backs.

Tumble-polished or natural rough stones may be wrapped like a bundle with thin silver wire and hung from a chain or thong to be worn as a pendant or earrings, and key chains, too, or bracelets, when mounted in this cage setting.

Bezel Setting

A cut stone, faceted or domed as in a cabochon, is usually set in a prong or bezel setting. For a bezel setting, lay the stone on the table and circle a narrow strip of heavy foil or plastic around it just to meet. When you have the exact size, cut a piece of bezel silver to this pattern and solder the ends together. Cut a base of 18-gauge sheet silver to the shape of the stone, and solder the bezel around it. Then insert the stone and with the handle of a table knife press the edges of the bezel tightly up against the stone. If it is to be set in a ring or cuff links, all the soldering should be done before you actually set the stone, because most stones will crack from the heat of even soft soldering. Bezel silver is "fine" silver, which has a higher melting point than sterling, and the base is usually of a heavier gauge than the bezel; these are important factors in soldering: the bezel will not melt while you are bringing the base up to temperature. However, a bezel may be made of the same material as the base if you are willing to have patience in using the torch.

A stone may also be set in a prong setting. For instance, two pieces of 16-gauge wire can be formed into a ring; on the underside, they can be close to each other—soldered together if necessary—and the part that shows can be flanged out to form a cradle for the stone. Solder several half-inch lengths of 16-gauge wire upright onto this cradle, and fit the stone into place. Then bend the wire up to form the prongs, cut them off at the desired length, and file them to a neat edge. Set the stone back in permanently by pressing in the prongs with a table-knife handle, and the ring is all finished. The number of pieces you solder on will be determined by the shape of the stone. A heart-shaped stone, for instance, could have three prongs, an oval shape four prongs, etc. The depth of the stone will determine the length of the prongs; a very deep stone might require more than a half-inch length of wire to start with. Bezels may be bought already formed for standard-size semiprecious stones, and ring blanks with prongs ready to receive a stone are also available; they merely need a final polishing.

Small pieces of table silver can be made simply with twisted wire, sometimes with no soldering at all. For instance, you can make a pickle fork from a twelve-inch length of 14-gauge round silver wire folded in half, leaving the loop about the size of a dime. Place the loop in a vise (protecting it, with leather, from scratching) and place the two free ends in the hand drill; then twist it loosely, leaving a half inch at the ends untwisted. Lay it on a steel block, and hammer the coils flat and then file the free ends to points, as in a two-pronged fork. Drill a small hole in the top edge of the loop, and with very thin wire string a colored bead through it to dangle in the loop. Some 20-gauge wire could be wrapped around the top for additional ornamentation, and this could be soldered on; with careful manipulation, it need not be. The bead ornament could be a little tumbled stone wrapped with fine wire, or a piece of branch coral or ivory, and this same idea can be used for a hair ornament by twisting just a short section at the top and leaving the prongs much longer. The prongs can be crimped into a hairpin shape with pointy-nosed pliers, and the ends should be filed a little blunt so as not to be dangerous.

To make a spoon, a dapping block is necessary for forming the bowl. You can make such a block yourself on a wood lathe by turning a small depression into a very hard wood such as rock maple. Place a flat piece of silver over the depression and hammer the silver into it with a ball-peen hammer or with dapping dies, which are steel forms made to fit exactly the depressions in the block. (A firm sandbag would serve the same purpose.) After forming the bowl of the spoon, you can solder it onto a twisted wire handle to match the fork.

Electroforming

There are other methods of making jewelry, some new and some old, and two of these methods are electroforming and granulation. Both are done on a preformed base: electroforming on any metal, but granulation usually on gold, because it is a difficult technique. Electroforming is merely electroplating allowed to run wild. Immerse a silver (or copper or gold) piece in the electrolytic solution; various factors will cause an irregularity in the deposit of the new metal onto the base. If you increase the temperature or agitate the piece, the rate at which the plating takes place will vary, and the piece will build up in an irregular pattern. Electroforming is difficult to control, and so duplicates are not probable with this method; single pieces can be made quite interestingly.

Granulation

Granulation is similar to your making of the pendant with the balls and wire soldered on, except that this most exacting technique uses minuscule balls and wires and no solder! You make the ornaments from snippets of thin wire heated on a bed of powdered charcoal; then coat them with an adhesive such as gum tragacanth. Set them in place on the base and bring the whole piece slowly to the temperature at which they will fuse to the base by capillary action. This is a very tricky technique, in which temperatures are crucial and ornaments are almost microscopic in size. Granulation is an ancient craft, probably practiced before soldering methods were known, and it is used today by meticulous craftsmen who enjoy the challenge just because it's there.

Niello, Vermeil, Married Metals

Niello is a treatment of silver (and sometimes gold) that looks like very dark oxidation against the brightness of the background metal. It is usually done by applying a mixture of metallic sulphides to engraved areas of the base. It is then fired; the firing fuses it to the background. Then it is polished to a slight luster. Vermeil is sterling silver gilded with 24-carat gold. Married metals is a method whereby thin pieces of different metals are soldered together like the pieces in a jigsaw puzzle; when all the pieces are fitted and soldered, they are treated as one flat sheet of metal, and the surface is polished so that the work looks like inlay.

Earrings. Thin silver sheet was rounded on a form, then half-round balls and wires were soldered on. Contemporary. Italian. Collection of the author.

Pin in married-metals technique. Brass and niello motifs were inserted into cutouts in a silver disk, and then the flat disk was soldered to a silver backing. Contemporary. Mexican. Collection of the author.

Filigreed buckle. Made from beaded silver wire, coiled, and soldered only at the corners. Contemporary. French. Collection of the author.

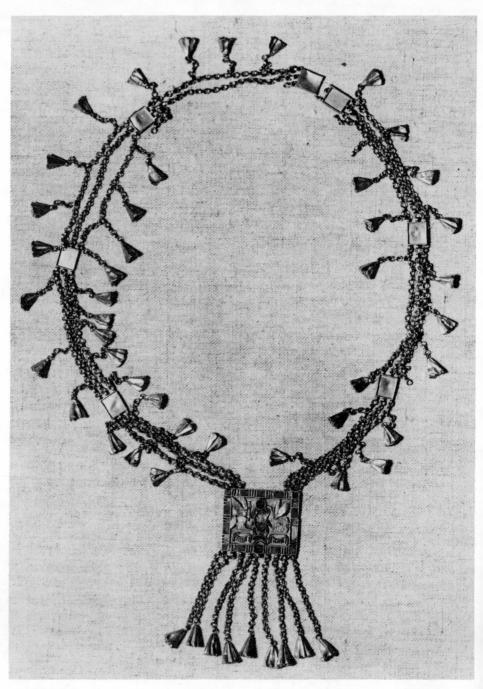

Pharaoh's necklace. Made from gold and silver motifs, and inlaid with lapis lazuli, it was possibly stamped from a form. Tenth to eleventh century B.C. Egyptian. Courtesy the Louvre, Paris. Cliché des Musées Nationaux.

Filigree

Filigree is a technique in which very thin wires are formed into coiled designs, then soldered or inlaid onto a base to make small pieces of jewelry. Sometimes thin strips of sheet metal are used on end instead of wire, and then no supporting base is needed, the metal being strong enough to keep its shape unsupported.

So, as you have learned by trial and error, most pieces are really simple to make, and once you have mastered the art of handling the materials you can go on to bigger and better projects. You will find that eventually you will want electric grinding and polishing tools, and if you send to a supply house for a catalog, you will find many tempting things in it, all designed to help you on your way to becoming a professional craftsman. Good luck.

Teakettle. Copper and brass sheet was raised on a stake in sections. Then the forms were soldered together and the handle riveted on. Contemporary. Israeli. Collection of the author.

SMITHING (FORGING)

Smithing, or forging, is the art of fashioning a shaped object from a flat piece of metal by hammering it into the desired shape. Just as the blacksmith works a horseshoe until it assumes the right proportions, so the craftsman works his precious metal until it is just right. Smithing usually refers to making a dish such as an ashtray, a bowl, or a teapot. There are two ways to do this: one is by "raising" it on a stake or mandrel, and the other is by "sinking" it in a sandbag. Both methods are carried out in the same way, the first one by hammering on the outside, thereby stretching the metal to raise up the sides, and the second one by hammering on the inside for the same purpose.

Smithing is not hard to do but requires patience, practice, and good tools. Large pieces that cannot be made by pressing them into a sandbag must be raised, by the reverse process of shaping them from the outside on a stake or anvil. The shape is gradually formed by hammering and constantly turning and annealing the metal. The end grain of a smooth piece of hardwood can be used as the stake, and a ball-peen hammer can be made by whittling a wooden mallet down to a perfectly smooth ball. Then the piece is worked by hammering and pushing the metal out toward the edges. This is done gradually, because if too sharp an angle is forced without first leading into it, the metal will tear. Raising the bowl from the inside is done by placing a flat disk on a sandbag; the principle here is the same, except that the piece would be free-formed, because the bag is soft and doesn't form a mold for the metal to shape into. This method is easy and can be used with charming results on copper or pewter. After the desired shape is reached,

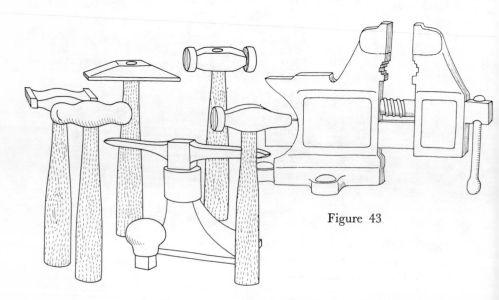

Figure 43

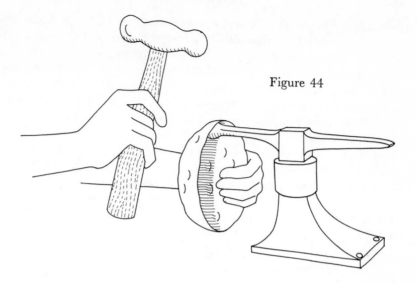

Figure 44

highly polished planishing hammers are used for the final finishing to rid the piece of the original hammer marks and to achieve a relatively smooth surface.

The process of raising is simple. Anchor a strong, sturdy vise to a strong, sturdy workbench, and into the vise set a stake. Place a metal disk against the stake and begin the hammering, which will change the flat disk to a raised bowl. Stakes and hammers come in many different shapes; the stakes are polished steel, the hammers are of steel, wood, or rawhide, and they are ball-peen, domed, flat-faced, round-faced, etc. (Figure 43.) Each tool has its specific use, but you should start with only the basic necessities, which can all be purchased in the hardware store. You will need the vise, a common T stake or a vertical dome stake (or a wooden bowl or other form somehow anchored to the workbench). You will need a ball-peen hammer and a propane torch on an asbestos work surface, tongs, a pail of water, and of course the metal disk, which could be copper for a starting piece. The metal should be heavy enough to keep its shape but not so hard as to be too hard to work; 16-gauge will be about right. Copper is inexpensive and easy to find—in a hobby shop if not at the hardware store.

Before you start to hammer, the metal should be annealed. This is done both to make the job easier and to prevent injury from the hammar blows. Working the metal hardens it, actually changing the molecular structure, and frequent annealings during the work are necessary to keep it malleable. To do this, simply heat the copper with a torch to cherry red, and then plunge it immediately into cold water. When you remove it, it will be nice and soft for working.

Place the edge of the disk on the stake, and keep turning it with the left hand while you hammer it with the right. (Figure 44.) Keep it moving, overlapping the hammer blows, and as you hammer the metal, you will see it begin to stretch and flange out where the sides of the bowl are being formed. Work from the rim toward the center of the bowl, annealing the metal frequently and being careful not to stretch it to the point where it will crack. Keep moving the work until you have formed the sides of the bowl, and leave the center area flat to form the bottom, on which the bowl must rest. When the shape is as you wish it, smooth away the hammer marks all over with a planishing hammer or with a softer mallet—rawhide, wood, or even plastic might work—and then smooth off the rough edge with a file. Polish the bowl and use it as is, or use it later as a base for enameling.

The experienced metalsmith has of course an array of tools, and will be very careful in his finishing; he will use assorted planishing hammers, electric grinding wheels, and polishes of various grits. He will use his tools until the bowl is smoothed over completely, or he will stop at any stage to leave hammer marks as part of the design of the piece.

Sinking a Bowl

Sinking a bowl on a sandbag is the same principle, but the work proceeds in reverse: from the inside. The hammering starts at the center, and the sides are formed out toward the rim. (Figure 46.) The bag should be filled fairly firmly with a medium sieve of sand: too fine, it will not be resilient; too coarse, it will not be receptive. Again, the metal should be annealed often, and using a rawhide hammer immediately after the annealing will do much toward softening the roughest of hammer marks.

Pewter disks can be sunk in a sandbag in the same way as copper, and pewter is a delightful metal to work with. It is butter-soft and malleable; it requires no annealing, but it does damage easily from too hard a hammer blow. It can be heated in the oven to about 275° and then can be worked

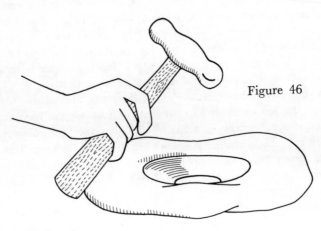

Figure 46

almost by hand; if a hammer blow should make a hole, it can be repaired by dribbling soft lead solder over it. Copper, on the other hand, hardens quickly and requires very frequent annealing, and silver is somewhere in between these two, being used most often for larger objects, such as teapots.

Smithing is really forging. Sculpture is made by forging metal into a desired shape, and bas-relief or repoussé wall sculpture is done by simply hammering the design in from the back on a sandbag until the desired depths are reached to make the sculpture stand out in relief. In-the-round sculpture can be done by forging individual pieces to shape and then welding them together to make a solid but hollow form. Jewelry and dinnerware that are made by hammering are forged, so, you see, forging is a versatile craft, and much can be done with a minimum of equipment and a little ingenuity.

What with plastics that look like metal and glues that act like solder, there are easy ways to do all kinds of things. But alas, they are not for the craftsperson who loves the challenge of the real thing.

SPINNING METAL

A metal bowl can also be turned, or spun, on a lathe by first making a wooden mold to act as the template. Fasten the mold (called a chuck) with the rim end at the headstock. Then center a flat metal disk against the base, and secure it in place by the tailstock. While the lathe is turning, start at the center of the disk and push the metal against the chuck so that it

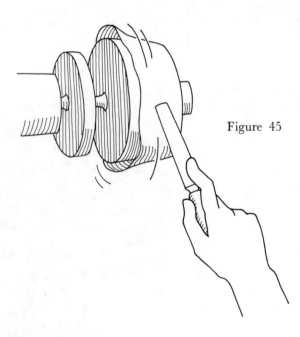

Figure 45

Upper-arm bracelet. Intricately worked in gold by repoussage. It was probably hammered around a stake to form a tube. Fifth century B.C. Persian. Courtesy the Trustees of the British Museum, London.

Brooch. Made of thin gold, repoussé. Minute ornaments were applied, possibly by granulation. Seventh century B.C. Etruscan. Courtesy the Vatican Museum, Rome.

Bead necklace. Coral, turquoise, and colored bone were shaped into cylinders. Then they were drilled, sliced, and polished into individual heishi beads. Sections were joined by links with silver balls added. Contemporary. Egyptian. Collection of the author.

Necklace. Fabricated from 14K gold wire, hammered and soldered. With three faceted diamonds pendant and a large polished agate. Contemporary. American. Ruth Pawelka. (top right)

"The Chestnut Tree." Made with sterling-silver branches, 18K gold leaves, and polished Persian turquoise for buds. The sections were each individually cast; then they were assembled and mounted on a slab of malachite. Contemporary. American. James Schwabe.

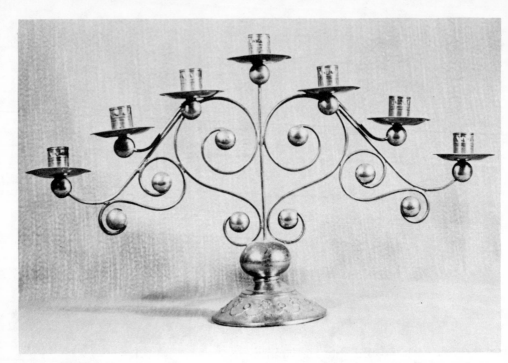

Candelabra. Tin motifs of half-round decorations were formed on a dapping block and then soldered together. Contemporary. Mexican. Collection of the author.

Candleholder. Forged metal. It was used either by jabbing it into a barn siding or hanging it from a beam. Early American. Collection of the author.

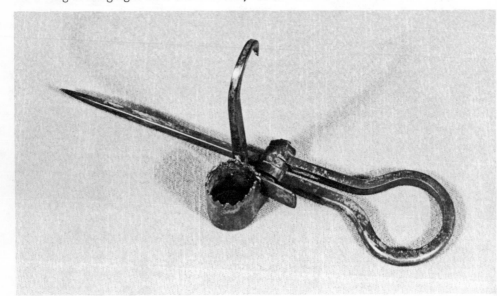

starts to take the shape of the mold. (Figure 45.) This must be done very gradually in order not to crease or tear the metal. There are special rounded chisels for this work; a smooth rounded stick like a broom handle might serve well, because it will not injure the spinning disk. Hold it against the revolving metal, shaping the bowl very slowly, a little bit at a time, always moving the chisel from base to rim—right to left. This is similar in theory to using a drape mold, by which an object is formed by making it assume the outside form of an existing model.

A soft metal such as pewter is particularly easy to turn on a lathe—so easy that great care must be taken not to push the chisel right through the wall. A brittle metal such as copper is much harder to work, and needs frequent annealing to keep it from creasing. All metal bowls, however, are spun the same way, by gently and rhythmically pushing them against the chuck, from base to rim, easing the metal into shape; and the chisel should be kept constantly moving from base to rim so that the mass of metal is moved uniformly.

It is difficult to spin a complicated shape, and so the chuck that you make should be a simple one, with reliance on good proportions rather than flamboyant design. When the bowl is finished, it can be polished with very fine steel wool, and then rouge or pumice, then scouring powder, and it is ready for use.

COPPER ENAMELING

The principle of enameling on metal is similar to that of glazing on ceramic. Enamels and glazes are both powdered glass, which is fused to the body of a piece by high temperatures. However, the methods of accomplishing this fusion are not the same, and the materials and equipment are not usually interchangeable. While a ceramic kiln is brought to a temperature of about 2,000° F very slowly, and then cooled slowly before it is opened, the enameling kiln comes up to temperature in about twenty minutes, and the enamels fuse in about three minutes, at a temperature of about 1,450° F. The enameled piece is then promptly removed from the kiln and allowed to cool at room temperature.

Enameling may be done on almost any metal if it is properly prepared. The metals ordinarily used by the craftsman are copper, silver, steel, and aluminum. The technique is the same for all the metals. Silver may burn before the enamel melts, and care must be taken to remove it from the heat on time; aluminum has a low melting point—1,200° F—and special enamels are needed that will fuse below this point; steel must be of special, low-carbon grade to accept the enamel; consequently, enameling is usually done

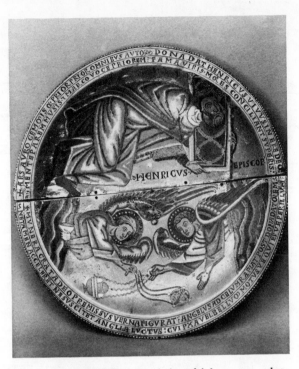

Decoration used on a reliquary. A "French" enamel, in which copper plate was engraved and then colored with transparent enamels. Circa twelfth century. English. Courtesy the Trustees of the British Museum, London.

on copper, which presents the fewest problems, and so we will concern ourselves with that medium.

While there are small, hot-plate-type kilns available, the most practical size has inside measurements of eight inches in width by eight inches in depth by four inches in height. This kiln will take a six-inch bowl or a seven-inch flat piece. Flat pieces are the easier to handle, and you don't need as much leeway in manipulating them in and out of the kiln; a bowl could be two and a half inches deep, but not much deeper. The enameled object is placed on an iron- or steel-mesh trivet called a spider, and the piece is moved in and out of the kiln by placing a spatula under the spider and carrying it. It is good to have several spiders on hand so that when one piece comes out of the kiln another is all ready to go in. (Figure 47.) In addition, some nichrome stilts are needed to rest the piece on if the bottom is enameled, because as the glass melts it will fuse to anything it comes in contact with, and the stilts allow a minimum of contact and can be easily pried off when cool.

The bottom of the kiln should be dusted with dry kiln wash to keep dripping enamels from sticking to the floor. The kiln wash can be brushed out from time to time, and along with it will come hardened bits of enamel that would cause trouble if allowed to fuse to the interior surface.

You will need a spatula with a long handle, and asbestos gloves are a wise precaution. You can buy a pair of copper tongs, or you can make them yourself by bending a long, narrow strip of copper sheet in half. Try to set up shop as close to the source of electricity as possible: sometimes not enough current comes through to heat the kiln properly if the plug is too far from the main line. The work area should be protected by asbestos sheeting placed under and around the kiln, and hot pieces as they are removed from the kiln should be placed on a thick asbestos pad while cooling. During the cooling period, they should be kept away from drafts, which could cause cracking.

The enamels usually come in powder form, but they may be bought in lump form and ground in a ball mill or with mortar and pestle. Then they must be sieved through a mesh; the finer the mesh, the smoother will be the final finish. Most prepared enamels are called "80 mesh." This means that the powder has been sieved through a mesh having eighty holes to the square inch, adequate for most purposes. Any speck of dust in the enamel will blemish the firing, and so any of the powder that is put back into its jar should be strained back in. Placing a piece of nylon stocking over the top of the jar with a rubber band is a convenient way to do this: the enamel is sieved on its way out as well as on its way in. In shaking or dusting the enamels onto the copper piece, always work on a clean piece of

Figure 47

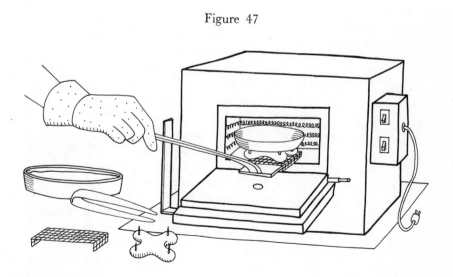

Figure 48

white paper; as you finish with each color, pick up the sheet of paper and sieve the excess enamel back into its jar.

The powdered enamels are dusted on dry, and on pieces with a sloping wall there must be something to act as a glue to keep them from sliding off. Sometimes a light spray of water will do, but usually it takes a solution of gum tragacanth to hold them. (Figure 48.) This should be made up at least a day before you start to work, so the gum can dissolve properly. To prepare the solution, put three or four lumps of gum in a half pint of water and allow it to set overnight. In the morning, strain it through cheesecloth or a nylon stocking, and add a few drops of carbolic acid to preserve it indefinitely; without the acid, it will keep for a few weeks in a cool place.

You can buy all sorts of copper forms from your craft dealer, such as precut shapes for pins, earrings, bowls, ashtrays, plaques, and such. Or you may wish to cut your own from sheet metal and form your own shapes on an anvil or a dapping block. The copper you use must be reasonably pure, and because commercial copper contains a large amount of zinc, it is safest to buy the sheet from your craft house. For a large piece the copper should be at least 16 gauge, but for smaller pieces 18 gauge will do, and plaques to be mounted might work out as thin as 22 gauge. The thickness in gauge is a standard rule applied to any metal: the higher the gauge the thinner the metal. Copper of 22 or 20 gauge can be cut with tin snips, but anything thicker than that will probably require a hacksaw or a jeweler's saw.

Hammer marks on the piece need not worry you too much, because when they are covered with enamel they may appear as facets do in a jewel, and be most interesting. Often, too, scratch marks can be incorporated into the design, sometimes applied purposely with a wire brush on a grinding wheel. French enamels are made in this way, a design being etched on the bare metal with a scribing tool and then many coats of transparent enamel fired on. The design will always show through these clear colors, and the many firings give the depth that is characteristic of this technique.

The last bit of preparation that must be made is the cleaning of the copper. To do this, first file the edges of the piece with sandpaper or a carborundum stone; they must be smooth, because the enamel will not adhere to a rough edge. Then scrub the piece with steel wool and cleanser—no soap, because that's greasy—and then with vinegar and salt. Wash it off with clear water, and dip it into a warmed pickling solution. This can be a solution of Sparex, which is available at the craft-supply shop, or 10 per cent sulphuric acid, which you can get at the drugstore, and which must be handled very cautiously: it is a strong corrosive solution. *Water should never be added to acid;* that causes spattering, and can burn severely; if you have to dilute it, always do so by adding the acid to the water, and not vice versa. Remove the piece with the copper tongs and wash it with water again. If it is clean and grease-free, it will hold a thin film of water, with no droplets. Wash it with water again and leave it to drain on a paper towel. It should be handled now as little as possible, and then only by the edges, because finger marks are greasy and the copper must be scrupulously clean in order to accept the enamels.

Small pieces of jewelry—or plaques to be mounted—are not usually enameled on the back, but heavier pieces should be, to prevent warping. This is called counterenameling and is sometimes done by collecting all waste enamels and sieving them back into a jar; this mixture is useful and can be interesting or at least adequate for counterenameling. Counterenameling is usually done in the first firing so as not to mar the inside of the piece in future firings. Jewelry pieces such as pins and earrings must have a bare metal spot on the back, on which to solder the findings later; if you wish to counterenamel them, leave a bare spot for the purpose. Anything that has been counterenameled must rest on a stilt through all firings; if it is placed directly on the spider, it will adhere to it in the kiln and you will not be able to remove it successfully.

Suppose you enamel an ashtray inside and out. Plug in the kiln, so it can warm up while you are working. Lay the ashtray upside down on a piece of white paper, and brush on a thin coat of gum trag. While it is still wet, dust it over with enamel, covering it generously, then turn it on its side and shake off the excess enamel. (Figure 49.) Place a stilt on a spider, and place the ashtray on the stilt, being sure that it is centered and steady. Allow the moisture to dry out by placing the whole thing on top of the hot kiln for five or ten minutes, then lift it up with the spatula under the spider and place it in the kiln, quickly closing the door. It takes from two to four minutes for

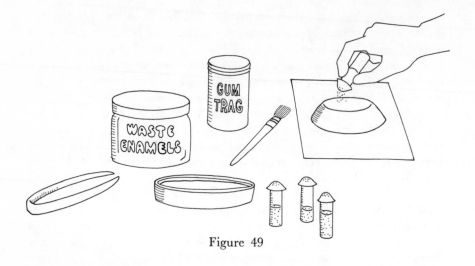

Figure 49

the enamel to fuse; open the door after two minutes and check to see if the piece has a smooth shine. Before it has quite fused, it has a pebbly, "orange peel" look, and then, when the whole surface becomes glossy, it is ready to take out. Slip the spatula back under the spider, lift the whole thing out, and place it on the asbestos sheet to cool. When it is cool enough to handle —fifteen minutes or so—repeat the process, this time enameling the inside of the ashtray. Brush it with gum, sprinkle on the enamel—sprinkling through the nylon stocking assures an even coat—place it on the stilt on the spider, and fire it. If the excess enamel on the white paper is not contaminated with other colors, sieve it back into its original jar. If it is contaminated, sieve it into the counterenameling jar.

Enameling and firing can be done any number of times on the same piece, each time in the same manner. Different colors may be laid on top of each other, or the same color applied again where perhaps it did not turn out well the first (or third!) time. Sometimes the enamel will fuse at a faster rate than the metal, which will cause it to pull away and form cracks while cooling. More enamel can be added, and the piece refired, which will usually mend the uneven surface. Sometimes rough black spots may form; these are called fire scale, and they can be removed with a wet carborundum stone or a wire brush on the electric wheel. That area can be enameled again and fired. Sometimes, soaking the piece in Scalex or a solution of one part sodium bisulphate to five parts water will loosen the fire scale, and then you can remove it by scrubbing it with an old toothbrush. If the fire scale cannot be removed, the piece will have to be discarded, for enamel will not take over fire scale. Usually the scale forms where the piece has not been sufficiently cleaned.

Enamels come in either opaque or transparent colors. If you wish to take advantage of the metallic hue of the copper, you will use only transparent enamels. The oxidation of the metal that takes place in the kiln will then show through the final colors of the enamel and form interesting, uncontrolled designs. It is a good idea to apply a coat of clear enamel, known as flux, as a first coat. In that way, oxidation will show through as beautiful golds, reds, and greens, and it can be incorporated into your design. Opaque enamels, on the other hand, will hide the metal completely, and in fact will hide any color that was previously fired on. So the results you are aiming for will determine which kind of enamel you use. If you want a lustrous, hazy design, you will use transparent colors; if you want a definite, hard-edge design, you can use all opaque colors or a combination of transparent and opaque.

Sgraffito

Sgraffito is an interesting technique in which a base coat is fired on, then a second color applied; when that is dry, it is scratched through with a pointed instrument to expose the base color. After firing, the scratched areas appear as the design and the second coat as the background. For repeat designs, you can cut a stencil from paper and anchor it on the piece with a little Scotch tape; then spray on gum trag with a hand or mouth sprayer, and dust the enamel over that. When the enamel is dry, remove the stencil and fire the piece, and the design will show up only where it has not been blocked by the paper. Many enamelists like to work on a base of opaque white or opaque black, and it is useful to know that if your piece does not turn out to your liking, you can apply a coat of either of these and start your design anew.

While the kiln is on, have three pieces going at once—one in the kiln,

Figure 50

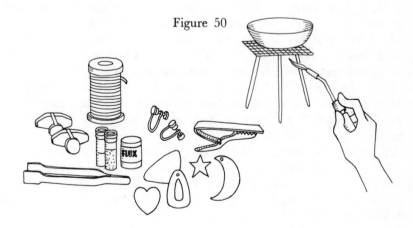

one cooling, and one being decorated. But watch the one in the kiln: it can be overfired and ruined very easily. If a piece is handled very much, you should pickle it between firings to remove any grease spots. If a piece warps in the kiln, placing a heavy weight on it as soon as it comes out of the kiln *might* bring it back to its original shape.

Backs for pins and earrings are put on with soft solder after the piece is finished. But there are special low-firing enamels that are used for silver, because silver has a lower melting point than copper; with these, a finding can be hard-soldered on first and then the enameling can be done. The reason is that the low-firing enamels have a lower melting point than the hard solder, and the heat will not be high enough to affect the joint.

Enameling may be done fairly satisfactorily with a hand torch by placing the piece on a tripod and heating it from underneath. (Figure 50.) The heat from the copper is usually enough to start the enamel melting; at that point you can play the torch directly on the enamel to help it along from above.

Beautiful things can be made in an enameling kiln. There are special kinds of glass that come in lumps and are handsome when they are fused onto a decorative wall panel. There are threads and beads for incorporating into a design, and there are underglaze colors to be painted on, as well as liquid slip or slush enamels that can be trailed on with a syringe. Silver or gold leaf can be used under any transparent color to give a sparkling, iridescent effect; puncturing the leaf with tiny pinholes allows the gases to escape, and in the kiln the leaf will become fused with the enamel. Lavender oil or saliva serves as a good adhesive, and can be applied with a small pointed brush where a very delicate design is wanted.

Cloisonné

There is the cloisonné technique, in which thin, flat, fine silver wires, or ribbons, are bent on edge to form little cloisons, or partitions. Each partition is anchored in place on the metal background with a little gum tragacanth, and when the design is completed, a clear flux is dusted on, which, when fired, fixes the cloisons firmly. They are then filled gradually with colored enamels and fired many times until the enamel is built up to the level of (or above) the edge of its cloison. Then both the metal and the enamel are ground smooth with a carborundum stone under water and polished with pumice powder. The cloisons are little more than $\frac{1}{32}$ inch in depth, but nevertheless it takes many firings to fill them, because too heavy an application at any one time will cause crazing or crackling of the surface. Pure (fine) silver has a melting point of about 1,760° F, so the repeated firings will not deform the cloisons. The old Chinese enamel work with flowers and leaves outlined in metal was done by this method, very patiently and very beautifully.

Cross, enameled in champlevé
technique, with jewels added.
Twelfth century. French.
Courtesy the Trustees of the
British Museum, London.

Censer. Made from bronze with copper and enamel cloisonné decoration,
with copper legs and rim. Seventeenth century. Chinese. Collection of the
author.

Plique-à-jour and Champlevé

Plique-à-jour is a technique in which the enamel fills an empty spot in the metal. This is fired on a mica sheet, because there is no backing to hold the enamel in place, and while the mica will support it, it will not adhere. After firing, when the mica is removed the plique-à-jour is like a clear jewel —translucent when held up to the light.

Champlevé (meaning "raised field") is done by etching a design in the metal with nitric acid and then filling in this etched field with enamel, giving, again, a sparking, jewel-like feeling. These two methods always require transparent enamel to set off the technique to best advantage.

Experimentation in enameling leads to many interesting things, and here, as in most crafts, experience and accidents and failures are the best teachers.

Figure 51

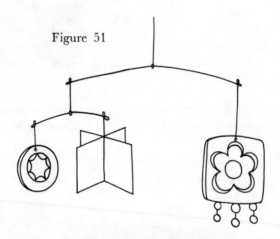

MOBILES

The principle of a mobile piece of sculpture is that all the components are strung together in such a way as to allow free movement of the arms and fins that make up the various units. Each unit is designed so that it can revolve and sway in the breeze, but each is balanced in relation to the others and no one obstructs any other. (Figure 51.) They can be assembled from all sorts of objects and can be made as light and airy or as large and massive as desired. Each unit consists of a rigid arm from which hangs a free-swinging fin, and the principle of construction is always the same, whether it is to hang from the nursery ceiling or in the middle of Grand Central Station.

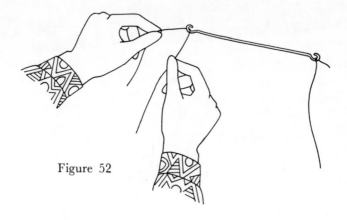

Figure 52

Suppose we make a simple mobile, using rigid clothes-hanger wire for the arms, and brass curtain rings for the fins. Let us make it five units long. In addition to two or three of these hangers, we need a tin snip, a pair of pointy-nosed pliers, some thin strong cord such as nylon bead-stringing or fishing cord, and six curtain rings.

Cut five lengths of wire into graduated lengths from three inches to eight inches, and with the pliers make a small loop on each end of these rods. Tie a piece of cord about two inches long to each loop of the smallest arm, which will be the bottom one, and tie a similar length of cord to one loop of each of the other arms. (Figure 52.) Then attach a curtain ring to the end of each piece of cord so that it dangles.

Now the units are complete, and all we have to do is find the center of gravity of each arm as the mobile rises from the bottom up. The formula for finding this balancing point is to assure that the length of the arm times the weight of the fin is equal on both sides—like a seesaw. It's a little complicated to come up with this "ounces times inches" figure, so we will just find each one instead by trial and error.

Place the shortest arm across your index finger and move it back and forth until you find the spot at which it rests horizontally. (Figure 53.) This is the center of gravity. With the pliers, bend the wire to a 45° angle at this point, and attach a piece of cord there, again about two inches long. String the other end through the empty loop of the next-longest arm and tie it in a bow. Now find the center of gravity of this arm, which is supporting the added weight of the bottom one, by resting it across your finger in the same manner. Bend it at this point (Figure 54), attach a cord at the angle, and tie it to the empty loop of the third unit. Then find the center of gravity of this third arm, which now supports the two below, bend it, tie it, and continue to string them in this fashion until the whole mobile is strung. Each arm consists of three main points: one end with the ring on it, the other

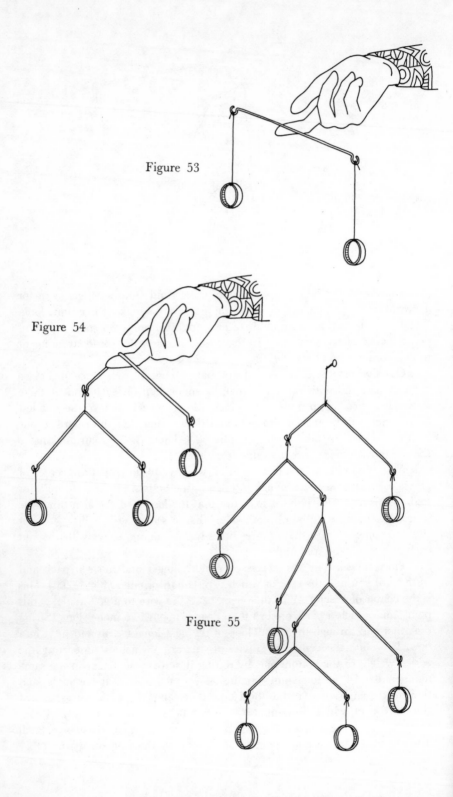

Figure 53

Figure 54

Figure 55

supporting the next arm down, and somewhere in between, the center of gravity, or hanging point. The lowest arm has rings hanging from two of these points, and the whole piece can be as many arms tall as you wish.

Attach a long cord to the center of gravity of the topmost arm and hang it from a nail where it can swing freely. Check the connecting cords to be sure that each unit clears the other ones as it swings around. Blow on it to keep it moving, and adjust the cords if necessary where you have tied them in a bow. Then secure these knots, and the mobile is finished. (Figure 55.)

The arms need not be graduated in length from the bottom to the top, just so long as they are able to swing freely without interfering with each other. The fins can be of any material that will catch the light as they turn, just so long as they can be supported by the arm without sagging. An easy mobile such as wind chimes, for instance, can be made without all those engineering principles simply by hanging objects from horizontal bars and letting them dangle pleasingly in the air. Each arm and fin balances and interrelates with the others, and as long as they are joyful in the interplay of light and movement, they have achieved their purpose.

4
Lapidary

GEMS

The cutting and polishing of gem stones is an art that is ages old, and in some remote areas of the world the craft is still practiced much as it was many centuries ago, the techniques being handed down from generation to generation. A grit was made by boiling down natural resins mixed with sand and then forming this into a pancake. When it was hardened, the abrasive disk was mounted on a hand- (or foot-) turned wheel, and when a natural rock was held against this revolving wheel, a rough stone could be brought to a nice polish and a jewel brought forth that was much prized. When the pancake became grooved from constant pressure, the grooves were put to use as a means of polishing-in an angular design; in this way, faceting came into being and jewels became more elaborate. When the pancake got too mis-shapen, it was simply melted down and re-formed with a little new material added, and there was never any problem getting supplies. There was always more resin in the trees, more sand by the river, and another rock to be dug up from the earth.

Today, synthetics are everywhere and life is not so simple. There are many kinds of grits, some of them containing synthetic gem dust, and many shapes of "pancakes"; one of the dilemmas now facing the gemologist is the difficulty in deciding and sometimes in distinguishing between genuine stones and synthetic ones. Synthetic gems are manufactured as exact replicas of natural gems, and are not to be confused with imitations. The synthetic is identical to the real in every way, while the imitation is merely a bauble meant for a plaything.

Synthetic Boules

All gem stones are crystalline minerals (with the exception of jet and am-
ber, which are formed from fossilized vegetation). At the end of the nineteenth century, a Frenchman by the name of Verneuil perfected a method
for structuring the crystals, and today any gem can be synthesized to be an
exact reproduction of the natural stone. The Verneuil method builds up an
aggregate of crystals by "growing" a boule. (Figure 56.) Various powdered
oxides are screened through a vertical hopper, then mixed with oxygen and
hydrogen. The gases are ignited, and a temperature of over 3,000° F is
reached, fusing the chemicals and changing them to a liquid, which then
falls in droplets onto the tip of a ceramic pin. The boule is built up drop by
drop, and by changing the formula of the chemicals, one can form the identical molecular structure of practically any gem. The process is quite simple,
but interestingly enough, the diamond, which has the simplest molecular
structure, has proved to be the most elusive, while the sapphire, which is the
rarest stone found in nature, is the easiest one to synthesize.

Diamonds are prohibitively costly to reproduce in quantity, but a close
first cousin called YAG, a garnet compound, is easily made, and it has
enough of the properties of the diamond to make it one of the most exciting
advances in gemology. It is excellent for jewelry, because it has a high ability to break up white light into its fiery components, and it is widely used in
industry because of its hardness and resistance to wear. The synthetic sap-

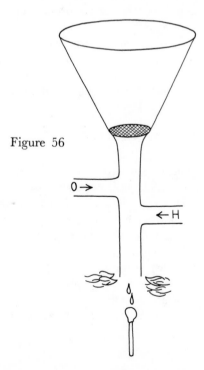

Figure 56

phires, which are known as spinels, are considered gem stones and can be colored chemically in the boule to resemble almost any other jewel; with the YAG and the spinel, the lapidarist today has a very extensive choice of gem materials to choose from, and all are suitable for cutting in the traditional ways.

The industrialist, too, is having a field day. The rubies that were used as the jewels in watchmaking are now spinels, and so all jeweled watches today are precision instruments, because the jewels, being less expensive than genuine stones, can be used more liberally at the critical points of stress. Solid-state transistors are made by etching a flat plate of synthetic crystal and imprinting it with an electrical circuit, thereby eliminating wiring. Probably, the trip to the moon could never have been made if these miniature components had not been perfected by scientists who saw the importance of this new world of gems.

Jewels such as opals, which are very fragile, are usually mounted on a backing, to strengthen them and give them more depth of body. This used to be done by cementing a facing of the gem material to a backing of glass, which didn't add much but made it more serviceable; this was known as a false doublet. Today, opals are fused to a synthetic backing, making them far more beautiful and far truer, being doublets of gem on gem.

Nothing is beyond the imagination. Rutilated quartz, which has dissimilar crystals imbedded in it, is being man-made, with strange effects going on inside it. Star sapphires are being synthesized and made more beautiful than Nature's own, and the only apparent difference is in the cost. Natural gems are still the most precious, but the upstarts are wholly acceptable and travel in the best of company.

All this has made life more complicated, and perhaps that is why lapidary get-togethers are such fun. The rock hounds are enthusiastic people, always willing to share their new discoveries, and no one can come away from a rock show without a feeling that all is right with the world, after all.

CABOCHON POLISHING

There are sedimentary deposits of gem minerals to be found the world over, and rock-hounding is a pleasant and popular pastime. The amateur gemologist takes great delight in hounding down interesting beds and collecting rocks that may or may not have intrinsic value but most certainly are of inestimable value to the collector. The mineralogist appreciates his rocks for what they are in their natural state: a round geode when cracked open might reveal a brilliant display of crystals, or an irregular chunk of stone when polished with carborundum paper might show up fiery streaks of metallic deposits, so he will often leave the stone to be appreciated with no further treatment. A lapidarist, on the other hand, is anxious to cut and polish his finds, and the cutting and polishing of semiprecious stones has until very recently been a specialized, time-consuming job requiring a shop full of equipment where each tool was designed to do one phase of the process. Today, one sophisticated all-purpose unit will do all the jobs, and it is possible now for the lapidarist to set up a whole shop on the kitchen sink.

The most usual way to work stones is into "cabs." A cabochon, the name of which stems from the word *caboche,* meaning cabbage head or bald head, is a polished stone domed on the top in the shape of a round or an oval, and flat on the bottom. Almost any pretty-colored rock can be easily transformed into a "cab" with a minimum of lapidary equipment.

The first step is to break the rock open and expose the inside, or heart, of the mineral, which is the crystalline formation, and this is done by cleavage. Make a score mark with a file to the depth of about an eighth of an inch, then set a chisel in this wedge; when you hit it with a sharp blow of a hammer, the stone will break in two. The rock can then be cleaved into as many pieces as desired by repeating this process, and each piece will be different, some perhaps not very interesting but some with beautiful possibilities worth pursuing further. There is an art to cleaving, because the rock should be broken up into pieces that will follow the crystalline structure; after a little experience, the lapidarist learns just where to start this process.

The next step is to cut away the excess material from the stone, so as to expose the inner structure to its best advantage. This is done with a slabbing saw and requires knowledge of the structure of stones and experience in cutting. The beginner would be wise to have this done at a rock shop; in the process, he will learn much about the structure and dynamics of working with nature. The slabbing saw is a circular saw with a thin steel cutting

Figure 57

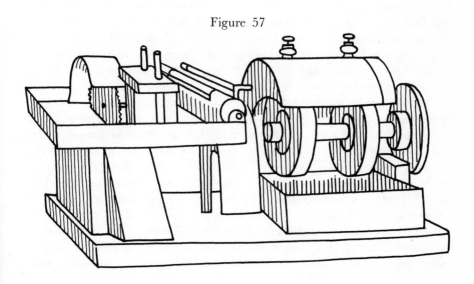

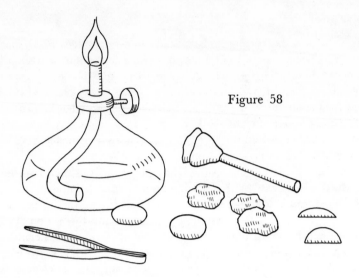

Figure 58

blade that is impregnated with diamond dust. Such a saw could be improvised for the cutting of the softer stones by passing the cutting disk of an ordinary shop saw through a "mud" slurry of silicon carbide to charge it. Once these steps are done, it is just a matter of patient grinding and polishing to produce a finished cabochon.

The grinding wheels are set up in sequence on an arbor, much as in a shoemaker's shop, and each wheel is used with its own grit—wheels of finer grit being used as work progresses. (Figure 57.) There are also units available that consist of one revolving wheel, using grit pads called laps, which can be changed as needed. These units obviously require less space than a whole arbor, and are good for the hobbyist, even though changing the laps is time-consuming. Whichever type is used, a constant drip of water on the grit is essential, both to keep the dust down and to prevent overheating, which could crack the stone; most lapidary grinding units come with a vessel that needs only to be filled with cold water. But if there is no vessel, a piece of rubber tubing can be attached to a dripping faucet, or a narrow metal tube can be soldered low on the side of a tin can or even inserted in a pail of water, which can then be set atop the grinding wheel. The tube can be bent so that it is aimed directly over the lap, and the flow can be started by sucking on it like a straw. As a matter of fact, a bent straw would do the trick. If the unit is not equipped with a drip pan, one will, of course, have to be placed in position to catch the water as it flows toward the floor. The wheel should not ever be used dry: the dust from grinding could be extremely injurious to health—and the stone could overheat, as well.

The materials needed for cabbing are few and simple. The stone is anchored to a dop stick, which can be a four-inch length of one-half-inch wood dowel. (Figure 58.) The adhesive is shellac, a mixture of sealing wax, beeswax, and lac, and is sold at the craft shop where you obtain your grits. The grits are of silicon carbide, and you will need two grinding laps, one a coarse, 100 grit and one a finer, 220 or 320 grit, plus two polishing laps of perhaps 400 and 500 grit, in cerium oxide. An alcohol lamp or a candle or a cigarette lighter, a pair of tweezers, some doweling, and a pair of goggles or a mask, and you are ready to begin.

Start on an oval cabochon, which is the easiest shape to cut. The rough stone should be no longer than about one inch by three quarters of an inch; it will have been slabbed into a more or less rectangular box shape, and will be one half to three quarters of an inch deep, with a flat bottom. Jewelry findings such as ring bezels come in certain standard sizes, and if you think you will be mounting the finished piece, then it is wise to buy a template to use as a guide for sizing, along with an aluminum marking pencil. You can scribe the stone to the proper shape with the aluminum and check frequently against the template as the work moves on.

Break off a chunk of shellac and, holding it with the tweezers, warm it at the top of the flame of the alcohol lamp until it gets just soft enough to press onto the end of the dowel. Wet your fingers to avoid their sticking to the hot wax, and pull the soft shellac down the sides about a half inch so that it binds well to the stick with no wobble. Then pick up the stone with the tweezers and hold both the stone and the dop stick near the flame. Warm them both just enough so that the stone adheres to the shellac when you press it on lightly. It is unwise to sink the stone into the shellac, because, during grinding, the stone should be clean; shellac getting into the lap will clog the grit and ruin it. Press the dop stick upside down on the table top to make a firm bond, and then set it aside to cool slowly.

When the shellac comes back to room temperature, it will be hardened and the stone will be firmly adhered, and you are ready to start grinding with the coarse, 100 grit. Turn the water coolant on to a constant drip or light flow directly onto the lap at a point just above where you are working; hold the dop stick lightly against the revolving wheel with both hands so that you start grinding at what will be the highest point on the dome of the cab. This of course is the center, which will have very little removed, and work will proceed down from this point on all sides, forming a slope like a little Mount Fuji.

Leave the center mound as high as you wish or grind it as flat as you wish by holding the dop stick to the wheel without pressure and letting the wheel turn against it as you rotate it from side to side, making a long sweep to the long ends of the oval and a shorter one to the narrower edges. Grind it away very gradually, so that the slopes are gentle, and when the stone is well shaped, you can change to the next-finer grit (the 220 or 320) and continue the shaping—refining it and starting now to smooth off the stone. The higher the number of the grit, the finer it is, and therefore the smoother the work. Once the shape is formed by a rough, low-number grit, the higher-

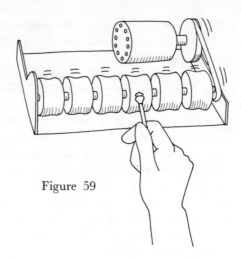

Figure 59

number laps will start the job of polishing, and so your grits in the final stages can go up to 600 or more. Keep grinding and polishing, and when the stone is finished, beautifully shaped, smooth, and glowing, you can rub it with a chamois cloth and it will sparkle like fine silver.

The perfect cabochon has an evenly sloped surface and comes to a gentle drop at the edge. To protect this edge you should bevel it; this might be done by first dopping the stone upside down and forming this chamfer before working the cab. A little heat will soften the shellac again, or a little ice water will make it brittle enough to undop and the stone can be removed and reversed for cutting. Chamfering to a 45° angle is always a good idea, because this rounds off the bottom edge and strengthens the base, making it less liable to chipping.

It is possible to buy rough-cut cabs that you need only to polish. And there is a beautifully designed, compact, motorized unit, available for polishing gems, that consists of six small vertical wheels each carved from rock maple. (Figure 59.) Moisten each wheel with a slurry of grit, progressing from a rough on the first one down to a fine tripoli on the last; the grits run from 325 to as high as 50,000. Put the cab on a dop stick and run it through the whole series of wheels, getting a smoother polish from each successive one. It is very important not to contaminate the wheels: a fine grit won't harm a coarser one, but even a speck of heavy grit will ruin a fine one, and for this reason the stone must be thoroughly cleaned before using each wheel. (The lapidary's shop, for this same reason, is always a neat one.)

Forming a cab is not the only way to work a rock. An interesting shape can be enhanced by grinding it with a carborundum stone, and sometimes a beautiful rock will even respond to hand working. Nephrite, which is classed as a jade, is found the world over, and it looks in the rough like a dull chunk of asbestos (which it is). But it can be blue Monterey jade from California, shaped irregularly on a carborundum wheel into a tie slide or belt-buckle ornament, or it can be soapstone from Alaska or China, carved by hand into a black Eskimo sculpture or a green smiling Buddha. Jadeite, which is considered the true jade, has a denser molecular structure than nephrite and takes on a glassier polish, and it is very seldom found in a random digging.

Agates, which also are found the world over, can be shaped and polished to any form that would best display the characteristic translucent color bands that appear in layers much like the rings of a tree trunk. Occasionally, when a moss agate is cleaved open, a whole landscape scene will show up; the craftsman then will joyously cut thin, flat slabs and polish each one lovingly, each successive slab revealing a slightly different "picture."

Tumbling

Quantities of rocks can be polished in lots by tumbling them in a hexagonal drum, which works like a clothes dryer. (Figure 60.) The drum is rubber-lined to keep the noise down, and the stones and grit are placed in it in a ratio of 10:1—five pounds of stones to about half a pound of coarse grit. The grit can be anything that is abrasive, and even coarse beach sand will do. The drum is half filled with water, then allowed to rotate for as long as is necessary to smooth off all the jagged edges of the rocks. As it turns, the stones are carried up and dropped down; this mechanical rubbing action takes about a week or longer to do its job. There is, of course, no control over the shape of the polished stone, but often such semiprecious gems as American turquoise matrix will be processed in this way to form nuggets, and small stones from the mines of Africa that are not fine enough for the diamond trade are sometimes finished by tumbling, ready to be used in expensive costume jewelry.

Quartz, which is the commonest of all minerals, falls into two general classes: opaque and transparent. An opaque stone such as chalcedony is

Figure 60

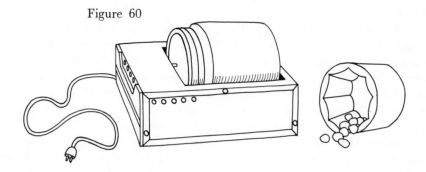

porous and can be stained or dyed but is seldom faceted. Others, such as rose quartz, amethyst, citrine, rock crystal, smoky quartz—all are transparent and therefore suitable for faceting.

All genuine stones are of course mined, but it is very unlikely that the rock hound would stumble on a precious gem in his digging. While a cab-cut jewel is usually less costly than a faceted one, because there is less labor involved, some precious gems such as opals and star sapphires are always displayed as cabochons in order to catch their inner fire, and they are very costly indeed. Rubies and garnets are often cab-cut to give them more depth of color, while a pretty bit of a quite ordinary quartz can sometimes be made to respond handsomely to an interesting faceted design. Irregular faceting can be done on a cabbing wheel, but the beginner might try his luck on an ordinary carborundum grindstone, which might or might not produce an interesting jewel.

Inexpensive store-bought jewelry is sometimes "real," and a good way to find out is by biting the stone. A real gem will feel hard and gritty, while an imitation one will feel waxy. This is a quick test for pearls and jade and coral, which can easily fool the eye but will seldom pass a tooth test. Imitations have their place, but not in the lapidarist's life.

FACETING

Diamonds are a form of carbon and are closely related to coal, which is affectionately known as black diamond; the significant difference between them is age. Carbon in the ground becomes hard coal in a few thousand years, but it takes millions of years for the molecular arrangement of diamonds to take form and to stabilize. That is why diamonds are so precious.

Diamond cutters are highly skilled craftsmen with a great deal of technical knowledge. They must know which way the crystals are structured: they must know at what angle the stone would best be displayed, and after the initial, and critical, cleavage of the stone, they must know exactly at what point to start the faceting in order to bring out the highest refraction of light.

Faceting cuts have improved over the centuries as more knowledge and better machinery have become available. The first facets were made simply to cover flaws in the stone, and in time more elaborate designs were introduced. The rose cut, considered very sophisticated, was the standard until about the beginning of the eighteenth century, when the brilliant cut was introduced; this classical faceting is still considered to be the most advantageous way to display the light dispersement of a round stone.

Brilliant-cut diamonds have fifty-eight facets, and to be perfect, each facet must be in a certain relation to the others. There are some gems, such as emeralds, that do not respond too well to the brilliant cut; they haven't the ability to refract light to the same degree as most other gems. So an elongated faceting was devised that would enhance the crystalline structure instead. This emerald cut is used today for the working of many gems, especially in the designing of modern jewelry.

All gems, precious or not, are classed according to hardness on an arbitrary scale known as Mohs' scale. The diamond is the hardest mineral known, and is given a rating of 10; all other gems fall below that in rank. Sapphire is the next hardest, with a rating of 9; topaz, 8; and so on down the line to soapstone, with a rating of 1. But the curve is not a gradual one —the numbers merely indicate an order. There is a greater difference between the diamond and the topaz, for example, than there is between the topaz and the soapstone. In the faceting process, diamond dust is the only substance hard enough to grind away the surface of a diamond, and so this is used routinely as the abrasive on the cutting tools.

The faceting unit is a small precision instrument somewhat like a record player; it can be set to very precise positions and will never waver. (Figure 61.) It consists of a flat, revolving wheel that is surfaced with a lap of diamond dust impregnated in copper. Adjacent to the wheel is an arm that extends out from an upright post; on this post is a calibrated protractor that can lock the arm into any one of sixty-four positions. The arm, which holds the dop stick, is locked in place so that it extends toward the lap at a given angle. When the stone has been cemented to the dop stick with shellac and the dop stick is clamped back into the arm, the arm is lowered so that the stone just touches the surface of the wheel, and the grinding begins. The arm is lowered a fraction of a centimeter at a time, and gradually a flat facet is ground away, always at this set angle. The metal dop sticks are notched, and after the upper, or crown, facets are ground, the stone can be reversed so that it lies in a precisely opposite position for the grinding of the lower, or pavilion, facets. While the grinding is going on, the surface of the lap is being cooled and lubricated with a constant drip of water.

Figure 61

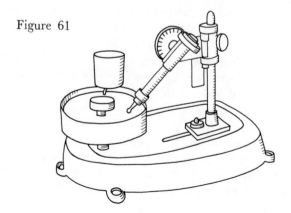

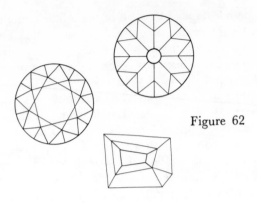

Figure 62

The stone is marked according to a predetermined plan, and only when the diagram is completed does the actual work begin. The brilliant cut is designed so that the upper third, or crown, has thirty-three facets; it widens to the girdle, the largest circumference, and then the stone narrows down again so that the lower two thirds, or pavilion, has twenty-five facets. The lower part of the stone has the facets placed so that they will complement the upper ones and give the best refraction of light, which is the whole *raison d'être.* (Figure 62.) Faceting heightens the dispersion of light, and the brilliant cut is used because this particular placement of the facets produces the best dispersion in clear gems. The stone is cut so that the crown, above the girdle, has a flat top and the pavilion, below the girdle, comes to a point. Those facets that are below the girdle shoot their lights upward and give the flat table the sparkle that is so desirable. Faceting is in effect a polishing, and so every surface of the stone will be put to the wheel.

The facets are planned in pairs and in series of eights, so that every eighth notch on the protractor would be used, and the arm is swung around to the opposing position for each pair. The first facet cut is the table, and then sixteen pairs are cut, radiating out from that in steps, down to the girdle. Then the stone is reversed and twelve pairs are cut on the pavilion. Then the bottom point is ground flat and the girdle is polished at a 90° angle.

It all sounds foolproof, and after eight or ten years of practice, it is— almost. It is never easy, because each stone is different and every facet must be exactly calculated so that the series of eights are positioned precisely with no overlaps and no space left over. Sometimes a hidden flaw might appear after work has been started, and then it becomes necessary to reconsider the pattern. Diamond cutters work in teams, and each man is a specialist in one particular phase; each rough diamond has been contemplated for many hours by many artisans before the design is actually decided on. The famous Jonker diamond weighed 726 carats (approximately five ounces and the size of a fist) before being cut into twenty superb stones, and many, many heads were put together before the cleaver struck the first blow with his chisel and mallet.

The brilliant-cut diamond is the height of lapidary art, but beginners should settle for something less. Quartz (with a hardness of 7) comes in many beautiful forms, and you can choose a small, transparent stone from the almost limitless assortment at your neighborhood rock shop. Shellac, which is a mixture of sealing wax, lac, and beeswax, is necessary. Tweezers, an alcohol lamp, assorted laps, and the faceting head with at least two dop sticks are all the tools needed, and you are ready to begin.

First, study the stone and decide just what to do with it. You might grind it in large, flat, angular, irregularly shaped surfaces and then set it into thin gold prongs for a pendant or a stickpin. The prongs have to come from somewhere, and so you should make a coming together of the angles at the pavilion. Then you could fashion a circle of gold wire to slip around this bottom cone so that as many prongs as needed can rise upward from there to anchor the stone in as many places as needed. (Figure 63.)

A good way to fashion a model for a free-form piece like this is to make one from soap. Carvers for decades have used Ivory soap because it cuts cleanly without chipping. Cut off a chunk the size of a walnut and start whittling it away with a small kitchen knife. When it is the size and shape of your rough stone, carve large, flat facets on it very gradually until you get an interesting interplay of planes and angles. Cement your model to a dop stick, using either warm shellac or melted candle wax, and set a piece of paper over the lap to prevent the grit from getting clogged with soap. Then set it into the arm in a position that allows one facet to lie parallel to the plate (keep it about half an inch above the lap to allow the rough stone to clear), and lock the arm in this position. Then ready the stone. Cut a piece of shellac about the size of an almond, heat it and the stone slightly, and press the stone in to a depth of about one eighth of an inch; then set it aside to cool. Never put the shellac or the stone directly into the flame: both would become brittle when cool, and likely to fracture. And always allow them to cool slowly, at room temperature. Remove the dop stick with the model from the arm of the unit, and replace it with the real one; the stone will then be in position to start grinding the first facet. Using calipers or a com-

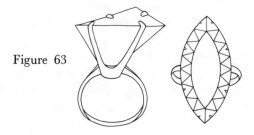

Figure 63

pass, you can check the stone against the model as you work, and when the facet on the stone matches the one on the model, switch dop sticks again (and again protect the lap from the soap) and set the angle for the next facet. Change back to the real one, grind it down, and so on until all the surfaces are cut.

A free-form stone makes a striking piece of jewelry and has the added advantage of being easier to facet than a symmetrical cut. Of course, the larger the surface, the more obvious any flaw will be, and the beginner's stone will surely not be flawless. But this asymmetrical design does away with the need for matching facets in pairs to form an octahedron, which can be very tricky: one out-of-line facet in a series can ruin the whole appearance.

While you are working, it is important that you keep notes as to the angles that have been set for each facet. When all the facets have been cut on a rough lap, then you can start the polishing by going over each facet with finer and finer laps until you are satisfied with its shine and sparkle.

When the stone is finished and mounted, you can clean the whole thing by placing it in a strainer and putting the strainer into a small pot with cold water and a little detergent. Bring it slowly to a boil, let it simmer for a few minutes, and then allow it to sit in the hot water until it cools thoroughly, to avoid a sudden change of temperature, which would surely crack it. Putting it in the strainer keeps it from touching the pot and accidentally overheating.

Rinse it under warm running water, set it in prongs, and hang it from a chain, ready to wear. Or you can use it as a stickpin, which is easily made by adding one extra prong and bending it down so that it lies parallel to the stone. File this "pin" to a point, and when you wear it, secure it with a kewpie catch, a small finding that slips over the tip and serves as a lock. But if the gem is to be mounted as a conventional pin or as a ring or in any form that requires soldering, the soldering must be done before the stone is put in, because the stone would crack under the heat of the torch. Epoxy cement requires no heat and on a roughened surface will hold forever, if you are willing to chance it.

Chunky costume jewelry can be made by collecting scraps of metal from other projects and melting them down and then plunging the molten mass into a pail of water. It will congeal in erratic volcanic shapes, and stones can be glued into the nooks and crannies to create handsome jewels, each a one-of-a-kind conversation piece. And the stones need not be all alike: they can be faceted, cabbed, tumbled, or even rough rocks, mixed or matched as the spirit moves. This is a far cry from faceting a diamond, but one thing does lead to another, and in due time perhaps this chunky jewelry will be made from platinum and set with your own diamonds—who can tell? Maybe even from stardust?

5

Leather

Handmade leather accessories such as bags and wallets and portfolios are handsome to look at and nice to the feel, and they will wear a long, long time. They can be made from natural cowhide, which is stiff, or from calf, which is softer, lighter, and more pliable; or from any of the many novelty leathers that are available—some stenciled to resemble zebra or leopard, some left with hair still on, some sueded in textures and finishes too exotic to imagine.

Leather comes in various weights and is sold by the whole skin, the half skin, and occasionally in small pieces or by the pound. In any case, except for the scrap leather, it is priced by the square foot, and usually it is more economical to buy it by the full skin. The weight that you buy is a matter of personal preference: usually, a 7-ounce cowhide is used for a bag, 6-ounce for a portfolio, and 3–4-ounce calf for a wallet. The tools you need might be found in a good hobby shop but more likely would have to be purchased from a leather-supply house.

Suppose you start by making a hand-stitched Italian-styled bag of cowhide with gussets and a flap. You will have strap hangers to attach the handles and a metal catch for the closing. In addition to those items, you will need a four-prong thonging punch, and if you wish to line the bag, you will also need a piece of skiver leather, which is very thin and is used just for this purpose; it comes in many colors and patterns. Then, from any sewing counter or supermarket, you can get beeswax, carpet or linen thread, large-eyed darning needles, single-edged razor blades, and some rubber cement. (Figure 64.)

A most important step in making the bag is the first one, designing the

Figure 64

Figure 65

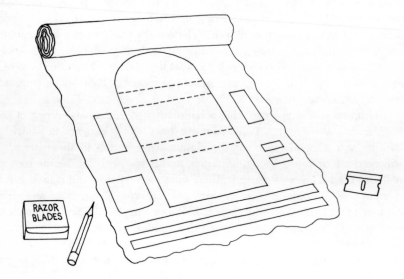

pattern, because everything must fit accurately. The bottom of the bag must be the right shape for the gussets, the flap must be related in size and shape to the size and shape of the bag itself, and all the pieces must be cut and fitted together perfectly before you start to work on the leather itself. If you are fitting the leather to something (such as a book cover), you should make an allowance for each seam by adding a quarter to a half inch, depending on the thickness of both the leather and the object you are working with.

Draw your pattern on heavy brown paper and cut it out. Then sketch the gussets, cut them out, and try them in place, trimming here and there until you get a perfect fit. This bag is designed all in one piece, so you must make allowances for the width of the gussets at the bottom as well as at the opening at the top, and the pattern will be a rectangle which will include the front, bottom, back, top, and flap. (Figure 65.) The gusset can be as

Overnight bag. Elaborate tooling was impressed with metal stamps on heavy cowhide. The strap hangers are stitched and riveted. Contemporary. Mexican. Collection of the author.

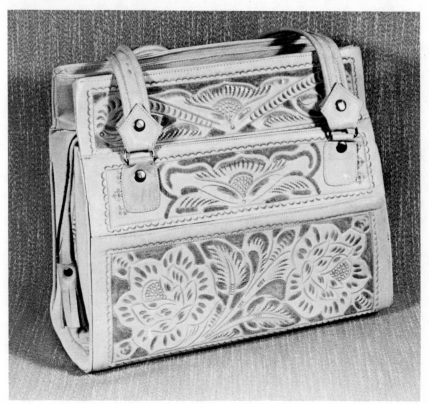

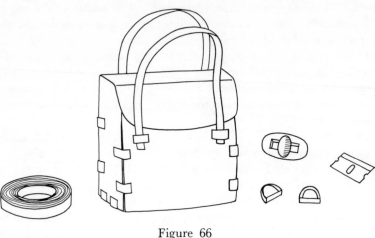

Figure 66

wide as is practical, say an inch and a half wide, rounded at the bottom, and as long as the length of the front of the bag from top to bottom. Pieces can be cut away or may be added to the paper with Scotch tape, and when everything fits together nicely, redo this adjusted pattern on a new piece of paper or on oaktag or slick cardboard. (Figure 66.) Make a pattern, too, of the handles as you wish them; perhaps two long and narrow ones, or a single wide, lined one—whatever seems to suit your design best. If all this engineering is too complicated, you can buy patterns from the leather-supply house, or you can perhaps adapt a commercial pattern to your needs.

Lay the leather right side up on a cutting board—a piece of masonite or a thick pile of newspaper will protect your table—and lay the pattern on top of the leather, also right side up. Be sure you place it so that you have an adequate length of leather left for the handles so that they will not have to be pieced. Draw around the pattern accurately with a sharp pencil, and then remove it. With a single-edged razor blade, cut cleanly into the leather along the pencil marks, and where the lines are straight use a metal straight-edge to guide and steady your hand. Cut out the gussets and handles in the same manner. Then try all your pieces together again to be sure of fit, and you are ready to sew.

Holes must be punched in the leather for all stitching, because pushing a needle through the leather will cause it to crack and tear. The holes can be made on the sewing machine by setting to a long stitch and running the machine with a heavy needle and no thread. This will work for lightweight leather, but a heavy leather requires the use of the thonging punch, which is a tool made of steel with four or more prongs, like a fork. The prongs are sharp and they make slits in the leather that allow the needle to slip through easily. With a compass, draw a line all around the edges of the bag where there will be stitching, about one sixteenth of an inch in from the edge; this will be the guideline to keep your holes straight. Lay the leather on a pad of newspaper (to prevent the tool from getting blunt), place the punch at one end of the guideline, and hammer it through the leather with an ordinary hammer. (Figure 67.) Lift it out, place the first prong in the last slit, and hammer this next set of holes through; by this means, the holes will be evenly spaced and so the stitching will be neat. Work along in this manner, punching holes all along the stitching edge, and all along the edges of the gussets, and the handles, too, if you wish. The stitching is used decoratively as well as purposefully, so you can decide now or later if you want to make use of this trim on the handles.

The thread should be used doubled, and should be pulled through the beeswax before knotting it, to give it added strength. White is customary, but it can be any color, matching or contrasting, and can be colored by dipping some cotton into a dye solution or into colored ink and then pulling the threaded needle through that before waxing it. In this way it will take the color but not get too wet. Start stitching at the center of the bottom of a gusset, matching it wrong sides together exactly to the center of the bottom of the bag. (Be sure that both gussets are exactly alike; otherwise the bag will be lopsided.) Stitch the front of the bag to the gusset with a running stitch going in and out of the holes, and end off your thread by weaving it in and out of the last few stitches; always have your doubled thread long enough so

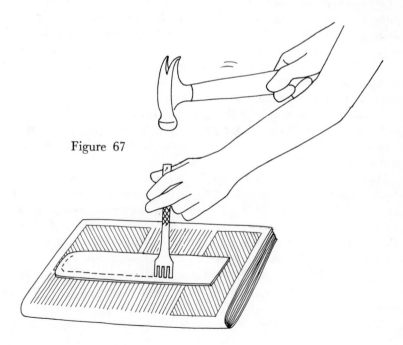

Figure 67

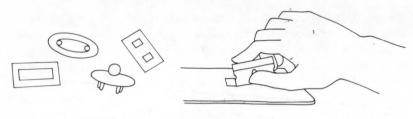

Figure 68

that you are not caught with an ending in a visible place. Sew up the other side of the front to the other gusset in the same manner, and then do the back. If you started the front stitching on the bag itself, then start the back stitching in the next empty hole of the gusset, so that the stitching will be continuous, with no empty spaces. Don't pull the thread too tight. When all the sewing is finished, press the stitching down with the handle of a kitchen knife so that it lies flat. And now you are ready to put on the findings.

Catches come in two pieces, one piece to be attached to the bag and one to the flap; so make a mark with a pencil exactly where they will go. The part to be attached to the bag has sharp prongs that go right through the leather and then are bent back on the inside of the bag to secure it; you can glue a piece of leather or felt to the back with rubber cement to hide these prongs after they are attached. The part that goes on the flap usually requires a rectangular hole to be cut in the leather. Do this very carefully with a razor blade or an X-acto knife, which has a small, very sharp blade, and cut it to the exact size of the opening, not of the whole finding: the rim must sit on the leather to anchor it. (Figure 68.) Insert the catch, and bend the prongs back onto the small metal plate that comes with it; this part of the catch has a finished appearance and will not have to be hidden. You may be able to design a closing that does not require a metal catch, or the size or shape of the flap may serve the purpose by itself; or you might want a bucket bag that has no closure at all. In any case, the bag is now finished except for the handle.

Put the metal strap hangers on the bag in the same way as the catch and then attach the handles to them by turning back the ends and stitching them closed. You might attach two of them to the gussets, or four of them to the front and back of the bag itself. Or you might just stitch the handles to the bag by shaping the ends neatly or by stitching a decorative piece of leather over the join to become a part of the design of the bag.

A cowhide bag need not be lined, but if you do wish a lining, glue the skiver to the skin before cutting it. Spread an even coat of rubber cement on the back of the skin, then carefully place the skiver down on it and smooth out air bubbles or lumps. When dry, the lining is treated as part of the skin, and the cutting is done as before. If you wish to put a zipper in the bag, attach it before assembling the pieces: glue it in place with rubber cement, and when it is dry, pierce the holes for the stitching. If you do this on the sewing machine, a piece of tissue paper under the leather will make it run through more easily.

You could stitch a pocket onto the inside or the outside of the bag and use the stitching as a decorative note, or, for purely practical reasons, you could just glue it to the inside with a strong cement such as epoxy. Rubber cement is flexible and won't harm the leather, but it does not have great strength under strain; on the other hand, epoxy is not really compatible with leather and might stain, and so you must use it with caution.

When the bag is completed, it should be waxed with Melowax or with a good grade of neutral shoe cream to avoid water spotting. If you want to dye it, you can use one of the commercial shoe dyes as directed.

A wallet is made in the same way, but here you would use a lighter-weight calfskin rather than cowhide, which is too thick for a small piece. A wallet usually has several small pockets, which are individually cut, and when you assemble the components, they are easier to work if you glue the parts together before stitching them. Sometimes it helps to skive a very narrow edge around the face of the pieces that are to be glued, because the glue will not hold on a slick surface. There is a special skiving knife that is very easy to use, or you can use a razor blade at an almost horizontal angle and shave away the thickness gradually.

For a conventional men's wallet, cut the outside piece about eight inches by three and a half inches, and then cut the pocket that holds the bills a little smaller all around to take into account the thickness of the leather when folded. (Figure 69.) A little wedge should be cut out from the center bot-

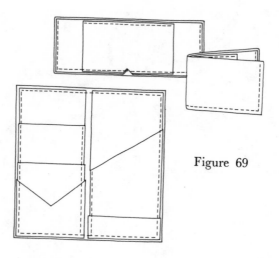

Figure 69

tom of this bill pocket so that there will be about a half inch at the center fold that is free of stitching, which helps avoid puckering at this point. You can add any number of pockets and half pockets (just so the wallet does not get too thick), and you can glue these pockets into place with a line of rubber cement an eighth of an inch in from the edges and punch the holes through all the thicknesses. Then the stitching is done all at once.

A French wallet, which is a large, single fold-over like a passport case, is easier to design and work with: here you would start with a piece of leather about eight inches square, and then fold it in half and stitch pockets to each half—as many and as varied as you wish. This type of design could also be made on a larger scale to serve as a portfolio or briefcase. You could use a tooling calf for either one so that you could imprint a design on it, or you might choose one of the fancy leathers. Generally, the patterned skins do not work up as neatly as a good-quality plain calfskin, but they are very tempting and certainly worth a try.

You could use lacing instead of stitching on any leather article by going in and out of the holes as in an overcast stitch. Very narrow strips of skived calfskin or goatskin are used as lacing, and the holes are usually punched with a round leather punch instead of with the thonging punch, to make the job easier. (Figure 70.) A special lacing needle can be used, or if you dip the end of the lacing into nail polish or Duco cement it will usually stiffen enough so that no needle is necessary. Lacing is used for a casual effect, while stitching can be formal and elegant if thoughtfully done.

Figure 70

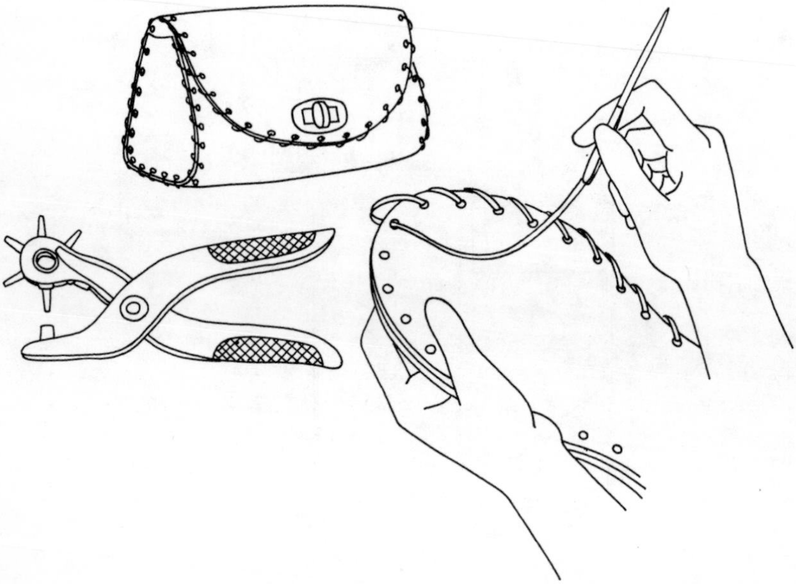

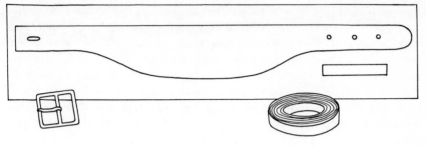

Figure 71

BELTS

Decorated leather belts have long been popular, and today we see tooled and antiqued leather used in a multitude of adornments—wristbands, motorcycle bags, hair ornaments, leg ornaments, chair covers, pipe-bowl covers, and so on to whatever strikes one's fancy.

Tooling is done on a specially tanned leather, usually cowhide or calfskin. The surface is such that it will retain impressions that are made on it, and these tooling skins are usually a little more expensive and a little more subject to nicks and scratches than other leathers. Once they are worked on and polished, they are very sturdy, but in their pristine state they must be handled with care.

Suppose you make a sport belt, using a fairly heavy tooling cowhide that will hold its shape. Sometimes you can buy belt strips that are cut and ready to attach to the buckle, but it is preferable to be able to cut your own in any shape you wish. You may design the belt to be contoured, wide in the back and narrowing toward the front, or scalloped, or in any form that will go around the waist, so buy a long piece of leather as wide as you wish.

For easy tooling, you can buy stamps in different patterns that will indent a design when pressed onto wet leather, but for your original design you will do your own tooling with an orangewood stick or a lignum-vitae—wood of life—scriber. Some antique leather dyes, a punch, a compass, a single-edged razor blade, and of course your buckle are all that is needed to start. All these can be purchased at your leather-supply house.

First you must make a paper pattern that will be the exact shape of the finished belt. The buckle has a bar and a tongue, and you must make cuts in the leather to accommodate them; the tip of the belt must slip onto the tongue, and you must mark the holes for this. The body of the belt can be any shape you want, but the end and the tip must be cut just to the width of the buckle. The length is to size, plus two inches' turn-under for securing the buckle at the end, plus four inches for slipping through the buckle at the tip.

Suppose you make a belt contoured so that it is two inches wide at the center back, narrowing gradually to fit a one-inch buckle in the front, and let us suppose that your waist is twenty-eight inches. The left end if you are female (right if you are male) will have two inches added for the buckle; the right end will have four inches added for the tip. (Figure 71.) Cut a long strip of heavy brown paper about thirty-six inches by four inches wide, fold it in half, and draw the shape fourteen inches long from the fold, which is the center back. Now open up the strip, extend it two inches on the left and six inches on the right, and cut it out.

The buckle will be attached at the left end, and so two inches in from that end cut out a small rectangle about an inch long and a quarter inch wide and slip the buckle into it to make sure it fits all right. Twenty-nine inches away from the buckle, make a hole with the punch, and now you can try it on for size. Adjust the hole if necessary, to make a good, snug fit, and you are ready to cut the belt from your leather.

Lay the cowhide on the table right side up, and place the pattern on it also right side up, anchoring it in place with rubber cement or masking tape. Draw around it with a sharp pencil marking all the holes and cutouts. Then cut on the drawn line with a sharp, new razor blade. Try to cut all the way through the leather in one stroke, as this will give you a neat edge. Now cut out the slit for the buckle tongue, and if you do not have a punch to make the hole on the tip end, your shoemaker will do that for you. It is a good idea to have another hole on either side of the original one so you can tighten or loosen the belt as need be. Round off the tip end neatly and test the belt on the buckle, to be sure it slips through easily without scuffing, and when all is right it is ready for tooling.

Hold the strip under cold water for a moment, just enough to wet the leather back and front but not enough to soak it. It is important that it be dampened all over so that there will be no water spots in any one place. If you can't complete the tooling in one sitting, you can dampen it again any number of times, but always wet the whole piece. Then place it between sheets of paper towels to absorb the excess moisture.

The designs used in tooling should be fairly simple and without too much detail. Leaves and flowers, birds and animals are usual, but a swirling design or a Greek key or initials in block letters are all possible, just so long as you design it to fit into the space allotted, leaving a half-inch border top and bottom so that it looks as though it belongs and is not just stuck on. Draw the design on tracing paper to exact size, and attach the paper to the damp leather with masking tape. With a gently pointed instrument such as a dry ball-point pen, trace every line of the design onto the leather. (Figure 72.) Remove the paper and accent the lines with the broad end of the orangewood stick; the shape of this tool will automatically impress tones of shading from the deeper edge to the shallower center. The harder you press and the more you go over it the darker the color will be. Thin decorative lines should be made with the pointed end of the tool to give contrast to the main design, and when the leather dries, those areas that have been worked over most will be the most prominent visually. For more contrast and a three-dimensional effect, you can actually cut into the leather and raise up small areas, as in the petals of a rose for instance. The tool used for this purpose is called a carving knife; it has a small sharp blade on the end of a swiveling post, and a T-shaped saddle at the top, where you rest your forefinger. With it, you cut around the lines to be raised—on dry leather—guiding the tool around the curves with pressure on the saddle. Carving must be done judiciously so as not to remove a section of the leather completely; use the tool at a slight angle to free the leather, but not enough to cause it to flap or tear off.

Another way to achieve a lot of contrast is to heat a tool such as dentist's probe and go over some of the areas to darken them. A design may even be burned in lightly by using an electric wood-burning tool.

When the design is completed, it should be finished off by an edging line placed about a sixteenth of an inch from the edge and running the full length of the belt. This is done with an edging tool made of lignum vitae, so called because it is strong and hard and will impart a glow to the leather as it is used. (Figure 73.) The tool is notched like a man with one short leg.

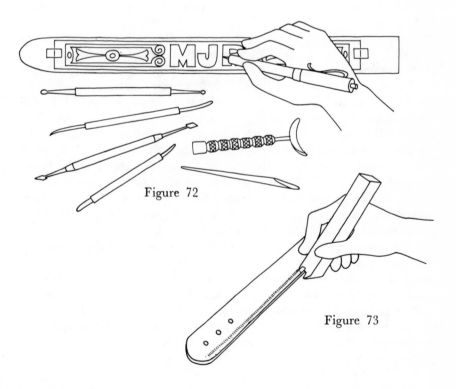

Figure 72

Figure 73

The long leg rests on the table, while the short leg scores a line as you move it along the edge. This could also be done by using an ordinary table fork—placing one tine on the leather and supporting it there by holding the second tine against the outside edge. This will keep your line straight and even.

When the tooling is all done and the leather dry, the belt can be left in its natural color or dyed with shoe dye, or it can be antiqued with special antiquing creams from your leather-supply house. Dyes and creams come in various woody shades—maple, cherry, mahogany, and others—and are applied to give a streaky or spotty, antique effect. To make a driftwood pattern, for instance, put a glob of the cream on a soft cloth and draw it along in one stroke the full length of the belt; the color will penetrate unevenly to give a striated effect. If you want a knotty look, dab spots of the dye here and there or apply it in a circular motion, and then apply it to the whole piece in long, even strokes to cover it completely; again, the irregular penetration of the dye will become the design. If your belt is heavily tooled, it doesn't really need the added effect of antiquing, and by the same token, antiquing gives enough interest to the leather so as not to need any other decoration. This is a matter of taste. Higgins inks or Luma or Dr. Martin's dyes from the stationery store will dye the leather evenly, as will the commercial shoe dyes. After you have used one of these colorings, you should wax the belt with Melowax, especially on the edges, to seal the dye in. Lastly, rub the edge all around with a piece of bone to give it a hard, smooth finish.

Now you are ready to mount the buckle. The leather must be thinned at the buckle end so that it will not be too bulky, and so you will shave off about half the thickness from the wrong side. (Figure 74.) This thinning of the leather is called skiving; it may be done with a special skiving knife, which is similar to a safety razor, or it may be done with a razor blade held almost flat to the leather, to shear off a little at a time. Skive about four inches of this end, and then attach the buckle by riveting, stitching, or gluing with a good-quality rubber cement. If the buckle has no "keeper" to hold the front end in place, then you must make one and attach it before you anchor the buckle. The keeper is a strip of leather, anywhere from a quarter inch to an inch wide, that straddles the belt just to the rear of the buckle. It can be stitched or stapled on the back, and it should be skived so that it will lie reasonably flat. (Figure 75.)

Belts may be designed so that no buckle is needed. They can be cut with long spaghetti ends, to be knotted to fasten. Or large holes can be punched and collar studs used as fasteners. Or Velcro fastening could be glued to the leather with Sobo glue, and then there would be no visible hardware. These are brass-hook-and-eye arrangements, or wooden or bone buttons. Or slits can be made in either end of the belt, and a handmade wood or silver "hairpin" can be inserted in and out of the slits to hold it together.

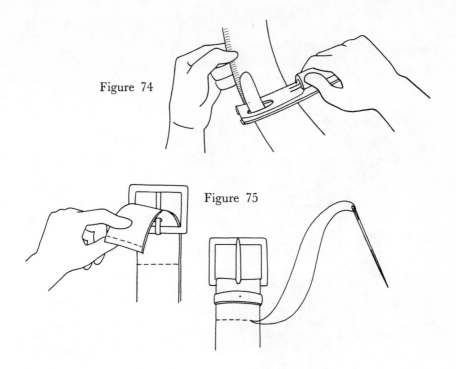

Figure 74

Figure 75

Leather can be formed by wetting it and pressing it on a mold. In tooling, for instance, some areas of the wet leather could be pressed onto a spoon back, or any hard surface that is shaped; if this is done from the back of the leather, it will raise it up on the front in a repoussé (pushed-out) effect. If it were done from the front, it would depress the leather, and these effects would actually form a bas-relief sculpture. Sandals with arch supports are made this way, by forming the leather over a plaster-mold shape. The leather will dry to the shape, and then it can be glued to foam rubber to help prevent it from collapsing.

If you wish a high gloss on your leather pieces, they can be treated with a leather lacquer, or with white shellac cut one part to three with denatured alcohol; these finishes tend to streak the dye, and so antiqued pieces are best just rubbed to a high polish. Leather dyes can be polished with Simoniz or a good shoe cream, but use any of these finishes sparingly, to avoid an artificial look. Leather needs to breathe in order to retain its beauty.

GARMENTS

Working with leather for clothing is the same as working with any other fine and beautiful material. Garment leathers are thin and supple and come in many colors and finishes. There are smooth leathers, sueded leathers,

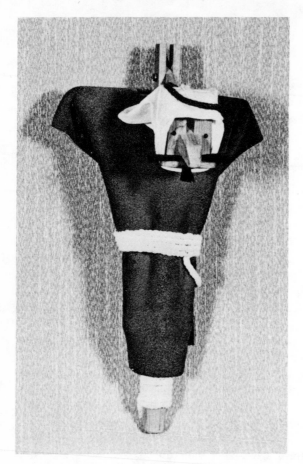

"The Arab." An imaginative sculpture made by draping pliable suede on a simple wood form. Contemporary. Israeli. Collection of the author.

leathers that are stenciled, crushed, gilded, even sequined. All are handled like fabric and can be sewn either by hand or on the sewing machine. Leathers are sold by the skin, and it takes from four to eight skins to make a dress, depending on the size—garment skins averaging about six square feet. Commercial patterns may be used, just so long as they are not too complicated and so long as they can easily be adapted for piecing where the skins dictate, because sometimes skins must be joined, and in such cases they should become part of the design, like a round yoke on a cape or a triangular yoke on a skirt, or a vest or pants.

For hand-stitching these soft leathers, there is available a special needle called a sword needle; it is three-sided and cuts through the leather with minimum damage. Silk or linen thread should be used if possible, but certainly never synthetic threads, as these are nonresilient and will tear the leather when pulled taut. For machine stitching, a piece of tissue paper put under the leather will keep it from slipping away from the foot, and the stitch should be quite long to avoid making the holes too close together, as this, too, will weaken the leather. Hems and facings can be glued down with rubber cement, as can trimmings such as furs or braids. It is wise to cut an identical cloth lining and sew it together with the leather to strengthen the seam and make the garment hang better. Or the leather may be "bonded" to a fabric lining by using rubber cement or bonding cloth, which will stiffen the whole thing (if that is what you want).

Suppose you want to make a sleeveless vest with a long fringe at the bottom. You will need two to four skins, depending on their size as well as on yours; perhaps the best way to judge this would be to cut a sample vest from fabric, using a commercial pattern. The fringe will be made by simply extending the length of the garment, and can be as long as you want it. (Figure 76.) You can then take the cut pieces of fabric to the leather store and measure them against skins to find the amount that you will need.

Only the main pattern pieces will be used—that is, one piece for the back and two pieces for the front, closing them with string ties. Perhaps you need not buy a pattern at all but can take an old shirt apart and use the pieces. Allow a little bit of extra turn-under at all the edges to take into account the bulk of the leather.

Figure 76

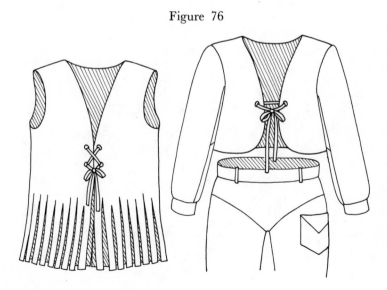

Lay your pattern on the skin with the right side up and draw all around the edges with a ball-point pen. Then cut the leather about a half inch outside these markings with a sharp pair of scissors or a razor blade. Stitch together the two shoulder seams, and the side seams from the armhole to the waist. Put the vest on, and make a chalk mark all around your waist where the fringing will start. Lay the garment flat on the table on a bed of newspaper, and with a sharp razor blade and a metal straightedge, cut the leather, from the chalk mark down, into thin strips about a quarter inch wide to form the fringe. (Figure 77.)

To make the facings, simply turn the edges under and cement them down with rubber cement, stretching the leather or nicking it with a pointy pair of scissors to make it lie flat on the curves. Cut six long spaghetti strings from the leftover leather, and stitch them in pairs down the front for ties, then trim off the fringe if you want it neat and even, and your vest is ready to wear.

Of course, this is a very simple garment; you can elaborate on it to your heart's content. You could cement another color for trim around the armholes, and glue this same color to the wrong side of the fringe length before cutting it.

Or you could use rivets or lacing, or hand- or machine-stitching in a contrasting color, to attach pockets or for other decoration. You could use a lambskin, fur side in for warmth, or you could line the leather with fur, thick or thin; furs are cut the same way as leather, but on the wrong side,

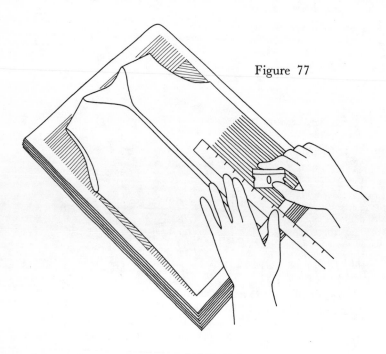

Figure 77

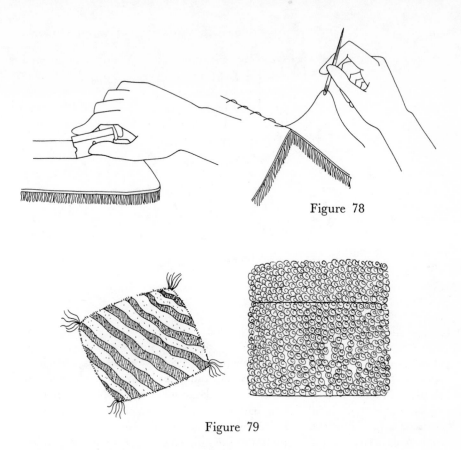

Figure 78

Figure 79

with a razor blade, just cutting through the skin and not shearing away the hair on the surface. Furs are sewn the same way as leathers, too, but butting the seams with an overcast stitch. (Figure 78.) This will avoid bulk at the joins, and the hairs will fill in so that the seams usually don't show at all.

Most leathers and suedes can be adequately cleaned by sprinkling them with yellow corn meal and, after five minutes or so, brushing it off with a dry, soft sponge or another piece of clean suede. Cornstarch has been used successfully, and an occasional vacuuming of suede is a good idea. Cleaning fluid should not be used; if a garment is to be commercially cleaned, it should be sent to a reliable cleaner who will process it properly. Furs also respond to the same treatment and will remain in good condition. Leather and fur garments should not be stored in plastic, which prohibits air circulation, but, rather, in paper or cloth bags that allow the skin to breathe and preserve its vitality. (Figure 79.)

A worn garment nearly always has enough good left in it to cut it down for something new. A jacket can be made into a vest, a skirt into short pants, and grandma's old coat into cushions or a car seat—and so much the better if it's mink.

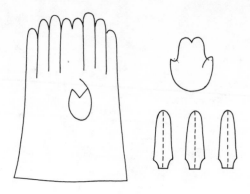

Figure 80

GLOVES

Leather gloves can be made from any pliable, stretchy leather, such as kid or deer or pigskin or lamb (with the wool inside), or from a stretchy garment leather. Making your own pattern for a classic glove is possible, but not too practical without help. Glove patterns may be gotten by writing for a catalog to J. P. Fliegel Co., P. O. Box 505, Gloversville, New York.

A pattern for a glove consists of the following: First there is one piece, for the back and palm of the hand, called the trank. Then there is the thumb, and an opening on the palm side where the thumbpiece will fit in; this opening is called the gouch. In addition, there are three pairs of strips that go between the fingers, called fourchettes. (Figure 80.) These fourchettes are stitched to the back of the glove between adjacent fingers, and then the palm of the glove is stitched to the fourchettes, closing them up to form the fingers. The thumbpiece is stitched into the gouch, and then it, too, is stitched up to enclose it, and the glove is complete.

All hands are different, and it is unlikely that the master pattern will be perfect for you. To make a pair of gloves uniquely fitted to your hands, you can adjust this pattern and make a new one that you can use time and again for a perfect fit in every pair. In addition to the master pattern, you will need a glove or a sword needle (blade-shaped), silk thread for stitching, a compass, a very sharp pair of scissors, and a Manila folder or similar oaktag board that will retain a clean, smooth edge when cut. And of course, the leather—approximately a half skin per pair of gloves.

On a piece of plain paper, lay your hand palm down with the fingers separated slightly and the thumb stretched out. With a sharp pencil, draw around your hand accurately. Take the compass and place the point on the

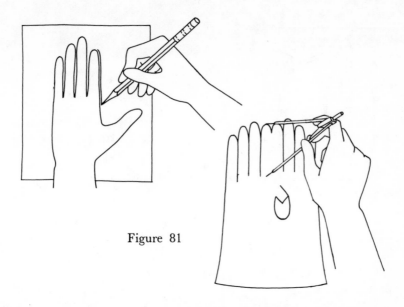

Figure 81

drawing at the center of the base of the index finger, level with the web between the index and third fingers. Open the pencil leg so that it comes just to the top of the index finger, and then place the compass in this same position on the trank pattern. (Figure 81.) If you have a shorter than normal finger, the pencil leg will lop a piece off the pattern. If your finger is longer than average, the pencil leg will extend beyond the pattern, and you will make your new pattern with a longer index finger. If your finger is short, then trim off the master as necessary, rounding the tip to the same contour that it was originally; if you need more length in any finger, Scotch-tape a small piece of oaktag onto the master, then trim that to conform to your own measurement. Repeat this measurement for each finger, and if your hands are different sizes, repeat it for the other hand too, so that each of your fingers gets marked on the master pattern.

Now the master pattern has been adjusted for all eight fingers and you are ready to transfer it to the oaktag to make your own personal pattern. Lay the master on the Manila folder, and trace around the outline with a sharp pencil or ball-point pen. If your hands are different, you will have to make two new patterns. As soon as you do them, mark them left and right, so that there is no confusion later as to which is which. Cut the new pattern out with a sharp pair of scissors, and now you are ready to make the thumb opening, or gouch, on this adjusted pattern.

The gouch has its base at the bottom joint of the thumb—almost at the wrist. On some hands, this joint may be higher than usual, and the opening would have to be placed higher on the pattern. To locate the proper position, just place the compass point on the tip of the forefinger on the draw-

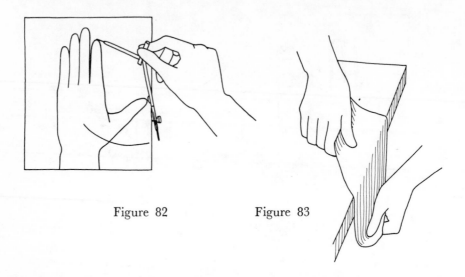

Figure 82   Figure 83

ing and describe a semicircle that intersects this joint. (Figure 82.) Repeat this on the new pattern. Where the arc falls is where the bottom of the opening should be for you. Lay the master pattern down on the new one, and line up the bottom of the gouch with the arc; draw in the gouch in its new position, and cut it out carefully with a pair of manicure scissors or a razor blade. Don't change the size or shape of this opening, because it is engineered to take the thumbpiece, and if it is changed, the whole glove will be out of kilter. Then measure the length of your thumb on the drawing, from tip to joint, and make any necessary adjustment as to length on the tip of the master thumbpiece.

If your fingers are very broad, widen the fourchette patterns a trifle, and if you have a very broad hand it may be necessary to add a fourchette to go down the outside of the little finger full length from tip to wrist. Men's patterns are cut fuller than women's, and sometimes it is more feasible to start with this fuller pattern, particularly in a sport glove.

So your personal trank is now transferred to a new oaktag, and you are ready to cut the leather. Mark one side of all the pattern pieces "right" and the other side "left," so that you will remember to reverse them for your two hands, always cutting the right one first.

Leather has about the same stretch up and down as it does sideways, but still it is best to cut the glove in the lengthwise direction of the skin. The skin should be stretched before cutting, so that the glove will fit snugly and not be baggy. To do this, roll up the leather in a damp towel for about a half hour, then remove it. While it is damp, stretch it by pulling it several times in each direction over the edge of the table. (Figure 83.) In this way, the leather gets stretched and the glove will be cut from a taut skin.

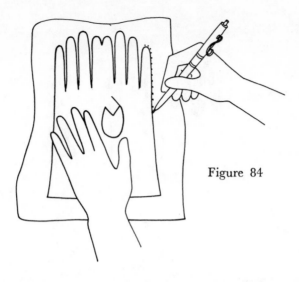

Figure 84

When the skin is dry, lay it flat on the table, right side up, and lay the trank pattern down on it. Make small dots all around the pattern with a ball-point pen, then lift it off and flip over the pattern for the other hand. (Figure 84.) Do the same for the thumbs and the fourchettes, and then cut everything out with a pair of scissors. Cut the fourchettes a little longer than needed, to be trimmed later at the tips of the fingers, when you reach that point in the sewing.

Cut the fourchettes in half lengthwise, sew them together in pairs at their broad base, and then sew them to the back of the trank. (Figure 85.)

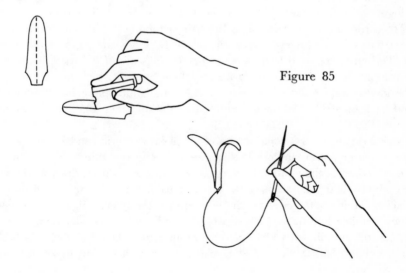

Figure 85

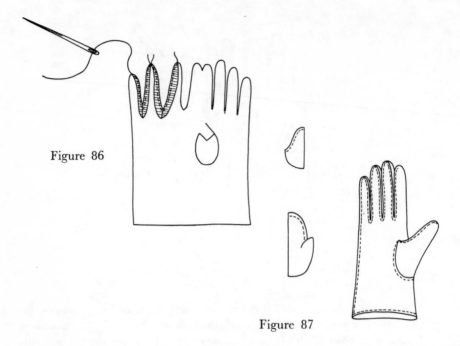

Figure 86

Figure 87

The fourchettes are angled at the base to take into account the web between the fingers, and so the long side is sewn to the back of the glove. Sew them in with a neat running stitch, wrong sides together, starting at the base and sewing up to the top of each finger. Leave an end of thread hanging; later, when you sew the fourchettes to the front, you can trim them to get an accurate fit at the tip of each finger, and then you can finish off the stitching. (Figure 86.) Start sewing at the index finger and go all around to the inside of the little finger: you will have one pair of fourchettes between each adjacent pair of your fingers—three sets in all. Now sew the palm of the trank to the fourchettes, and lastly sew up the outside seam of the trank to enclose it completely. Now you can try on the glove, putting your thumb through the gouch, and it should fit perfectly. Sew the thumbpiece into the gouch and try it on again, trimming the thumb at the tip if necessary before sewing it up. (Figure 87.)

Fabric gloves or a combination of leather and fabric can be made without a master pattern by crocheting fourchettes to separate palm and back pieces. To make the two-piece trank pattern for these gloves, draw a straight line about eight inches long on a piece of oaktag and lay the hand down, placing the index finger along the line. Spread the fingers slightly, and then draw another line outside the tip of the little finger parallel to the first; stretch the thumb out wide and trace around the whole hand in this position. (Figure 88.) Make each finger as long as need be, but make them all

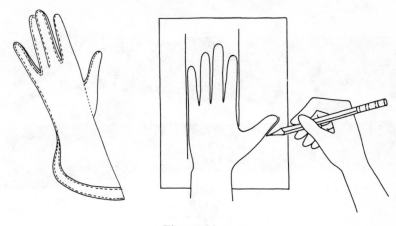

Figure 88

the same width, because it looks much better if they're all uniform; then cut the pattern out, using the two parallel lines as the outside cutting lines. You will make four fabric pieces from this one pattern—two backs and two fronts, right and left—and you can make the gloves longer or shorter by extending the outside lines to go higher up the arm or cutting them off shorter at the wrist. Join the two parts of the trank with a crocheted strip about a half inch wide all around the glove to close the fingers up. This piece can be sewn in, or worked right in, with a sharp-tip crochet hook. The gloves could be made from any fabric to match any costume for any season of the year; they could have a leather palm for driving or be made from fur for skiing, or adapted into mittens for extra warmth. Instead of crocheting them, you could use a stretchy knit fabric for the fourchettes; this might or might not work out well.

Leather gloves should be cleaned professionally; or, if the leather is washable, they should be rinsed in cold-water soap designed for fine woolens. Dry them flat on a towel, and when they are still a little damp, ease them on the hand to shape them, then finish the drying. Fur gloves can be tumbled in a brown paper bag with corn meal, which will remove the dirt without drying out the skin.

Good leather that is fresh and flexible is very strong and will take a lot of abuse, but if the skin is dried out, it will tear very easily. For all the labor involved, it is advisable to use the best material you can afford, and then take the best care of the finished piece that you can, to preserve its life.

Woodcut. Made from a pearwood block. This wood has almost no grain, and so the print is smooth, without the usual grain lines. Contemporary. American. Elizabeth Bramsen.

6

Graphics

Printing from a wood block is done by cutting away everything that is not wanted, and leaving just a design that is raised on the surface of the wood. As the ink is rolled over the surface of the block, it will be received only by the raised portion, and therefore only that portion will register on the printing paper. Any design raised from the background is in "relief," and so this is known as relief printing.

The materials needed for wood-block printing are quite simple. The wood that is used can be just about anything that is solid enough to carve and retain its contours. Sugar pine is used by most artists, being easy to get at any lumberyard, but different woods can be used for different effects. A fine-grained wood is used for a delicate drawing, and a grainy wood is used for just the effect that it creates by being grainy. Sugar pine is a good workaday wood, being smooth to cut in either a loose or a tight design, and still it has enough grain to make it interesting in printing.

Three wood chisels of different-shaped gouges are enough to start with. One should be a small round gouge, another a larger round, and one a small V gouge. An X-acto knife, a single-edged razor blade, some printer's ink, and a small rubber brayer or roller are needed; also some turpentine, a piece of window glass for rolling out the ink, plenty of newspaper to protect the work table, and lots of rags for cleanup.

The Japanese, who are very adept at this craft, have a pad made of tightly interwoven bamboo leaves called a *baren,* which is used to rub over the paper so that it will make contact with the ink. You can use the back of a tablespoon to do this. They also use rice paper of different weights and textures to print on; we have found these papers to be the best for the purpose, and they are readily available in any hobby store. Oil-based printer's ink is the most satisfactory paint to use, but with experimentation you may find water colors such as poster paints or tempera colors quite adequate for your job. Different kinds of paper might be tried out too, just so long as they are absorbent enough to receive and to hold the ink without smudging. You will find that fast-drying colors such as poster paint will take well on thin paper. A heavier, oil-based paint needs a heavier paper; you should judge your materials by balancing them one against the other. Rice paper is always more interesting when torn than when cut, and so it is a good idea to buy large sheets and tear them to whatever size you need, by folding the paper neatly to the size of the block and tearing it along the fold. You will find that it tears easily along one edge but not along the cross-grain edge, but if you wet this edge with a small brush dipped in water, it will weaken and tear easily.

Suppose you cut a block for a print that will be six inches square. The piece of wood should be the same size, that is, six inches square, and about a

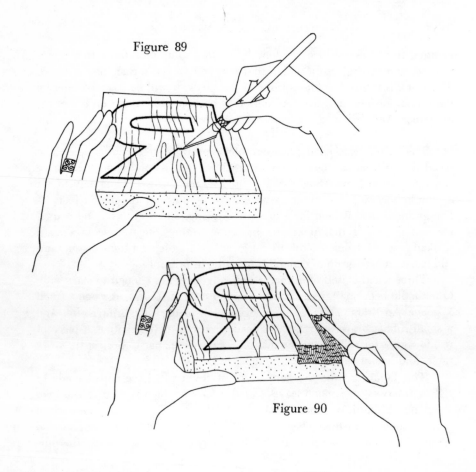

Figure 89

Figure 90

half inch thick, because this thickness is the easiest to handle in the cutting.
Draw your design on paper and then transfer it to the wood, remembering
that it will be in reverse on the print; things such as letters or numbers must
be cut into the wood in reverse to print correctly, the block being in effect a
negative. A simple way to do this is to put your finished drawing on thin
tracing paper, turn it over, and with a carbon trace it onto the block from
the back. When the design is accurately drawn on the wood, you are ready
to start carving.

Start cutting by tracing around the drawn lines with the X-acto knife
held at right angles to the block. When all the lines are scored, then you can
start gouging out the background. (Figure 89.) This first cut will protect the
design from being marred by the larger chisel point: by making this first cut
with the knife, you can use your chisel to cut in at right angles to it, and
it will be stopped by this break and not nick into your drawing. (Figure 90.)

The wood left in relief to be printed should be at least as wide at the
base as it is at the surface, so that it will not break away from the block. To
achieve this, the knife should be held perpendicular to the surface of the
wood so as not to undercut, and a clean line should be cut to a depth of
about an eighth of an inch. For gouging away small, delicate areas, you can
go against the grain, but for large areas it is safer to cut with the grain, so
that it will not splinter: the sharp, V-angled chisel is good for hard-to-get-at
places, the round one for larger areas. In places where you wish a little
roughness and interest, do not cut deeply; a little of the ink will remain on
these spots to add character and shading to the print. The charm of a woodcut lies in the fact that it is not too even and exact; slips of the chisel are not
always catastrophic, but on the contrary might be incorporated to add interest.

When the background is all cut out (and if you do not wish the print
to have a border, the part around the edges, too, must be cut away), wipe
the block off with a cloth to free it of all dust, and you are ready for printing.

Take a blob of printer's ink and put it on the window glass. Thin it a
little with turpentine, spread it on the glass with the brayer, and roll the
brayer back and forth over the glass for a full minute to charge it completely
with ink. Then roll the charged brayer several times over the raised design
on the wood block. Pick up a paper by the two upper corners and bring it
carefully to the block, making contact along the bottom edge. (Figure 91.)
Drop it down by lowering the held edge, and the ink will cause it to adhere
to the block. Once this is done, the paper must not be shifted or it will
smudge. Rub over the paper with the *baren* or the back of the tablespoon,
making contact at all points between the paper and the raised printing lines.
(Figure 92.) When you are sure all areas have been contacted, lift the paper
up by the two upper corners, and quickly peel it off the block. (Figure 93.)
Now you have made a print. This first printing, or proving (it is called an

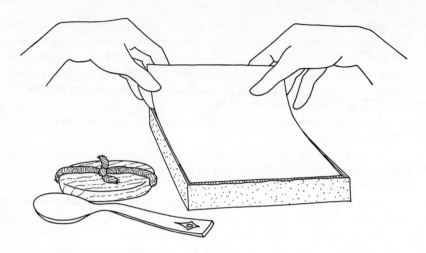

Figure 91

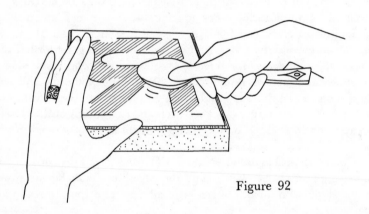

Figure 92

Figure 93

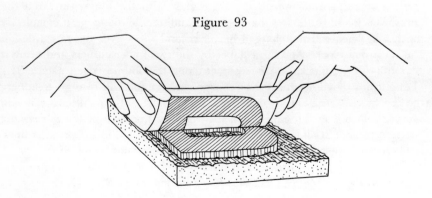

artist's proof), is done to see whether more carving away is needed on the block. If any marks are on the paper that shouldn't be, it is because you have not cut away deeply enough. If anything is not there that should be, chances are that you have cut it away and it will never be retrieved, but perhaps you can save the block by adjusting the drawing.

Wipe the block off with turpentine, and recut where it is needed; run another proof, and when you are satisfied, you can start printing in earnest. Charge the brayer and ink the block for each print. Allow the prints to dry for at least an hour before stacking them, and when you are finished work, clean the block and the brayer with turpentine. A wood block will make many prints before wearing down, and different-colored prints can be gotten by cleaning off the equipment and laying out new ink on the glass.

Wood-block prints are often mounted with the torn edge of the paper left exposed. They should be glued carefully to the backing with a dab of library paste and glassed for protection and framed. If you prefer, they can be mounted conventionally by matting and framing.

Multicolored prints are made in the same way, but a different block is needed for each color. The blocks are all exactly the same size, and you transfer the design to each identically. You cut away each block entirely except for areas that are to be in one color. For instance, a blue house with red chimney and green shutters will require three blocks—one for each color. In the first block, you cut everything away except the parts of the house to be blue (and will the sky be blue?). In the second block, only the red chimney will remain in relief, everything else to be cut away, and in the third only the green shutters remain. Perhaps you will want a fourth block to outline everything in black—a fourth color.

When you use multiple blocks, you must have a register mark in the same place on each block so that the same piece of paper can be laid down accurately for each color register. This can be done by leaving an identical little triangle uncut on the two bottom corners of each block. Place the paper exactly on these triangles as it is run through each successive printing, and if care is taken, the register will come out right; that is, the colors will each register in the right place on the paper. It is easier of course to do a design that is more abstract, so that a slight error in placing will not spoil that print. One ruined print, however, does not ruin the day: just start another one. Practice will make perfect.

As in all printing methods, one color may be used on top of another to make a third. If you wanted to make your house blue, the chimney red, and the shutters purple, you would require only two blocks. You would cut the first one away except for the house and shutters; the second one, everything but the chimney and shutters. A red printing on top of blue will make the shutters purple, and so you have eliminated one block. A blue house, yellow chimney, and green shutters would be done by the same trick—yellow on blue making green.

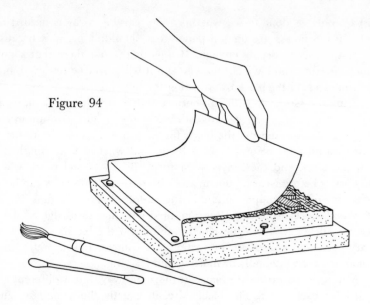

Figure 94

Provincetown Color Printing

Another method for making multicolor prints is called Provincetown color printing. This is great fun, and not as taxing to the patience. In this method, you cut one block. Place it on a larger board and anchor it down with several nails to keep it from shifting. Cut your paper about four inches longer than you need it, and tack it to the board at the head of the block to keep it from shifting, too. (Figure 94.) Now with a brush or a Q-Tip ink in all the areas on the block that you wish to be blue. Lay your paper down over the block, make contact with the *baren,* and then lift it off, leaving the tacks in place. Wipe the blue ink off the block, and paint all the areas to be red. Draw the paper down onto the block, print that area, and carefully lift it off, again. Clean off the red ink, apply green where it is wanted, pull down the paper, print, lift off, and there is your blue house with red chimney and green shutters, and only one block cut. Of course, obviously, you could with care do this whole operation at once by very carefully inking in the various sections. If you are not a purist, you might also use a brush to accent areas on the print that were not included in the inking.

A self-confident artist can make a multicolor print from a single block by printing up the largest masses first and gradually cutting away areas for successive printings, so that the part of the block that will register becomes smaller and smaller. You ink the palest background color onto a pristine uncarved block and make a complete run of, say, twenty-five proofs. Then paint a massive design on the block, and carve away everything outside that.

Ink the block in a little deeper color and make a second run on top of the first, so that the prints are now in two colors: the background and the broad design on top of that. Clean the block, sketch some broad detail on with paint, and again cut away everything remaining. Ink on a darker color and superimpose another run; the prints are now in three colors.

These steps can be repeated until nothing remains of the block but the thinnest, darkest accent lines. Of course the block itself will wear out in due time, and those last lines may not register too well; it will take practice to recognize the point of no return.

This process is best worked from a linoleum block, which is easy to cut, and it certainly raises the simple linocut to a sophisticated art.

Linoleum Blocks

Linoleum blocks are used in the same way as wood blocks, and they may be purchased in a hobby shop along with sets of small chisels. It is very simple to make your own blocks, by gluing a piece of uncoated, inlaid linoleum to a plywood base the same size and brushing it over with a coat of white poster paint to give contrast so that you can see your drawing better as you cut it. Linoleum is much easier to cut than wood, because you don't have the grain to contend with, and it can easily be cut in soft, amorphous designs. It does not make as interesting a print, however, because it has no grain to impart "texture." There are advantages and disadvantages to both mediums, and the beginner will probably be wise to start with a linoleum block and graduate to the more difficult wood block. The method of printing is identical.

Printing on Textiles

You can print on textiles in the same way as on paper, except that here the block is placed on the fabric, instead of vice versa. Lay the material flat on the floor on a bed of newspaper, ink your block with textile paint, and place it carefully on the fabric. Step on the block, shifting your weight around so that contact is made at all points. Remove the block (carefully again), ink it for the next position, place it down, and print it. You can repeat this as many times as you wish, for an all-over pattern on draperies, for instance, or perhaps as a border on denims, or a single motif on a set of place mats.

Whatever your medium, when you are finished work, clean your blocks thoroughly and wrap them in newspaper for protection. They can be used again many years hence, as good as new.

Other Print Media

There are many ways to transfer a design by this printing method. A "block" can be made by cutting a raw potato in half and carving a simple design into the cut surface. A cut onion will transfer an interesting pattern of circles, or wavy lines if it is cut at an angle. A roll of corrugated paper printed on end, a ball of steel wool, the teeth of a comb, a piece of burlap, the end grain of a plywood board—anything that will pick up ink can be used to transfer that ink to another surface. Pieces of matchsticks glued to a piece of cardboard could be a block, and so could bits of wire screening or cardboard cutouts. An ink pad can be made by folding soft absorbent cloth or paper toweling into a thick pad and putting it into a flat container with some kind of "ink"—water-color paints, liquid dye, food coloring, beet juice, old coffee or tea. The field is only as limited as your imagination, and imagination should never be constrained.

Duco Prints

You can make an interesting kind of print by drawing with Duco cement on a piece of window glass to make a relief "block." (Figure 95.) Draw your original design on a piece of paper just to size, and lay the clean glass over the paper. With a new tube of Duco, trace the design onto the glass by squeezing the glue out in a trailing movement; allow the Duco to dry without disturbing it, and when it is hard it will adhere to the glass in raised coils. Mix some artist's oil color on a clean palette, and with a small rubber roller pick up the paint and roll it lightly onto the coils. Then fill in some of the larger open areas by applying paint directly to the glass with a brush, so that your print will not be just a drawing. Now take a piece of paper—colored construction paper is good—and place it carefully on the glass. Rub over the paper with your fingers, making contact with the block wherever you can without creasing the paper. Peel the paper off in one quick motion by grasping the edge with clean fingers, and you have made a

Figure 95

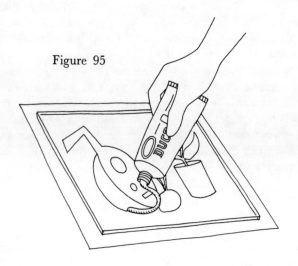

print. The outline, where the Duco is raised, will be most prominent, and the color of the paper will be part of the design, with the brushed-in areas just adding a note of interest. The plate should be inked fresh for each print, and the color can be changed by wiping the coils lightly with turpentine and cleaning off the roller, too, with turps. Poster paints or acrylics can be used if you work quickly, before the paint dries on the block. For these water-based paints a soft, absorbent paper is best, such as rice paper or newsprint.

COLLAGRAPHS

Another way of producing interesting prints is by making a block or plate from a low-relief collage. Spread a layer of acrylic medium or gesso on any support that will hold it—a piece of masonite or cardboard or plywood. Scatter around found objects such as a leaf, a bit of lace or window screening, or a piece of crumpled paper; and when the medium starts to set a little, stipple or carve a design into it, for background effect. When it has hardened, apply a coat of medium (or Elmer's glue) over the whole thing, and as soon as that is dry you can start to make prints. (Figure 96.)

An even quicker way to make a plate is to just place objects on the background support, then cut a piece of heavy aluminum foil large enough to cover completely and wrap around to the back. Cover the back of the foil with a coat of spray adhesive, and lay it on the collage, bringing it around to the back to make it a secure covering. Press it all over with your hand; it will conform to the raised design, and you will have anchored the objects in place and created an aluminum plate.

The collagraph you make from this plate can be either a relief print or

Figure 96

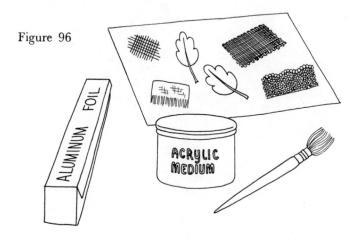

an intaglio print, depending on your method of inking. If you roll the ink on with a brayer so that it just reaches the high points, it will come out as a relief print. If you apply the ink with a squeegee and then clean off the surface so that the ink remains only in the depressions, it will produce an intaglio print. One would be the reverse of the other—black where one is white, and white paper where the other is black. This could lead to some interesting ideas for series printing. You can also ink the plate in several colors to make a multicolor print in one run-through.

The serious artist uses etcher's ink and an etching press. It is possible, however, to make a very satisfactory collagraph with thinned oil paints and the back of a spoon, coupled with lots of elbow grease.

RELIEF PRINTING BY OFFSET

Relief printing may also be done by the offset method. Here you ink up the block as before and run a new, clean roller over the block carefully, just once. (Figure 97.) The design will be picked up by the clean roller, and you

Figure 97

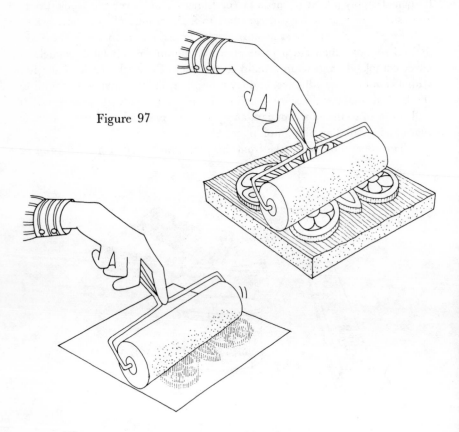

can transfer it to paper by simply rolling it on. You have to work carefully and surely to avoid smudging. The circumference of the roller should be equal to the length of the block, in order to get a proper register. For example, if the design is three inches long, then the roller should be one inch in diameter—the circumference being approximately three times the diameter. This is a very quick method, and prints can easily be made of anything that is raised from the background—some tree bark or a piece of driftwood, for instance. By taking a print of wood grain or corrugated cardboard or wire screening, and then superimposing another print, of a drawing or an object, on top of that, you can easily create a print with "texture."

Offset prints can be made on any flat surface—a chair back, a tray, even a cylindrical lamp base. Usually an oily type of ink is required, because this will remain wet through the two stages of transfer. This offset method is often used for pulling a proof to check the design in the more sophisticated procedure using a press. The preliminary proof taken this manner is known as the artist's proof.

Rubbings

Rubbings are made by placing a clean piece of paper on a relief surface and rubbing it all over gently with the side of a crayon or pencil. You would tape the paper taut to the "block" and then rub it completely over, lightly and evenly, so that every part of the design that is raised will register on the paper. If the design is depressed, the background will show up and the design will appear as the untouched color of the paper. This is the method used for taking old tombstone rubbings and is ideal for a reproduction of anything that cannot be transported into the studio. Rubbings can also be made by using a roller or a stiff cloth dabber with a very thin, even coating of oil paint. The roller should first be run over a piece of waste paper to remove excess paint so that the rubbing will not have splotches on it; this is a quick method and might work out with a water-based paint.

Monotype Printing

Monotype printing is the process of making a one-time print (which cannot be duplicated). It can be made from any "plate" and by any method that will not allow a repeat. For instance, if you press a piece of paper flat onto a wet palette you will have made a print; obviously, you could never repeat the design that you have just created, and so it is a monoprint. Most mixed-media printing will result in a one-of-a-kind print. If you make a print from a wood block and then fill in some areas by hand, it will be unique. If you make a print from a lithography stone and run it through again, but this time off register, it will be unique. If you dip string in paint and lay it on paper, it can make a print that will never be repeated, and therefore is unique, a monoprint.

Artists usually produce prints in limited editions, and the more limited the run the more valuable is the print. There is an interesting story that has been handed down through the ages about willow-pattern china. It seems that once upon a time someone inadvertently sat on a still-wet blue Chinese painting and then sat down on a white plate, thereby transferring the painting to the plate. In this way, a whole new fashion came into being: ever-popular willow-patterned china. True or not, it is interesting to contemplate that a reproduction of a rare painting done centuries ago can now be found in every five-and-dime store across the nation. The value of a print, therefore, must be carefully judged.

The making of prints by traditional methods is a time-honored craft, and the true artist will do it the hard way, just as it was done centuries ago. The Goya etchings are prime examples of metal-plate reproductions, and Toulouse-Lautrec's lithographs are perhaps the best-known stone examples in our time. The artists didn't have any quick, easy methods; they used trial and error, as we must.

LITHOGRAPHY

Lithography is planographic printing in which the plate, or master, is made on stone. It is the freest form of printing, because the design is simply drawn on the stone, and the lengthy preparations necessary in relief or intaglio printing are not needed here. The principle in lithography is that grease and water do not mix. The drawing is made with a grease crayon called tusche, and then the stone is wetted with water. The printing ink, which is grease-based, will adhere to the stone only where the tusche is, and will be repelled by the water everywhere else. The printing paper will harmlessly absorb the clear water, and receive impressions only from the inked areas.

The printing should be done on a lithographic press, which exerts a pressure of fourteen hundred pounds, but successful prints have been made in a studio workshop by experimenting with different kinds of paper, more or less ink, and different kinds of ink. (Figure 98.) In some cities, there are art schools and museums or colleges that might be willing to do the printing for you on their press; this is worth investigating.

Limestone is generally used, the best stones coming from Bavaria. They range in texture from the blue, which is hard and close-grained, to the yellow, which is the softest and coarsest. A good, new stone will cost about a hundred dollars, but used stones can be rented or purchased from a graphic-arts supply house quite reasonably. The stone must be prepared for printing, so as to be free from scratches and any traces of grease that might be left

from a previous job. This is done by rubbing the surface of the stone against
another hard surface—usually two stones are rubbed together—with a grit
such as a paste of powdered carborundum or pumice. (Figure 99.) The
two stones are covered with the solution and then rubbed together until the
surfaces are smooth and flat. As lithographs are usually not very fine in line
(compared to etchings, for instance), you may wish to leave the stone heavily grained instead of polishing it smooth, to give the effect of casualness to
the print. Once the stone is polished to your liking, cover it with a clean soft
cloth, and handle it only by the corners to avoid finger marks, which could
ruin your prints. It should be kept covered until you are ready to start work.

The supplies needed are simple but exact. Liquid tusche and tusche in
stick form (called lithographic crayon) are used to draw the design. The
tusche is grease-based—made from wax, soap, and lampblack—but differs
from printer's ink, so that they are not interchangeable. In addition to the
tusche, you will need printer's ink, a brayer, and a piece of window glass to
roll the ink on; small amounts of powdered rosin, talc, gum arabic, and ni-

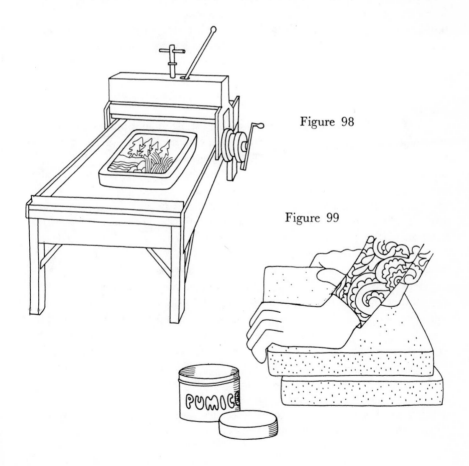

Figure 98

Figure 99

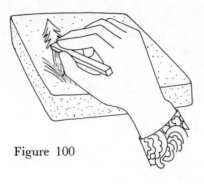

Figure 100

tric acid; lots of soft, clean cloths, three or four clean jars, a camel's-hair brush, and gasoline to clean up.

Your preliminary sketch may be roughed in reverse directly onto the stone with Conte crayon, which will not interfere with the tusche. A more accurate method is to draw it on thin tracing paper with a tusche crayon, place the paper face down on the stone, and go over the drawing with a blunt pencil, thus transferring it to the stone in reverse. Because the stone is a negative, the design is always laid on in reverse and the print will come out as a positive. However you put down your initial sketch, you can check it by holding a mirror up against the stone to be sure it is all right. This first, suggestive drawing can be easily rubbed off with gasoline if it isn't to your liking.

Once your idea is transferred to the stone, you apply lithographic crayon and liquid tusche to the surface of the stone. These are greasy materials and will attract the ink, which is also greasy. When you pull a proof, the paper will be printed only where there is grease; water prevents the ungreased areas from picking up the ink. For this reason, it is important that there be as little handling of the stone's surface as possible. Fingerprints are greasy and would end up on the print, and so it is a good idea to rest your hand on a piece of clean, soft cloth while working.

All kinds of drawing and painting techniques can be used in lithography. Sharp, clean lines are made with the crayons, which come in varying degrees of hardness; the higher the number the harder the crayon and the sharper the line it will produce. (Figure 100.) Toning may be done by using the crayon flat to give shaded effects, and liquid tusche may be used as a wash, or may be drawn on with a pen to give the strongest, blackest lines. For a sharp, clean edge, you may scrape the tusche off the stone gently with a razor blade, and for a fuzzy effect, rub it over with a soft cloth, dampened perhaps with a little gasoline. Dabbing it with the cloth also gives the effect of lightening it, for you are then picking up the tusche and making it less dense. Applying the tusche with a clean, dry sponge or spattering it with a toothbrush will also give interesting effects.

When the tusche design is on the stone just as you wish it, play a fan on it until it is thoroughly dry, and then you must set it so that it will be firmly established. In a small, grease-free jar, mix equal amounts of the rosin and talc and cover the top with a piece of nylon stocking to act as a sprinkler. Dust the stone over with this mixture and it will set the tusche onto the surface. After a few moments, brush away the excess powder with a few light strokes of a soft cloth; then you further set it to prevent the grease from spreading into the open pores of the stones. This you do with gum arabic, after which you use nitric acid solution to etch the cleaned-up design into the stone so that it will remain there through many printings. Mix a few chunks of the gum with about eight ounces of water to the consistency of light cream. Let it stand a half hour and then strain it through a nylon stocking into two jars, half in each. To one of the jars, add two teaspoonfuls of nitric acid, very slowly. *Always add the acid to the water,* never vice versa, and always do it slowly and carefully: it spatters, and an acid burn can be very painful.

Now brush the stone over lightly with the pure gum solution with the soft camel's-hair brush. Leave the gum on for about one minute, wash it off under running water, and stand the stone on edge to drain. The pores of the stone have now been closed by the gum solution, and the tusche design has been fixed in place. Now brush on the acid-gum etching solution, and after eight or ten seconds wipe it off with a clean, damp cloth. This etching solution dissolves out any remaining surface grease and drives the heavier tusche into the stone. It must not be allowed to remain on so long that it dissolves the drawing too, so now rinse it very thoroughly under running water and then stand it on edge to drain.

Have all your paper cut to a size slightly smaller than the stone, and lay one piece on the stone, positioning it in the proper place. With chalk or pencil, mark a small right angle on the stone at the bottom corners of the paper, to serve as your registry marks for the entire run. Each new piece of paper must be laid down accurately all at once, and so these guides are a necessity.

Now you are finally ready to start printing. Put a glob of printer's ink on the piece of window glass and roll it with the rubber brayer for about one minute, until the roller is well charged with the ink. (Figure 101.) If the ink is too thick to roll smooth, add a little turpentine or linseed oil to thin it: it should have the consistency of a thin paste, not quite liquid and a little tacky. Wipe the stone with a wet sponge—it must always be wet when printing—and then ink it with the charged roller. (Figure 102.) The ink will be repelled by the water, which in turn has been repelled by the tusche, and the ink will take only where the grease drawing has been made.

Now lay your paper carefully on the stone, using the registry guides, and anchor it in place with masking tape. Lay a large blotter on top of the paper and play a rolling pin or a clean brayer across it many times with as much pressure as you can muster, being sure to cover all areas. (Figure

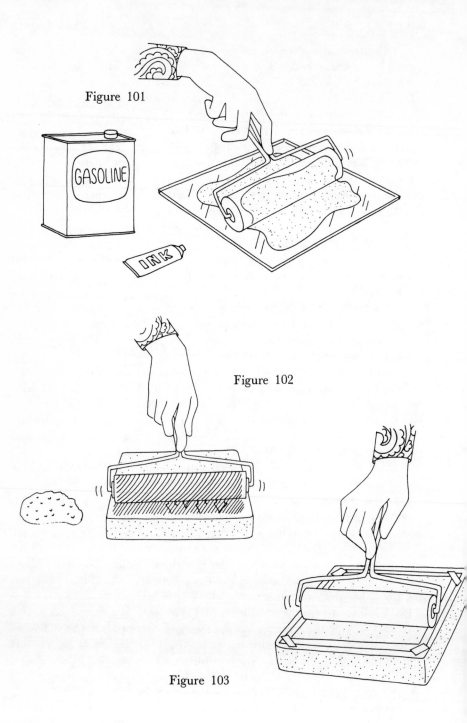

Figure 101

Figure 102

Figure 103

103.) Then remove the blotter, lift off the paper, and, we may hope, you have pulled your first proof. Working without a press may or may not be successful. It could depend on the quality and absorbency of the paper and the thickness and viscosity of the ink. Sometimes a cheaper paper and thinner ink will succeed where better quality did not. A lightweight paper may be used dry, but a heavier paper should be dampened slightly by placing it between two damp blotters for about twenty minutes, to make it more absorbent. But, each time, you would wet the stone again, ink it up, and make another print.

A stone can be used for just so many prints before the tusche becomes worn out. The first prints are usually the best, and for that reason you see numbers in the lower left-hand corner of professional work. The lower the number, the more valuable the print. For instance, if the number is 7/50 it means that this is the seventh print out of a run of fifty. If you were purchasing prints, ⚹1/50 would be the most costly and ⚹50/50 would be the least expensive of the run.

As you pull your prints, hang them on a line with clothespins, in the order in which they come off the press, and when they are dry, they can be numbered. When they start to look bedraggled, your run is finished.

. Lithographs may be colored with water-color paints when the ink is dry, but usually they are left as black-and-whites. A true color litho, of course, requires a separate stone for each color run, but a simple way to do a multicolor litho is to clean off the stone with gasoline to remove the ink and most of the tusche, and then to wash it with clean water. You will find that ghosts of the original drawing remain and it is very simple to apply tusche again where you want a new color. In this method of printing, color is used mostly to fill in masses, and because the ghost of your outline still remains, it is easy to know where to put the new tusche for a new color. It is important not to lose the registry marks when you clean off the stone.

When you are finished with this particular run of prints, clean the stone thoroughly with turpentine and then wash it well with water. Grain it down with grit to remove all ghosts, wrap it carefully in soft cloths, and store it upright to prevent scratching. If well cared for, it will last a long time and be receptive to many new designs.

ETCHING

Etching is a process of printing that is done by biting into a metal plate with acid and then forcing damp paper into the incised design, which holds the ink. This is known as intaglio printing: intaglio means cut in, or engraved. Etching can produce the most precise lines of all the printing methods, and some of the greatest works of art to come down through the ages were done by this intaglio method.

The face of the plate, usually copper, is covered with an acid-resisting wax called a "ground." The design is then cut in with an etching needle just deep enough to scratch through the ground to the surface of the metal. The back of the plate is covered with a "stop-out" varnish to prevent the acid from attacking it, and then the plate is immersed in a bath of nitric acid and water. It is allowed to stay in the acid bath just long enough for the lines to be lightly etched, or "bitten in." It is then washed and dried, those areas that are to remain light in the print being painted with the stopping-out varnish to protect them, and the plate is put back into the mordant so that deeper and darker lines will be etched in. The etching process is repeated in this manner until the darkest lines of the drawing are bitten in. In the printing process, the shadings are obtained by the fact that more ink stays in the deeper lines and so these areas will print darker; the deeper the incising the darker the line.

When the etching is finished, the plate is cleaned of all stop-out and then covered with an oil-based printer's ink. The surface is wiped off, and the ink remains in the depressions, ready to be transferred to paper. Etching is usually done on a commercial press, and here, as in lithography, perhaps a museum or a printing shop or an art school will do the actual printing for you. But with perseverance you will make some prints yourself. (Figure 104.)

Etching may be done on several kinds of metal. Zinc is less expensive than, for example, copper. It is softer and will not produce as many sharp prints as copper, but this need not concern the beginning etcher unless he

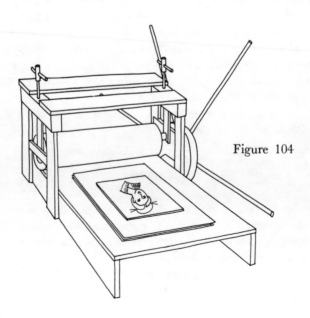

Figure 104

plans on running off hundreds of prints. Aluminum plates are effective and will retain the design indefinitely, and because they are not always highly polished, they can be used in the rough state for interesting backgrounds. Copper plates are expensive and give a different line from zinc, for example, but, traditionally, copper plates are considered to be the best. One might try etching a piece of plate glass with acid, and perhaps interesting prints could be pulled from such a "plate." Some very hard plastics or rubbers might also serve.

Suppose you start by etching a simple design on a zinc plate. You will need wax ground and stop-out varnish, ink, turpentine, and paper; a piece of glass and two brayers; nitric acid and a shallow rust-proof pan; rubber gloves, a hot plate or torch, and lots of newspaper and small rags.

It is important that the edges of the plate be beveled so that they will not tear the paper during the printing process. You can do this rounding by filing and sanding them until all rough edges are smoothed away.

The plate must be clean for the wax ground to adhere properly. Scrub it with a very fine grit so as not to scratch it: tooth powder with a little white vinegar is a good metal cleaner. Then wash it with detergent and rinse it with clear water, repeating this until no droplets form, which means that the surface is then grease-free.

There are many kinds of grounds, but this acid-resistant wax is usually made from beeswax combined with asphaltum and some sort of varnish. Heat the metal on a hot-plate, and while it is still warm rub it over with a lump of the ground wrapped in a casing of fine cloth; an old handkerchief makes a fine dabber. It must be a soft material so as not to scratch the surface of the plate.

Lay the ground on, completely covering the plate with a thin, even coat to a depth of about one sixteenth of an inch; then you are ready to transfer your design to it. Do the drawing on thin tracing paper and then lay it face up on a flat, hard surface, remembering that the plate will be a reverse of the finished print (and of the original). Carefully lay the plate face down on the tracing paper, bring the edges of the paper up, and tape them to the back of the plate. Turn the plate face up, and with a very sharp pencil go over the drawing to impress it onto the ground. (Figure 105.) If you are working with two colors, which requires two plates, you can repeat this process on the second plate, tracing only those areas on the first plate that are to be in the first color, and the other areas on the second plate for the other color. Another way to transfer the identical design to a second plate is by offsetting it, that is, by pulling a print and immediately setting it face down onto a second (or third or fourth) plate. The ink will be wet enough to transfer the drawing—by offsetting it—onto the new ground. After you have transferred the design to the ground and scraped through the wax to the surface of the metal, the acid will make the actual imprint in the plate

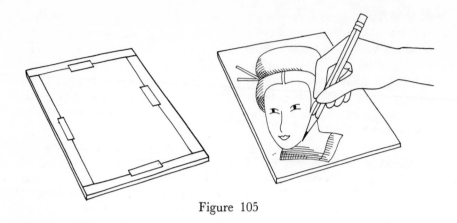

Figure 105

by etching, or biting, into it. It will dissolve the metal away, and this biting action will take place wherever there is exposed metal. Any instrument that will cut through the wax can be your "needle"—a thin nail, a penknife, a dressmaker's wheel, an orangewood stick, a spoon, even a needle—just so that you reach through the wax ground to the metal.

After your whole design is cut through the wax, the back and edges of the plate must be protected from the acid eating away at them too. This is accomplished by coating them with stopping-out varnish. This varnish is made from rosin dissolved in turpentine, with a little lampblack added to make it visible. It is applied with a brush all over the back and all four edges to keep the acid from wantonly attacking the plate.

Now that the plate is exposed where you want it etched, and stopped out everywhere else, it is ready for the acid bath, which is the etching agent. You will require a vessel that is large enough to submerge the whole plate, and in order to avoid an interaction of metals, such a pan should be made of Pyrex or Corning Ware or porcelain. The acid used for the mordant is usually nitric acid in a 10 per cent solution. Mixing acid is a very dangerous procedure, and great caution should be observed. *The acid should always be added to the water,* and never vice versa: each molecule of acid reaches for many molecules of water, and so there must always be a surplus of water in order to keep the mixture from spattering up, which could cause a serious burn. Put nine parts of water into the pan, and then very slowly add one part of acid. (Sometimes hydrochloric acid is used as the mordant; your supplier can advise you as to which is the better one for your particular job.) It is advisable to wear heavy rubber gloves, wash your hands often, and keep the water running in the sink so as to dilute the acid as it goes down the drain. You can neutralize the acid when you are all finished by adding washing soda to it until the solution stops foaming; but if you have a septic system, you should first rinse the plate in a tub of water and then dump the tub; otherwise the acid will destroy the bacteria that activate the system.

Lay the plate in the acid bath, and move it around a little to allow the bubbles to escape. (Figure 106.) Leave it in for one or two minutes, then remove it, rinse it in running water, and blot it dry gently with a soft cloth. You have now etched in the lightest lines, and later will return the plate to the mordant to etch in the darker ones. To keep some of the lines light, they must be protected from further biting in. To do this, apply stop-out varnish with a small brush to those areas you wish to remain light, and then put the plate back into the mordant to etch for another five minutes. Remove it, wash it, and stop out the next shadings. Repeat this process three or four (or ten) times, until all the shadings, from light to dark, are made. The more times a line is subjected to the acid bath, the deeper it will be and the darker it will print.

When your drawing is completely etched into the metal plate, clean it thoroughly with turpentine to remove all the wax ground and all the stopping-out varnish, and polish the surface with toothpaste and then with detergent and water. Now you are ready for printing.

In intaglio printing it is necessary for the paper to reach down into the incisions to grab the ink. For this reason, a soft, strong, flexible, absorbent paper is needed. Water-color paper is good if it has been well soaked beforehand. Or a heavy rice paper that has no sizing may be dampened by putting it between two wet blotters. The paper is always used wet so that it will press into the etched areas without crumpling, but not so wet that it will repel the ink or cause it to smudge. Consequently, you should always put the paper between blotters before printing, either to dampen it or to remove excess moisture from it. For the printing, you will need newspapers, a tube of

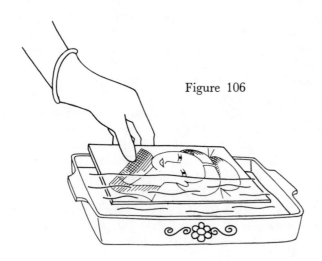

Figure 106

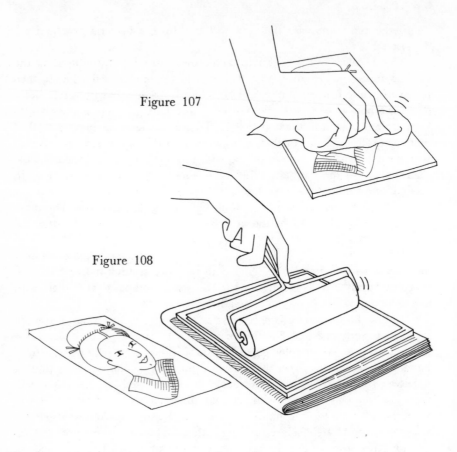

Figure 107

Figure 108

printer's ink, some turpentine, a sheet of window glass to roll the ink on, two rubber brayers, and lots of soft, unsized (washed) cloths formed into small pads. Everything in intaglio printing should "give" a little, and so you rest the plate on a bed of newspaper and protect it on top with "blanketing." The blanketing is usually made from thin felt cut a little larger than the plate, or some heavy cloth or thin foam rubber.

With one of the brayers, roll out the printer's ink on the slab of glass, thinning it with a little turpentine or gasoline if necessary so that it thoroughly charges the brayer. If the copper plate is heated a little beforehand, it will better accept the ink. Roll the inked brayer back and forth across the plate in all directions, recharging the roller if necessary, and then, with a pad of cloth, wipe the whole plate over to force the ink into all the lines and etched-out areas and to remove the ink from the surface of the plate at the same time. (Figure 107.) This will take several wipings with clean cloths. When the surface is clean and your design shows up clearly in the color of the ink, you are ready to pull your first proof.

Put the plate on a clean bed of thick newspaper, face up, and carefully place the dampened printing paper on it. Cover the paper with a sheet of dry paper and blanketing and roll the clean brayer over it, back and forth, as many times and with as much pressure as you can muster. (Figure 108.) Remove the sheets, and if the lines were etched deep enough and wide enough and the paper is soft enough and absorbent enough, you will have pulled your first print.

The professional printer, of course, uses an etching press, which has a flat bed and a roller that is adjustable to give as much pressure as he needs. However, because we are printing by hand, we make do with what we have available, and one of the difficulties of doing it by hand is to keep the paper in position while printing it. If you do find your paper shifting, it is possible to tape it to the newspaper bed with masking tape. The tape can stay permanently attached to the newspaper and just be attached to each piece of the printing paper as it is placed on the plate, in a sort of hinge arrangement. Instead of the brayer, a bamboo baren, as employed in wood-block printing, might work better; or perhaps something softer, such as a paint roller made of foam or felt, or a rubber roller from a wringer-type washing machine. A thin rice paper might come through with better results than a heavy quality printing paper.

After you pull your first print, lay the paper flat on a smooth surface to dry, and examine it. If the darks are not dark enough, it could be for one of several reasons. Either the plate was not etched deeply enough, or it was not inked sufficiently, or not enough pressure was applied on the paper to force it into the deepest lines. Try inking it up again and applying more pressure in different directions before you decide that the plate must be re-etched. If it is necessary to re-etch some lines, then of course everything else would have to be stopped out again before putting the plate back into the mordant.

A soft effect can be obtained by leaving a light film of ink on the surface of the plate, or by drawing some ink out of the etched lines with a piece of tissue to give a blurry, hazy appearance.

You might prefer to prepare the plate by the reverse method of etching in the darkest lines first and the lightest ones last. You would apply the ground and the stop-out varnish, and then needle in just the darkest lines and etch them for five minutes in the acid bath. Then you would remove the plate, wash it, and needle in the next-lighter shadings; etch them in, and then repeat the process for these tones. If you do this for as many different shadings as you wish, the original lines will be the deepest and the darkest, because they will have been in the acid for each successive biting in. The last lines that were needled in will have had only one period in the mordant and so will be shallow and will show up as the lightest lines on the print. You would have to check the ground and the stop-out frequently to be sure that there was no breakdown exposing the metal, but you might, even so, come up with some interesting results.

Aquatints

Aquatint is a version of etching in which large areas are bitten in to create loose masses of shading rather than individual lines. This method does not require the use of an engraving tool; the ground is laid on very thinly by dusting a light coat of powdered rosin over the plate through the meshes of a nylon stocking. The plate is then heated from below either by resting it on a tripod and playing a torch on the underside, or by resting it directly on a hot-plate for a few minutes. When the surface becomes shiny, the rosin is fused and the ground is ready to be worked on. You can scratch through this rosin resist with your thumbnail, or with a pad of steel wool, a matchstick, a comb, or a piece of sandpaper. You can rub some of it off with turpentine or scrape it off with a penknife. When you put it into the acid bath, the areas that you have scraped away completely will etch the deepest; the light scrapings will etch the shallowest, and the untouched rosin areas will emerge as a fine mesh, having a pebbly or grainy surface. You can make a print using only the soft tonal quality of this type of ground, or you can use this quality in combination with hard line etching, as the old masters often did.

Once the ground has been laid, you must be very careful not to damage it by resting your hand on it. A good way to avoid this is by constructing a "bridge" to rest your hand on. Cut a thin piece of plywood about four inches wide and a little longer than the width of the plate, and nail two half-inch "legs" to each end. This can straddle the plate and serve as a support for your hand while you are working.

Drypoint and Mezzotint

Drypoint and mezzotint are classed as etchings although technically they are not, because they are not subjected to the etch of the acid bath. Drypoint is done by actually cutting into the plate with an engraving needle, and because no acid is used, no ground or resist is needed, but the tool must be very strong and sharp to cut into the metal; and so this needle is usually made with a steel or a diamond point. Some engravers like to use a little vaseline, colored with lampblack, to lubricate the needle as it is cutting and to make the lines visible as they are worked. Any cutting by this direct method will raise a burr, or ridge. In drypoint the burr is left, but in engraving it is removed by a scraper, which is a flat-sided needle that removes the roughness without affecting the drawing. After this a burnisher is used to flatten and smooth out any unevenness, and the plate is ready for printing.

Mezzotint is done in the opposite way. Here a burr is raised over the entire plate, and the lighter tones are then put in by leveling down this burr. The cutting tool here is called a rocker, and it is a curved, serrated blade with a wooden handle that nests in the palm of the hand. (Figure 109.)

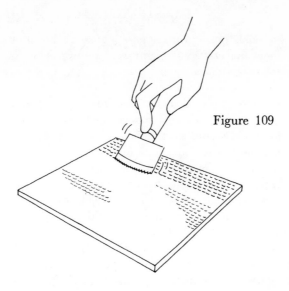

Figure 109

The tool is rocked across the plate, constantly moving from right to left (unless you are left-handed, when the motion would be from left to right). The plate is completely burred in this manner, and if a print were pulled at this point, it would appear to be solid black. The middle tones are then put in by flattening some areas with a scraper, and then the lightest ones are made by further flattening with a burnisher, which will polish the plate down to its original smoothness. Large masses of shadings can be produced by this technique; it is often used in combination with drypoint or line etching. Today the craftsman reverses the mezzotint procedure by leaving some of the metal flat for the light tones. He puts in the next-darker shadings with a tool called a roulette, which is like a serrated dressmaker's wheel, and then he uses a scraper to tone down some of the burrs raised by the roulette. Finally he uses the rocker for the darkest colors. This is cheating, but the final effect is the same.

The drawing for drypoint and mezzotint may be done directly on the metal plate with a ball-point or a felt-tip pen. The print will be in reverse, and if you are engraving words, it is best to do your lettering carefully on thin tracing paper, then transfer it with a carbon by placing it face down on the plate and taping it in place so that it won't shift. With some abstract designs it doesn't matter whether the print is a positive or a negative of the original, but you must always keep in mind that they will print in reverse, and so if it does matter, you will by habit do it correctly.

A raised effect on the print can be obtained by etching the lines deeply into the plate and by using a heavy, quite wet paper. The paper will be forced into the lines, and when it is dry it will retain the impressions, much like papier mâché. In fact, prints made in this manner can be done with no ink at all, being three-dimensional sculptured pieces that have, in effect, come out of a mold. These prints require a great deal of pressure, and if you are serious about this craft, you might want to investigate the studio presses that are adaptable to different methods of printing and are relatively inexpensive.

When you have finished a run of prints, clean your plate thoroughly with turpentine and store it with a coat of vaseline to protect it. A plate may be ground down and repolished to take a whole new design, or the deepest-bitten lines may be retained and used for another drawing by incorporating them. To grind down a metal plate, stones of various grits are used. These stones should be just of a size to hold flat in your hand, and rounded so as not to cause scratches in the metal from rough edges or corners. Arkansas stone followed by Scotch stone will give a fairly smooth finish, then a paste of fine pumice or rottenstone in any kind of oil, and finally a good copper polish, and toothpaste. Toothpaste is, of course, a grit, and it is the best finishing polish—being both a cleaner and a smoother in one. Electric buffers can be used but are inclined to make the surface wavy, which would interfere with the printing.

Old etching plates are good for a new mezzotint, and they also make interesting wall sculptures by etching them clear through to the back: stopping out would be done only in some areas to retain forms, and the rest of the metal could be completely bitten away. Sentimental plates such as an engraved wedding invitation are sometimes mounted on a box cover with epoxy cement as a memento of happy times; and if you no longer want a copper plate for any purpose, it can be used as a base for copper enameling, with unusual results. (*Basse-taille,* or French enameling, is done on engraved copper.)

Printings made from two or more unrelated plates by imposing one impression on another is also an interesting technique, especially for multiple-color work. By etching and/or engraving say two or six or ten designs, you can obtain a color print that would be very acceptable, because today, in all art forms, the possibilities are limited only by the ingenuity of the craftsman.

SILK-SCREENING

Silk-screen printing had a burst of popularity in the 1930s. Artists took to this "new" medium with great excitement, and today it has become a craft with endless applications. It is used on paper, cloth, and glass, in factories, studios, and home workshops. New methods of screening through silk have been devised, with photographic stencils the most recent and most versatile.

A basic method for silk-screening is the glue-and-tusche method, in which a design is put onto silk with a grease-based tusche pencil, and then a water-based glue is brushed over the whole screen. The tusche is dissolved out, leaving bare silk where the grease-based ink can penetrate to print. This

Silk-screened greeting card. Printed in three colors, it required three screens. The middle motif and the border were blocked through all three printings to remain in the white of the paper. Contemporary. American. Courtesy Conception Abbey Press, Conception, Missouri.

is a glue-resist method, in which the glue acts to block out the screen wherever one does not wish the ink to get through; only those parts will print where the tusche design has been eliminated. All methods of silk-screening are variations of this blocking-out principle.

You can buy a kit containing all the equipment you need, but being a true craftsperson you would not do that. You will gather materials from hither and yon, and start your project from scratch.

From the lumberyard you will need a 2×2-inch Grade A stock to make the frame for the screen. If your screen is approximately 6×12 inches, you need three feet of lumber. From the hardware store, you will need four small angle irons, a box of small carpet tacks, LePage's mucilage, some masking tape, some kerosene, a small, inexpensive brush, and some shellac. From the craft-supply house you get the tusche—which is a grease ink in liquid or pencil form—silk-screen ink for printing, some turpentine, and a

rubber squeegee for spreading this ink on the screen. Also, you need the silk
—at least four inches wider and longer than the frame, to allow for the turn-
under.

The silk can be special silk-screening silk, which is a very high-quality
fine mesh, or you can use organdy, nylon, or even cotton if it is not too
tightly woven and is strong enough to withstand the scrubbing that it will be
subjected to. The most time-consuming part of the whole process is making
up the screen, but once it is made, you can use it practically forever by
washing out the old design and applying a new one; for this reason, it is well
to use a good-quality cloth.

First, you must make the frame on which the silk will be stretched. Cut
the lumber into four pieces—two of six inches and two of twelve. Butt the
ends together to make an accurate rectangle, and strengthen each corner
with an angle iron. (Figure 110.) (You could instead use a sturdy wood picture frame for this.) Start to fasten the silk to the frame by laying it on with
the grain running true in both directions, and then tack it lightly at the center of each side. Work one side at a time by tacking on either side of that
first tack at one-inch intervals, pulling the silk tight as you go along and
keeping it true to grain. When this side is all done, pull the silk taut and
tack the opposite side the same way—from the center out to the ends. Start
with the two long sides and follow with the short sides, always pulling the
silk as tightly as possible and always keeping it on grain.

Now cover the lines of tacks with long strips of masking tape for protection, and trim the silk even with the frame for neatness. (Figure 111.) Turn

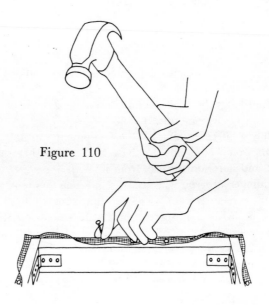

Figure 110

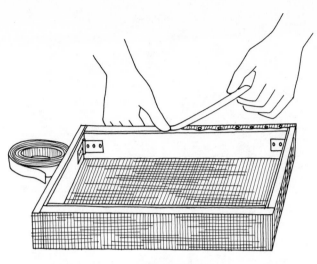

Figure 111

the frame over, so that the silk is on the bottom, and cut four lengths of the tape, one for each side. Fold them in half lengthwise and fasten them to the inside edges of the screen, half on the silk and half on the wood. (Figure 112.) This is the face-up side of the screen; the tape serves to keep the ink from seeping under the wood. Now shellac the tape and half an inch of the silk next to it, to seal it completely.

If you plan to make many prints, you will want your screen hinged to a base so that your prints will always register in the proper position. The base should be a smooth board at least two inches larger all around than the screen. If you plan to use several screens, even of different sizes, a formica board with one half of two loose-pin hinges strategically placed and permanently attached makes an excellent bed. Then your screens can all be hinged

Figure 112

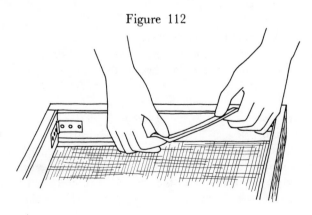

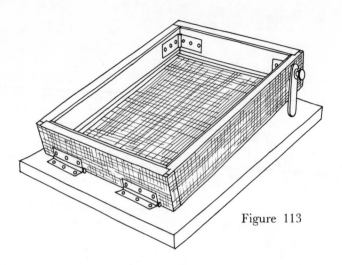

Figure 113

to match these halves and your base is always ready to use with any one of the screens by slipping the pin in or out as needed. There should be no play in the frame when it is raised and lowered for each print. If all your screens are hinged to mesh exactly with the half on the base, you need only take out the pin and change screens to be ready for work with a new color or even a new design altogether on a different-size screen.

A leg stand is a big help in keeping your hands free. Your screen will open like a trap door—with the hinges at the far end. (Figure 113.) About two inches from the front of the screen, fasten a small piece of wood about four inches long. You can use a pop stick or a wooden ice-cream spoon fastened with a long, artist's pushpin. Or drill a hole in the stick, and hang it on a nail driven into the frame. This way it will be free-swinging and will drop of its own weight each time the screen is raised. The purpose of this leg is to keep the screen propped up while you take out a finished print and insert a new piece of paper.

To insert each piece of paper in the right position for printing accurately, you will need registry guides. Place a piece of paper the actual size of your finished print in position under the screen. Scotch-tape a strip of cardboard to the base along the bottom edge of this sample piece. Halfway up one side of the paper, tape another piece of cardboard to the base. (Figure 114.) The cardboard pieces will be your permanent guides to insure the proper registry of each print; as you insert each piece of paper for printing, you will line it up by these guides, which are always left in place on the bed.

Any good-quality paper can be used, and any kind of colored ink, but it is best, for a start, to use the prepared oil-based silk-screen inks, which may be thinned with turpentine to the consistency of very heavy cream. For applying the paint to the screen, use a squeegee. This is simply a rubber spreader the width of the screen; a piece of matboard serves the purpose very well and can be discarded after use.

All your initial preparations having been made, you are now ready to prepare your screen for printing. Draw your design on paper, place it in exact position under the screen, and Scotch-tape it to the base. Now trace it directly onto the silk, using a tusche crayon for the design and liquid tusche for masses and texture. You can make stippled or dappled effects with the side of the crayon or by dabbing the liquid on sparingly with a sponge. Very thin lines can be drawn on with a pen, and the tusche can be sprayed or spattered on with a toothbrush. If you use a light touch, the mesh of the silk will remain slightly open, and will be able to receive some of the glue, so the ink later will not penetrate as easily. By controlling the amount of tusche and by feathering out the edges with a soft cloth, you can make your design as soft-edge or as hard-edge as you wish it.

When the design is done just as you want it to appear on the print, let it dry for an hour or so; then mix the LePage's glue half and half with water, and brush the whole screen over with this mixture. (Figure 115.) Allow it to dry for fifteen minutes, and apply another coat of the glue. Allow this coat to dry for a half hour or longer to be sure it is quite dry, before you dissolve out the tusche. The tusche is dissolved by kerosene, and the

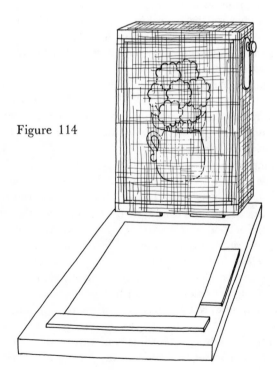

Figure 114

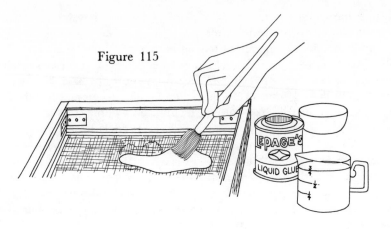

Figure 115

glue can be washed out only by water; the places where the glue remains will become the background on your print, because no ink can pass through these coated areas. Soak a rag in kerosene and scrub the silk on both sides until the tusche is all washed away. The water-soluble glue will remain on the screen except in the tusche areas, where it will wash away along with the grease. When the whole design shows as clear silk, wipe it with a dry cloth; when it is thoroughly dry, you are ready to start printing.

Place your paper on the base, lined up with the registry guides, lower the screen, and pour about two ounces of ink along the full length of one edge of the screen. Remember that your silk is on the bottom of the screen and that the wooden sides of the frame form walls to retain the puddles of ink as you spread it. With two hands, hold the squeegee in an almost upright position and push or pull the ink along the full length of the screen. (Figure 116.) The ink can go only through the clear silk; where the glue blocks it, it will not print, and so wherever there is this obstruction, the paper will remain its original, background color.

Rest the squeegee against the opposite side of the screen from which it started, and raise the screen. The leg will drop and keep the screen raised while you remove the paper, which has now been printed. Insert a new piece of paper, lower the screen, and drag the ink across to the other side. Rest the squeegee, raise the screen, and you have another print. It is as easy as all that, and you can print many times before having to add more ink. If your screen clogs up, clean it with turpentine and pour in fresh ink. If you use a rubber squeegee, keep it clean, too, wiping it now and then with a turpentine rag. For a change of color, just wash the screen and the squeegee thoroughly with turpentine to remove all traces of the old ink, and proceed with a new color.

When you have made all the prints you wish of this particular design, you can clean off your screen and put it away for use at a later time. Clean

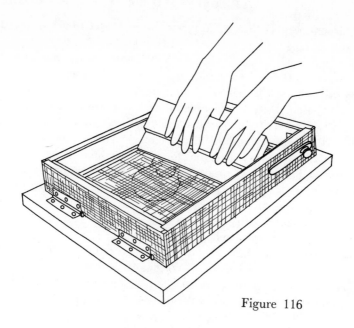

Figure 116

Figure 117

it with turpentine, and then scrub it with warm water to get rid of all the glue. It can then be used for a new design.

For a multicolor job, you will need as many screens as you have colors, blocking out each time all the areas not supposed to register in the color you are then using. You will make each screen from the original sketch, being sure that the original is accurately placed each time with the registry guides. For designing a bowl of fruit, for instance, you might want red apples, yellow bananas, and orange oranges. Because red and yellow make orange, you will need only two screens—a red one for the apples and oranges, and a yellow one for the bananas and oranges. The yellow printing on top of the red should give orange, so that a third—orange—screen will not be necessary. You will prepare the first screen by omitting (blocking out) the yellow bananas with glue and printing with red ink, and the second one by blocking out the red apples and using yellow ink. (Figure 117.)

The prints take at least an hour to dry and should not be stacked immediately. They may be laid out individually or hung from a line with clothespins till dry. It is better not to do a second printing on them until they are thoroughly dry, because of the danger of smudging.

Cutting Stencils

Cutting a stencil and adhering it to the silk is another method of screen printing. You may use special stencil paper, cut with a stencil knife, or you can use heavy white bond paper, that has been wiped over with turpentine or kerosene to make it somewhat translucent. The stencil knife has a short, sharp-pointed blade, and with it you cut away all positive areas—that is, all the areas you wish to print. Whereas, before, it was the glue that blocked out the ink, now it is the stencil paper that will not allow anything to register through the screen except where you cut it away. Draw a cartoon to size, and then cut a piece of stencil paper to the exact size of your original so that it engages in the registry marks. Lay it on the cartoon, trace the design, and then cut away all the design parts that are to be printed. Lay the finished stencil on the bed, lower the screen into position, and squeegee the ink across the screen. This first inking will act as an adhesive and will bind the stencil to the screen.

Stencils may be made for a short run, of five or ten prints, by simply adhering torn or cut paper to the bottom of the screen by this inking method. You could cut your paper carefully into a thought-out design or tear small pieces and overlay them to form an abstract pattern. Flat ferns or leaves might be adhered to give a reverse print; the leaf would be in the background color, and the ink would come through to show it up in silhouette. Anything that would adhere to the bottom of the screen would in theory produce a print.

The lacquer stencil that comes with a glassine backing is used in the same way. This method allows for very delicate designing, because the glass-ine backing holds the design in place until it is affixed to the screen. A special film-adhering liquid is used, and then the glassine is removed and the screen is ready for printing.

Photographic stencil film provides another method of blocking out the silk. The principle is like that of a photographic negative; an emulsion allows areas to wash out that have not been hardened by exposure to light. These stencils are processed as in photography and then adhered to the screen. The photo-stencil procedure allows for the most freedom of design, because one can take a picture of anything, with no manual dexterity involved. It is used commercially for printing on textiles, plastics, glass, ceramics, and other materials. Reproductions on canvas of great art are done by this method.

For simple work with poster paints or tempera, perhaps the easiest method is that using imitation shellac. The design is painted on the screen with LePage's glue, and then the whole screen is covered with imitation shellac, applied with a squeegee back and forth. When thoroughly dry, the glue is washed out with water applied to both sides of the silk; the shellac remains, and the screen is then ready for use with a water-based paint. The shellac is resistant to water, and when the printing is finished, the shellac can be cleaned off the screen with denatured alcohol. Acrylics and casein paints are not suitable for silk-screening, because they harden quickly and would clog the screen in no time. Beyond that, there appears to be little restriction in the art of silk-screening.

"Layers." Wassily Kandinsky. 1932. Mixed media, tempera and oil, on a wood panel. A composition made by the placement of forms of lights and darks, for which this artist is best known. Courtesy Nathan Cummings Collection.

7

Painting

PAINTING

Painting, they say, is a coming together of happy accidents. The professional artist with long years of study behind him can manage to make these happenings more happy and less accidental, but this same professional is never satisfied, because he is never quite sure when he has finished a painting. Anyone can learn to paint, but one can become an artist only through constant application and criticism. The most important ingredient is work, and it is very hard work. Unlike other forms of art, it cannot be spoken, or played, or heard; it must be put down, to be seen and pondered.

All painting is done on a support, which is the surface onto which the paint is applied. Traditionally, oils were used on a canvas support, water colors on a paper support, frescoes on a plaster support, and so on. Inasmuch as the artist today is not bound by tradition, all manner of supports are now used for all manner of media. There are rigid supports such as canvas board, wallboard, plywood, masonite, and there are flexible supports such as paper, linen, cotton, burlap. Traditionally, the support was given a ground coat of gesso to seal it and make it receptive to the paint, but today the artist experiments with different kinds of grounds, perhaps sealing the pores by simply applying a coat of varnish to isolate the paint, or perhaps working on a raw surface to achieve an unusual effect as the paint is absorbed.

All artist's paints are made of pigment bound with a medium. Oil paints are bound in linseed oil and are miscible with turpentine. Acrylics are bound in a synthetic polymer and are soluble in water, but they are usually classed with oil paintings, because ordinarily they are used on canvas. All the other paints are classed as water colors—casein, egg tempera, gouache,

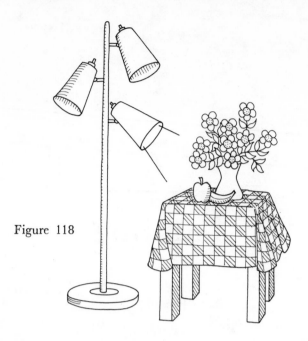

Figure 118

inks, aquarelles. Of this group, each is called by its own name, except aquarelle, which is the only one commonly called water color. It is pretty confusing, and of little consequence, but for exhibitions and juried shows, it is important to know which class a painting belongs in. Mixed media is a fairly new category; it means simply that more than one medium has been used, ink with aquarelle, for example, or tissue collage with oils.

In the Northern Hemisphere, a north light is the best one to paint by, because it is constant. Eastern, western, and southern exposures change from hour to hour as the sun changes position, and if a northern exposure is not available, an artificial light should be set up, especially if you will be working over a long period of time. The light and the easel should be marked as to position, so that at the next work period the shadows will still be the same. In art schools the position of the model is marked on the floor with chalk, and the student makes marks too, for the position of his easel, so that from day to day the model is seen in exactly the same way.

In realistic painting or drawing, the source that the light comes from is important. A strong light coming from one side will accentuate highlights and shadows, and all forms in painting must come from these lights and darks. (Figure 118.) So, for the beginner it is important to have the subject well defined by properly placed lighting. Abstract art seemingly ignores conventional form, but the true artist has had years of experience in realistic work, and the form comes through into his painting without his giving it a thought.

Some teachers start the beginner off by throwing a very strong light on the subject to make the student see only masses of light and dark—body and

Still life. Francisco de Zurbarán. Oil on canvas. A splendid composition of simple objects with interest dependent on light and shadow. Early-seventeenth century. Courtesy Museo del Prado, Madrid.

body shadow. If you paint a picture of an apple on a table, the apple will be floating in space unless it has a shadow to anchor it in its place, because nothing exists without a shadow. As you get more proficient in "seeing," these strong contrasts are no longer needed, and then a softer, more natural lighting can be used. Once you are familiar with how the shadows fall, you can paint objects intuitively, and only then are you ready to start on the road to abstract painting.

It is necessary, too, to learn to squint. In painting realistically, you must put down exactly what you see, but with the eyes wide open you see too much. Squinting will narrow your vision and make the lights stronger and the shadows deeper, and extraneous patterns will be filtered out. Squinting also helps to put things in their proper perspective: identical objects in the background and in the foreground are not identical in a two-dimensional painting (the one in the background appears smaller as it recedes; the farther away it is, the smaller it gets), and squinting will help you to see this proportion. Suppose you put two twelve-inch rulers on a table, one at the front edge and one at the back. Now stand back and hold a pencil at arm's length; with one eye closed and the other one squinting, mark off with your thumbnail the length of the nearer ruler. Hold that position, and squint at the farther ruler. You will find that the farther ruler appears much smaller

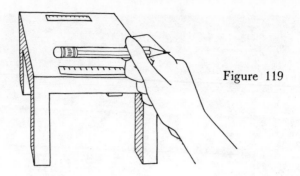

Figure 119

when lined up with the pencil, and this is how it must appear in the painting. (Figure 119.) All proportions are measured in this manner. If you are doing a painting from a still-life setup of fruit, for instance, the largest object might be a pineapple; measure off the size of the pineapple and, keeping your thumb at this mark, measure all the other fruits by their relative size to this one. While perspective and distance may not be important in this particular painting, you will have established the size and proportion of each object as seen in relation to the others. In a study of the human figure, for example, you will find that the head will go into the body about seven times; points of reference can be marked off on your canvas so that each part of the anatomy will fall in the right place. (Figure 120.)

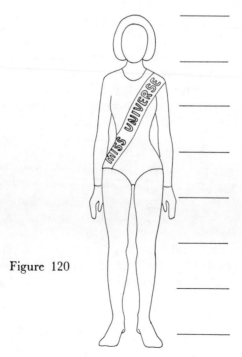

Figure 120

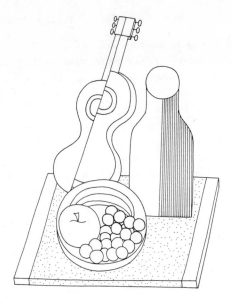

Figure 121

ABSTRACT PAINTING

Abstract painting got started when artists decided to take liberties with the rules that had been instilled in them. Up to Renaissance days the people were hungry, and painters usually depicted samplings of food in their work. Fish, loaves of bread, and fruit were all true to life, to be admired and relished, giving vicarious pleasure. Later, when there was less hunger, artists started to take liberties with subjects, and color and composition became a more interesting challenge than exact likenesses. Perspectives started to change, and along came such artists as Cézanne, who painted fruit on a table as though he were walking all around it; some areas were done as if from an eye-level, head-on view, and others as if from a bird's-eye view, all mixed up on the same table.

Cubism went even further, and artists started to paint with a "universal" perspective: a mandolin painting by Braque shows every aspect of the instrument as though it had been dematerialized and then put together again as an idea out of thin air. (Figure 121.) Modern art becomes an art of invention and innovation, with a basis always of solid background and knowledge. If Braque had not painted mandolins from every angle and Cézanne had not painted apples from every viewpoint, they certainly could not have put a painting together with universal perspective. And that is why an experienced artist can paint a picture with such impact, and that is why the beginner must work hard to establish the basic rules. Love is not enough.

There are certain terms used in the studio that one should be familiar with. The "medium" refers to the vehicle that is used to carry the pigment.

In oil painting, the vehicle is basically oil and turpentine, which is sometimes mixed with other substances according to the preference of the artist. "Priming" refers to the first coat (of anything) that is put on the porous canvas. This prime coat is used to protect the canvas so that it will not be attacked by the vehicle of the paint: in due time, the oil and the turpentine would rot the canvas support and the painting would disintegrate. And priming is usually done on a slick surface, too, so as to give the paint something to grab onto. Traditionally, gesso was used for this prime coat, but today there are synthetics that serve the same purpose, maybe. Time will tell. The "underpainting" is the preliminary work sometimes done to put in the forms and general composition of a painting. "Scumbling" is a technique in which a thin coat of opaque paint is overlaid and then pushed around to give an effect of movement. "Glazing" is a thin coat of transparent paint usually held in dammar varnish; this is an overpainting to heighten the luminosity of a surface.

VARNISHING

"French varnish" or "retouch varnish" is a light film that can be used while work is in progress. It combines with the paints and gives a temporary protection, but doesn't seal the paints in. "Final varnish," on the other hand, is a covering and sealing agent, and the two should not be confused. The expression *alla prima* is used to denote a painting that came out just right first time around: sometimes an expression of thought is expressed by the first strokes of the brush on the canvas, and sometimes it seems to take forever to get things right; when they are right first off, the painting has been done *alla prima*—quickly and decisively.

One of the cardinal rules in oil painting is "fat over lean." Oil paintings dry by evaporation, and so the paint must have a surface exposed to air so that it can breathe. The medium used is oil, which is fat, plus something else such as turpentine, which is lean, and each successive layer of paint must be no "leaner" than the one beneath it. This lean mixture would dry more quickly and would form a hard film over the fat one, preventing it from evaporating, and it would never dry.

It is important to look at and to study all kinds of art, and one of the best tools of learning is to copy paintings done by old masters. In doing this, you will become conscious of how the paint is applied: every artist has his own "brush stroke," and it is like a signature. You will also begin then to notice nuances of color and shadings, and actually doing it yourself will help to teach you the ability to transpose from eye to canvas. What the hand puts down is not always what the eye has seen: something often gets lost in the translation, and by studying the masters, you can find and correct your own errors, and by self-criticism and perseverance you will learn much.

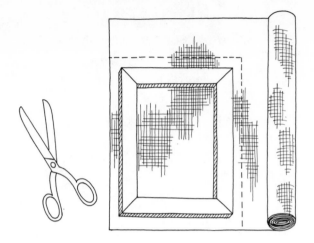

Figure 122

STRETCHING CANVAS

Canvas for oil painting can be bought already stretched in stock sizes. These are sized to a tried and true formula of design: 12×16, 16×20, 24×30, etc. Stock frames come in sizes to match these canvases and are less expensive than having a frame made to order. However, if you wish an odd size—say a street scene where you wish a definite horizontal effect, or a vase of flowers that you want to be tall and thin—then you can have a canvas stretched professionally by your fine-arts supplier, or you can buy the canvas and stretch it yourself. Canvas is sold by the yard, and sometimes you can pick up remnants from a roll. There are many grades, ranging from inexpensive, coarse cotton to finest linen, which is quite expensive, but all of them are much cheaper to buy by the full roll. (Figure 122.) Rolls run from six yards up and are about fifty inches wide; this is a lot of canvas for one amateur painter. A group sharing a roll could, however, save a fair amount of money.

Stretchers are sold by the inch: a 10×15-inch canvas would take two 10-inch and two 15-inch stretchers, and the canvas is cut at least one inch larger all around, that is, at least to 12×17 inches. The stretchers are notched to dovetail into each other at perfect right angles, and once they are assembled you are ready to mount the canvas. (Figure 123.) All you need are small carpet tacks and a hammer. Be sure that the stretcher is truly squared by pushing each side against the corner of a doorjamb, which is a right angle, and manipulating it until all the edges run straight.

Center the canvas on the stretchers as accurately as possible, keeping the grain true—the threads running truly vertically and horizontally. Bend the canvas over the stretcher edges and hammer a tack part way in at the

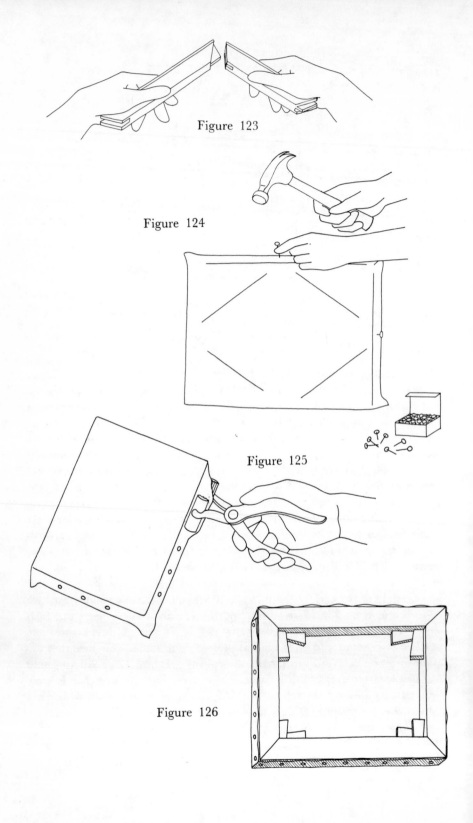

Figure 123

Figure 124

Figure 125

Figure 126

middle of each side. Pull the canvas taut and, working from the center toward the corners on all four sides, hammer a tack on each side of that first one on side 1, then do the same on sides 2, 3, and 4. (Figure 124.) Now you will have three tacks lightly placed in the center of each side. Put two more into side 1, and continue in this manner so that all sides are stretched simultaneously toward the corners, keeping the grain true all around. Place the tacks about two inches apart and hammer them only part way in, so that if any unevenness occurs they can be pulled out and reset. When you have worked your way out to the corners, pinch up the canvas between the thumb and forefinger, fold it over into a neat mitered edge, and tack it down. Now, if the canvas is well set and stretched as tightly as you can, with no ripples, hammer the tacks all the way in.

There is a tool, called stretching pliers, that enables you to pull the canvas tighter than you can by hand. These pliers are about two inches wide, with corrugated fulcrums at the jaws. (Figure 125.) With the pliers, grab the canvas and press one fulcrum against the stretcher to pull it as tight as possible, then put your tack in, and continue along the sides until all the tacks are done. Canvas made of an open-weave material such as burlap will not stand the strain of being pulled so tight, but regulation artist's canvas will withstand a great deal of pressure, and these pliers are a big help. Primed canvas is ready to use as soon as it is mounted, but unprimed material should be coated with several coats of gesso to fill the pores after stretching.

Along with the four stretchers, your dealer has supplied you with eight little wedges called keys. Lay the canvas face down on the floor and place a key into each slot at the ends of the stretchers, two in each corner. (Figure 126.) Holding a hammer vertical to the floor, knock these keys in as far as they will go. They will serve to push the stretchers out and tighten the canvas still more. If at any time bulges appear in the canvas, they can usually be worked out by sponging the back with water; while it is drying, shrinkage will occur and the bulges should disappear.

Sometimes a painting mounted on stretchers will warp, especially in large sizes. This is usually due to the wood of the stretchers being "green," or not well aged. The best way to avoid this is to make your own stretchers, using a good grade of lumber and raw artist's linen. At first it will seem difficult to do and cumbersome, but when you are turning out pictures at a good rate, it becomes part of the job, and it will certainly save you a lot of money.

At the lumberyard, purchase the best grade of 1×2-inch white pine, and $\frac{1}{4}$-inch quarter-round molding. Cut the 1×2 to the size desired, and lay the "frame" out on the floor, butting the ends (not mitered). Fasten the corners together with corrugated or Scotch fasteners, being sure the corners are squared off, using a carpenter's square as a guide. (Figure 127.) If the size is very large, brace the corners with thin lengths of wood such as lattice

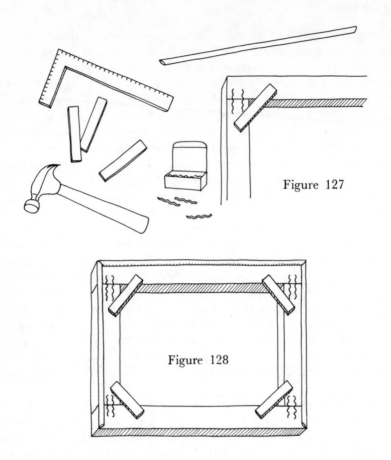

Figure 127

Figure 128

strips. Carefully turn this rectangle over, and reinforce it on the other side in the same way with a fastener in each corner.

Now cut the ¼-inch molding to the size of this frame, mitering all the corners. It will be placed all along the outer edge of the 1×2s to keep the canvas away from the wood, so glue these moldings onto the front, outside surface of the frame. (Figure 128.) When it is dry, the stretcher is complete and ready to take the canvas. Use a raw canvas for this stretcher; the most satisfactory canvas for painting has a close weave, is linen, and comes from Belgium. Actually, any material may be used as a support for paint. A good grade of linen will last literally forever (what is "forever"?), but artists have used, as the spirit moved them, burlap, dish toweling, bed sheets, nylon stockings, unbleached muslin, anything, and perhaps with the proper grounding these, too, might last forever.

Preprimed canvas, whether it be linen or cotton, must be stretched tightly, but raw linen need not be, because when you put the priming coat on, it will shrink the linen and make it tighten automatically. Spread the linen on the floor, place the stretcher on it, molding side down, and cut it about two inches larger than the stretcher on all four sides. Then, with small carpet tacks or a staple gun, tack the center of all four sides to the back of the stretcher. It is important that the grain of the fabric be true, and a certain guide for this is that when you have these four tacks in place, a diamond shape will take form on the linen from tack to tack. When you have thus trued up the grain, fasten the linen on all four sides simultaneously, rotating the frame so that tension is maintained as you go around. Miter the corners carefully and trim off excess linen around the edges.

Now the raw canvas is ready for priming. The purpose of this prime coat is to protect the canvas from the oil of the paint, because if this oil is absorbed by the cloth it will cause rotting in due time. For centuries, priming has been done with gesso (from the hardware store); it comes in paste form to be thinned with water to the consistency of heavy cream. Using a large brush or roller, apply one coat to the surface of the canvas, brushing it on in one direction, and when it is dry, put on a second coat, brushing it in the opposite direction, and then, just to be sure, a third coat. This application of the primer will stiffen the canvas, making it more substantial, and will also shrink it so that it will now be taut on the stretcher. The gesso should be allowed to dry for a day or two before you start to paint.

Sometimes an artist working in acrylics will use a priming of Knox gelatin—one package to one cup of water. This also serves to close the pores and strengthen the fabric, and being transparent it is sometimes more desired than the white, opaque gesso. Artists sometimes, too, employ white-lead house paint or white acrylic, and some artists use no prime coat at all, just working on the raw support. Rembrandt used gesso.

OIL PAINTING

Painting in oils may be done on many different surfaces. Stretched canvas was considered necessary in times past, but today experimentation with the support is as important as experimenting with the medium or the technique. Rigid supports such as masonite (untempered) are very acceptable, as are wallboard, plaster board, celotex, plywood, cardboard, even paper.

Perhaps you will not like to work on so rigid a surface, and so softer materials can be used: burlap, linen, cotton, silk, monk's cloth, all of which may be stretched on wooden frames to make them taut but still flexible. Perhaps, as a beginner, you will want to start with a prepared canvas board from your art-supply store. (Figure 129.) Many serious artists use masonite panels, because these are easily stacked and don't take up as much room as stretched canvas; also, they are resistant to almost everything, including damage in transportation. A panel may be cut to any size, and when primed with two or three coats of gesso to make a white absorbent background, it is ready for work; but gesso gives a rough, chalky surface, and if you wish to

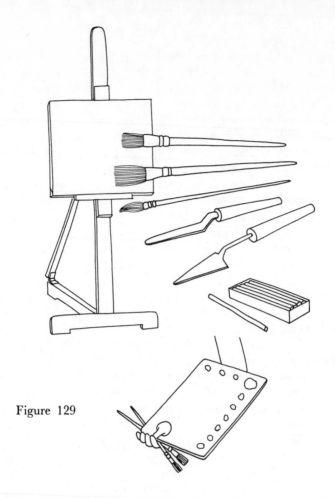

Figure 129

cut down this texture, you can brush it over with a very dilute solution of clear gelatin—about one teaspoonful to a pint of water. Ordinary white house paint of any kind can also be used as a prime coat.

Canvas can be purchased already stretched in stock sizes, and your art dealer will probably stretch one for you if you want an odd size. This canvas is primed and ready for use, as are the canvas boards, but if you wish to stretch your own canvas, your dealer will have a selection of both cotton and linen by the yard, primed, double-primed, and unprimed. The price will vary with the quality, but today practically all artist's canvas is of enduring quality. Cotton canvas is firmer to paint on than linen, and linen seems a little slicker, inviting one to more delicate brushwork and finer detail.

You may wish to start with an imaginative painting, or with a still life that you have set up to paint as you see it. Perhaps you would like to use a combination of both—using the forms as they exist but colors from your imagination. However you decide, you must first set up your palette. It is best to have a white-surfaced palette, so that the colors you lay out are seen truly: any other color behind them will interfere with the refraction of light. However, a 12×12-inch piece of masonite or shellacked plywood will do, or you might buy a pad of palette sheets, which are disposable, or use a piece of freezer paper or aluminum foil. The colors you buy are a matter of taste: any color may be mixed with any other color; theoretically, you need only the three primary colors plus black and white. This of course is putting it on a very elementary basis; the number of colors you buy will depend on how much you wish to spend. Artist's oils are not all priced alike: each company makes several grades, and different brands also vary in price. Some colors, too, are more expensive than others: the reds are high, as are some yellows. In general, the more expensive the line the better the quality, but this can be a matter of personal preference. I have bought very inexpensive oils that I have had pleasure in using and, on the other hand, have had some very expensive tubes that I have found distasteful for one reason or another. White is a very important color; there are several kinds—zinc white, titanium white, and flake white being the most widely used. My own preference is for titanium, for both its color and its consistency.

Brushes come in a great variety of sizes and shapes. The shapes are classified as "flats," which have a straight edge with fairly long bristles; "brights," which look like sawed-off flats, and "rounds," which are long-bristled with pointed tips. One of each, medium-sized, medium-priced, would be good for a start to see which type you prefer. Brushes for oil painting are nearly always bristle, but for fine, detailed work you may want one sable-hair brush, which applies the paint more smoothly than do the bristles.

Your easel can be as elaborate or as compact as you please. Perhaps, for a start, the best arrangement would be a table easel, which will hold a canvas up to 16×20 inches. Floor easels come in many different sizes; some are wood, some aluminum; some have folding, spiked legs to take outdoors and stick into the ground to resist the wind. The floor easels always have an adjusting attachment on the back, which may be raised and lowered to anchor different-sized canvases; the back leg can be raised or lowered to change the angle of the canvas so that it catches the best light for working, with no reflections.

Every experienced artist sets up his palette exactly the same way once he has worked out the most convenient arrangement for his own preferred colors. My own palette is arranged with the yellows and reds along the top, greens and blue down the left side. More white is used than any other color, for it is used to soften, lighten, and change the hue of all other colors, and for that reason it is always laid down in the upper left-hand corner of the palette, isolated so that it will not become contaminated.

Next to white, I lay out palest lemon yellow, then cadmium yellow deep, Naples yellow, yellow ocher, sometimes an orange, then into light red, medium red, and alizarin crimson. A small dab of each does for a start until you get into your painting and know just which colors you will be needing

"Young Lady in a Park." Mary Cassatt. About 1880. The source of the lighting was of primary importance in achieving the luminous quality of the Impressionist painters. Courtesy Nathan Cummings Collection.

most. I use very little burnt sienna or umber—the old masters used a great deal of both raw and burnt sienna and umber—but if I do want them, I still have room for them at the top right of my palette. Down the left side I lay a pale green next to the white, then a Hooker's green deep, viridian green, cerulean blue, ultramarine blue, and perhaps a Prussian blue, which I prefer to black. If I want extreme darks I mix alizarin crimson or Prussian blue with black or umber, but very seldom do I use black alone. The center of the palette is always left bare for mixing.

A double turpentine cup is clipped onto the right side of the palette, one cup for cleaning your brush between colors, and one for thinning the paint. You can buy large cans of odorless "turpentine" at the hardware store, and some artists like other prepared thinners that you can get from an

"Self-portrait." Albrecht Dürer. Painted originally on parchment, this exquisite rendering was later transferred to canvas. Fifteenth century. German. Courtesy the Louvre, Paris. Cliché des Musées Nationaux.

art-supply dealer. A medium of one part linseed oil to two parts turpentine is popular, and to this some artists add one part dammar varnish. Sun-thickened linseed oil, or stand oil, is choicest, and you may buy this in small jars; you can make your own by placing the oil in a shallow dish and letting it stand in the sunlight until it becomes viscous.

And now, with your colors all laid out, your canvas in an upright position, and plenty of rags or tissues, you are ready to start an oil painting. Dip your brush into turpentine, pick up a blob of color, and transfer it to the mixing area in the center of the palette. Pick up a blob of another to mix the color that you want; for instance, a reddish purple will take mostly red, a bluish purple will take more blue, and adding white will change the feeling altogether.

"Boys Wrestling." Paul Gauguin. 1888. A striking example of action with simplified forms in broad color fields. Courtesy Nathan Cummings Collection.

Head of a Woman." Alexej Jawlensky. 1910.
Oil on board. This artist was a highly gifted
member of the Blaue Reiter group, who, like
the Fauvists, used pure, exuberant color to
express ideas. Courtesy Nathan Cummings
Collection. Photo by Malcolm Varon, New
York.

"The Theatrical Producer." Georges
Rouault. About 1912. Oil on paper. A
superb expressionist, this artist could
portray a feeling with just a few bold
lines. Courtesy Nathan Cummings
Collection. Photo by Malcolm Varon,
New York.

"Head of a Woman II." Georges
Braque. 1930. A modern application of
universal perspective through the use
of interlocking planes. By one of the
founders of the Cubist movement.
Courtesy Nathan Cummings Collection.
Photo by Malcolm Varon, New York.

Start drawing in your forms with broad strokes of the brush, and don't be concerned if, first shot, they don't look right (*alla prima*), because you can work oils over and over. You may, if you wish, sketch your drawing in lightly with charcoal or a soft pencil; it should then be fixed with a light spray of varnish to prevent muddying of the colors. While you can also sketch in your forms with paint, your finished work should never look as though it were a drawing in paint; in the end, the lights and darks are what will make the forms. Light colors will bring an object forward, and darks will push it back. A round object will have highlights on its nearest point and will appear to recede if you gradually deepen the darks. If you are working from a still-life setup or from a model at odd intervals, you can set up artificial lighting, which will remain constant at any time of the day or evening.

For modern abstract or impressionistic painting, the imagination can take over. The former means that you are abstracting the essence of the subject being painted, and the latter means that you are putting down your impression of that subject. Distortion is acceptable, and the important thing in this kind of painting is sureness of line and color. Confidence, which comes from familiarity with your medium, and experimentation are helpful as you try out different surfaces and techniques. A palette knife, which is a flexible spatula, is another tool to work with; you can create interesting large areas of color and shading with the knife, and you can build up the paint and texture it. It spreads the paint differently from the way the brush does, and a combination of brush and knife can be firm and productive. With the knife, no vehicle (turpentine) is needed: just lift blobs of color with the knife and mix them on the palette, then apply them to the canvas, using both the edge and the flat surface of the knife to get different effects.

Oils take a long time to dry, and so you can work a canvas in a different area at each sitting until the colors start to get too muddy from overworking. Then it is necessary to put it away for a few days to let the paints set a little. If the colors seem to dull out in some areas, you can spray those areas with retouch varnish, which is compatible and does not interfere with past or future work but will bring the color up true. Oils can be worked over and over, and if you don't like what you have done, you can cover the whole thing over with white and start fresh, or perhaps cover just part and leave what is good. Oil canvases may be restretched if necessary: sometimes stretchers may warp and need replacing, or sometimes you might want to diminish the size of a painting for one reason or another.

Gesso is used as a primer on porous material such as burlap or raw, unprimed linen by stretching the material on canvas stretchers or tacking it down to a rigid surface such as wallboard or cardboard, and then applying three thin coats with a brush or roller, each coat going in a different direction to insure good coverage. This primer seals the pores of the material, which would otherwise absorb too much of the oil in the paint, but if you

"The Outskirts of Paris." Vincent van Gogh. 1887. The artist achieved perspective by the gradual fading away of his famous brush strokes into the distance. Courtesy Nathan Cummings Collection. Photo by Malcolm Varon, New York.

wish to retain the original color of the support, the pores could be sealed by using white shellac instead of gesso. Usually a white background is used in modern painting, because any color underneath will influence the color on top, and for that very reason the old masters used a muddy color as background to deliberately tone down the colors in their subjects. Landscape artists often used gray, while portrait artists used sepia; Rubens used a green underpainting, and then a thin glaze of red on top of that, because these complementary colors gave off a vibration that imparted the famous glow to his flesh tones.

Oils are sometimes used in combination with casein or acrylic paints. The latter two are water-based paints that come in tubes and are handled in the same way as oils; they may even be used as a priming coat on raw canvas or masonite. Ordinarily, the purpose of using them in combination with oils is to get a fast-drying underpainting, which will be dry in about twenty minutes, ready to be finished off with the oil colors. (Casein and acrylic paints are very hard on brushes, and it is best to have special, inexpensive brushes for them. They should be washed immediately in soapy water when you are through.) Oil paints are sometimes used effectively as a thin wash on water-color paper, or in combination with other oil-based media such as wax crayons and oil pastels. An interesting technique known as wax encaustic is used by mixing beeswax with turpentine one to one, with a few drops of dammar varnish added as a binder; this emulsion is kept warm on a hot-plate and used as a medium for the oil colors. Some artists like to add a dash of stand oil to this mixture; this makes it a little looser to handle but gives more brilliance to the colors. Wax encaustic imparts a fluidity and luminosity to a painting that is not possible with conventional media.

Brushes should be cleaned after every work period, first with turpentine and then with a mild soap and warm water: Hold a bar of soap in one hand and rub the brush gently on it for two or three minutes until it rinses clear. The bristles should then be smoothed in the direction they are meant to go, and allowed to dry flat and undisturbed. They can be wrapped in a band of newspaper to preserve the shape.

Final varnishing of an oil painting should not be done until the painting is at least a year old. The oil in the vehicle takes that long to dry, and varnishing prevents the evaporation of the vehicle; it would try to escape through the back and in due course would rot the canvas. When dry, the painting should be cleaned gently with a little soapy water. The final varnish can be either sprayed on or brushed on, and it will not change the character of the work. Varnishing is optional, and once the varnish is dry, any oil painting can be refreshed periodically just by wiping it with a damp cloth, soapy or not.

WATER-COLOR PAINTING

The term water color refers to a painting medium in which the pigments are suspended in water. Every pigment needs a vehicle to hold it together, and many different vehicles may be used. In general, media fall in two classes— those bound in oil and those bound in water. Water alone is not enough to bind the pigment, and so usually a glue is added; the glue may be gum arabic, as in aquarelles; egg yolk, as in egg tempera; milk glue, as in casein; or even soap or glycerin, as in finger paints. Fresco painting was done by using pure pigment on wet plaster, which acted as the binder to hold the color in place.

There are opaque water colors, and there are transparent ones. To the purist, the only true water-color painting is in the transparent aquarelle

"Divers." Fernand Léger. 1942. Water color. An unusual medium for the expression of this artist's well-known flat style. Arbitrary color and shading are used to simulate action. Courtesy Nathan Cummings Collection. Photo by Malcolm Varon, New York.

technique, because all other media are opaque and therefore can be re-worked. Some opaque paints may be made more or less transparent by the use of a great deal of water while you are painting, but this of course dilutes the amount of pigment carried in the brush, and so the brilliance of aquarelle is never really achieved by imitation. Aquarelle, being transparent, is a difficult medium to work in, because corrections cannot be made: each stroke that goes onto the paper is final. There is no white in this medium, because all whites are opaque; lightening is achieved by using more water and thus diluting the color. If white is added, the medium becomes a gouache.

Water-color painting must be done on an absorbent support, usually paper. Paper for this medium is specially sized so that the water will neither spread nor be repelled, but will flow on smooth and controlled. It comes in

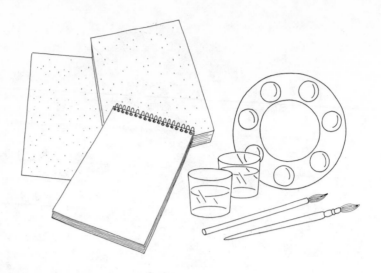

Figure 130

different weights, such as 72 pounds and 140 pounds; these weights refer to the fact that one ream of the paper weighs 72 pounds, or 140 pounds, as the case may be, and it stands to reason that the heavier the weight the better the paper. The 72-pound is recommended for the beginner: lighter than that, it will buckle, and heavier than that, it becomes very expensive. Some artists like a rough-textured paper with a lot of "tooth"; others like the smoother, cold-pressed surface, which absorbs the color more smoothly and with less texture. Some like to work on a block on which the paper is anchored on all four sides, and some on a pad; some prefer to buy single sheets of handmade rag paper. These things are all a matter of personal choice, but of course the best quality that you can afford is the best for you to use. (Figure 130.) There is a great deal of waste in water coloring, and some days are discouraging—not one good picture has been produced but an awful lot of paper has been used up.

As a rule, the paper should be thoroughly wetted before you start work. If the paper is of high quality, it may be held under running water for a few moments or soaked in the bathtub for twenty minutes. Good-quality, 100 per cent rag paper is extremely strong, and it has been said that it is the most durable background support known. If it is of lesser quality, it can be wetted by brushing up and down and sideways with a clean, large brush or a clean sponge. After wetting, it should be stretched so that it will not buckle under the onslaught of water that is in store for it. This you can do by tacking it to canvas stretchers just as though it were cloth. Tack it at the center of all four sides, and then with gentle pressure pull it taut and tack it all around. When it is almost dry, remove it from the stretchers and let it lie flat on the table while you are working.

Another way to stretch paper is by laying it wet on a piece of cardboard of the same size and smoothing it from the center out to free it of wrinkles. As you do this, the paper will stretch, and you can then turn it under and tape it to the back of the cardboard to keep it taut. Because the cardboard will become wet in the process, countersoak it on the back to prevent warping. You do this by laying the whole thing on wet newspaper and weighting it down while it dries. Stretched paper that has dried may be rewetted by sponging before work; most artists work on damp paper.

A white plastic or metal palette should be used. It should have small cups along the sides to hold the colors, and a flat area in the middle for mixing them or for lightening them with water. Some water-color palettes come all set up with cakes of color laid out. These, however, are not usually the best-quality paints, and for serious work the tube colors are recommended. Water colors will dry on the palette or in due time in the tube itself, but they can usually be softened up again by adding water. The palette can be covered with plastic wrap to protect the laid-out colors between work periods, but if a color dries, simply adding a drop or two of water should be enough to liquefy it again.

Water-color brushes can be of any soft hair, such as badger, camel, or ox. However, the most important factor in the brushes is that they be able to hold the liquid and the pigment, which is in suspension; red sable brushes are the best for this purpose. They can be quite costly, and so the beginner can start with just one square-end sable and two or three pointed-end camel's-hair or Japanese bamboo brushes. Two jars of water (one for rinsing the brush and one always to be clean for mixing), some colors squeezed into the palette wells, lots of cleansing tissues, and a flat surface to work on, and you are ready to begin.

Suppose you start with an outdoor scene, which is usually begun by brushing in a pale wash for the sky. In the mixing area, put a small amount of blue paint and add water to it until you get the color you wish—the more water the lighter the color will be. Apply it in long, wet strokes from left to right, then pick up the paper by the bottom corners and move it back and forth to spread the wash. For a cloud effect, pick up some areas of the color with a ball of tissue or a clean, dry sponge to expose the white paper. Water colors are put on from lightest to darkest, and being transparent, they cannot be worked very much or they become muddy; an understated water color is always better than an overworked one.

After you have laid on this background wash, start the design—a heavier blue-green for the water, a yellow-green for the grass. (Grass in the sunlight has a great deal of yellow in it.) While the paper is getting drier, you can make subtle gradations of mass color; in a sunset, for instance, you can blend pink and orange and violet to give a hazy melding of the tints;

as the paper dries more, the brush strokes will take on a sharper focus, so that figures, trees, and any objects close up would be put in last, with the lines becoming progressively crisper as the paper gets drier.

In doing a still life or a portrait (which is very difficult in water color), you must plan the design well in advance, because the use of white space is very important. It is difficult to correct a mistake in aquarelle, and white space can never be retrieved successfully if it is once touched with color; one way to preserve areas of white is by "masking out" with rubber cement. Brush this on where the white is to remain pristine, and when the painting is finished, strip the cement off; a white, untouched space will be exposed.

In a representational painting, it is wise to sketch the drawing in with pencil before wetting the paper; washes are not used so much here, and the paper can be nearly dry for working. In a modern abstract or nonobjective work, some areas can be made wet for a hazy, limpid effect, and other areas left dry for sharp impact; large masses of color can be laid on and then broken up with a dry brush well charged with pigment: the wet and dry spots on the paper will supply striking contrast. Sometimes one dab from a square-end brush can give just the note of interest needed, and at other times a stroke or outline from a soft, pointed brush is just the thing. The sable hair is characterized by the way it bellies out in the middle, holding the pigment there, and then comes to a fine tip. Very long, thin, unbroken lines can be gotten with this sable brush. On the other hand, a Japanese water-color brush, which is round-tipped and more flexible, will give a softer drawn line. The suitable brush for any effect becomes a matter of preference for the individual artist.

If the bristles of an almost-dry square-end brush are charged with pigment and then separated, one bold stroke can give an interesting rhythmic effect, such as is found in the bark of a tree or in the combers in a seascape. Leaves on a tree can be made by washing in masses of light green and then stippling in dark greens and browns with an almost dry stubby brush; clusters of flowers can be made by spattering with a toothbrush or a sponge. Painting in aquarelle is most attractive when it is done in a light, suggestive way. New strokes should be invented and practiced because every problem is different, and the handling of the medium is all-important. It takes a lot of time and patience to acquire facility in this medium.

Some artists like to mount their finished paintings by gluing them to a cardboard backing with white library paste. If you wish to do this, it is advisable to experiment first, because your particular paper might not take well to the paste. If all is well, don't forget to counterglue the cardboard on the back, perhaps by gluing on white sketch paper, or even brown wrapping paper, to prevent warpage.

Water colors should always be matted and put under glass for protection.

ACRYLICS

There are a great many new, synthetic painting media classed loosely under the term acrylics. Whether these plastic paints will take the place of conventional oils or water colors, and whether they will be as durable, time alone will tell. Certainly, for the modern artist in a hurry they have advantages over other media. They dry quickly, they will cover almost anything, they retain their brilliant colors outdoors as well as in, and they can be cleaned up with water.

Acrylics may be worked thick and opaque, like oils, or thin and transparent, as in water colors. In competitive art shows, the rule usually is that acrylics under glass are classed as water colors, and those not under glass are judged as oils. They may be used on any surface except an oily one—although even here it's not a hard and fast rule, because there are some plastic resins that are oil-compatible. The polymer acrylics are the ones generally used by the artist; it is important to read the labels before buying, because they are not always compatible one with the other; vinyls, epoxies, and other polymers are all different chemically and are usually not interchangeable.

The young painters have taken to acrylics with much enthusiasm. These dry almost immediately, and a painting may be finished and ready to hang in a few hours. Colors can be used one over the other without fear of muddying, and hard-edge designs such as were never possible with oils are easily achieved with this medium. They may be used as a thick impasto or thinned with water or medium for use as a thin, transparent glaze. They also can be used as an underpainting for oils, being dry enough to take the oil glaze in a matter of minutes. Oils should not be used under acrylics or with acrylics, but because these plastics dry to a hard, impermeable finish, oils may be used on top of acrylics with no adverse reaction. The support used is best primed with gesso, but even this is not necessary: a prime coat of acrylic will serve quite well on even raw linen canvas. The support can be canvas, wood, masonite, cardboard, paper, glass, plastic, anything.

Brushes of any sort may be used, but they will not last long in this medium, and it is advisable to use inexpensive ones. They should be kept in a jar of water while working and when not in actual use. Nylon ones are best, because the bristles do not absorb the water, as natural bristles do; any natural-bristle brush will swell and deteriorate if it is soaked in water. Acrylic paints harden very quickly on the brush, and so as soon as a working period is over they should be washed thoroughly in water with soap or liquid detergent. Spills should be cleaned up as soon as possible with a soapy cloth, and it is wise to allow the rinse jar to settle; then the liquid can be drained, and the jar, along with the rubbery residue, can be discarded. Unlike oil or water-color paints, acrylics cannot be softened once they have been exposed, because they become set by chemical change. For that reason, only enough paint should be set out to do a half hour's work, and then it is time to start a fresh palette.

Various prepared additives may be used to achieve various effects. There is a gel that will retard drying time and that also makes the paint more transparent. There is medium that is used instead of water to give more body to the paint and that also serves as a final varnish. (The nomenclature of different manufacturers varies, so, again, it is important to read the labels.) There is modeling paste that will thicken the paint and allow for a heavy, sculptured effect, good especially when you are working with a palette knife. None of these additives will change the color or hue of the paint, and all are useful for their purpose.

Acrylic is a very strong adhesive, and because it dries colorless, it is used widely for collage and for relief paintings by adding aggregates of all kinds to give body, texture, or volume. Sand, cement, vermiculite (which gives bulk without weight), talc, powdered marble, clay, asbestos, crushed stone, slate, sawdust, shredded foams—although these, being plastic, might react chemically—almost anything can be bound in this medium. And by the addition of dry pigment, you can create your color while you are forming the surface—visual as well as tactile. The paint as it comes is also strongly adhesive, and aggregates can be bound to the colors just as they come from the tube.

The palette for acrylics should be smooth-surfaced, because a porous material would prohibit cleaning off the paint. Glass, Saran Wrap, aluminum foil, freezer paper, all make excellent palettes, with the mixing area in the center, where the colors can be mixed just as they are in oils. (Figure 131.)

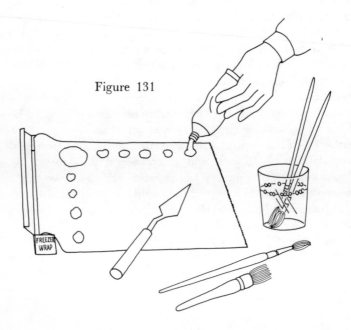

Figure 131

If they are being used as water colors, a water-color palette of porcelain or plastic may be used, and then washed clean as soon as work is finished: the longer these paints sit, the harder it is to remove them. And in this technique, the outcome of the painting will depend on the amount of water that is used with them. For opaque painting, as in gouache, there would be little water; for thin, transparent washes as in aquarelle, there would be much water. Medium is not used for water-color techniques on paper, because the additional binder is not necessary, nor need the paper be wetted unless great puddles of water are expected. These paints can be "gone over" without too dire effects; however, because they are emulating water color, it is best to stay with the idea of spontaneity. As in aquarelle painting, a better quality of paper will produce a better picture, and serious artists use good sable brushes when they work in this delicate technique.

Egg tempera is very successful when it is used with acrylic paints: one egg yolk to one cup of water is used as the medium. When the paint is dry, if it is briskly rubbed with a soft cloth a beautifully luminous quality will buff up. These acrylic "water colors" need not necessarily be put under glass: they don't need the protection, for they can be easily cleaned with soap and water. However, glassing any water color enhances it.

Acrylics are great fun to work with, but established artists who are used to working in oils usually go back to them, finding more satisfaction in the more difficult medium. Water colorists accustomed to truly transparent aquarelles are not happy unless they, too, are working to overcome the inherent difficulties of their medium. But this era of new media is very exciting, and horizons of the expanded palette are limitless indeed.

CASEIN PAINTING

Casein for painting is a very old medium, the binder in this case being an adhesive made from milk. Casein was used in ancient times for very detailed work, because it could be relied on to stay exactly where it was put. In recent years, the formula has been improved to the point where modern artists have been tempted to use it. It is classed as a water color.

Casein paints are versatile. They can be used on almost any kind of support; they can be used in a water-color technique or they can be squeezed directly onto the palette and used with a palette knife just like oils; colors may be used one on top of the other; in their thick state they will cover, or if used thinly they will allow some underpainting to show through. The colors have great brilliance and strength, and usually the final painting is less gentle than a water color.

Casein is water-soluble when moist but insoluble when it hardens. Laid-out paint cannot be saved for another session. Brushes will gum up and so should be rinsed often; they should be washed well in warm, soapy water when work is done. A porcelain palette is recommended, because the paint will not stick to this slick surface, but the sparkling-white plastic cartons in which eggs come from the supermarket make ideal palettes—twelve color cups and a mixing area, all ready, disposable, and free.

As a water-color technique, caseins are used today where artists a generation ago used gouache or tempera for opaque effects. But they may also be used with oils, as the underpainting or preliminary "sketch." Oils can go on top of casein, but not vice versa, because in using mixed media the rule of "fat over lean" must be followed. An oil-based paint is "fat," a water-based paint is "lean," so the fat paint must never be sealed in by the lean one. Another way of expressing that maxim might be "slow-drying after fast-drying."

Casein can be applied to any kind of absorbent paper, gesso panels, gesso-primed canvas, plaster, plywood, or cardboard. If the rough, chalky texture of the gesso seems unpleasant, it can be toned down by applying a coat of very dilute clear gelatin—one teaspoonful in a pint of water. If gesso panels are used, they should be of untempered masonite: the tempered kind has an oil finish that will repel artist's materials. If casein is used on water-color paper, the picture should be matted and framed as a water color; and if it is used on gesso panels or canvas, the picture should be varnished for protection and then treated as an oil painting. There are special casein varnishes, and a dammar-varnish spray is satisfactory.

EGG AND WAX MEDIUMS

Through the ages, many formulas have come down for special effects in painting.

Egg tempera, for one, is an ancient medium that was ordinarily used for the religious panels that we see still glowing on the walls of our art museums. It may be made up and stored in a tightly closed jar with a film of water over it to further exclude air, and it will keep for several weeks.

Carefully break a very fresh egg into a strainer or egg separator, and allow the white to drain away. Pick up the yolk in the thumb and forefinger, and hold it over a half cup of distilled water. (The water bought for your steam iron is distilled.) Pierce the bottom with a clean needle, allow the yolk's contents to fall into the water, shake it up to mix it thoroughly, and use it instead of water while painting. Dry pigment can be ground up right into the medium if you need large quantities, or it can be used to soften up those old poster paints that you have been saving for a rainy day. Egg tempera can be used on gesso panels or on good-quality rag paper. Very fine, meticulous work can be done with tempera and tiny brushes, or freer, broader effects can be achieved with larger brushes. When it dries, the glue of the egg will have made it as permanent as any medium known.

Egg-oil emulsion is another formula that can be used with water-based paints to give them even greater luminosity. The water and the oil of course do not mix, but egg added to the mixture will emulsify it, and the oil and water will become compatible.

To one whole egg add an equal volume of linseed oil; mix them well, then add one volume of water (equal to the combination). Shake this up well, strain it through cheesecloth, and keep it in the refrigerator, just taking out small amounts as needed. A little dammar varnish added to this medium will thicken it and make it a little more viscous, if that is your pleasure.

Wax emulsion is still another medium that imparts a beautiful heightening to either water-based or oil-based paints. This is made by slowly heating one part of white beeswax in six parts of water, with a few drops of clear ammonia. When the ammonia fumes are all gone, it means that the wax has become emulsified, and it will now be compatible with the water or oil. You can add this mixture to egg-tempera medium for use with casein or tempera colors, or you can add it to turpentine for use with oil paints. If you buff it up with a soft cloth when it is dry, it will give a beautiful sheen to your painting.

Wax encaustic is another very old technique in painting that has been revived in recent years. It is great fun to work with, but it is a little cumbersome, because the wax medium must be kept warm and liquefied while you are painting. A muffin tin to keep the colors in and a cookie sheet for a mixing palette, both kept warm in a pan of water on a hot-plate, are serviceable for this purpose. (Figure 132.) The vehicle is made by carefully heating about five parts of white beeswax and one part of linseed oil, with a little paraffin or carnauba wax added to harden it. The more beeswax you put into this medium, the more difficult it is to work it, so you can play around with the ratio until you find a proportion that you like. Because beeswax never dries really hard, the others are added to give a stiffening to the finished work. The microcrystalline modeling waxes are very good for this purpose; perhaps you can get some from your dentist.

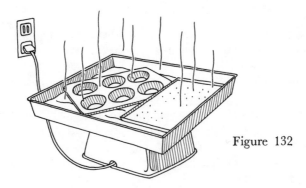

Figure 132

Portrait of a young girl. Encaustic on board. Done with a heated palette of tempera and beeswax. This technique was the forerunner of easel painting as we now know it. Second century A.D. Egyptian. Courtesy the Louvre, Paris. Cliché des Musées Nationaux.

When the mixture is melted, fill the heated muffin cups about half full, and mix in as much dry pigment as you wish in each of the cups. Use two or three of the cups for a clear vehicle to lighten your colors as you work, and paint your picture with a palette knife. Brushes can be used, but they are difficult to control, because the medium hardens almost immediately.

When you have finished your painting, lay the picture flat on a table and play a heat lamp (or, with utmost care, a torch) over the whole surface to fuse the wax and get rid of any unevenness. When it is dry and hard, buff it up with a soft cloth, and it will glow and sparkle as in no other painting technique.

PASTELS

Pastels are pure pigment compressed into stick form, with little or no binding vehicle. They are a little like chalk, and for this reason, the support on which they are used is very important. It must act as the binder, by entrapping the particles of pigment to keep them from flying away. So pastels are always done on a surface that is rough. Special velours paper, sandpaper, velvet, and water-color paper with a heavy tooth are all suitable to work on.

Pastels are not blended on the support, as are the liquid paints. Each spot of color uses a different stick: once the tooth is stroked with the pigment, it cannot hold any more; this initial laying on of color is the final laying on. A good set of pastels will consist of several hundred sticks—each one of a different hue.

Oil pastels are worked similarly to true pastels, but they have an oily binder and are more like wax crayons. They may be blended and can be used on any kind of paper or cardboard, and they are useful in the classroom or for outdoor sketching. They are not, however, considered a true art medium.

Pastels are usually worked in a delicate pattern, befitting the delicacy of the medium, and pastel drawings should be handled with care to avoid smudging. They should be sprayed with charcoal fixative when finished, and should always be framed under glass with a mat for protection.

"Russian Girl Dancing." Edgar Degas. 1895. Pastel. Even in this difficult medium, the artist was able to catch the movement of a fleeting moment by quick sketches and a mastery of perspective. Courtesy Nathan Cummings Collection. Photo by Malcolm Varon, New York.

Portrait of the poet Li Po. By Liang K'ai. Chinese.
Done in the early-thirteenth century, this is a splendid
example of sumi-e. Classified among Japan's National
Treasures. Courtesy Tokyo National Museum.

SUMI PAINTING

Sumi painting, or sumi-e, is one of the oldest art forms known to oriental culture, which is pretty old. In its ancient, true form it was a meditative art, and literally translated means "painting from the head." Each process in doing a painting was a ritual as important as the painting itself. The sumi ink was made from pine-tree soot, animal glue, and incense. While rubbing the ingredients together, the artist would meditate, and when the fragrance of the incense came through his thoughts, he knew it was time to start his painting. It took many, many years of work and meditation before an artisan could be considered an artist, and a proficient artist in sumi-e could do a whole painting with one brushload of ink.

Sumi-e is black-and-white painting in its simplest form. It may be called abstract in the truest sense of the word, because everything is left out of the painting that does not have actual meaning, and only the essence is abstracted. The manner in which this is achieved is by the shading of the lines.

A few simple tools are needed, and while you are easily able to use substitutes and the effect might be the same to the uninitiated, you really are cheating yourself. Black ink can be used with a water-color brush on mimeograph paper, but part of the result of a good sumi painting comes from the discipline of learning to handle the materials.

The brushes used for sumi-e are made to hold a great deal of water without having to recharge; each line must be continuous, and so the brush must hold enough color and liquid to make the line without lifting. The oriental artist had brushes for specific purposes made from various kinds of hair—horse, sheep, deer—shredded bamboo for special hard effects, wool for soft effects. For our purposes we will settle for two Japanese water-color brushes made of badger hair, one large and one small. These brushes have bamboo handles and the bristles are set into a metal ferrule. The best brushes have a continuous ferrule—no seams—and the bristles have been set by hand; a continuous-ferrule brush is quite expensive and deserves good care. It will last a long time.

The color that is used is called sumi, and it is still made from pine soot mixed with oil, glue, and carbon black. It comes in stick form and it is rubbed on a stone called a *suzuri* to liquefy it for use. The suzuri is an oblong dish of stone (or slate) that is deeper at one end than the other. A few drops of water are placed in the deep end, and the sumi stick is dipped into this water and then brought up to be rubbed on the shallow end, or mound, with a circular motion. (Figure 133.) As the stick is rubbed, it forms a paste. It is brought back to the water and back again to the mound with the circular rubbing motion, and the more it is rubbed, the more stick is dissolved and the darker the ink becomes. In painting, the ink is always picked up from the mound, and as this is soon used up, it is necessary to

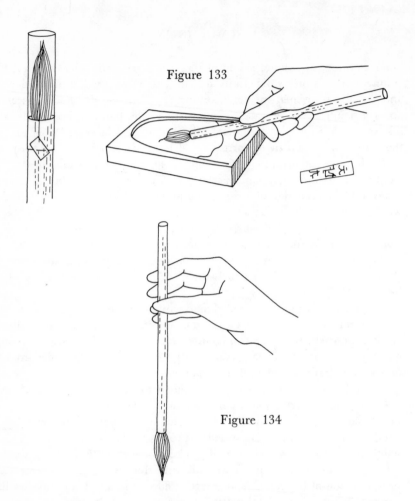

Figure 133

Figure 134

prepare more while working, so two little dishes of water are kept alongside the suzuri. They are used for making more ink, and also for wetting the brush and so extending and lightening the color of the ink.

Japanese rice paper is used for sumi painting. This is a thin, highly absorbent paper, which is placed one sheet at a time on a flat, hard board covered with white flannel. This serves both as a working surface and as a pad to help absorb excess moisture from the ink.

All human elements are important in sumi painting. The posture should be good, the arm relaxed, the elbow free. The brush is held perpendicular to the paper between the thumb and all four fingers, and the strokes are made with the whole arm. (Figure 134.) Broad strokes are made with the large brush; thin, dark accent lines with the smaller brush. Now that we know all the elements of sumi-e, let us do a sumi painting of bamboo shoots, a traditional Japanese subject.

Place a piece of paper, smooth side up, on the flannel board. Wet the brush thoroughly in water, and then remove the excess by stroking it on the side of the dish, always keeping the brush to a sharp point. Pick up ink by laying the brush flat on its side on the mound of the suzuri where you have prepared the sumi. Apply the stroke to the paper in a long sweep, never going over a stroke—no corrections are allowed. Absolutely. The first, palest strokes are made by holding the brush almost flat and horizontal, and the amount of pressure put on the brush will determine the width of the line. If only the tip of the brush has been inked and the brush is drawn sideways along the paper, the stroke will be shaded from dark at the tip edge to pale at the base edge, which holds water but has not been inked. The older stalks are painted with this broad, pale stroke, while the new shoots, which have more life, are painted with short, dark, staccato strokes to give a feeling of youth and vitality bursting forth. Each stroke should be practiced many times as an exercise before you start to paint, because there are only two elements in a sumi painting—the stroke and the composition—and both must be decisive. The older stalk will appear rounded, because the absorbent paper will catch the advancing dark and the receding light colors; the young shoot does not in reality catch so much light and shadow, and the inking of the brush is more even—not so much contrast here between the tip and the base. Nothing else goes into the painting—just a section of bamboo stalk, the old plant fading away and the new one springing to life. During the course of one session, you will do perhaps a hundred paintings, and you will be fortunate if there is one good one.

Some traditional Japanese objects for painting are crabs, dragonflies, and roosters, and each of these has a point of strength that must be stressed. Whereas in the bamboo it was new growth, in a crab the claws are the most important feature; they must be very strong and bold, ready to grab for food. A dragonfly's body is its strength; it must be formed in a strong decisive stroke, with the wings delicate and elusive. A rooster's identifying mark is the cockscomb; a few soft strokes can form his body, but his comb must be proud and strong. A bird or fish has a beady eye, flowers have stamens and pistils, a fruit has a stem from which it gets life. These are the most prominent features, and they must be shown as such. And so sumi painting portrays the essence of the object, and all tributary strokes must be subsidiary.

The signature can be a fanciful calligraphic symbol; if you know someone who can translate your name into Japanese, you can have a true signature. Japanese characters are not written phonetically, as in English, but rather, they conjure up an image, and one's signature can be very poetic. In a bamboo or a flower painting, a dark leaf or a stamen placed at a strategic point can be balanced by the signature symbol, which is also part of the painting and so must be placed with regard for the whole composition: every element in a sumi-e is important to the whole.

In olden days, each owner of an important painting placed his own red seal on it when it became his. That is why in museums today you may find Japanese or Chinese paintings with many seals imprinted on them. The seal is sometimes used today more for a decorative spot of color than for anything meaningful, so that if it is used, it, too, must be placed advantageously in the picture. Some art-supply stores sell sets for sumi painting that come complete with seal, but the serious artist will want his seal made to his own design, and these are hand-carved from ivory or from bamboo roots.

When you have finished painting, your brushes should be washed thoroughly in plain warm water. When they are clean, put them in your mouth and draw them to a fine tip. The saliva acts as an adhesive, and they will retain this point indefinitely until they are ready to be used again. Thin, flexible bamboo mats are used to keep the brushes in tip. The brushes are rolled up in these mats, which allow them air circulation as well as protection while they are drying. Another way to protect the bristles is to roll a sleeve of heavy acetate around the tip and secure it with Scotch tape; this will keep the hairs from getting bent.

Once you get used to the discipline of sumi painting, you will find it one of the most relaxing and gratifying of all the art forms. Much about art can be learned from sumi painting, because all art is composition, and with so basic an example, every point becomes clarified and knowledge has been gained that can be used in every other form of art. True sumi painting involves the whole person, and can be likened to yoga in the feeling of well-being that it imparts.

FRESCO PAINTING

Mural painting is usually done with modern synthetic paints and has little relation to fresco buono, the time-honored craft practiced by the artists of early times. This true fresco is done by applying pure color to a wet plaster surface; as the plaster dries, a chemical reaction takes place so that the pigment becomes an integral part of the support. Fresco was employed by the wealthy ruling class and the Church for interior decoration; easel painting was not yet known. The artist was considered an artisan, and a prince or bishop simply hired this artisan to work directly on the walls of his palace or church. Because so much area had to be covered, it was common for the master craftsman to do the preliminary cartoons and the assistants to do the actual painting. (Figure 135.)

The surface on which the painting is done is a layer of fine lime plaster, about one fifth of an inch thick, called the *intonaco*. It is applied to the wall fresh each day, and covers just as much area as can be painted in eight hours, or before sundown; the area is called a *giornata*—a day's work—and frescoes usually have seams like a jigsaw puzzle, each piece representing one

"The Brazen Serpent."
A fresco buono painted
the dome and the wall
Michelangelo painted
on his back on scaffolding.

Michelangelo Buonarroti.
on a spandrel between
of the Sistine Chapel.
the ceiling while lying flat
It took him four years,

from 1508 to 1512. Courtesy Vatican Museum, Rome.

giornata. The plaster is freshly mixed each day from good-quality white cement and fine clean sand in the proportion of three parts of cement to one part of sand. Some artists prefer a mixture of marble dust and sand, the better, they say, to hold the pigment. The masonry surface of the wall, which is called the brown coat, is wetted down, and the white, intonaco coat is applied smoothly with a trowel, ready to receive the section of the cartoon that will be done that day.

The cartoon, or *cartone,* is drawn on heavy paper, and then the entire drawing is gone over with a sharp stylus, pricking it into the paper. (Figure 136.) Two cartoons are made, one to be used for reference and one to be cut up for each giornata. The day's cartoon is laid on the wet plaster and outlined with a pointed wooden tool, and then powdered charcoal, which is held in a thin cloth bag, is dusted over it so that the design gets transferred through the little holes. The sketch is now on the plaster, ready for painting. (Figure 137.)

Pure powdered pigments are used, and they are ground in water to

Figure 135

which a little lime has been added to hasten the chemical bonding with the lime of the plaster. The colors that are used must be lime-proof; that is, they must be alkali-resistant, or they will be attacked by the caustic, causing them to disintegrate. The day's work must be all done before the plaster dries, because a new giornata is added from the cartoon each day; so the artist must have everything well planned for each day's work.

Fresco painting is done in a flat technique, and rather thinly so that the white background can be allowed to come through enough to impart a luminous quality to the colors. It is never overworked or heavy, and for this reason the cartoon is worked up complete in every detail so that it can be reproduced on the wall with a minimum of indecision. In early times, paper was scarce and quite often the master would sketch the cartone directly on the brown masonry wall. This was done in a red earth color and is known as the *sinopia*. The assistants would study the sinopia very carefully, then plaster over it with the intonaco coat, and paint on that from memory!

In 1967, when Italy was flooded, many of the buildings housing great art treasures were ruined. To save the frescoes before the buildings collapsed, a very interesting technique was devised by which the plaster coat could be removed from the masonry wall and these precious works could be retrieved.

A sheet of soft muslin was pasted to the fresco with a water-soluble glue. On top of that was glued a heavy canvas to give it support, and when the glue dried, the canvas was pulled away from the wall. With it came the muslin, and with that the whole intonaco layer of plaster. The whole thing was laid face down on the floor, and a heavy canvas backing put on it, and then a rigid board. It was turned over, and the original canvas-with-muslin was soaked off the face with water. Thus the precious frescoes were removed intact, now mounted on wood panels and ready for installation in place when the buildings were repaired. In some cases even the sinopia was saved by the same method but with stronger glue, which actually removed the pigment from the masonry wall without disturbing the design.

A similar technique is employed in the restoration of old paintings: the backing is removed by various solvents, and the pigment is transferred intact to a new support. This can be done to even inexpensive prints by offsetting them onto a new support. If they are coated with acrylic medium and then soaked to remove the original paper backing, the ink will remain in the resin and the whole thing can be transferred to a new surface. So a newspaper article or a magazine picture can be saved for posterity.

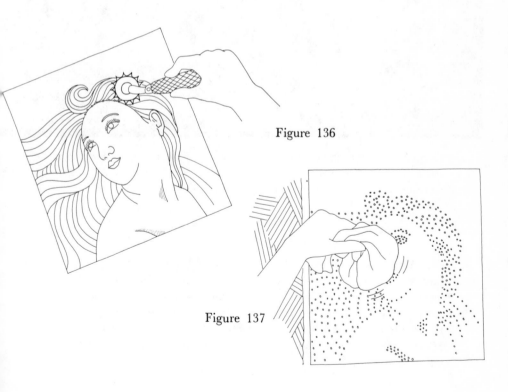

Figure 136

Figure 137

Garden with an ornamental pool. A fresco showing a view of a whole scene, using universal perspective. Fourteenth to fifteenth century B.C. Egyptian. Courtesy the Trustees of the British Museum, London.

Acrylics are said to be almost indestructible, and the young artist today finds them useful in a fresco secco technique—dry, or false, fresco. As a matter of fact, the caustic action that is present in wet lime is not much of a factor in the dry plaster, and practically any type of paint can be used. Synthetics are one great advantage that the artist of today has over the artisan of yesteryear. Modern materials are changing the scene, and time alone can tell us their value.

PICTURE FRAMING

Today artists are painting huge canvases and putting a minimum amount of framing around them. Frames for large canvases can be very costly, and artists are simply mounting them with narrow pieces of thin wood for protection rather than for enhancement. These thin strips are called lattice strips; they may be purchased at the lumberyard or art-supply store in raw wood to be stained or painted, or they may be gotten from framing shops all finished with a silver or gold metallic edge. Usually they are not mitered but are nailed directly to the stretchers, with butted ends. (Figure 138.)

A normal-sized painting in a normal-sized room needs a proper frame, and the type of frame used can make a picture or ruin it. Oil paintings are ordinarily put into a substantial frame, which might be made of flat

"Cattle inspection." A freely painted fresco. It appears that the colors were laid in and then the outlines added. The minerals in the earth provided the brilliant, lasting colors. Fourteenth century B.C. Egyptian. Courtesy the Trustees of the British Museum, London.

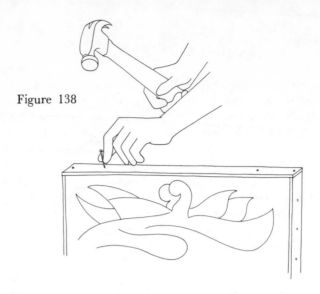

Figure 138

molding or angled in to give the effect of depth or angled out to make the picture stand away from the wall. Some pictures need a flat frame and would look lost in a deep shadow box, while others require this effect of distance to show them off to advantage; still others need a very simple frame so as not to detract from the subject matter.

Water colors and prints are usually framed with a narrow molding, and because they should always be matted for protection, the matting becomes an important element to be considered; it can be as wide or as narrow as the picture demands or as your space permits.

Old frames can be picked up in secondhand stores and restored, and plain wood frames in stock sizes can be purchased in the supermarket to be enhanced in a variety of ways. You can order special sizes from your art-supply dealer and paint or gold-leaf them yourself. Making your own frames from molding is of course the most work, but it is also the least expensive and the most satisfying from a creative point of view. So we shall now proceed to make a frame from scratch.

Purchase from your lumberyard half-inch stock in two-, three-, or four-inch width, depending on how wide you wish the frame to be. Measure the four sides of your picture, and add enough length to the lumber to take care of the mitered corners—the wider the stock, the more extra length you will need. There is a formula for this measuring that is handy to know: length of sides plus width of molding times two. For instance, a 20×30-inch frame in a three-inch molding would take 20 inches plus 3 inches plus 30 inches plus 3 inches, multiplied by two. The total length of lumber needed for this frame is 112 inches, or roughly nine and a half feet. However, it is very easy for the beginner to make a wrong cut in mitering, and it is always advisable to buy a few extra inches just in case. Also, the lumberyard does not sell such odd sizes as nine and a half feet.

If you wish to leave the frame in raw wood, try to get chestnut or hickory or oak stock, but if the frame is to be painted, common No. 2 pine is adequate and certainly the easiest to saw; oak is a very hard wood and requires much elbow grease. It is also important to have a good miter box for a raw-wood finish, because mistakes will not be hidden under paint, and a good box and a good saw will help you to make a smooth cut at the angle desired. In addition to the lumber, you will need Elmer's glue, one-inch brads, and odds and ends of stains or paint for finishing.

The inside edge of the frame should measure a quarter inch smaller all around than the picture, to allow a seat on the back to hold it in place. For a picture 20×30 inches, the window measurement of the finished frame would be $19\frac{1}{2}\times29\frac{1}{2}$ inches. Every store-bought or professionally made frame has a rabbet, which is the recessed edge on the back of the molding in which the picture rests. If the lumber dealer will do this millwork for you, so much the better, but we will assume that you have no rabbet, and so we will later improvise a way to keep the picture in its place.

Cut the four pieces of wood, mitering them as carefully as you can, and assemble the frame on newspapers on the floor. If there are any bumps at the joints, file them down with a coarse file until you have a good, square fit at all four corners. Perhaps some unevenness would be better filled in than filed off, and if this is the case, you can add some sawdust to glue and use it as a filler. You will probably find that both filing and filling are necessary to align the corners neatly. When all the joints fit well, coat both edges of the mitered corners with glue, and assemble the frame flat on the floor. Before the glue has set hard, hammer brads into the outside corners, so that each mitered edge is nailed to the adjacent one. It is best to do this before the glue is set, because the shock of hammering might undo the glue job, and hardened glue is difficult to repair. Allow it to set overnight, sand off the excess glue, and round off the edges of the frame with a file and then with sandpaper. If you are using a hard wood, you will find that having predrilled holes for the brads will make that job much easier; a good way to do that is to set the drill into a vise and use it as a drill press—applying the wood to it rather than vice versa.

Now the frame is assembled, and we must conjure up some way to hold the picture in place instead of by the professional rabbet. This can be done by using a right angle at the back of each corner, a quarter inch from the window edge, making an outline 20×30 inches; this would also serve to strengthen the joints. Instead, thin strips of wood could be glued along the back, forming a rectangle that would keep the picture from shifting. Also, small nails or carpet tacks could be placed on the back at intervals along the edge of the picture, once the painting is in place. (Figure 139.)

Now you have a raw-wood frame made up and ready to take a finishing treatment. If you have used a good wood with interesting grain, it can simply be finished with an oil stain made by using artist's oils in turpentine, or

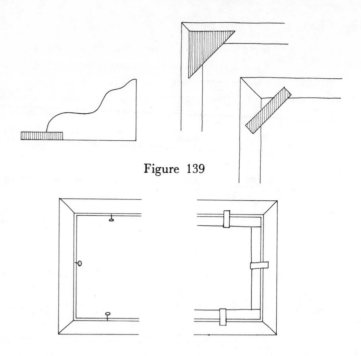

Figure 139

you can use a commercial penetrating stain. Then you can wax it with a paste wax and it will be all finished. If you wish to give it a weathered or wormy-chestnut appearance, you can hack at it with an ice pick or a can opener, or you can play a torch over it lightly to burn in an interesting effect of old driftwood. After it is stained, you can antique it by brushing on a thin coat of off-white oil paint and immediately wiping it off. Raw-wood frames—or old frames washed with detergent to remove old wax—can be painted any color with acrylic paints, oil colors, or regular house paint.

Polychromed Frames

An interesting polychrome effect can be gotten by sealing the pores of the wood with shellac, gesso, or any flat, white paint. For the main coat, mix three parts of turpentine with one part of dammar varnish, and squeeze art-ist's oil color into this medium directly from the tube; use a disposable tin and an inexpensive brush, because the mixture is difficult to clean up. Paint on this basic color and allow it to dry thoroughly; then apply as many different colors right from the tube as you wish, brushing them on and lightly wiping them off almost immediately. Each color will leave just a streak behind, and the picture can be enhanced by picking out the colors from the painting itself. On a commercial molding where there are several grooves, or profiles, it is interesting to paint each profile a different color; the whole effect might be tied together by antiquing it with a neutral coat such as raw umber or burnt sienna.

Gilded Frames

A frame done in oil colors should be protected, after it's thoroughly dry, with a coat of semimatte varnish. In fact, if you wish to isolate each color so that there is no intermingling, you can apply a coat of the varnish between adjacent colors. After the final coat of varnish, you can gild the frame by rubbing on a good paste wax mixed with a bronzing powder. This method of wax gilding is attractive and is done by saturating a soft cloth with the wax, dipping the cloth into the gold powder, and rubbing it briskly onto the wood. The more dry powder you pick up, the more will transfer off and the brighter the finish will be. You can make the gilding more permanent by heating the wax and adding a few drops of dammar varnish, which will act as a binder. Or you can buy a prepared gilding wax to be used according to directions.

Textured Frames

For a textured finish, a build-up of gesso is used. Gesso is a thick, white, chalky paste, which can be bought in an art-supply house or perhaps from a hardware store. It can be thinned with water to be brushed on as an under-coat, or it can be applied thickly with a palette knife, to be textured when almost dry for a carved or sculptured effect; dry pigment or any water-based paint such as acrylic or casein can be added to the gesso to color it. An easy way to apply interest to a frame is to prime the wood with a base coat of white gesso and then apply a coat of colored gesso; before that is quite dry, scratch through it to expose the white in a design of scrolls or wavy lines— you can use a small piece of comb to do this. This *sgraffito* pattern could tie in with the design of the painting. When the gesso is dry, you can polish it to a shine with steel wool or leave it rough and chalky. You can gild it lightly by wax gilding, or shellac or varnish it so it will shine and not soil so easily.

If you are using gesso to get a deep, carved effect, or to repair a heavy antique frame, apply it to the wood without thinning it. Put it on in thick globs, and when it is nearly hard you can carve it with an orangewood stick or a toothpick or a dentist's probe. (Figure 140.) If you wish a deeply sculp-

Figure 140

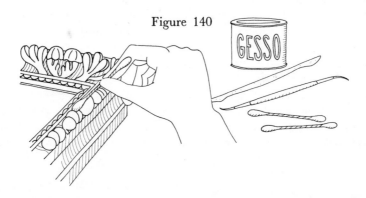

tured treatment, you must build the gesso up slowly in layers, allowing each application to dry overnight; it is heavy, and will cave in of its own weight if applied too thickly all at once. When it is built up and carved as desired, allow it to dry thoroughly and then shellac it for protection before further handling.

Restoring Antique Frames

Antique gilded frames are usually very handsome, and can easily be restored to retain their original feeling. First, the frame should be gently cleaned with a little mild soap or detergent on a soft cloth. (Soap may not get all the dirt off, but detergent may be too harsh for the old gilding; you have to judge this for yourself.) When it is dry, brush on a thin coat of a neutral-color oil paint—raw sienna, yellow ocher, Venetian red, burnt umber—and immediately wipe it off with an absorbent cloth. The color will remain in the depressions, and the gold (or silver) elevations will be exposed. The more you wipe off, the more metallic surface will show and the more ornate the frame will look; these frames have an innate nobility, and for that reason it is best to treat them simply. If the frame is in poor condition, it can be repaired first with gesso and then gilded to match the original before you start to antique it. Gold powders come in many different shades from pale yellow to rich red bronze, and they can be intermixed. They should be applied with bronzing fluid (banana oil) or with shellac if you have no banana oil. Gold leaf is by far the most beautiful finish of all, and it can be used if your preliminary work is good enough to warrant the application of this real gold.

Antiquing frames in the conventional manner is done with a base coat of oil stain that is shellacked when dry, and then a gold coat is painted on and wiped off before it hardens—in five or ten minutes. If the wood is new, a prime coat of gesso should be used; if it is old and dirty, it should be cleaned with paint remover or turpentine before you start work. Gesso or wood putty can be used to build up broken decorations; the acrylic media with modeling paste or plaster added are easy to work with and have a built-in binder because the medium itself is a glue. Metallic paints have improved to the point where it is sometimes difficult to distinguish them from real gold leaf. If you want a quick job, use the new media, but if you want a fine, craftsmanlike job, stay with the old, tried and true.

Inserts

An insert may be used with a plain frame to give it added interest. This is simply a second, smaller frame placed inside the first, as a rule finished in a different color from that of the main frame. If the frame is made from flat three-inch stock, for instance, you could make the insert from half-inch

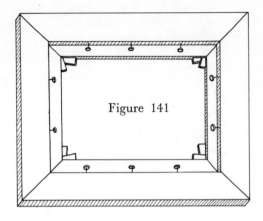

Figure 141

stock and paint it white or gold to set off the picture. The insert is mitered and assembled in the same manner as the frame and attached to the window of the frame to give much the same effect as a mat; if you already have devised a rabbet to anchor the picture, then the insert is merely decorative. (Figure 141.) But if not, then it could be planned to be useful as well as decorative: By being placed on the face of the frame overlapping the window by a quarter of an inch all around, it would form a rabbet, and then you could anchor the picture from the back with tape or tacks. This is a good way to mount masonite panels or canvas boards, and it also makes a neat contemporary frame for a painting on stretched canvas.

In the case of stretched canvas, the main frame would be cut exactly to the size of the stretchers, and then a strip of narrow stock could be glued onto the face of the frame to form the anchoring rabbet. If you wished a shadow box, or effect of depth, you could fasten the insert to the back of the frame instead of to the front, and then build up the back of the insert with thin strips of wood to form the rabbet.

An insert gives a professional look to a handmade frame because the lumber stock is plain and the insert at the window edge lends interest to the flat wood. This same idea can also be used on the outside edge of a frame to give it more importance there: half-round or quarter-round molding can be used as effective decoration. Many lumberyards carry small precut orna-ments and devices that may be glued onto flat stock and perhaps gilded in contrast to an antique finish on the main profile of the frame. An insert and an outside molding could also be added and the frame built up in this man-ner to very handsome proportions.

Unusual Framing

Another effective treatment for a modern picture is to make a narrow frame and mount the whole thing on a solid piece of beautiful wood, or on plywood or masonite. (Figure 142.) This is particularly good with an ab-

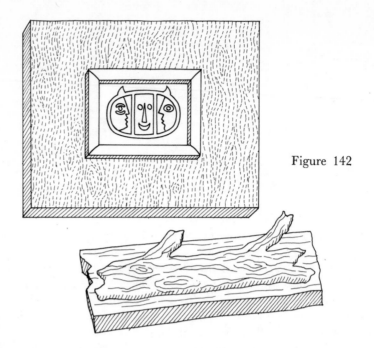

Figure 142

stract painting or a bas-relief or an enameled plaque. Veneers are used to good advantage on a flat frame to set off a modern work of art; any common stock can be used as a base for veneering, which is quite an inexpensive procedure. Pieces of driftwood or unusual specimens of any sort might be mounted on veneered plywood to set them off to good advantage, and the edges of the plywood can be finished off with a backband or with adhesive veneer strips, which are available at the hardware store. Framing a canvas directly with a backband gives good protection to it and prevents the edges from being damaged.

Any molding can be carved into, and anything can be added onto a frame, just so long as it serves its purpose, which is to enhance a painting. A fine piece of art work deserves to be shown to its best advantage, and the suitability of the frame is very important. Overframing can detract from a painting just as much as underframing, and the artist should know instinctly just how much is enough.

MATTING

Prints and water colors should be framed under glass for protection. A mat is used, both as decoration and as a buffer to keep the paper from contact with the glass, for moisture sometimes forms on the inner surface of the glass and would be harmful if it touched the picture. A mat is similar to an insert

in that they both are additions to the frame and they both enhance the picture, but where an insert is usually of wood and is exposed, a mat is usually
of matboard (textured cardboard) and is placed under the glass, where it
serves its useful purpose.

A mat may be quite large, to set the picture off to its best advantage, or
it may be just a narrow strip serving to keep the glass away from the paper.
A standard-width mat is an inch and three quarters, and because the bottom
tends to look narrower by an optical illusion, the mat is usually made a little
wider at the bottom in order not to appear skimped. To decide on the best
width for your mat, take four pieces of white paper and lay them on the picture so as to form a frame. (Figure 143.) Move them in and out on the
painting until you have a pleasing arrangement, being sure to cover at least
a quarter inch of all four edges of the painting so that there will be no daylight showing through when it is mounted. Then measure this inside window
and you have a starting point.

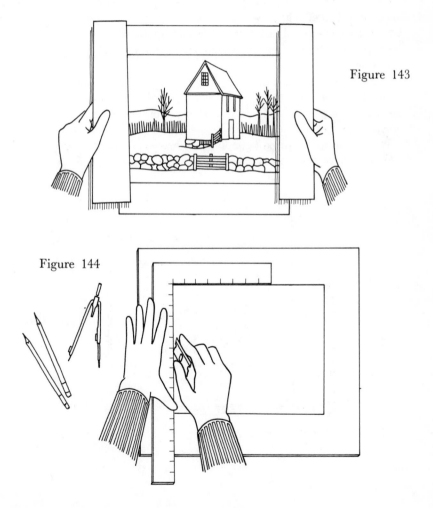

Figure 143

Figure 144

Measure off the outside of this trial mat and then cut a rectangle this size from your matboard, using a single-edged razor blade and a metal rule as a guide. Now measure the width of all four sides of the mat as you have it set up. This is easily done by using a compass open to the width of each side in turn. Holding the point of the compass at the outside edge, draw the pencil leg straight along the matboard. When all four sides are drawn on, true them up with a metal rule and you will have marked off the "window" of the mat. Cut this window out very carefully with a razor blade, working away from the corners so that if the blade slips it will not cut into the board (the window will be discarded, but the mat should be kept as neat and clean as possible). (Figure 144.) When the window is freed from the board, remove it and put the picture in its place. When you have placed the painting exactly right, with all four edges covered by the mat, pencil in a faint dot in each corner of the painting. Remove the mat and put a few strips of gummed tape on the back of the picture, leaving half of the tape free. Lay the picture down and position the mat on top of it, with the dots as guides, and the gummed paper will anchor it in place. (Figure 145.) Turn the whole thing over, and secure it firmly with more strips of tape. Then tape a large piece of heavy paper or cardboard to the back of the mat to serve as protection for the picture.

Matboard can be purchased in an art-supply store, and as it is sold in large sheets, one board will make several mats. The windows that are cut away may be used for mounting smaller pictures or as supports for casein or acrylic or even for oil painting.

Matting may also be done with ordinary cardboard or thick wallboard or with fancy papers or poster board, which comes in many colors. If you

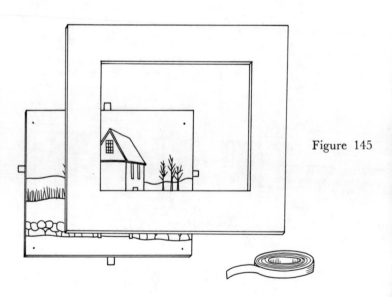

Figure 145

wish a special color of mat, you can paint almost any type of board with
tinted gesso or with any water-based (or oil) paint, remembering to paint
both sides to prevent warpage.

Special effects on mats are easy to think up: a French mat, for instance,
has lines drawn close to the window edge in different colors: first, perhaps, a
narrow black line, then a wider red line, and finally a very narrow gold line,
about an eighth to a quarter inch apart. The lines should be drawn very
carefully, with the aid of a metal guide rule and a fine drawing pen and ink
(a felt-tip pen might work, but it might smudge). Silver or gold leaf could
be applied in a crackle effect to set off a print or painting to handsome advantage. Mats can be covered with a variety of materials depending on how
stately you wish to make the picture: linen, cotton, burlap, grasscloth would
look well for a casual treatment, while silk, velvet, moire, brocade, or fancy
rice papers would be suitable for a more formal work. If the mat is to be
covered, almost any rigid backing may be used—wallboard, cardboard, even
a flat wood picture frame.

Covered Mats

Let us cover a mat with linen, which is the fabric most commonly used
for this purpose. The material can be coarse or fine, pure linen or synthetic;
you will also need some white library paste and a pair of sharp little manicure scissors. Cut the piece of cloth an inch and a half larger all around
than the mat, and then brush the mat all over with the library paste—face,
edges, and back. Lay the linen flat on the table carefully; lay the mat down
on top of it, face down, and gently pull the linen taut all around, being sure

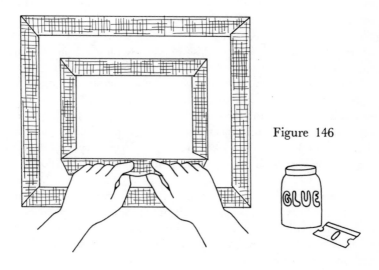

Figure 146

to keep the grain true. Pull the outside edges around to the back, and anchor the linen down with masking tape to prevent shifting. Pinch up the corners between your thumb and forefinger to form a neat mitered joint, and cut off the excess material with the scissors or a razor blade. Now turn the whole thing face up and smooth the front down with a soft, clean cloth to get rid of any buckles or lumps, and then cut away the window, leaving at least one inch excess all around for turn-under. Make a diagonal cut into each corner exactly to the mat, and bring the material around to the back on these window edges. (Figure 146.) Glue and then tape these edges to the back, and when all is done place the mat between paper towels and put it under a heavy weight overnight. It should be dry and flat by morning, ready to receive its picture. If you decide to use a light, delicate material, it is best not to apply the glue to the face of the mount, but only in narrow ribbons on the back; the glue could seep through the material and leave a stain.

Another way to cover a mat is by cutting strips of material and mitering them on the face of the mount, which requires less material because there is no waste. To do this, cut four strips, each an inch and a half larger all around than the four sides. Glue them onto the face of the mat, and at each corner pinch up the material as closely as you can to make a 45° mitered angle. With a very sharp razor blade, cut off the excess material, leaving a flat, clean mitered joint. Now turn under the outside edges and the window edges as before, and the mat is completed.

Cutting Glass

Glass for framing is not difficult to cut, but it can be dangerous because of the splinters; an auto-glass or mirror store will do this job for you quite inexpensively. If you wish to do it yourself, you will need a glass cutter from the hardware store, a small jar of kerosene or any kind of oil, and a metal carpenter's square, window glass of good-quality single thickness can be used. Lay the glass on a bed of newspaper, dip the cutter into the oil, and with the square as a guide, draw the cutter across the glass in one clean stroke. Tilt the glass up and tap it gently from underneath just outside the scored line, and "bend" the excess up and off. Using the square to get a true right angle, repeat the process on the adjacent side. Measure the glass so that if possible only these two cuts will be necessary. You may polish the edges if you wish with a wet carborundum stone, but this should not be necessary.

When you frame a picture under glass, a rabbet is necessary, because the glass is heavy and should it fall out it could be dangerous. If you are making an artificial rabbet or using an insert for this purpose, be sure the strips of wood are strong enough to hold the glass, and reinforce the glue with small screws or brads to make it quite secure.

Mounting Prints

Sometimes a delicate print or painting or photograph needs to be mounted on a backing before it can be handled for framing. To do this, you will need a heavy matboard or wallboard, brown kraft wrapping paper, and wallpaper paste or thinned library paste. Spray the painting with a light fixative varnish such as that used for charcoal drawings, brush the brown paper with clear water, and brush both sides of the matboard with glue. Mount the picture on one side of the board and the kraft paper on the other side, smoothing them out with a soft cloth. Then place the whole thing under a pile of books overnight, and when it is dry you will have a firm, rigid mount, ready for framing. The kraft paper acts as a counterglue to prevent warping; this type of "wet mount" should dry perfectly flat so that there will be no "pull" from either side. This in general is the way precious paintings are restored, but for a valuable work it is recommended that you have it done professionally, for the expert restorer knows the chemistry of materials and has had the experience of handling them. Old things, like old people, become fragile and need special care.

GOLD LEAF

Gold leaf applied to a picture frame will impart a richness and luster that no other finish can give. Gold leaf is pure gold (as silver leaf is pure silver), and while it is expensive and there are imitation leaves available, for the work involved and the beauty of the end result, it is worthwhile using the genuine article. Gold leaf is made in several shades from yellow gold to red gold, 16 carat to 24 carat, and it is rolled to the thinnest possible film. It comes in the form of a book, each page about three inches square. The professional gilder will rub a camel's-hair brush through his hair to give it a static electricity charge, enabling him to attract the leaf and pick it up without having to touch it. But we will use a leaf that is backed with tissue paper, known as patent leaf, and the process that we will use is known as "gilding in the wind." This leaf comes in book form; each leaf has a margin of paper around it and you will handle it by that edge of paper. If you are working on a narrow frame, you can cut or tear strips of leaf, but you must always leave an edge of the paper to hold onto. Never touch the leaf with your fingers—it is too delicate.

The leaf is adhered to the frame with gold size, which you can purchase in the art-supply store along with the leaf. This is a clear liquid and the best thing to use, but spar varnish or shellac will also do quite well. Some small brushes and soft cloths and the undercoating colors are all the equipment needed.

First prepare the frame by sanding it smooth, and then apply a good

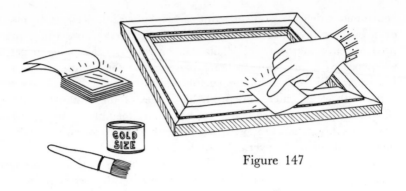

Figure 147

coat of the undercoat to seal the pores. Metallic finishes should always be backed by certain colors to set them off to best advantage: in the case of gold, a red undercoat is used; in the case of silver, blue, yellow, or black is best. This undercoat can be any type of paint: a hard enamel will allow the leaf to go on smoothest, but acrylic or oil or flat house paint serves the purpose adequately. Brush it on as evenly as possible, and when it is dry rub it briskly with steel wool to get rid of any bumps or specks. Then you are ready to apply the leaf.

Brush on a coat of the size with a small brush; if the frame is large, work on one side at a time: the operation can be stopped at any point and picked up again later. When the size is almost dry—tacky to the touch, in about twenty minutes—it is ready to receive the leaf. Pick up one page of leaf by the paper edge, and place it face down on the prepared wood, pressing it down with your finger on the paper backing. (Figure 147.) The leaf will stick to the tacky size; after rubbing the whole back surface of the paper, lift it off by a corner; the gold will have been transferred to the frame. Repeat this process over the whole frame, and where spots are missed, as they are bound to be, simply apply more leaf in the same manner, until you are satisfied with the coverage. Sometimes it is more interesting not to cover the frame completely, leaving some undercoat showing through, but as a rule the sheets of leaf are overlapped to give complete coverage. If there are depressions in the profile of the frame, the leaf can be pounced into them with a small paintbrush or a soft Q-Tip. If the gold does not stick, it is because your size is too wet or has been allowed to dry too much. You can apply more size on top of the gold for repairing spots. It is colorless and will not harm the leaf.

When you have applied the gilding to your satisfaction, allow it to dry overnight, and then burnish it to a high gloss by rubbing it with a soft cloth or a piece of leather. (Figure 148.) Metallic finishes will tarnish, and if you wish to protect the sheen, wax it with a good wax such as Simoniz.

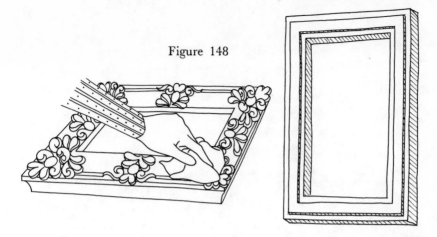

Figure 148

Silver leaf is applied in exactly the same way; however, you may wish to tarnish (oxidize) it right away for an antique effect. Purchase some sulphur powder from your druggist and dissolve a teaspoonful of it in a glass of water. (Or you could mash up a hard-boiled egg in water and thereby release enough sulphur to do this job adequately.) Paint it on the areas that you wish to be oxidized, and as soon as the color is dark enough, wash it off with clear water. Then dry it thoroughly and shellac it. If it gets too dark, you may have to remove some of the oxidation with pumice or toothpaste before shellacking, or else you might add a little new leaf here and there to pick up some bright highlights.

Antique frames may be restored by this same method, first repairing them with gesso, then shellacking the restored areas and proceeding with the leafing. A heavy frame that is badly soiled could be antiqued first with oil colors, and then the leaf could be applied: in this way the leaf would stay bright and not be spoiled by too much handling. Touches of leaf can be applied in the same manner to silk-screened greeting cards and to paintings— oil or water color. The size will make it adhere to almost anything, and there are many avenues that the craftsman might explore to further enhance his handiwork.

Ceramic coil pot. Made from fine, thin-walled clay with the decoration painted on. It was made, possibly on a potter's wheel, about 2500 B.C. and excavated intact more than four thousand years later. Chinese. Courtesy Tokyo National Museum.

8

Ceramics

CLAY

All ceramic objects are made of clay, and all clay is worked in the same manner, no matter what method is used to shape it. It should be moist enough to squeeze easily, but not so wet that it loses its firmness; it must be kept damp while working, and it should be allowed to dry out slowly when finished. If work in progress is to be put aside for any length of time, it must be kept moist, because new wet clay cannot be added to it once it is dry. So it should be wrapped in a damp cloth, which has to be kept damp either by wetting it periodically or by covering it with a plastic to keep the moisture in.

A heavy piece must be allowed to dry evenly. The drying will take place from the outside in, and if any section dries too fast it will crack and break away from the still-damp areas. It should dry in a cool place, away from heat and sun, and the exposed surfaces should be checked often. If cracks do appear they can sometimes be repaired by wetting the adjacent areas and then forcing a paste made of the clay with water into the crevice. Drying it on a masonite board or on anything that will not absorb water is a good idea, and covering it with a heavy cloth such as denim will help to keep the drying uniform.

To enable the clay to "mature," all the moisture must be driven out of it. Drying it in the air rids it of absorbed moisture; then firing it in the kiln gets rid of the chemically bound moisture. Various clays have differing maturing points, and usually chemicals are added to commercial clays to make them more stable and predictable. But it is possible to dig your own clay out of the ground and use it as is. The composition of the earth varies from place to place, and certain types of pots are indigenous to certain areas: pottery made from clay dug in America's Midwest is much different from that made from native Japanese clay. Belleek china, which is fine, translucent, and creamy in color, is made from a clay that is found only in a certain part of Ireland. But regardless of origin and regardless of the appearance of the final product, all clays are handled in the same way.

There are special terms that are applied to different stages in the maturing process. When a wet piece has dried in the air for a day or so it becomes "leather hard." At this stage it is firm enough to handle, and this is the best time to do the finishing work on it: smoothing, repairing, decorating. It is still cool to the touch. In four to six days it becomes "bone dry," warm to the touch, pale in color, and extremely fragile. This is known as the "greenware" stage.

The greenware must be bone dry before it goes into the kiln, for the first, "bisque" firing. When it comes out of the kiln it is known as "bisque ware." It is now "mature" and sturdier, ready to be glazed. Bisque ware is not practical for use, but such ornamental objects as figurines are often left unglazed.

It is possible to glaze the piece at the greenware stage and put it through a single firing; it is known then as a "one-fired" piece, but this is risky, because the glaze may trap moisture or air in the clay and cause an explosion, or the glaze and the clay may have different maturing points, so that underfiring or overfiring could occur. Ceramists are now producing pieces that can be made from start to finish in a few hours: in the ancient Japanese raku technique, a low-fired, groggy piece is not only completed in one day but it is taken directly from the hot kiln and placed in a bed of wet eucalyptus leaves, there to undergo the mysteries of reduction. The smoky fumes created by doing this use up the oxygen, thereby changing the composition of the oxides, which in turn causes them to change color. This reduction firing can be achieved by introducing bits of straw or wood into a hot kiln via the peephole; and by the same token, leaving the peephole open at the end of the firing cycle will bring in extra oxygen, to result in the changes of an oxidation firing. Technicians today are working on the effects of introducing various chemicals into the firing process, thereby producing subtleties of color never before dreamed of. But many chemicals cause dangerous conditions and should not be attempted by the amateur. Salt glazing, for example, releases chlorine into the air, and for that reason, while it produces an interesting textured glaze, it is no longer used.

There are many different types of clay used for various methods of forming. In general, they range from a smooth liquid for slip casting to a smooth solid for hand building, up to a rough, coarse clay for wheel throwing and a very heavy, groggy, rough texture for sculpture. But porcelain, which is smooth and fine, can be wheel thrown, and raku, which is usually hand built, contains at least 30 per cent grog to allow for the rapid escape of chemically bound water. Your art-supply dealer will help you choose the

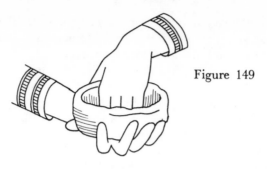

Figure 149

right one. Regardless of tactile quality, all clays are plastic when wet and brittle when dry; they all go through the same process to reach maturity.

A ceramic dish can be made by any method that comes to mind while you are holding a chunk of clay; just manipulating the clay into a form is called the pinch method. (Figure 149.) This of course is the simplest way to

Bowl built by the pinch-pot method. Fine white clay formed the body, then black slip and white slip were applied and the design was made, partly by painting and partly by sgraffito. Unglazed. Contemporary. American. Collection of the author.

form a piece, the clay simply being pummeled into a shape, and you may call it finished at any point that you desire. Depressions can be made by simply pressing down with the thumb, and extensions formed by gradually pulling and squeezing the clay out to where you want it. These pieces can end up having a certain naïve charm and can be satisfying to a beginning worker. Clays and glazes are available that can be fired in the kitchen oven, and some, called "self-hardening," need no firing at all. Painting these with acrylic paints for decorative purposes allows wide freedom of expression, with guaranteed instant success.

Two time-tried techniques of hand building are the slab method and the coil method. With slab building you roll the clay out like a pizza crust, cut it into sections, and then weld these flat slabs of clay together to form the base and sides of a dish or the walls of a sculpture.

In the coil technique, you roll out many "ropes" of clay and then coil them one on top of another, so that they rise up in a spiral somewhat in the manner of basketmaking or like the beehive placement of coiled lines on the deck of a shipshape sailing vessel.

Unglazed painted animal figure. Hand formed. Made from terra cotta and decorated with colored slip. Contemporary. Peruvian. Collection of the author.

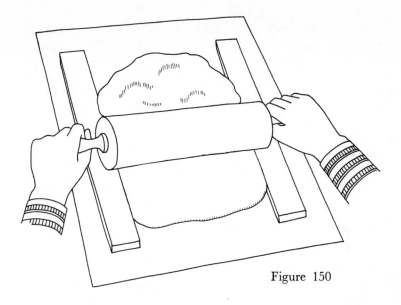

Figure 150

HAND BUILDING

Suppose we make a rectangular ashtray by the slab method. A masonite board or the rough side of a piece of oilcloth makes a good surface to work on, because the clay will not slide around on such a surface. A rolling pin or a thick piece of doweling, two strips of wood about a foot long and a quarter inch thick, about three pounds of moist clay, and a small kitchen knife are all the materials needed.

Place the two strips of wood on the board about ten inches apart to form guides to help you roll the clay to an even thickness. Put a pancake of clay between these guides and start to roll it out. (Figure 150.) The clay will gradually level off to the height of the guides and then will automatically roll out evenly. Using a piece of five-by-eight note paper as a pattern, roll the clay out a little larger, and then place the paper on top of the clay and cut the clay to size with the knife. This slab will be the base of the piece. Set it aside, and then roll out a new chunk of clay; from this, cut four pieces as long as the sides of the base and as wide as you wish the tray to be deep. These sides will be welded to the base, and to make them stick, you must roughen all the edges of the base and of the side strips where they will join together. To do this, make small scratches all around the edges of the base slab and along one long edge of the side strips with the point of the knife. (Figure 151.)

Now put a little clay into a bowl and mix it with water to form a thin

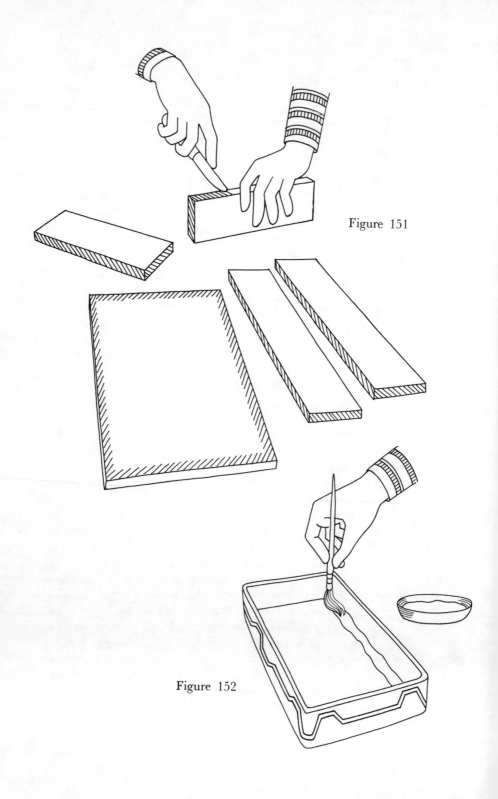

Figure 151

Figure 152

paste. This is called slip; it will act as the glue to weld the pieces together. With a small brush or your fingers, apply the slip to the edges that you have scored, and lay the strips along the base at right angles to form the walls of the ashtray. Pinch the strips together at the corners, run a little slip down the inside of these joints, and smooth it into the cracks with the handle of your knife or with a matchstick or a pop stick. Add slip wherever there is a sharp angle that needs to be rounded off: glaze will not adhere to a sharp edge. (Figure 152.)

Set the piece aside overnight to dry, and when it is firm enough to handle, smooth it all over with a damp sponge, blending in the slip and rounding all the edges. Then the piece is ready for decoration. Because of the large, smooth expanse and general simplicity, this type of work lends itself well to underglaze decoration. This can be done with underglaze colors or with engobe, which is colored slip, or perhaps by scratching in an incised design. When you are finished with the decorating, set the piece aside until it is bone dry, and then it is ready for firing.

COIL BUILDING

In the coil method of hand building, small chunks of clay are rolled into coils about the size of a finger and built up one above the other to form bowls and vases. This method is widely used in some pottery centers, because there is a certain charm to these pieces that cannot be duplicated in any other way.

To make a coil, take a chunk of clay about the size of a plum, and roll it into a rope about ten inches long. Make a dozen of these, and cover them with a damp cloth to keep them moist and pliable. Because coil pieces are usually round and deep, we will proceed to make a bowl that is both round and deep.

Take the first rope, lay it flat on the work surface, and coil it around and around itself to form the base, making it as broad as you wish. Taper the end of the rope by pinching it narrow, and then start a new coil by tapering the next rope too, so that the thickness where they join will be the same as it is along the length of the coil. Score both tapered ends, apply a little slip, and weld them together. Continue coiling, but now start building upward to form the walls of the pot. (Figure 153.) As you go along, coat the crevices between the coils inside and out with just a dab of slip, using an orangewood stick or your finger to seal them tightly together and smoothing the top coil down onto the one beneath it. The important thing is to be sure that the coils are well sealed each to the other with no spaces in between and no air pockets to cause trouble in firing, for trapped air can cause the piece to explode in the kiln. Continue adding the coils to build up the wall, perhaps shaping it wider as you raise it up and perhaps narrowing it down

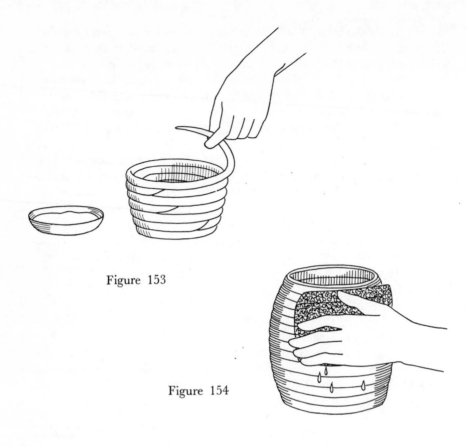

Figure 153

Figure 154

again at the mouth. You can make a smooth wall, or you can leave traces of the coiling to give a decorative effect. In either case, the rim should always be well smoothed off, to give a finished look. This can be done with a sponge while the clay is still damp, or you can allow the pot to dry thoroughly and then rub it upside down on a piece of coarse sandpaper that lies flat on the table. Or you can put a drop or two of water on a smooth table top and rub the rim back and forth in a circular motion (Figure 154); then you can round off the sharp edge with a damp sponge. If the wall is to be perfectly smooth, do the best job that you can with the damp sponge, and when the piece is bone dry, smooth it over with sandpaper. You can then decorate the pot with underglaze painting, or if the coil effect is to be retained, use the sandpaper perhaps to accentuate the design by rubbing away some of the slip at the joints. Coil pieces are usually interesting enough in shape and design not to need underglaze decoration, and an opaque art glaze is sometimes the most pleasing way of finishing them.

A weed pot with sprigged-on necks. Coil built. The low-fire, earth-brown glaze is in keeping with the natural, persimmon form. A different method of construction or type of glaze would have changed the visual and tactile quality. Contemporary. American. Collection of the author.

SLIP CASTING

Slip casting is the usual method followed for reproducing ceramic pieces in quantity. Slip is a liquid clay of the consistency of heavy cream; chemicals have been added to it to make it homogeneous in solution. Slip used as a glue in welding together moist clay is made simply by suspending clay in water, but in casting a whole piece from slip it is important that there be enough elasticity to allow the piece to pull away from the mold without cracking. So clay mixed with water is not adequate for this job; chemicals must be added, and this more sophisticated product should be purchased from your craft-supply dealer. Slip comes ready to use in liquid form; if you prefer to mix it yourself, you may buy it in powdered form. If you buy it as a powder, then you must mix it with water at least two days prior to using it, and stir it frequently during that period to be sure that it homogenizes thoroughly. An egg beater or the mixing attachment on an electric drill is good for this. Slip that has hardened can be put back into the jar and stirred up well to liquefy it again, adding as much water as is necessary to bring it to a heavy-cream consistency. All lumps must be screened out before pouring slip into a mold, and so it should always be stirred and strained by sieving before use. Strainers are available for just this purpose, but an adequate job can be done by using cheesecloth or window screening or nylon mesh.

Slip casting is done in a plaster mold. Plaster has the property of extracting moisture from the clay, and in slip casting you leave the clay in contact with the plaster just long enough for a wall about an eighth of an inch thick to form. The plaster absorbs the water from the area closest to it and then gradually pulls away water from deeper in. So if you were to leave the slip in the plaster mold too long, the wall would get thicker and thicker, and eventually you would find that all of it had solidified, and instead of an empty pot, you would have a solid form in the shape of the mold.

Try making a set of simple mugs—no handle and wider at the mouth than at the base. These can be cast in a one-piece mold, because there are no undercuts. You will need the mold and cheesecloth or a mesh nylon stocking tied over the mouth of the slip jar to strain automatically as you pour; an orangewood stick or tongue depressor to release the rim of the finished mug from the plaster; and a fettling knife, which is thin and flexible, like a small spatula, for trimming the mugs once they are removed from the mold.

Pour the slip into the mold right to the top, and as the water is absorbed by the plaster you will be able to see the wall of the piece starting to form. Allow it to sit for perhaps twenty minutes and then check the thickness of the wall. When it is as thick as you wish it to be—an eighth to a quarter of an inch—pour the excess slip back into the jar, straining it through the screening to rid it of lumps. (Figure 155.) (No sense adding lumps to the slip only to have to remove them later.) With one quick motion, pour back just as much as is still liquid, and leave the remainder undisturbed in the mold, which will continue to draw moisture from it. When it begins to get really dry, it will start to shrink away from the plaster. (If the mold is fresh and dry, this will take about half an hour. You can cast many pieces in one day, but each will take a little longer than the previous one, for the mold gets wetter with each casting.) When you see this shrinkage start, give it a little assist by loosening the mug all around the rim with the

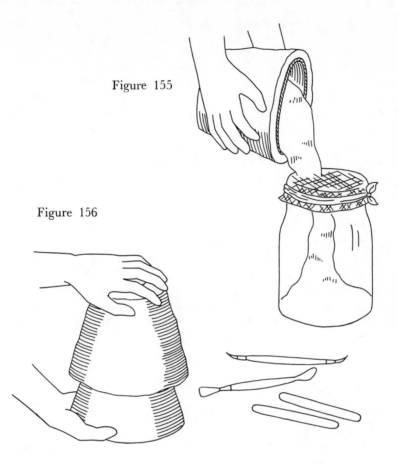

Figure 155

Figure 156

orangewood stick, holding it at right angles to the plaster wall. This will free the piece from the plaster, and drying will continue evenly all around until the clay is hard enough to remove from the mold.

To remove the mug, turn the mold over and catch the mug in your hand as it drops away from the plaster. (Figure 156.) It is safest to allow it to remain in the mold until it is quite hard before doing this, for this type of clay misshapes easily; once you have poured off the excess slip and loosened the rim, the mug can remain in the mold indefinitely to dry. When it is leather hard you can smooth off the rim by trimming it with the fettling knife; a design can be incised at this leather-hard stage if you wish. When it is bone dry, smooth over the whole piece with a damp sponge or sandpaper and then apply underglaze decoration if you wish. If you are making a matching set of anything, it is wise to decorate all of them at the same stage; in this way, they will match up as closely as possible. When the set is all finished, cover them with a light dust cloth, and put them aside to be bisque-fired when you have enough pieces done to fill the kiln.

Two-piece Molds

Now suppose you make a vase. You will want to make this in a two-piece mold. The method of pouring is the same, but you cannot see into the mold, and so you must judge the thickness of the wall by the pouring hole. This is an extension of the mold into which you will pour the slip and out of which you will later drain it. The mold also has "keys," which mesh to give an accurate closure so that the slip does not run out through cracks created by improper alignment. Put the mold together, carefully matching the keys, and tie it securely with a narrow strip of cloth. The mold must be leakproof, but if any leaks should develop they can usually be stopped up with a chunk of wet clay; have a little of that around for emergency use. If your mold is a new one, it is a good idea to set it in a large pan, so that if it does leak the slip will not run all over the place. If it leaks that badly, you will probably have to discard it and make a new one.

Pour the slip into the mold, through the pouring hole, right to the top. (Figure 157.) It is sometimes necessary to add more slip: the level sinks when the moisture is absorbed. Check it in twenty minutes or so, and when the wall at the pouring hole is as thick as you want it, pour the excess slip back into the slip jar, and allow the mold to set undisturbed until the visible

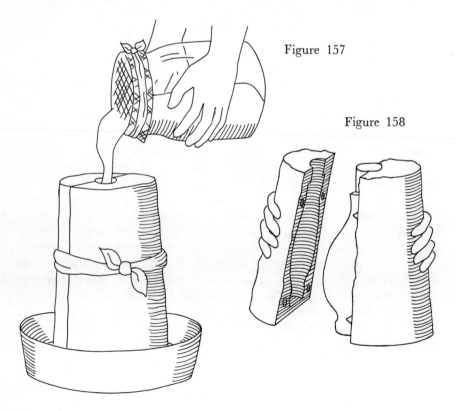

Figure 157

Figure 158

wall is leather hard. Then remove the tie and carefully "break" the mold open. (Figure 158.) If it is hard to open, that is because the slip is still too wet, so wait a while, until it opens easily. Remove the clay piece carefully so as not to dent it, and with the fettling knife cut off the stovepipe pouring hole, which is attached to the top of the piece. This should be cut away while the piece is still moist, because when it is dry the whole thing becomes brittle and easily damaged.

Set the vase aside to dry, and when it is hard enough to handle, trim away the mold marks with the fettling knife; these appear as jagged lines down the sides of the pitcher where the two pieces of the mold were joined. Rough edges should also be trimmed off and sponged smooth; then the vase can be decorated, and when it is completely dry it is ready for firing.

A mold that is made in more than two pieces is cast in the same manner. Put the mold together very carefully, being sure that all the keys match up so that the pieces will fit exactly and there will be no leaks. In pouring, jiggle the mold once or twice to be sure the slip is getting into all the crevices. When you are ready to remove the object, break the mold open very carefully, pulling each piece away in the proper direction, so as not to strain the clay. Naturally, the more pieces there are to the mold, the more spots there are for trouble to occur. It is suggested that the novice practice on simple molds before attempting a complicated casting.

Press Molds

A press mold is used in exactly the same way as any other plaster mold, except that it is very shallow and a chunk of moist clay can be used instead of liquid slip. The clay is pushed and pressed into the mold until it has reached all the nooks and crannies of the plaster. As it is pushed into place, moisture is being extracted both by your fingers and by the plaster, and it becomes firm enough to handle almost immediately, so by using a little piece of wet clay as a dop stick, you can lift it right out and set it aside to dry. (Figure 159.) If slip is used or if the piece is large, it should be allowed to remain in the mold until it dries enough to fall away of its own accord.

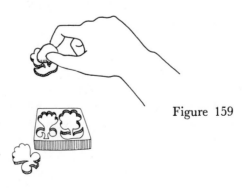

Figure 159

Jasper-ware vase. A Wedgwood-blue body with intricate white motifs applied by sprigging on. Eighteenth century. English. Courtesy the Trustees of the British Museum, London.

A small ornament made in a press mold can be sprigged onto a cast piece by welding it on with a little liquid slip in the leather-hard stage. Some of the finest table china and decorative porcelains are made in this way, because slip casting is the only ceramic technique in which the wall can be made as thin as desired.

WEDGING CLAY

Any clay that is to be turned on a wheel must be prepared before you start to work on it. The process of preparing is called wedging, and it is necessary to do this to free the clay of all air that may be trapped in it. The better the clay is wedged, the less likelihood there is of trouble in the kiln: an air pocket will expand in heating; and if it is trapped and has no way to get out, it will explode. If there is an explosion in the kiln, not only the faulty piece is ruined but possibly other pieces as well; anything falling on a glazed piece will adhere to it, and the shattering fragments could break other bisque pieces.

The safest method for wedging clay is to cut it many times. Attach a small block of wood to each end of a ten-inch length of piano wire—or any thin, very strong wire; the wood pieces will serve as handles to protect your hands. Lay a large chunk of moist clay on the table and cut it in half with the wire. (Figure 160.) Pick up one half and throw it with force onto a wood or masonite board; then pick up the other half and throw it down on top of the first. Cut the piece again at right angles to the first cut, and throw both halves down one on top of the other—hard—and repeat this process for five minutes. This should knock any air bubbles out of the clay, and if you plan to do much wheel throwing, you might wish to make yourself a wedging board, which makes this tedious job much faster.

To make a wedging board, use a 12×12-inch piece of half-inch plywood, and drill two quarter-inch holes, one in each of the two back corners. Drill a small hole through the top of each of two quarter-inch dowels that are about eight inches long, and hammer a carpet tack into each dowel, near the holes. Then glue the bottom ends solidly into the holes in the board. The board lies flat on the table, and the two dowels rise up at right angles at the back corners. String a piece of piano wire tightly through the holes in the top of the dowels, pull it taut with a pair of pliers, and fasten it securely by winding it around the carpet tacks. In wedging the clay on this

Figure 160

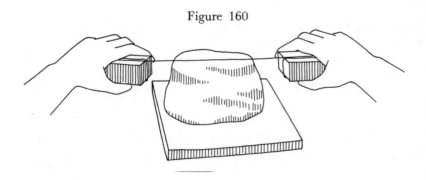

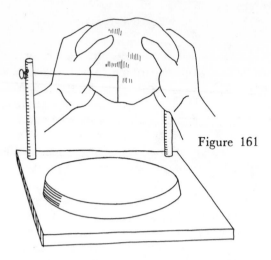

Figure 161

board, you will pass the clay across the wire to cut it, and so the wire must be as taut as you can make it. (Figure 161.) Hold the chunk of clay in both hands, cut it, and then slam it down on the board one half on top of the other half. Pick it up in both hands, cut it at a different angle, slam it down, and pick it up again. Repeat this for two minutes, which should be long enough by this method. Sometimes you will see little air bubbles on the cut surface of the clay; part of the trick of getting rid of them is the violence with which you throw the clay down. The harder the better.

After the wedging, you may set the clay aside for future use by wrapping it in a wet cloth and storing it in an airtight container or plastic bag. If you plan to make a set of anything, all pieces similar, such as bowls or mugs, you can weigh out similar amounts of clay and store them individually, ready for use. The clay should always be wedged a few times immediately before using.

Plaster Batts

Some potters wedge the clay by kneading it as a baker kneads dough, while others prefer the cutting method. Whichever you choose, the end result must be the same: the clay must be rid of all trapped air bubbles. Each ceramist finds his own foolproof way.

If the clay is very wet, you can dry it while wedging by throwing it onto a plaster batt. A batt is easily made by brushing the inside of a pie plate with soapy water and filling it with plaster of Paris. The soapy water acts as a separator, and when the batt has hardened, it can easily be removed from the plate. It is always a good idea to have several batts at hand.

THE POTTER'S WHEEL

A pot thrown on the wheel has a different feel and look from a pot built by hand. (Figure 162.) The process of turning, or "throwing," rearranges the molecules, just as hand hammering of silver changes the structure of the metal. The experienced craftsman can easily tell one type of work from another. Commercial clay such as Jordan or Monmouth is easiest for the beginner to work with, but it is possible to dig clays that are usable, and many areas have enticing beds of white, red, or gray clay that are fun to try out. But they must be washed to remove impurities, meshed (strained), and then dried to a workable consistency. Usually it is necessary to add chemicals to make them less brittle, or "short." It can be a long job of trial and error. Wheel turning requires patience and practice, and it is best to begin with a clay that is known to be easy to manage.

Start with a small chunk of clay and wedge it thoroughly. When you are reasonably sure that there are no air bubbles left in it, form it into a round ball and throw it (literally) onto the center of the wheel; whether the wheel is at rest or turning is a matter of preference for each potter. This takes much practice. The clay must be perfectly centered in order to bring it up. It must adhere securely to the base, and if it is to do this, the base should be almost dry; if the base is too wet, the clay will slither around. You can lift the clay off and throw it down again as many times as necessary to get it centered, and only when this is accomplished can you start pulling up

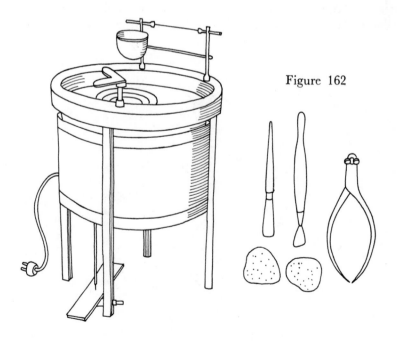

Figure 162

the pot. Wet your hands, place them around the outside of the ball, and press them gently together as the wheel turns. This pressure from both sides will further center the clay, and in a short time your hands will stop wobbling and the cylinder of clay will start rising up true. If after a few moments your hands are still being pushed from side to side, it means that the clay was not centered accurately enough to start with, or perhaps that you are applying more pressure from one side than from the other: you must then ball up your clay and start all over. Once it is centered, increase the speed to maximum and raise the clay up and push it down (with the heel of your hand) a few times to wedge it further, and then it is ready to be formed into a pot. Reduce the speed by about half, and holding your hands on the outside of the clay, raise up a tall, thin cylinder. Then press your two thumbs down on the top, with your fingers running down the sides, and as the wheel turns you will now be forming the inside of the pot. Keep wetting your hands, and every so often dribble a little water into the pot with a small sponge to keep it free-turning.

When the hole in the top gets to be about an inch deep, place two fingers of the right hand on the inside wall and the left hand on the outside wall. By applying more pressure on the inside hand, you will start to open up the pot and form the desired shape. (Figure 163.) Reduce the speed a little as you apply pressure from both hands—more from the right one to widen it, more from the left to make it narrower and taller. As the opening gets wider you can gradually move your whole right hand into the inside, and then you can start to shape the pot and make the wall thinner at the same time. It is important that the hands face each other at all times. Unsupported pressure from either hand will immediately cause the pot to twist.

Figure 163

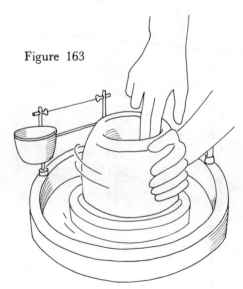

Always keep a little excess water in the pot for lubrication, but if too much collects, mop it out with your sponge. As the wheel turns, you can judge the proper speed: too fast a wheel will cause the piece to fly off or get lopsided, too slow and it will drag, with the same result. You can open and close the pot as often as you wish, and you can make it taller by pressing it from both sides or shorter by pressing down on the top. A wheel-thrown piece is difficult to make very thin, but you should try to keep it of a uniform thickness; the base usually ends up heavier than the walls, but you can cut this down later, at the leather-hard stage.

It is difficult to make a narrow neck on a wide pot; this is best accomplished by collaring. In this technique, the neck is formed wide and then pressed in by holding both hands on the outside of the pot and pressing them gradually and gently together to achieve the desired narrowness.

When you have brought the pot up to the desired shape, the rim will probably be crooked. While the wheel is turning, hold a hatpin or a long needle horizontally a little way down from the top at a steady height, and the excess clay will be sliced right off. (Figure 164.) Pull this strip away with a quick motion, and you have an even, straight rim to be rounded off later with a damp sponge. If you wish the base to be much narrower than the top, as in a pedestal effect, use a tool such as a round-blade table knife or a stiff, looped-wire sculpturing tool or a large hairpin and hold it against the base where you wish to cut away, applying gradual pressure. Here again, the excess will fall away. And if you want to trim clay from the sides of the pot, you can hold the hairpin parallel to the wall and trim it just where you wish.

Now that your pot is perfect, you can inscribe a design in keeping with

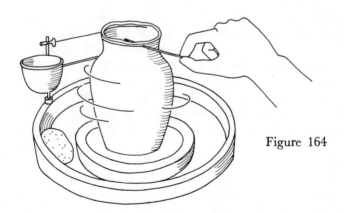

Figure 164

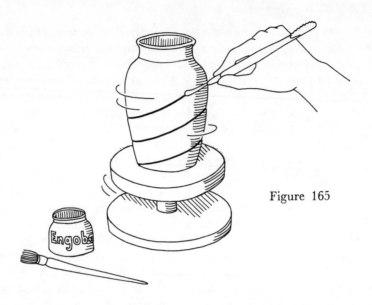

Figure 165

the character of wheel-thrown pieces. This could be a circular or spiral incised design, which is made by holding a pointed sculpturing tool or perhaps
a nut pick against the piece while it is turning. (Figure 165.) If you keep
your hand level, you will have a circular band, and if you move your hand
from base to rim it will be spiral. This same design could be applied by
using engobe (colored slip) with a small or a large brush. Wheel-thrown
pieces are sometimes only partly glazed, the glaze being brushed on decoratively to become a part of the whole design.

It seems picayune to make do with hairpins and kitchen knives. There
is a wide assortment of tools available for both pottery making and sculpture, but very often just the right tool for the job is a makeshift one. However, two modeling tools from your art-supply dealer, one large and one
small, and a fettling knife will serve almost every purpose. Potters save all
kinds of odds and ends: jars, of course, for mixing slip and glazes; bits of
screening for forced straining; burlap for pressing on a wet piece to make an
interesting texture (it will burn out in the firing); a piece of comb for
inscribing a design; pop sticks, medicine droppers, toothbrushes for spattering. The wet clay is like a piece of dough and will accept any impression
that you want to make on it.

When your piece is leather hard, you may if you wish make a foot on
the bottom. Set the piece upside down on the center of the wheel, and
anchor it gently with a few globs of wet clay placed around the outside rim.
With the wheel turning slowly, start cutting away, with the wire-loop modeling tool (or hairpin), from the center outward, toward the outer wall of
the pot. Stop about a quarter inch from the outside edge and remove the
clay gradually, so as not to go right through the bottom of the base. Cut

away until you have gone in about a quarter to a half inch, depending on how thick the bottom was to start with, and always leaving that quarter-inch rim, which is called the foot. The purpose of making a foot is to thin the bottom and also to provide an unglazed surface to rest on in the kiln. If there is no foot on the piece, it should be glazed on the bottom, and then you run the risk of having puddles of glaze collect on the bottom and fuse into lumps, adhering it to the stilt.

Before the pot hardens, you might paddle it to flatten it in spots, or gouge out chunks with a melon-ball cutter, or cut away parts of the top to scallop or to make indentations. You can decorate any greenware piece by applying engobe when the piece is wet or underglaze colors when it is dry. In a wax-resist decoration, wax or hot paraffin is brushed on in a design and then the piece is brushed all over with engobe or glaze. The wax will burn out in the firing, leaving the original background color in the form of the design. In a wheel-thrown piece a design can be made just by indentations of the fingers as the pot turns, and this may be all the decoration needed.

In throwing a pot, you will find it easiest to get it centered by throwing it directly on the wheel. However, a good piece is sometimes ruined in removing it, and to overcome this problem you can work on a base that you can lift right off. A base can be a round plaster batt or a six-inch circle of masonite; it can be anchored dead center to the wheel by small chunks of moist clay placed around the edge. Run the wheel for a moment to see that the base is centered, then throw your clay onto it. In this way, when your piece is finished you can lift it off, base and all, to set aside to dry. If you prefer to work directly on the wheel, you can cut your piece away with a length of piano wire, lift it carefully by its base, and set it aside. If you are doing only one pot, you can leave it in place on the wheel and it will shrink away of its own accord in a few hours.

The old potters always used the kick wheel, and they say there is an advantage to it in that the wheel is better controlled than the electric wheel. However, this is a matter of personal preference and experience, and certainly electrification has made life easier. Where electricity is not available, the kick wheel, which is operated by foot, surely has its place. Craftspersons still produce beautiful pieces on hand wheels, revolving a simple turntable with one hand while forming a clay pot with the other. This takes skill and practice, but you might try it.

GLAZING

Glazing is done on ceramic pieces to seal, to protect, or to decorate. Usually a piece is glazed completely, but sometimes only the outside is covered, or sometimes only the inside to make it impermeable and still retain the interest of an unusual clay body. Sometimes the glazes are used just here and

Bud vase with high-fired glazed body and unglazed foot. It was wheel-thrown, then the sides were paddled to flatten them, and the foot was added later. The tiny hole was formed by closing the top to a pinhole and then blowing into it to open it up. Contemporary. American. Collection of the author.

there to enhance the intrinsic design of an object; and sometimes a clear glaze is used to show up an applied design.

Glazes are a mixture of chemicals that are mixed with other chemicals that are known to melt at a certain temperature and then form a hard, glassy surface when cooled. The ceramist might concoct his own glazes, but there are many prepared ones on the market that are both interesting and satisfactory. They come as a liquid ready to use or as a powder to be mixed with water. In powdered form they are added to water and stirred to a heavy-cream consistency in a ratio of perhaps two parts powder to one part water; sometimes a little gum tragacanth is added to the mixture to make it more adhesive. Glaze is occasionally applied to a greenware piece, but in general it is better and certainly safer to do a bisque firing to allow the piece to mature before glazing it. Greenware pieces, and glazed pieces may be fired at the same time if the firing is sufficiently slow.

There are several ways to apply glaze, all of them satisfactory, and the method you use depends on how many pieces you have to do and how much work space you have to do it in. In any case, you should have a handy basin to catch the drip, a wire cake rack for draining, some flat sticks for stirring, and some empty jars in case you need them for something. Always stir the glaze just before starting, because the particles are in suspension in the liquid and you want them all dispersed so that they will give good coverage.

Tile, with engobe decoration and transparent glaze. Nineteenth century. English. Collection of the author.

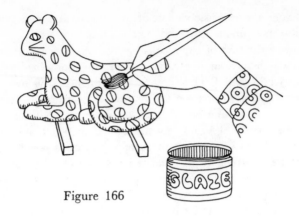

Figure 166

For glazing one or two pieces, or when you are using several colors, it is simplest and neatest to brush the glaze on. Water-color brushes are fine for this purpose, but they are expensive; your ceramic-supply house has good sable brushes for under a dollar. These brushes are capable of holding a lot of the solid material in the mixture, whereas ordinary bristle brushes will pick up mostly liquid and your piece would be cheated on the glaze. Dip your brush often into the glaze, because most of it is adsorbed onto the clay on the first stroke. (Figure 166.) Brush the glaze on the entire outside of the piece in one direction, then do the inside in one direction. By this time the outside is dry enough for the second coat—in the opposite direction, at right angles to the first. Then do the inside, then the outside, then the inside again. Three coats in all. The reason for brushing in different directions is to be sure that all the surface gets covered; any areas missed at first will be covered next time around. Put only two coats on the bottom of the piece unless it has a foot, because the bottom of a foot is usually left unglazed.

Test the thickness of the glaze by pressing your fingernail into it. It should be about one sixteenth of an inch thick. Scrape a little off with a knife if it is too thick, add a little if it is too thin. Then set the piece aside to dry, with as little handling as possible.

Pouring the glaze gives good coverage to a ceramic. Pour glaze into the inside of the piece and swish it around quickly so that the inside is completely covered with a thin coating, and then pour the excess quickly back into its jar. Place the piece upside down on the rack over the basin to drain. The rack may be a cake rack or simply two pieces of thin wood or other rigid "tracks" spaced so as to support the piece. (Figure 167.) Pour glaze over the whole outside, using a brush to touch up places where the glaze has skipped, and then with a knife scrape off most of the glaze that is toward the bottom of the piece, so that you won't have lumps forming there during the firing. The bottom edge or the foot should be wiped absolutely clean of glaze for about a quarter of an inch up, just to make sure. Kiln shelves must be kept scrupulously clean. (In the kiln most glazes will tend to run down and can cause trouble if they have been applied too thickly.) Pour all excess back into the jar, cover it tightly, and store it for future use. Always label the glaze as soon as it is prepared, because you cannot identify a glaze by its color. Glazes will keep indefinitely, and if they harden in the jar just add water a little at a time and mix thoroughly to get rid of lumps. Little bits of leftover glaze may be stored in a waste jar; the mixture will form an interesting unknown when used on an odd piece.

Dipping is another very quick and easy process, but for this method you need an even larger amount of glaze than for pouring. Put the glaze into a large bowl, hold the piece with just the thumb and forefinger, and dip it in and out. Place it upside down on the rack to dry, and touch up the finger marks with a brush dipped in the glaze. The reason for drying it upside down is that the glaze will be thicker at the top of the piece, and as it tends to run down in the kiln, it will be absorbed by the sides, rather than forming icicles on the bottom in the firing.

Spraying is another method; it is most satisfactory but not recommended for the amateur potter. It is of utmost importance to have a good ventilating system, with an exhaust fan and a spray booth to pre-

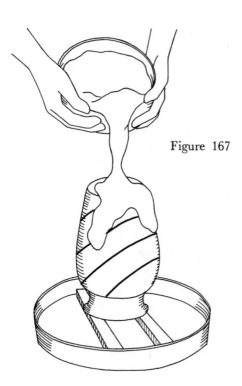

Figure 167

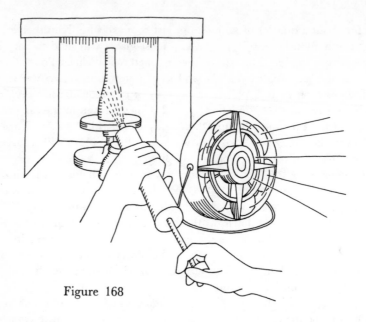

Figure 168

vent inhalation of the glaze. (Figure 168.) If you wish to experiment, set up a turntable inside a large carton set on its side, and charge a spray bottle with glaze. Keep the piece turning on the turntable, and spray on several thin coats. This method is the best one when you wish to intermingle various colors of glaze. It is also the most wasteful method, and the most dangerous to your health.

Different glazes may be used for the inside and the outside, or a glaze may be dribbled on the rim and allowed to run down to mingle with the main color. Certain glazes are made especially to run and so create a haphazard design; these might be brushed on here and there on the piece for an interesting effect. When the glaze is quite dry—about two hours in a warm, dry room—the piece can be placed in the kiln for firing; a glazed piece may be put aside indefinitely until you have enough pieces to fill your kiln. For that matter, ceramic pieces at any stage will keep. Just throw a light cover over waiting pieces to keep the dust off.

Glazes come in various finishes—high-gloss, semigloss, and dull (or matte). Certain glazes are nonflowing; that is, they may be applied in dabs to a vertical wall and they will not "move," or run. Different types of glazes may be intermixed: if an opaque glaze is too dull, it could be mixed with a little colorless high-gloss to give it luster, but most colors can be had in any type; a clear glaze, for instance, which is ordinarily applied over underpainting decoration, can be had in high-gloss, semigloss, or matte finish.

Pyrometric cones melt (or deform) at differing temperatures, just as glazes melt (or mature) at differing temperatures. In the zero series, the higher the number the lower the melting point. Cone 04, for instance, deforms at 1,940° F, while cone 018 melts at 1,240°. (Figure 169.) In the straight series, the higher the number the higher the melting temperature. Cone 5, which is the beginning of the stoneware temperatures, melts at 2,156°, while cone 10 goes all the way up to 2,300°. It is therefore important to know what cone to use for a particular glaze, and to record that information on the glaze label for future reference.

Almost all glazes used to contain lead and were poisonous. Up to a few years ago, most potters knew that they had to avoid prolonged contact with the skin, wash their hands thoroughly when they were finished working, and never put a glaze brush in the mouth. This is not farfetched, for many artists in other fields work with a spare brush between their teeth or lick a brush to give it a fine point. Modern potters no longer use leaded glazes, but these old precautions can do no harm, and even today edibles should not be stored in a handmade pot, because a glaze just might break down if subjected for a long period of time to the acids in foods or drinks. It is rumored that the fall of the Roman Empire came about not because of debauchery per se but because the generals' wine was stored in ceramic jugs and just about everybody got lead poisoning.

Figure 169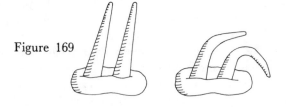

KILN FIRING

Kilns can be fired by various kinds of fuel. There are gas kilns, electric kilns, and kilns fired by wood or coke. In far countries there are whole villages engaged in the production of ceramic ware; they dig their kiln out of the side of a mountain and keep it going by feeding it whole trees rolled down from the top. The villagers spend perhaps six months making the pots, and then they fire them en masse for as long as a week or two. There is much jubilation when the kiln is finally cracked open to culminate a half year of work. But we will concern ourselves here with the stacking and firing of a simple electric studio kiln. (Figure 170.)

Clay, which is dug from the ground, is formed basically of silicon, aluminum, and water. It is bound together by two kinds of moisture: surface or absorbed moisture, and that which is chemically bound. Any ceramic piece in the unfired stage is fragile, because both these kinds of moisture are still

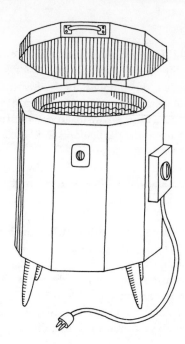

Figure 170

present. The absorbed moisture is dried out by allowing the piece to stand in a cool, dry room, and it is important that the article be dry before placing it in the kiln. It is also important that the drying process take place slowly to avoid cracking the clay. When the greenware piece is free of external surface moisture, it is known as bone dry, and then it must be subjected to a very high temperature in order to drive out the chemically bound moisture. When this is achieved, the clay is mature—hard and durable.

Different clays and glazes mature at different temperatures, and it is important to know this factor before firing a piece. Earthenware clay, which is used by most beginners, will mature at about 1,950° F and will disintegrate at 2,220°; some stoneware clays, however, just start to mature at 2,220°. The same thing is true of glazes, only more critically so. High-gloss glazes in general will be burned out at a temperature that is just starting to melt a matte glaze. Red glazes of any sort burn out quickly, and ordinarily are done in a separate firing, for a shorter period of time.

To make life easier for the ceramist, pyrometric cones have been devised, so that knowing the maturing temperature in degrees is not necessary. These cones are small, pyramid-shaped objects, manufactured so as to melt at a given temperature, and each is given a number. Clay bodies and glazes are sold under this number, and so the potter speaks of a cone 06 glaze or a cone 2 clay. Every kiln has a peephole, and the cone is placed upright in a little pat of clay in front of the peephole so as to be easily visible during firing. The kiln is stacked with pieces that will all mature at the same temperature, and when the pyrometric cone melts, the pieces are done and

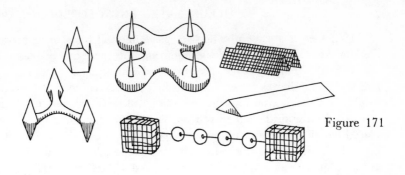

Figure 171

the kiln is turned off. Some kilns are equipped with pyrometers, which register the temperature, and some cut off automatically when the desired temperature is reached, but they all operate on the same principle. The average kiln takes about eight hours to fire to cone 07.

The electric studio kiln is like a firebrick box. It may open either at the top or at the front, and for each firing the pieces are stacked as efficiently as possible on removable shelves. The shelves rest on supports, also removable, which can be bought in different heights. Glazed pieces must rest on stilts, which are small, star-shaped objects of varying sizes having an upright nichrome wire or other support at each point of the star. (Figure 171.) The purpose of a stilt is to keep the area of contact at a minimum, because as the glaze melts it will fuse to anything it touches; if a piece is not steady on one large stilt, it may be rested on several small ones.

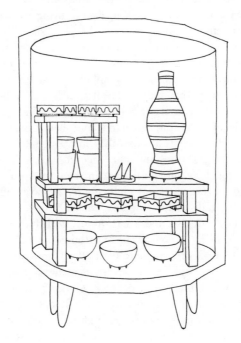

Figure 172

Half shelves are useful when you have one tall piece to be fired. Since the kiln should be used fully for every firing, this piece can be placed to one side and the remaining space can be stacked with smaller pieces resting on a half shelf. The shelves are each set on three or four supports, all of the same height. In stacking, you must leave room on the lower shelves to place these supports for the next shelf to rest on, being sure that no glazed pieces are placed too close to them. Bisque and glazed pieces can be fired at the same time, the bisque pieces stacked one on top of the other, but there should be at least a quarter inch of "daylight" all around a glazed piece. (Figure 172.)

Then, lastly and very important, there is the kiln wash. This is a mixture of china clay and flint in equal parts mixed to a paste with water. The kiln wash is brushed on the floor of the kiln and on the top side of all the shelves, as a protection against dripping glazes. It repels any spilt glaze, which then may be just lifted off instead of having to be hacked at with a chisel to remove it. While a small amount of spilled-over glaze actually does no harm, it is advisable to try to keep the kiln as clean as possible. Glaze left on the shelves will create bumps and pits so that supports do not have a level surface to rest on and stacking becomes very difficult. If pits are created, they can be filled in with a thick paste of the kiln wash to level them off.

All the furniture needed is available at your craft-supply dealer. There are many more items that may be used for firing unusual pieces, but those mentioned are necessities and all are made from special materials that will withstand the high temperature of the kiln. And so, having all the equipment necessary and all the pieces ready for firing, you may stack the kiln.

When you turn the kiln on, leave the peephole plug out, and prop the cover open a crack for about an hour to let all the moisture escape from the kiln. (Be sure that everything is bone dry before you place it in the kiln.) Then hold a mirror in front of the peephole. If there is moisture present, the mirror will fog up; if this happens, wait a little longer before closing everything up tight. Until you are familiar with your kiln it is a good idea to use two cones side by side, the left-hand cone being of a lower temperature. When that one bends, it is a signal that in about half an hour the kiln will reach proper temperature and the second one will melt. Remove the peephole plug just long enough to peek in each time you check.

Firing time averages about eight hours, and cooling time at least that long—preferably half as long again. Special firings such as overglaze and luster take only about two and a half hours, with four to five hours' cooling time. When the firing is completed and the cooling time has elapsed, open the door slightly and prop it there for half an hour to avoid a sudden rush of cool air. The first sight of a successful firing is very exciting, but don't chance a catastrophe by being too hasty. A good practice is to leave the kiln unopened overnight; in the morning crack it open gradually, and remove the pieces only when they are cool enough to handle with your bare hands.

If a stilt adheres to the base of a piece it can usually be pried off when it is cool, but if too much glaze has collected at these points it must be ground off with a carborundum stone or wheel. If the glaze has dripped down the side of the piece to form a lump, this, too, can usually be ground off and if necessary touched up with fresh glaze and fired again. A piece may be fired any number of times, with the same or different glazes each time.

There is special equipment available for special firing problems. Footed pieces, for instance, may be rested on triangles instead of on star stilts. These are long, narrow, triangular rods, and the piece rests on the sharp upper edge—always with the purpose of minimum contact. You may fire a series of six-inch tiles at one time without the use of shelves by using a special holder designed for this purpose. You may fire beads after glazing by inserting a piece of nichrome wire into a bit of firebrick and stringing the beads along as if on a clothesline, being sure that they do not touch each other. Nichrome wire is very useful in the kiln: you may use it to repair broken elements in the kiln itself, and you may even fashion a stilt from it, provided the piece resting on it is not too heavy; it withstands high heat, and it can be used for many special problems.

There are clays and glazes on the market that are self-hardening or that may be "fired" in the kitchen oven. Some of them are quite good, and certainly worth trying if professional equipment is not available. Your art-supply dealer probably knows someone in the community who will do firing for you if you wish, at so much per cubic inch.

Ceramic kilns come in all sizes and shapes and are relatively inexpensive for the hobbyist. Before buying your own, though, you must check your studio wiring to be sure that you have enough current coming in. Anything with heating elements requires a safe and sound electrical system. Extension cords are not advisable, and your kiln should be set up as close as possible to the source of electricity.

MOSAICS

In ancient days, when man first decided that perhaps his mud floor could be improved upon, the covering he chose was a mosaic. The word mosaic means made up of small pieces, and he did not exactly choose his materials: they were the only ones available to him. He picked up stones washed smooth at the seashore, and bits of glass, which is basically made of sand,

Figure 173

"Archers of the Guard." A mural for a palace made from ceramic bricks. The decorations were applied directly with slip, engobe, or glaze. Fifth century B.C. Persian. Courtesy the Louvre, Paris. Cliché des Musées Nationaux.

and set them into a firm foundation of well-packed mud. (Figure 173.) And so the first mosaic work was conceived. If the artisan was an artist, so much the better; he might be hired to decorate a public building, perhaps a place of worship, and so the making of designs became important and the craft was raised from the practical to the ornamental.

Essentially, mosaics are still made in the same way as they were in those olden days; but today we don't pack them into mud, because we have found other materials that we consider superior. The "small pieces" that we use are man-made from ceramic or glass, and the binding media are various types of cement ranging from fine plaster to heavy, coarse concrete. The ceramic and glass tiles that are used are called tesserae. They are three quarters of an inch square and a quarter of an inch thick; they are glued to a rigid surface, and the spaces between them are filled with the grout. Outdoor mosaics are usually grouted with mason's mortar, so as to be weather-resistant, while indoor ones are usually handled more delicately, with a smooth, white cement to hold them in place. A kitchen counter for a country lodge would be treated in a rougher fashion than the same counter for an elegant town house, and a wall that is exposed to the elements would by necessity be stronger than a protected room divider. But they are all made in the same way.

Suppose you were to make a small coffee table, two feet square, with a butterfly design in the center. The tesserae come in six-inch-square sheets, and so you will need sixteen sheets of assorted colors, about half in background colors and half for the design; a tube of Elmer's glue; a straightedge ruler; a tile nipper, which resembles an old-fashioned pair of ice tongs; a package of grout; a stiff scrub brush, and lots of rags. The backing on which the tiles will be laid should be ¾-inch plywood, the easiest to handle and the least likely to warp. (Outdoor or marine plywood is the best, and a must if you plan to use the table outdoors.) Everything can be purchased in a tile shop or a good hardware store.

Shellac the board on both sides to prevent moisture from seeping in, and set it aside for two days to dry. Draw a full-scale sketch of the butterfly, transfer it to the plywood either before or after the shellacking, and then you are ready to begin the mosaic. Apply a heavy coat of glue about an inch wide along one edge of the plywood. You could start anywhere, but the table will look neater if the tiles at the edge are evenly lined up, and so it's best to start with the borders. Stand the straightedge against the edge of the board to be sure you are getting the tesserae on straight, and put them down into the glue one at a time as close together as possible. (Figure 174.) Press

Bench or table made from cement mix with fired stoneware-clay motifs set in. Framed and mounted in oiled walnut. Contemporary. American. Susan Hughes.

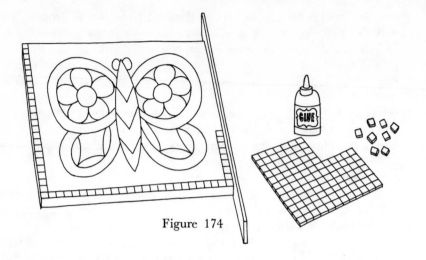

Figure 174

them down with the edge of the ruler, and repeat this all along the other three edges. Now that all the edges are neatly done and out of the way, you can start gluing in the center with the butterfly design. The design will be built up by starting with whole tiles in the middle and then gluing out toward the edges of the wings and body; here, irregular pieces are needed, and it will become necessary to cut some tiles to fit into small spaces. To do this, place the tile nipper on a tessera and cut off little pieces until you have the shape you need. (Figure 175.) Complete the gluing down of the butterfly, using whole tiles and pieces and filling in the spaces as closely as you can with the tesserae.

When the butterfly is finished, you can work in the background by glu-

Figure 175

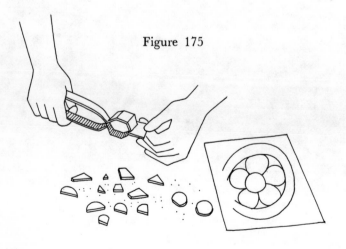

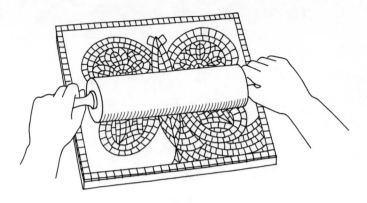

Figure 176

ing up small sections at a time. Keep in mind that the background will have an effect on the butterfly, just as it would in a painting: a static background will keep the butterfly static, and a background with movement will make him come alive. Movement is achieved by the direction that the tiles go in, and if the butterfly is just in the air the tesserae could be placed in a rather haphazard design suggesting airiness. But if he is in a field with a brook and sky, those things could be suggested by laying nipped tiles vertically for the grass, horizontally for the running water, and in a cloudy effect for the sky. It is a good idea to do a full-scale "painting" in crayon and then follow the direction of your strokes in the laying of the tiles. It is best to use variegated tesserae for the background unless you wish a monotone color. Mottling will hide unevenness and make for a more professional look.

Use the straightedge to even off the straight lines of tesserae, and as each section is finished use a rolling pin or a dowel to smooth it down and to level the tiles. (Figure 176.) Mosaics are seldom completely level, but the better the job now, the stronger the surface will be.

When the table top is completely tiled in, apply the cement to fill in the crevices and to make the surface smooth and level. Put this grout in a bowl and mix it thoroughly with water until it is just thick enough not to be runny. Brush it generously over the whole surface of the piece, forcing it into all the little spaces between the tesserae, and then scrape off the excess with a rubber spatula or a piece of stiff cardboard. Allow it to dry for an hour, wipe the whole surface gently with a damp, soft cloth, and let it dry completely overnight. Then scrub it over with a stiff brush to remove all the grout from the surface, but don't disturb the cement that remains in the cracks, and after a day or two it will be set hard enough so that you can spray it with a clear silicone waterproofing to protect it from soil and spots.

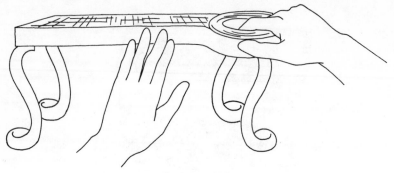

Figure 177

The exposed edges of the plywood can be finished off the same way with the tesserae, or you might use one of the adhesive tapes that are available—plastic, wood, metal; there is a large choice. (Figure 177.) Backbanding from the lumberyard can be mitered to form a gallery all around the edges, or you could make an edging from half-round or quarter-round molding.

Legs for completing the table can be bought at the hardware store in any height. You could make them yourself from 2×2-inch lumber stock, or you could use the pedestal from an old table. You could apply a mosaic directly to a store-bought table for a handsome conversation piece.

The same plywood table could be made for outdoor use by setting the tiles directly into mortar. In this technique, you make a form from wood strips on a piece of outdoor plywood, and pour cement into it to whatever depth you wish. The mosaic design is then set into the grout, complete, in

Figure 178

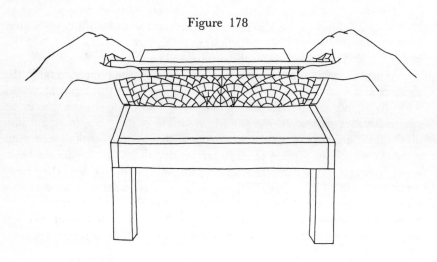

one fell swoop. To do this, lay the design out on any smooth surface with all the tesserae in their proper places, and then brush the whole top surface with LePage's glue. Lay a large piece of heavy brown wrapping paper on the design, covering it completely, and with your fingertips gently rub over the whole piece to be sure that all the tesserae become securely glued to the paper. Then pick up the paper by two corners and lay the whole thing, tiles down, into the wet cement. (Figure 178.) Smooth it over and allow the cement to harden for an hour or two; soak off the brown paper with water-laden rags, and there is your design embedded. When the table is quite hard and dry, scrub it with a stiff brush to clean off any cement that might be spoiling the tesserae. No further grouting is needed here, because the cement has filled all the cracks between the tiles. In this "reverse" technique of applying a mosaic, it is important that the grout be of just the right consistency. If it is too dry the tiles will not be anchored solidly, and if it is too wet they might be swallowed up.

Two-headed serpent. A mosaic ornament made from chips of turquoise and shell set into a wood form. Fifteenth century. Aztec. Courtesy the Trustees of the British Museum, London.

These two methods, one direct, the other indirect, are for the making of all true mosaics. However, materials of all sorts may be used as both tesserae and grout; the choices are endless, even to setting stones and bits of glass into a base of well-packed mud!

A patio for the back yard could be made from stones or slate or round slices of tree trunk set into a heavy concrete mixture; a stall shower might be made from conventional tesserae set with a fine white waterproof grouting; and a room divider might be made from chunks of jewel glass set into a clear-resin binder. Marbles, marble chips, bits of stained glass backed by aluminum foil for increased light refraction, coins, anything that strikes your fancy can be used as tesserae, and anything that will adhere it in place can be used as the grout. Materials unheard of five years ago are on the market, just waiting for your curious mind and agile fingers. There is little outlay for the materials, and the final result can be a thing of beauty to give lasting enjoyment to its creator.

Birds. A room divider, 6×2½ feet. It is made from glass and ceramic tesserae mounted on plywood paneling. Contemporary. American. Max Spivak.

9

Glass

LEADING STAINED GLASS

The mounting of colored glass as window decoration goes back to antiquity. Where other crafts had their beginnings as necessities—such as clay pots for cooking and jewelry for barter—stained glass was always ornamental. Today, with modern technology, stained-glass mountings have reached monumental proportions. In the 1950s, a building was erected at New York's Kennedy International Airport that displayed a mural window 317×22 feet containing nearly a thousand decorative panels held together by reinforcements of iron and steel bars. A far cry from the original concept.

Colored glass is basically made from sand mixed with soda and lime, with some metallic oxides added. Different colors are obtained by using assorted oxides; by fusing the ingredients for varying lengths of time and in varying proportions, different types of glass are formed. Common glass melts at about 1,470° F, and various chemicals may be added to the molten glass to give it specific properties. The addition of more lime makes it stronger; the addition of more soda can lower the melting point dramatically, and sometimes it is necessary to do this in order not to burn out the desired color. Reds, for example, will almost invariably deteriorate if exposed to too high a temperature, and in fact, the old ruby glass that is so prized by antique lovers had to be stained or flashed onto clear glass, because the red could not withstand the high temperatures of the melting kiln.

The chemicals that are used to make glass are fused in ceramic pots in a "pot furnace"; then the molten mass is put into a spreading kiln, where it is flattened into sheets. Commercial glass is flattened mechanically by pressure, and the little irregularities that are desirable for aesthetic refraction are few. The best stained glass is called "bottle" glass; this is made by blowing

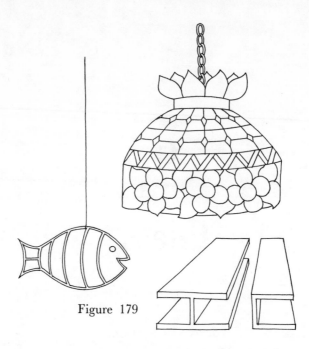

Figure 179

the glass into a square-bottle-shaped mold. The neck of the bottle is then cut off and the four sides and the bottom are cut away to make five slabs. This type of glass gives the best refraction of light; it is, of course, the purpose of ornamental glass to do so. European glass is usually superior to American glass in both visual and handling qualities: it is easier to cut and more pleasant to handle in general; it is also more expensive than the American varieties. Glass is sold by the large sheet, or scraps by the pound.

The lead that is used between the pieces of glass is extruded in long, narrow lengths, and these strips of leading are called cames. (Figure 179.) The cames are channeled, so that the glass is held in place; there is one sixteenth of an inch between pieces of glass. The channel can be single, on one side only, forming a U; or double, on both sides, forming an H. The cames come in several widths up to about one inch, the most practical for general work being the quarter-inch. They are very flexible, and they must be stretched just before use to make them taut and straight. This is done by stepping on one end and pulling as hard as possible on the other: you will find that a six-foot length will stretch about six inches. The lead is toxic, and so any little nicks or abrasions of the skin should be promptly taken care of.

The "light table" is very desirable in serious work with stained glass, for it helps to check the placement of colors and their relationship to each other. (Figure 180.) It can easily be made by placing a piece of heavy plate glass on two-by-fours or on two stacks of books and putting a soft light under the glass. The background under this viewing surface should be white, to give the proper diffusion of light, and so the table underneath should be covered with white paper.

The glass and cames will come from your craft-supply dealer, and the rest of the tools from the hardware store. You will need a plywood board to work on, a glass cutter, and a metal straightedge for guiding the glass cutter; a package of one-inch nails and a small rubber hammer; a single-edged razor blade for cutting the lead; an electric soldering iron, and putty or some sort of glazing mastic for reinforcing and waterproofing the piece. You will need a spool of soft solder (60 per cent tin and 40 per cent lead) and oleic acid, which has been found to be the most satisfactory flux for this job, allowing the freest flow of the solder.

Cutting the glass is not difficult, and it becomes easier with practice. You should do the cutting on a thick pad of newspaper, or better still, on a piece of carpeting, which will harmlessly catch and hold the splinters that are bound to appear. (Figure 181.) Dip the glass cutter into kerosene or any oil to lubricate it, and with the straightedge as a guide draw it firmly along the glass, holding the cutter perpendicular between the first two fingers. Tap

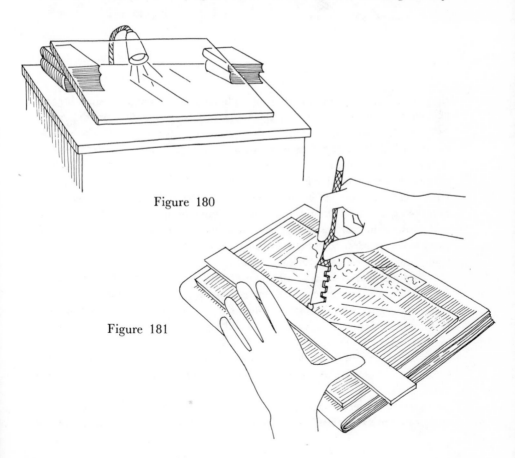

Figure 180

Figure 181

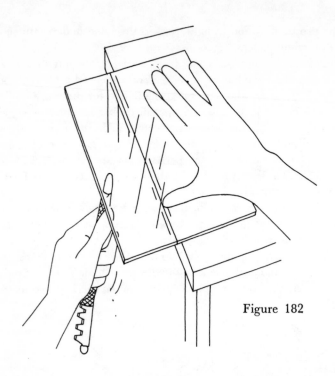

Figure 182

the glass gently from underneath on both sides of the cut, and then break it by holding it over the edge of the table and bearing down on the excess. (Figure 182.) It is important to break the glass as soon as it is scored, because, strangely enough, a "scar tissue" develops and the break will be difficult if you wait too long. The notches on the glass cutter are for grozing off—chipping off small pieces where the break has not been clean. You can cut curved lines or circles the same way, holding the cutter perpendicular and then grozing off small pieces one at a time. Sometimes an injury to glass will cause it to run just like a run in a nylon stocking; cutting a concave form is the hardest to do successfully, because the angle of cutting is constantly forming the basis for such a run.

Suppose you make a small panel of leaded glass, about 5×8 inches, either to insert in a window as a pane or perhaps just to hang where it can catch the light. This rectangle will have the equivalent of seven lines of leading in each direction, and so you will need 7×5 inches plus 7×8 inches of came. Two 6-foot lengths of the leading, therefore, will be enough. Because the piece will be made up in various colors, it will be best to buy a few pounds of assorted glass scrap, so that you can have a mixture to choose from.

First, a pattern of the design must be made: this is called the cartoon; it is drawn to exact size. This cartoon will be broken up like a jigsaw puzzle, with lead cames separating the pieces; therefore you should draw the lines on the cartoon one sixteenth of an inch wide. Number each section to avoid mix-ups later, and make a carbon copy of this cartoon, numbering and all. Then color the two drawings with crayon or water color to represent the colors of each piece of glass. Set aside one of the copies, to be used later for reference in assembling the piece, and cut the other one into pieces following the drawn lines. Once the cartoon is made, you are ready to begin work.

Lay the cut-up pieces of the cartoon on glass of corresponding colors, and trace around them with a grease pencil—or glue them on—and cut each piece of glass according to its pattern. Cutting curves is difficult, and it must be remembered that every concave curve must have a matching convex curve to fit into the double channel of the came. (Figure 183.) It will be easier for the novice to cut straight lines and to plan the cartoon with this in mind.

When all the pieces necessary are cut to exact size, assemble them, on the light table or on white paper, according to your master cartoon. The leading will be done on the wooden board, but the light table enables you to study how everything will look, and to make any changes desired. When the design is in its finished form, with all the pieces of glass in place, it is ready to be leaded.

Start the leading at the top left-hand corner; for your rectangular project, the outside edges must be at right angles. Hammer nails lightly into the plywood board, forming a right angle, and in that way you will obtain a support to keep the outlining came in position. The outside leading will be single-channel, U-shaped came, and all the other came inside the rectangle will be double-channel, H-shaped came. Your piece will be 5×8 inches, and

Figure 183

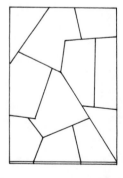
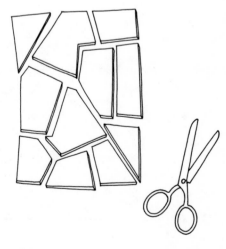

so you will miter two pieces of U came, one five inches long plus an extra inch for leeway, and one eight inches long plus an extra inch, cutting them with a razor blade. Form the angle by butting them against the nails, apply flux with a small brush, and solder them together by holding the end of the spool of solder against the join, and applying heat with the tip of the soldering iron. (Figure 184.) Now insert the top left-hand piece of glass into the open channels of these cames, and tap it lightly into place with the rubber hammer. Cut two lengths of H came to fit the two exposed edges of the glass, and hammer them very lightly into place. Place a few nails along the outside of the horizontal came to hold it there, and insert the next right-hand piece of glass into the exposed channel of the perpendicular came. Tap it lightly into place, cut the came for the bottom of that piece of glass, tap it into place, and fix it there with a few nails. Add new lengths of came and new pieces of glass in this manner until your piece is completely filled with glass, each piece leaded to a snug fit. Trim off any excess from the first two pieces of U came, and then solder on the other two pieces of outside U came so that your rectangle is fully enclosed, and hammer a few nails outside to keep it steady. (Figure 185.) Then apply flux, and solder every join. Now flip the piece over carefully, and solder every join on the reverse side; once it is soldered on both sides, it will become quite strong and rigid.

If you wish to reinforce and waterproof it, force the glazing compound into all the channels with a putty knife; this will cement the glass in place. Press the came down flat with the handle of a table knife, scrape off the excess putty, and scrub the whole thing with detergent. You may put the piece into place as a windowpane by using pane molding, or you may nail it into a

Figure 184

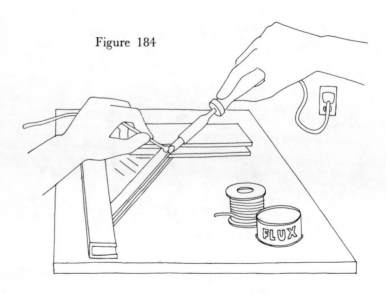

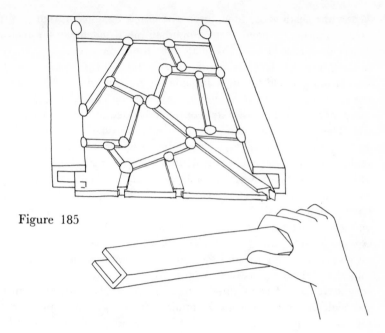

Figure 185

picture frame or place it on an easel with a light behind it to show it off to advantage.

This method is used for all types of leaded-glass windows, whether they be small panes or great church windows—even commercial façades. Large areas must be reinforced with a bar of rigid metal such as steel or brass, which you would incorporate into the design of leading and solder to the back of the piece at intervals of about every twelve inches. The lead itself will be flexible enough to adapt to wind and temperature changes, but too large an expanse would cause it to buckle without the added support of the steel.

Stained-glass Lampshades

In making a stained-glass-panel lampshade, you would follow the same steps. To make the pattern for a small shade, cut a circle with a radius of about fourteen inches, from paper, and cut a smaller circle, with a radius of about three inches, out of the center. Cut the circle open, and manipulate it until it assumes an enclosed shape that pleases you. Then trim away the excess so that the edges just meet. (It will look like a cone with the tip cut off.) Mark the paper into an even number of identical panels, and use these wedge-shaped pieces as the pattern for cutting the glass.

Cut the required number of glass panels, and lead them in three separate sections, using H came for the ribs and U came around the rims. On each section, leave the outside channel of the extreme right hand exposed.

When the leading is done, prop the three sections upright on the work board, and gently bend them around to meet and make an enclosed form. Insert the exposed pieces of glass into the three open came channels, and holding them in place with masking tape, solder all the joins.

H came could be used throughout, and then you could add a skirt at the bottom and a crown at the top by extending the pattern and cutting new pieces of glass from these extensions, to be added onto each panel.

The curved glass that is used to form flower-shaped shades is made by heating the glass in a very slow kiln by either a slump mold or a drape mold; Tiffany-style shades are made by employing a form or mold for providing support while working, and the pieces of glass are sometimes glued to the form (if transparent) and "leaded" with copper foil, a flux of zinc chloride being used. In a mobile, each piece of glass is leaded individually, and each surrounding came is soldered to itself, end to end. Lead is extremely flexible, and if the angles are not too sharp, one piece of came will go all around the glass and then just be soldered where it meets itself. You may then join the pieces by soldering them together in a few places, or you may leave them freestanding or hanging. You might solder them to a rigid rod such as copper or brass to simulate flowers growing, and perhaps insert the "stem" into an interesting bit of driftwood. You could extend them out from the wall on rods to catch the light from a pin-up lamp behind them, or hang them in a doorway from little copper rings or hang them in the garden to sway in the breeze. If leaded glass is used in a protected place, puttying is not necessary, but if it is to be outside in stormy weather, it is advisable to putty it for protection and strengthening.

Jewel Glass

Slab glass, also known as faceted or jewel glass, is often used to form solid walls when it is set in concrete. This glass comes in slabs an inch or more thick and can be cut with a hammer and chisel, becoming faceted like a jewel. Chips of jewel glass may be set in a bed of epoxy resin to form table tops or decorative wall plaques. Solid hanging ornaments can be made by gluing chunks of slab glass together in a ball shape and then gluing strips of copper foil to the joins to simulate leading. Liquid solder from a tube will give the same effect, and if it is too bright the metal can be oxidized with liver of sulphur.

Imitation Stained Glass

There are many ways of imitating real leaded stained glass. One way is to use sheet lead and colored casting resin on a piece of clear glass. You cut the sheet lead (from a plumbing-supply house) into strips about three eighths of an inch wide and glue them to clear glass in a design so that they outline areas just as leading would. Pour colored resins into the enclosed spaces, and when they are dry an attractive translucent piece is ready to be mounted.

A fun method for the children is to shave colored crayons onto pieces of wax paper and place another sheet of wax paper on top of them. Press the whole thing with a warm iron, and the wax paper will become transparent, with the colors laminated in. You can then cut the sheets into shapes and tape them to a windowpane with black or colored plastic tape. Colored tissue paper pressed onto wax paper should achieve the same effect.

There are transparent "stains," which are just painted onto clear glass to imitate stained glass, and there is liquid steel or brass, which may be applied as leading for a decorative effect. Narrow strips of thin aluminum, tin, or copper may be folded in half to make channels for inserting glass, or they may be used as a tape and glued on to give the effect of leading. Pieces of stained glass can be glued to a sheet of clear glass or plastic with a transparent glue such as Duco or epoxy, and "leading" then applied by any method that comes to mind. Sometimes it is not possible to back up glass with light; in this case the refraction can be caught by backing the piece with aluminum foil and placing a light in front to heighten the refraction. The purpose of glass in a decorative scheme is to catch and break up rays of light, and any way that this can be achieved is acceptable.

Chunks of colored glass washed up on the beach and smoothed by the sea are fun to work with. Old bottles lying in the desert sun become bleached to shades of violet, and these nostalgic scraps have special meaning today.

FUSED GLASS

Fusing stained glass is a delightful craft to work in and can be very satisfying, but it takes time and patience to get used to the handling of the glass. Beginners in this medium must go through a trial-and-error period, which, alas, must be done for each different type and color of glass.

Domestic stained glass is fairly constant in its composition, because of the rigid controls of American technology, and once the craftsman has determined the properties of each color, the results of fusion will be predictable. Imported (European) glass is less constant in properties from sheet to sheet, but it is more interesting in its refraction of light, perhaps because the controls in manufacture are not so strict. Each color has its own coefficient of expansion, that is, its own melting point and rate of contracting while cooling, and so all glass being fused together must be compatible in this respect or the piece will shatter while it is cooling. Reheating glass of any kind to its melting point makes it fragile, and this is why every artist must do his

Sculpture. Made from multicolored fused-glass shapes attached to welded steel rods. Mounted on a wood block. Contemporary. American. Susan Hughes.

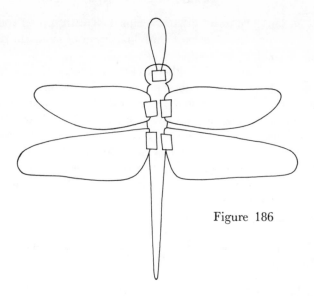

Figure 186

own experimenting to determine the critical points of the particular materials he is working with.

Many unusual things can be done by fusing or melting glass in a kiln. An individual piece can be fused into a different shape, such as a soda-pop bottle melted down to become an ashtray. Several pieces can be fused together to form an interesting varicolored piece. Nichrome wire might be formed into a simple shape, such as a fish or bird or animal, and pieces of glass can then be placed within these cloisons and melted to assume the shape of the wire. If a hanging piece is wanted, a small loop of the wire can be attached to the glass with masking tape; the tape will burn away, and the wire will become imbedded as the glass melts, to serve as the hanger. Nichrome wire has a very high melting point, and for that reason it is useful in the kiln—it withstands high temperatures. The elements in a studio kiln are made from nichrome wire, and so it is always handy to have some around for emergency repairs anyway.

Suppose you wanted to fuse a flat motif of a dragonfly with a long, narrow body, and with four large, light wings superimposed on it. (Figure 186.) Choose five pieces of glass of about the shapes and colors desired, and test them in various ways by laying the wings on the body until the design is pleasing. Fix them in place with a small piece of masking tape, and then tape on a wire loop for hanging.

In general, handling glass in the kiln is somewhat akin to glazing on ceramics; the glass will stick to anything it touches while fusing, and it will "run" or spread to some extent and will mold to the shape of anything that it rests on. So you must coat the surface on which glass will be supported with kiln wash or talc; this will act as a parting powder and prevent the glass from sticking. To do this, paint a kiln shelf with several coats of kiln wash, and then sift a dry layer onto that. Flat sheets of mica can be used instead of the wash, since the melting glass will not adhere to mica.

For our fusing we can use either a ceramic kiln or an enameling kiln, but in either case it is most important that it be cooled slowly—eight to twelve hours. Lay the glass design on the shelf, and place the whole thing carefully in the kiln. Heat the kiln slowly to about 1,460° F; this should take about two to three hours. The door should be left open slightly for the first hour or so to slow down the heating action, then closed. After a while, peek into the kiln through the peephole; when you see the edges of the glass become rounded, you know that it has started to melt and to fuse. Turn off the kiln, and crack the door open for a minute or two to halt the heating; then close it tightly, and do not open it again until the kiln is thoroughly cooled, usually overnight. Then remove the glass, which should now be fused into one piece, a beautiful, translucent dragonfly, ready to hang from its wire loop.

Molding Glass

In making a formed piece such as a bowl, it is necessary to use a mold to contain the glass, which would otherwise flow freely with no restriction. A mold may be made by scooping out firebrick to a desired shape, or from clay that has been bisque fired (never glazed, because the glaze would fuse with the glass). The mold cannot be too deep, because the glass would just melt into the bottom, or perhaps never even reach the bottom.

Coat the mold with kiln wash as you did before with the kiln shelf, and place a rectangle of glass on the rim. (Figure 187.) Place it on a shelf in the kiln and fire it slowly, as before. As the glass melts, it will take the shape of the mold, and for this reason it is called a slump mold: the glass slumps into it as it becomes soft. A drape mold is made in reverse: the clay bowl is turned upside down, and the sheet of glass rests on the outside base, to melt down the outside of the mold. (Figure 188.) The sides of the bowl will perhaps not come out regular, but this adds interest to the piece just so long as the edges have melted to a smoothness. In fusing glass on a mold, it is important to watch the heat carefully: not enough heat, and the glass will not

Figure 187

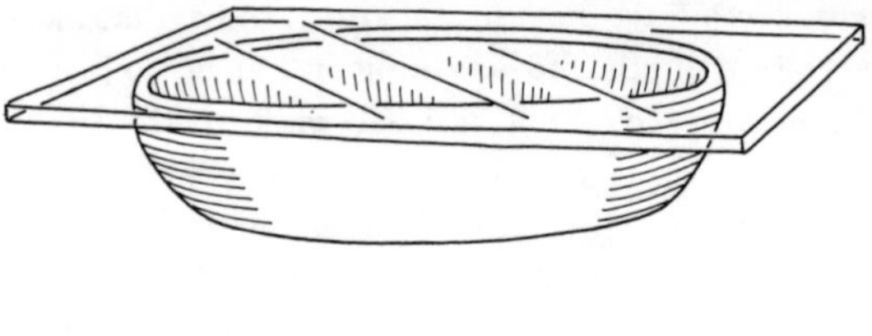

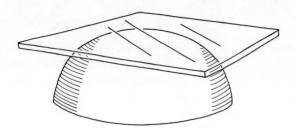

Figure 188

assume the shape; too long a heating period, and it will just flow down to melt into a blob.

A design may be painted on with ceramic paints, or with powdered enameling glass. These are fused in the kiln, usually at a lower temperature, but, again, they must be cooled slowly. The higher the temperature required, the longer it takes to fire the kiln and the longer it takes to cool it off. So the cooling period is always in direct relation to the firing period— usually one and a half to two times longer to cool down than to fire up.

Fusing single flat pieces of glass enhances their appearance, by rounding all the edges and giving them an appearance of fluidity. (Figure 189.) Single fused pieces can then be used for various effects. They can be glued with epoxy resin to a clear-glass or plastic sheet to make a mosaic. A hole can be drilled with a lubricated carbon drill and they can be strung up to make a mobile. Pieces can be glued to a glass sheet to form a design and the background filled in with any kind of grout, such as cement or plaster, or sand mixed with acrylic medium or Elmer's glue. They may be wrapped with lead came to form a chunky wall hanging, or glued together and the joins filled up with liquid lead or steel to give the effect of leaded jewel glass. This technique is also used to build them around a lampshade form; lighted from the inside, they make a handsome fixture.

Glass bits can be put into a glass caster cup and fired to make a paper-

Figure 189

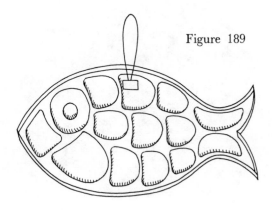

weight. Or they could be set into clear epoxy or acrylic resin to make a pendant or a nut bowl or a huge standing sculpture. Glass can be fused onto copper forms, but since the melting point of glass is usually quite high, one might find that the copper melted before the glass did. These are the experiments that make the craft interesting, and we don't really want a predictable success every time, do we?

GLASSBLOWING

Glassblowing is an ancient craft, probably perfected by the Phoenicians. Blown pieces dating back to ages before Christ have been discovered in diggings in the Holy Land, and modern technology has not been able to surpass in beauty the color and luster of these ancient pieces, sometimes enhanced by the passage of thousands of years.

The basic composition of glass has not changed much, still being the fusion of silica, soda, and lime. But today other chemicals are added and the craftsman has a choice of colored or clear water-glass canes, which are sticks of glass obtainable in a craft-supply store; he can choose to work with soft glass or hard glass. Both come in solid rod form or in hollow tubing, usually in four-foot lengths. Pyrex glass has been treated to be hard and durable but requires a high temperature to form it. Flint glass is more fragile, more liable to fracture, but it requires less heat and so is easier to work with.

Glassblowing is a serious undertaking, requiring elaborate equipment and very special facilities.

Glass fish. Made from glass colored with metallic oxides, it was probably sagged into a mold of clay and sand. Fourteenth century B.C. Egyptian. Courtesy the Trustees of the British Museum, London.

Candleholder. Made from colored glass that was blown into a pewter form. Art Nouveau. Nineteenth century. English. Collection of the author.

In a commercial glass factory the glass blowers work in teams out of a melting furnace in which the glass melts and remains viscous. The molten glass is gathered on the end of a blowpipe, and this "gather" of glass is blown on the pipe at a temperature of about 2,600° F. An assistant has another small molten gather on the end of a pontil, which is an iron rod, and when the bottle is blown to size, he fuses his gather to the bottom of the bottle with the pontil extending out from true dead center. Then the blower snips the neck off the blow rod, and the shaping of the lip begins. The assistant sits in an arm chair and rotates the pontil over one of the arms while the blower shapes the neck with a carbon paddle, keeping the piece at about 1,500° by putting it in and taking it out of the open blow furnace. When the blower has shaped the neck and lip, the pontil is snapped off and the bottle goes into an annealing oven, or lehr, where it remains for about two hours. Then it is brought slowly to room temperature, and then it goes to the finisher for final polishing, and possibly to an artist for decorating: sandblasting, etching, or engraving.

FLAME-WORKING

Simple flame-working of glass may be done with a hand torch and a few tools on an asbestos workbench. (Figure 190.) Necessary is a small carbon paddle and a pair of forceps or tongs, which are used to shape the molten glass; a carbon or asbestos block or a firebrick, which is used to stub the glass to form a level base on which the finished piece can stand; a few corks; some rubber tubing; a file, and a few dentist's probes. A pair of asbestos gloves should be kept handy in case the hot piece should fall; it would burn right through the floor if not retrieved pronto.

When you are working with glass, the canes are heated and then pulled out (or stretched) to make thin areas, or heated and then pushed in (or compressed) to make thick areas. (Figure 191.) Pieces may be added one to another, again by heating so that the parts melt and fuse together, and canes may be flattened and broadened at the ends by pressing them against a paddle. The heating process is always done gradually: the cane is moved back and forth through the flame over a much larger area than is actually needed, and it is kept rotating constantly. This is to assure that change in temperature will be gradual along the whole length of the rod; too sudden a change in any one spot will surely crack the glass. Heating glass causes it to expand, and this in turn causes internal stress, which may result in fracture; the danger can be lessened by annealing, which tempers and toughens. This is done by very slow, gradual heating and then very slow, gradual cooling. It is a good idea to anneal your canes ahead of time, so that they will be ready to use when you want them.

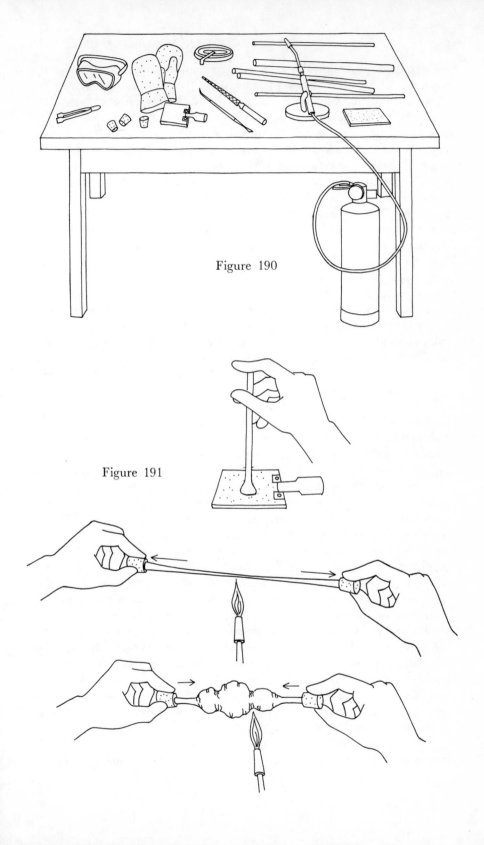

Figure 190

Figure 191

To do the annealing, lay a cane down on an asbestos sheet and play the torch the full length of it, using just the tip of the flame. Slowly increase the temperature by moving into the blue cone, which is the hottest part of the flame. When the glass is glowing pink, withdraw the flame gradually until a soot forms. Leave the glass undisturbed, and allow it to cool for about an hour. When it is cool enough to pick up with your bare hands, it will be more malleable than before, and stronger too.

For working, the torch should be on a stand so that the flame will be stationary, allowing both hands to be free to hold the rod horizontally. The flame should point away from you, at about a 45° angle. Heat the cane slowly and gradually by passing it through the flame just above the blue tip, rotating it all the while. Work on an area of about two inches at a time; and in order to heat this area without cracking it, you must heat a larger area, by moving the rod from side to side in the flame, heating about an eight-inch span. As the rod warms up, gradually lessen this area until the flame is concentrated on the center two-inch section; when this starts to bend, it is ready to be pulled or pushed—or blown if the rod is hollow. The cane must always be kept moving and rotating in the flame: too much heat in any one place will cause it to sag irretrievably.

Once you understand the principle of flame-working glass, you are ready to start a project.

Suppose you make a small sculpture of a snail carrying his little hollow shell on his back. The body will be made from solid rod and the house from hollow tubing. You will be heating several portions of the rod in series to form the humps of the body, so score a piece of the rod at about fourteen inches and break it off. This should be long enough so that you can hold it at either end without burning your hands. Start the flaming about four inches from the left end, where you will soon concentrate the heat, and gradually work the flame toward the right end, to warm up an eight-inch section so that there is no sudden change of temperature along its length. If the ends become too hot to handle, you can insert them into corks or into small pieces of rubber tubing for protection. Have the flame of the torch about an inch long, and start flaming in the yellow area. Gradually bring the rod closer to the tip of the blue cone, moving and rotating it constantly; then decrease the area that you are flaming, concentrating the heat toward the left end. When the center two inches of that hot portion becomes wobbly, it is ready to be compressed to start forming the sculpture. Still rotating the rod, push your hands together slowly, so that the glass will thicken in this softest spot and form a blob; you have now made the first shape in the sculpture. Repeat this process to form three blobs, one right next to the other, forming the body of the snail—always heating up the areas adjacent to the spot you are concentrating on.

Now heat the last section, and with a quick pull stretch the glass out to form the neck; then pull the excess rod right off the main piece. It will

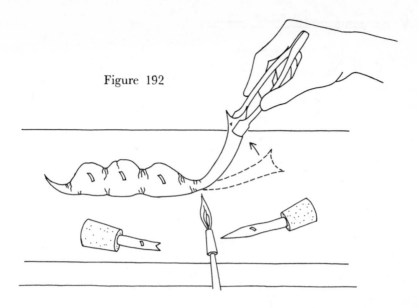

Figure 192

break away where it is thinnest. Quickly stub the body down onto the carbon block; it should still be soft enough to flatten on the bottom so that it will have an even surface to sit on. If it doesn't flatten out this one time, heat that area again and stub it down again until it sits steady. Allow it to cool; then with a file score off the excess rod on the left where you have been holding it, and take the torch in your hand to flame the finishing touches. Heat this tail end to smooth it and round it off; heat the neck, and with the forceps lift it to an upright position while it is malleable. (Figure 192.) This flaming will allow you to manipulate the neck into an interesting position and at the same time will soften the broken edge and thicken it to form the head of the snail. If you wish, you can heat thin pieces of the rod while you are working on the head and add them on as feelers, using just the heat to fuse them into place.

Now put the body aside and work on the shell. This will be made from hollow tubing blown into shape. Cut a fourteen-inch piece of rod and insert one end (the right end) into a small piece of rubber tubing to form a mouthpiece so that you can blow into it without burning your lips. Put the torch back on its stand and heat the rod slowly and gradually, and when a small section toward the left end becomes cherry red you can make it into a bubble by carefully blowing into it via the rubber tubing. You can reheat it and blow into it as many times as you wish, until it is the right size for your project. (Figure 193.) Break away the pieces of excess tubing on either side of it by flaming and pulling them away, and as soon as the glass breaks off, you can flatten the point by stubbing it on the carbon block. Then flame it again to smooth it off and close it up if you wish.

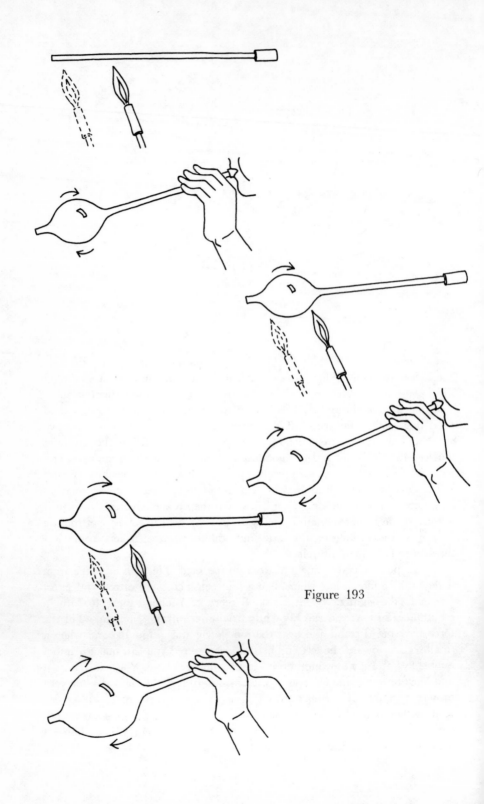

Figure 193

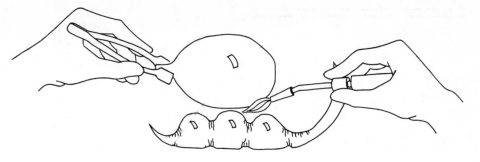

Figure 194

Now you fuse the snail and the shell by flaming them simultaneously, and the piece is finished. This first attempt may or may not end up as what it set out to be, but with practice things will improve. (Figure 194.)

There are, of course, many other things that can be done with the molten glass. Shapes can be formed by pinching and twisting and snipping with tongs, pincers, and pliers. Forms can be shaped by paddling the hot glass with carbon paddles, and by carving into it with a dentist's probe or with any heat-resistant scribes or files. Blown pieces such as goblets or vases can be made, the size depending largely on how well you are able to manipulate the hot glass. The glass cools quickly in the air, and blowing a large bubble is difficult. One way to get around this is by blowing in series: instead of one large bubble, a vase formed by heating and blowing successive sections could be interesting. And working in front of a mirror is helpful.

Colored glass rods are available, but you can obtain you own colors if you put transparent ceramic glaze stains (coloring oxides) into hollow tubing. Lay the tube on the asbestos pad and bring it slowly and carefully to high heat when the glaze will melt and fuse to the glass, which can then be worked into a design. Stained glass could be fused to a clear rod: a glob or "gather" of the colored glass might be fused to the end of a solid rod to make a swizzle stick, or to the end of a hollow rod to make an ice-cream spoon. If two pieces of glass have a similar coefficient of expansion, and you have a great deal of patience, success can be yours, eventually. Glassworking does take practice.

Working a Vase

We here will work on a simpler scale, using preformed tubing to take the place of the gather and blowpipe, and a simple torch instead of the melting furnace.

Suppose you try your hand at blowing a clear vase with a band of color for decoration. Take a length of tubing about fifteen inches long, and fit one end of it with a small piece of rubber tubing as a mouthpiece. Flame the

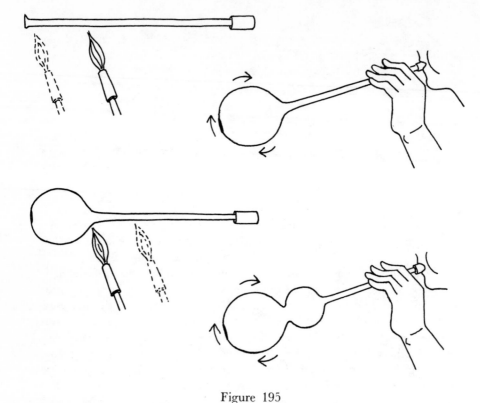

Figure 195

other end of it, turning it constantly in the torch, to a depth of six to eight inches. Then concentrate the heat on the very end and flame it until it is almost molten. Quickly stub it on the asbestos block so that the end is sealed, and then you will be able to blow into it without the air escaping. Also, this stubbed end will serve as the foot of the vase, and so you should have it level and broad enough to support the height of the piece. Flame the rod just around the footed area for about one minute, or until it becomes cherry red, then remove it from the flame and immediately blow into it. While you are blowing, keep the tube revolving so that the bubble will form evenly all around and the vase will be symmetrical. Keep repeating the heating and the blowing; progress up the tubing gradually, until the vase starts to take shape. It would be wise not to try to blow it too thin until you have mastered the art a little. For a first try, an hourglass shape might be easiest to attempt, because you are then not overlapping the heated areas to the point of spoiling what you have already created. (Figure 195.)

　　After you have blown the glass to the shape you wish, you can now decorate it with, let us say, a spiral band of color. For this you will use a length

of narrow colored cane called a string or snake. Apply this or any other embellishment while the vase is still attached to the blowing tube. Applying
decoration is a tricky job requiring a steady hand and good manipulation,
for both the blown piece and the thin rod must be brought to temperature
simultaneously so that they will fuse together without one being so hot that
it will crack the other. Hold the vase by the blowing rod with the right hand
and the snake with the left, and start to flame them slowly. When the decorating rod becomes flexible, move them a little higher in the flame; there the
rod will remain flexible, but the vase will not become distorted. Starting at
the bottom of the vase, lay the end of the colored rod on, and rotating the
vase slowly, lay a spiral and continue the length as far as you wish. (Figure 196.) At the end of the spiral simply pull the snake away and it will
break off. Now take the vase back into the hot area and flame the colored
spiral to fuse it tightly onto the clear water glass and also to smooth off any
rough spots. Now the decoration is done.

If you wish to add a handle, you can do it in much the same way.
Flame the end of a rod (or hollow tube) for a length of about five inches
and heat the two ends of this five inches a little longer, until they are molten. Place these sections on the heated vase, the free end attaching near the
rim of the vase, and the attached end fusing to the vase lower down to form
the bottom of the handle. Pull the rod away to break if off, flame it at the
top and bottom to smooth the joints, and pat it with the carbon paddle to
secure it and line it up accurately.

Now, if the decoration is completed, the vase is ready to be removed
from the blowing rod, which has been attached all this time. Hold the vase
with an asbestos glove on and flame it at the point where it is attached to
the blowing rod. When the rod is hot enough to sag, pull it away quickly,

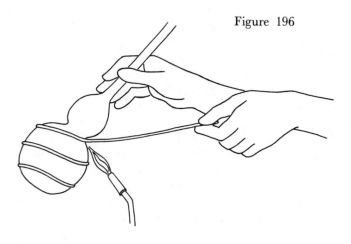

Figure 196

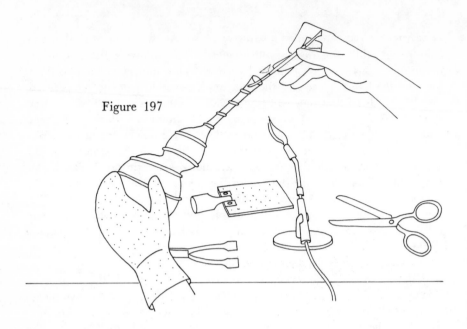

Figure 197

and nip the top of the vase with a pair of scissors to open it up. Now, while rotating it in the flame, open the neck gradually, using the probe and the forceps and the carbon paddle until it forms a lip; you can form a pouring spout too if you wish. (Figure 197.) When it is opened as much as you want, flame it to smooth it completely, and the piece is now finished. Set it on the table to see that it sits straight; if not, flame the bottom and make it level by stubbing it while it is still hot.

Another method of glassblowing is to attach a piece of tubing or rod directly opposite the blowing rod to serve as a pontil. This enables the craftsman to hold onto the piece with both hands, but also heightens the possibility of distortion. While the right hand does the work of turning and guiding the glass, the left hand must be in perfect co-ordination, so that the work is not pulled out of kilter. A stand can be made by notching a V into an upright piece of 4×4-inch wood, which will allow the tail end of the tubing to rest in it while working. This stand can be placed to the left of the flame, and can be moved farther away as the work on the cane progresses to the right. The commercial glass blower making scientific instruments for chemists and for medical research uses a lathe, which holds his tubing always in perfect alignment; the artist craftsman, however, usually wants more freedom for spontaneous work.

All workers in an art-glass factory are highly skilled and experienced. Working in glass is very sensitive, and every step is a crucial one. But practice breeds confidence, and if, at first, success looks dim, try again.

10

Textiles

The dyeing of cloth is an ancient craft. In biblical times, it was discovered that everything growing would yield a color when treated in a certain way, and so the making of dyed goods became one of the first professions known. Experimentation with natural vegetation is fascinating if you have the time and patience. Here are some dyes from nature that you might like to try out. Most of them are not fast-color, but the addition of a mordant such as salt, white vinegar, or washing soda may help to set them.

Milkweed or yarrow boiled in an iron pot will yield a warm yellow, but the same weeds cooked in a copper pot will give a soft brown color. Of course, even this is not certain, because it will depend on what you use to stir the mass with: a freshly cut twig will add its own juices, and a metal spoon will change everything. Berries will yield a bluish or reddish purple; sumac leaves or walnut shells, a yellow-brown; goldenrod, dandelion, or buttercups, a rich yellow, while the thick taproot of dandelion produces a brilliant magenta. So do beets, of course, and carrots will give forth orange. Tea and coffee, as we all know, are pretty permanent browns, and most barks yield a yellow-brown—except cherry, which gives red-brown, and birch, which gives a silver-yellow. And so, I leave you to experiment.

The dyeing of materials for rugmaking is not difficult and is the best way to achieve the desired colors for the strips or yarn that is used. The commercial dyes available in the supermarket should do an adequate job for the beginner, but the experienced rugmaker will probably prefer the more intense dyes, which are available from the supplier of rugmaking materials.

It is desirable to have the colors a little uneven, as this will give a softer effect when the rug is completed, and so the dyeing is best done in small

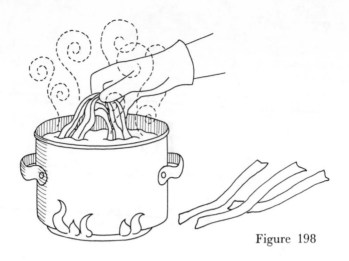

Figure 198

lots. Various vessels will affect the dyes in various ways, and rather than take too many chances, the process should be carried out in impervious glass or enamel pots, and wooden or plastic spoons should be used for lifting and stirring. In dyeing yarns, it is best to do them in the hank, but if they are already formed into balls it is chancy that enough color would penetrate into the core to be successful. Materials, which can be any old thing but preferably made of wool, should be cut into strips about three inches wide for ease in handling. Then they should be washed thoroughly and left to dry until ready for their dye bath.

In a large pot put three quarts of water and a half cup of white vinegar and bring it to a boil. The vinegar acts as a mordant, to bite into the material and fix the color. Dissolve a package of dye in a small jar of hot water and add it a little at a time to the boiling pot. Wet your material and wring it out, then dip an inch or so into the dye solution to check the color. If it is not strong enough, add more of the concentrate from the small jar. If it is too strong, add more boiling water, and when the color looks right put in several handfuls of the wet strips—as much as the pot will hold—and boil them gently for half an hour, stirring them occasionally. (Figure 198.) Then remove the strips, wring them out, rinse them several times in clear water, and hang them up to dry or put them into the clothes dryer if you wish.

Grading Colors

Most of the dye has been lifted from the solution by this first batch of cloth, and if you put in another batch of the wet strips, they will come out a paler shade of the same color. You can use this lighter shade, or you can add more of the same color to deepen it, or you can add enough of a new color to change the shade subtly so that it blends with the old. Do as many strips as you want to in this manner, adding dye and/or liquid as needed. You could make a whole rug in shadings of red, for instance, or you could start with a red dye and add a bit of purple to each dipping. In due time the red would be all absorbed and the true purple would dominate, but in between, the strips would range from purple-red to red-purple and the blending would be perfect.

The whole idea of hand dyeing is to get a graduation of color that will give the rug a spectrum like a maple leaf in autumn. So we try any way we can to make the yarn shade itself. One way is to tie the strips in loose knots; the dye will penetrate less where the knot is, and thus come out uneven. Part of the strip can be held out of the pot and then put in for the last ten minutes of boiling, to make it a lighter shade than the rest, or part of the strip can be removed and more dye added for the last ten minutes. Some strips can be added to the pot later than others, some removed earlier, or anything you can think of to make the hues come out graded. When old, commercially dyed garments or blankets of wool are used, it is difficult to remove the color, and you must take into account the fact that the background material will affect the color; if you need to get a pure color it is advisable to start with a white cloth.

Unbleached, or "raw," yarn can be dyed by the same method, and beautiful variations of color can be obtained with this natural material.

Spinning Yarn

Some people like to make their own yarn, and this is quite easy to do with a simple spinning wheel. Natural fibers, such as wool, cotton, or hair, are cleaned and puffed by stroking or "carding" them between two flat, oblong metal brushes until they are light and fluffy. Then, with a puff held in the left hand, small amounts of the cleaned fibers are plucked out con-

Figure 199

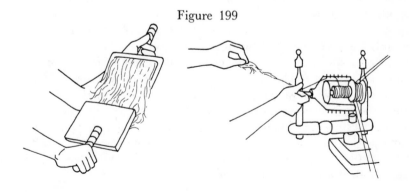

tinuously with the right hand, and rolled between the thumb and forefinger to "felt" them. These are fed, also continuously, into the wheel through a narrow tube which leads them to a revolving spindle, which twists the short strands into continuous thread. (Figure 199.) The spindle is activated by a treadle, and the amount of tension that is applied to the constantly spinning fibers will determine the thickness of the filament. The tighter it is held and the faster it turns, the thinner the thread will be, and hand spinners usually like to vary the tension to create random interest throughout the yarn.

The raw wool still has the natural lanolin in it, which makes it soft and enjoyable to use, and boiling it in a mordant will of course remove this natural oil. But, on the other hand, never having been treated, it will accept the dyes easily and with grace. Interesting enough, but not really surprising, is the fact that the dyeing can be done in the oven just as well as on top of the stove. This is known as "steaming"; 350° for thirty minutes will do the job nicely. Sometimes a few drops of glycerin in the dye bath will help the color to set and to keep the wool from stiffening from the harsh treatment it is going through.

RUG HOOKING

Hooked rugs may be made from heavy yarn, from strips of old blankets or worn clothing, from scraps cut from fur, from raffia, in fact from bits and pieces of any material that is strong enough to be pulled through a small hole with a large crochet hook.

There are several types of hooks that can be used. A hooker used with one hand that automatically produces uniform loops, and an automatic shuttle-type hooker that requires both hands to operate, make the work go very fast. Both hookers are worked from the back of the rug, and both cause a certain amount of strain and psychological push to get the work done. The easiest, slowest, and most pleasurable hooking is done with the old-fashioned crochet-hook type that has a chunky wooden handle for comfort in holding. (Figure 200.) This one is worked from the front of the canvas, and you can watch your work in progress and easily change from short to long loops. It is certainly the most relaxing of the three to work with.

The backing can be of burlap or of monk's cloth, which is more pliable and easier to handle. The cloth must be stretched on a frame to keep it as taut as possible while working, and this frame can be store-bought—on legs, with a tilting device—or it can be made from a flat wood picture frame or constructed from 1×1 lumber in any convenient size. If you wish to work in your lap, you might want a small frame, rolling up the excess material to keep it out of the way and anchoring it back with a large safety pin. If you like to work at a table, the frame must be high enough off the table to allow

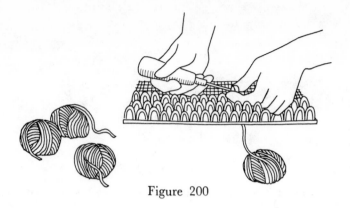

Figure 200

access for the hook. A low frame can be raised by nailing a piece of wood into each corner to form a leg to give it the desired height. An old wooden card table can be made into a good frame by cutting out the center and tacking the monk's cloth to the empty rectangle. (Figure 201.) The tacking might be done with thumbtacks or artist's pins, or by hammering carpet tacks into the frame and then anchoring the material to the tacks with curtain pins. However it is done, it is important that it be taut. The piece can be as small as a piano-stool cover or as large as a ballroom-size rug—all are worked in the same way.

Suppose you make, from rag strips, a small area rug to lie at the foot of your favorite chair. The size of the strips is a matter of personal preference but a quarter inch is a good general average: thin strips will make up into a more delicate-looking rug than wide ones. A narrow strip will give the

Figure 201

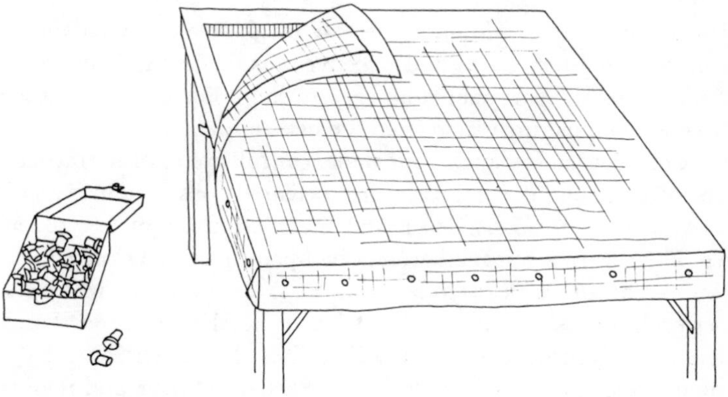

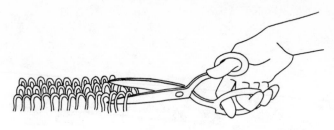

Figure 202

effect of gros point if it is hooked close together with short loops. A heavy strip with a long loop, on the other hand, can give an effect of free design and casualness. A long loop will work up much faster than a short one, because the loops need not be so close together. The rug will look sparse in the hand, but when it is laid on the floor the loops will fall over to fill in among one another. The loops can be cut open to make the rug softer-looking: you use a pair of long shears, insert one blade into a row of loops and cut them in half at the tops. (Figure 202.) An interesting pattern might be formed by leaving some sections looped and other sections cut, a monotone rug can be given a design just by cutting the loops in a regular pattern. For example, a rectangular rug might have alternating stripes of cut and uncut loops, or a round rug of uncut loops might be perked up with scattered circles of cut loops.

All kinds of materials can be used—silks, wools, blanketing, suiting, trousers, skirts; the length of the strips is not important. In general, materials should be stripped on the straight of goods, as that is the strongest line, and the width should be not less than three sixteenths of an inch. Old materials should be washed before stripping, and you can fade and soften colors if necessary by hanging them wet in the sun. There is available a little stripping machine, which automatically cuts three strips of material at a time—a big help and great timesaver.

Use a backing of good-quality two-ply monk's cloth, which you can buy at the local upholstery shop, and a conventional hooker from the needle-point counter in a department store or yarn shop. For the frame, use an inexpensive wooden picture frame from the five-and-ten.

First off, you must sketch your design in full color with crayons or felt markers, or by gluing down cutouts from colored construction paper. When it is as you wish it, take a ruler and mark off the sketch into one-inch squares. Then, with a felt marker or a ball-point pen mark off your monk's cloth into squares to scale, such as one inch to six inches, or what you wish. Number each square on the sketch, and then number them on the cloth to correspond. All you have to do now is follow the sketch for color as you work along. A simpler way is to draw your sketch full scale and then trace it onto the backing with carbon paper. Always leave a two-inch margin around the edges for turn-under; to prevent raveling, put masking tape around this border or run up a guard stitch all around it on the sewing machine. Mount the backing onto the frame with thumbtacks, and you are ready to start work.

If the frame is large, you can rest it on a chair back to be comfortable; if it is small enough, you can rest it on the arms of the chair you are sitting in. Both hands must be free to work. You can start the piece anywhere and go in any direction, but the rows of hooking are obvious and will form a pattern; leaves, for instance, should be done in the way that they are veined, flower petals in the way they grow. Hold the yarn with the left hand under the backing, insert the hooker from the front into a mesh, and pick up one loop to the surface; disengage the hooker, insert it into another mesh about a quarter inch away, and bring up another loop. Continue along in this manner, making rows of loops back and forth or around and around. With very little practice, you can bring your loops up to a uniform height, or you can alternate sections of long and short loops, as you will.

Hooked rugs can be worked in any design or color—quiet, conventional birds and flowers, or wild, colorful abstracts. It is necessary, of course, to do a conventional rug in a neat, orderly way. Two people can work the same pattern, using the same kind of yarn, and each will come up with a completely different end product; the personalities will show up almost as in handwriting. However, it is possible for several people to work on a rug successfully by deciding beforehand on techniques such as length of loop and thickness of pile, and then to use an automatic hooker, which can be nearly foolproof.

As a rule, the whole backing is covered with hooking. Interesting pieces can be made by leaving sections of the backing bare. These areas might be dyed with the use of a small brush, or a design might be painted on directly. They might be filled with a completely different material such as fur or pompons glued on with rubber cement; or they might be embroidered with unusual stitches; or, odd bits of yarns or grasses could be knotted into place.

Figure 203

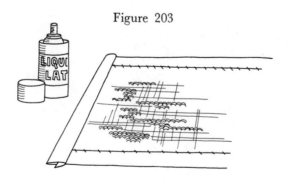

When the monk's cloth is all filled in to your liking, take it off the frame and remove the masking tape from the edges. Fold each edge into a double hem and stitch it to the back. (Figure 203.) You can brush or spray the back with liquid latex, which will help to keep the loops from raveling and will also serve as skidproofing. If you wish to fringe the rug, you can do it with yarn by a simple knotting. Allow about five times as much yarn as the fringe length is to be, double or triple it, then loop and knot the strands through the edge of the hooking about every half inch. (Figure 204.) Long fringe is not practical for a rug, but if you are planning to use the piece as a seat cover or a wall hanging, where the fringing would not be dangerous, it can be as long and as decorative as you want. Pompons, too, make an interesting edging, and can easily be made by winding yarn around the tines of a fork and then tying it up through the space between the two center tines. (Figure 205.)

Hooking a rug with yarn is done in exactly the same way as with strips. It is more beautiful, I think, than a strip rug, but it is also costly; while cot-

Figure 204

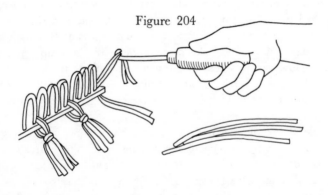

Figure 205

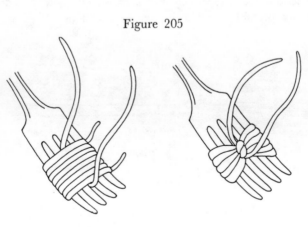

ton and synthetic yarns are satisfactory, they will not look or wear as well as wool. Wool doesn't soil as readily as the others, and because it has a natural spring it is pleasanter to work with and not as tiring to the hand.

Small rugs can be washed in the bathtub by scrubbing them lightly with a soft brush and detergent. Larger rugs can be taken out in the winter-time and cleaned as the Scandinavians do, by sweeping them with fresh, clean snow. In this way, they don't get too wet and the snow picks up the dirt, leaving them fresh and clean and not too long in drying. In the days when oriental rugs were handmade from silk or from wool, the artisans washed them in the river and then spread them out to dry in front of their shops. The river water removed the excess dyes, and then the sun and the trampling of many feet softened and blended the colors. So they were always mellow, even when new.

A rug too big to handle in the bathtub can, of course, be cleaned with the modern foaming synthetic cleaners made for that purpose. It is not ad-visable to use anything that requires brush scrubbing; we must treat our handmades with tender loving care.

KNOTTED RYA RUGS

Knotted rya (or ryijy) rugs, which originated in Scandinavia, are most beautiful, perhaps because of the type of knot, which gives a heavy, luxuri-ous pile, but more likely because of the type of yarn. It is a thick, loosely spun, twisted wool yarn known as Persian twist, which has a particularly shimmery look when it is cut. It is dyed to brilliant colors, and in the process of knotting, it is always used in combination with other, blending shades.

The backing for rya work is a specially woven one with a linen double warp and a heavy wool woof, so tightly beaten (woven) that it forms ridges. Every half inch, there is $\frac{1}{8}$-inch space in the woof, and it is here that the needle is inserted to make the knot. A large crewel needle is used with three lengths of blending yarn, each thirty to forty inches long. Work progresses in straight rows, from left to right from the bottom up, and it takes two stitches to make each knot. The needle is inserted from right to left, and every stitch goes around one set of warp threads.

Suppose you make a rug with a soft green-yellow background and several rectangles scattered about in dark blues and purples. (Figure 206.) To make it interesting, you would need three blending shades each of green and yellow, and two each of blue and purple. I would add one or two shades of dark red to strengthen the purple. It takes about three and a half ounces (one hank of 2-ply yarn) to cover a six-inch square, so these twelve hanks would make a runner about 24×30 inches with loops an inch and a half long. If you cut each hank in half, you will have your threads cut to about thirty-six inches (which is a good working length) and ready to use.

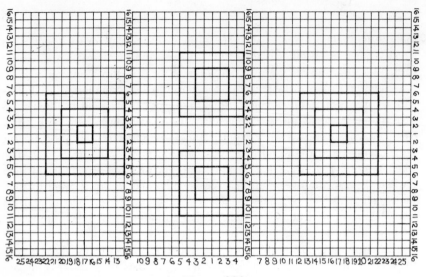

Figure 206

First, make a chart on graph paper showing where the dark rectangles will be; shade them in with crayon to give yourself an idea of what blends of yarn to use. The graph should be quite accurate, so that you will know when and where to pick up a new color, but once you have experience in this craft you will not need the graph but can work spontaneously as you go along. It is helpful to have several threaded needles on hand, so that colors can be changed readily; each needle is threaded with three lengths of yarn, with at least two blending shades.

Start the first needle with three shades of green; for the next threading use two shades of a dark green and one of dark yellow. For the third threading, try two threads of lighter green and one of yellow, and so on, always changing very subtly. In this way, no area ever becomes monotonous, and there is always the shifting of light that is characteristic of rya knotting.

Start in the lower left-hand corner of the backing, leaving five or six warp threads free along each side to be turned under for finishing. From the front, insert the needle down into the seventh hole, then back up into the sixth one, and pull it through, forming a loop with the fingers of the left hand. (Figure 207.) From the front, insert the needle down into the eighth hole, then back up into the seventh, and pull this one tight to anchor the first loop in place. For the loop stitch, hold the yarn down toward you with the left hand; for the anchor stitch, hold the yarn up and away from you so that when pulled tight it will automatically anchor the first stitch. Continue across the row in this way, alternating loops and knots, and then work the succeeding rows in the same way, always from left to right, making a stitch in every hole from right to left. Make the loops as long as you wish: they should be at least three quarters of an inch, and may be as long as two inches, but don't alternate loops long and short, because then you will lose the surface effect. If you want the effect of some high areas and some low areas, have clusters of the different lengths, so that they will show up as islands. As you finish each row, slip a scissors blade into the loops and cut them to make the shag.

Work the rectangles right along with the background as the rows progress; now you will be using blues and purples with an occasional red thread added. Here is where an accurate graph will save you time: if you have flecks of color sketched in place, you will know which threads to use. Not all rectangles need be the same, nor should the background be duplicated all over; however, it is helpful to keep notes as to the shades used in case you want to refer back to an area.

When the rug is completely filled in, turn back the edges to hem it. It can be used as is, or fringed if you want.

It is difficult for the novice to picture how the rug will look when finished. The colors are blended to give a feeling of movement, but the blending might not come out to your liking the first time around.

You can purchase rya rugs in kit form, one of the few packaged crafts that can be considered a real art form. The designs are well planned, and they come complete with all that you will need. They come to you directly from Scandinavia, and may be ordered from very good needlework shops.

Knotted rugs, of course, are not limited to this particular technique. Almost every country that has a cottage industry in rugmaking has a special way of tying knots that is all its own. The Moroccans are among the most skillful in this craft, using a loosely woven warp that hangs from a bar so that it is accessible from both sides. They use short pieces of yarn—about

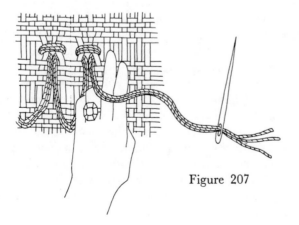

Figure 207

four inches—pushing it through from the back with one hand and knotting it on the front with the other. Whole families work on a rug together, and their fingers fly with unbelievable speed. They learn this trade from earliest childhood, and the most efficient members of the group are the very young, whose fingers have not yet been slowed down by age.

An easy type of knotting is done with a rug hooker or a crochet hook on a burlap or monk's-cloth backing. The yarn is cut to about five times the length of the pile, then it is doubled and pulled through the holes of the fabric and knotted by pulling the ends through the loop. These are not true knots, and this type of rug should be treated with a liquid latex backing to secure the threads in place. Knotting can be done in combination with other weaving techniques—it can be worked into the backing of a simple woven design to make a wall hanging or cushion. Wool or linen will give the most interesting effects, but any type of thread can be used. Some of the new synthetics might work well, and the imagination can dictate the rules of order.

WEAVING

The principle of loom weaving is always the same, regardless of how simple or complicated the mechanical apparatus is. The threads of the fabric are interlaced by the process of passing woof threads alternately over and under warp threads; just a few standard ways of doing this are the bases of all types of cloth. The warp thread is securely attached to the loom, and different weaves are obtained by varying the way the woof threads are handled. The simplest pattern is over one, under one, from right to left, and reversed on the way back, from left to right; but the woof threads could go over two warp threads, under two, over two, and so on across the whole warp, giving a ridged effect. And if these picks were advanced by one thread on every row, then a diagonal weave would emerge. If the woof were to go over two and under one warp thread, a different effect would be produced, and so on through innumerable combinations.

Anything that is woven follows these principles. (Figure 208.) They apply to basketry, in which an odd number of "spokes" are interwoven with dampened "weavers" such as palm leaves, grasses (sweet grass will retain its delightful odor forever), vine stems, or even willow wands. They apply to cane seating, in which moist cane is laid in from back to front and from side to side through holes in the frame of the chair itself, and this forms the warp; this warp is then woven vertically, horizontally, and diagonally, with a one-to-one tabby weave, thus forming the traditional open octagonal design so familiar to lovers of antique furniture. They apply, too, to rush seating, in which thick, damp, twisted rush fibers are woven around the rails of the chair seat so that the frame of the chair actually becomes the framework of the warp.

Dionysus and child. An intricate weaving used to serve both as a decorative hanging and the practical purpose of warming the cold wall of the palace. Wall tapestries were the forerunners of paintings. Sixth century. Coptic. Courtesy the Louvre, Paris. Cliché des Musées Nationaux.

Indian beading, beaded bracelets, handbags, hair ornaments—all are made on the same principle of forming a web from a warp and a woof. In this technique, beads are added onto the woof thread as the interweaving progresses, and this is but one way to achieve elaborate results from a simple process.

A professional loom is a complicated piece of equipment, but many patterns can be worked out on it by the experienced weaver who knows the rudiments of weaving techniques. Looms for the hand weaver range from two-harness all the way up to sixteen-harness, and cloth can be woven as

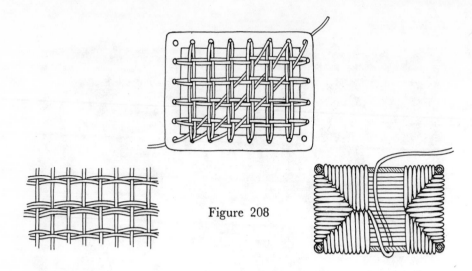

Figure 208

Figure 209

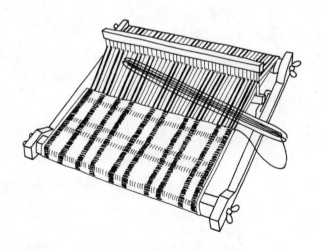

wide as a hundred inches. The larger the size the more complicated the loom is to thread, but of course the larger it is the more intricate are the effects that can be achieved. (Figure 209.) The setting up of a loom varies with each type, and the instructions for warping each one are obtained from the manufacturer, but all looms are set up in the same basic manner.

There are special names given to each part of the loom, and the sequence of setting up the loom for work goes like this: The warp threads are attached at the back of the loom to the warp beam, which keeps them taut. Then they are threaded through the heddles, which are upright bars on the harnesses that keep the threads in proper sequence. Next they are placed in the notches on the reed, which help to keep them in place; lastly they are secured to the breast beam at the front of the loom. The harnesses are attached to pedals, and each pedal raises a shed or opening through which the shuttle can pass to form picks, or rows. These picks make the woof (or weft) of the cloth, and every so often these woof rows are beaten down with a batten to keep the lines regular. Various looms will have differing accessories, but all operate on this same basic principle.

Before the warp is prepared for weaving, a work sheet should be drawn up with all the necessary information listed: the width of the cloth, so that the tension of the woof can be kept constant; the length of the piece, so that the warp threads are long enough, and always allowing an extra foot or two at each end for knotting; the color of the warp threads, and the color and texture of the woof threads, as well as the frequency of repeat. If the design is conventional, such as a plaid or a chevron or a formal stripe, there is no room for deviation, and correct count is very important.

Some types of design require special looms. Intricate designs can be produced on a Jacquard loom; this has an elaborate setup in which the warp threads pass through a series of cards perforated in such a way that the design is formed by the influence of these cards on the sheds (the raised warp threads) through which the woof threads pass. Monsieur Jacquard invented this loom in France in the eighteenth century, itinerant weavers used it in America in the nineteenth century, and IBM machines are setting it up for the weaver of the twentieth century. In Gobelin weaving on a tapestry loom, the woof threads are secured by tying them around individual warp threads, similarly to the interlocking stitch of Scandinavian rya weavings. But the principle of weaving is always the same: interlacing vertical threads with horizontal ones to form the web of the cloth.

Needle weaving as done by primitive craftsmen is similar to tapestry work; it makes a good project for the beginning weaver. Intricate patterns can be achieved, because the design is laid in by weaving back and forth across small areas of warp threads so that each area is worked individually. Suppose we set up for a small rug.

The needle-weaving loom is very simple. You can construct it from 1×2-inch wood strips made into the form of a rectangle, placing the top and bottom strips on top of the side ones so that these side pieces will not interfere when you pass the needle back and forth. Insert eye screws or carpet tacks, spaced a half inch apart, along the top and bottom bars, and warp them up and down with a thin, strong thread in a neutral color, such as carpet warp or fishing line. It is important that this warp be strong, because it will be the framework of the rug and will have to support the rest of the work. It must also be taut; if you wet this warp thread, it will shrink a little and then tighten as it dries. Use three strands together on the edges to make the selvage, which should be especially strong.

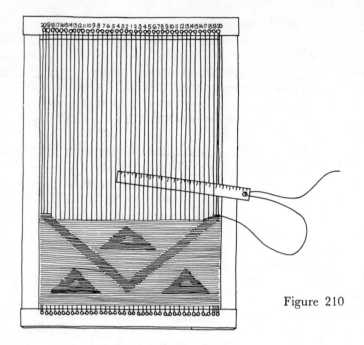

Figure 210

String any number of warp threads and, starting at the center, number them in duplicate out from the center to each side, using a felt marking pen on the wood. Draw the design on squared paper, with each vertical line representing one warp and each horizontal line one woof thread. Number these similarly so as to give an accurate graph to follow. Each square will represent one pass of the needle, and each one will be stitched in individually, so that the design can be repeated as many times and in as many places as you want. You can fashion a long "needle" or shuttle from a ruler by drilling an eye in one end to carry the woof thread, and you can also use this shuttle as the batten to pack the woof rows down as work progresses.

Usually, this type of weaving is done in a geometric design of triangles or diagonals or stylized figures, and each row of design is expanded or contracted by one thread. (Figure 210.) This is called "stepping up" or "stepping down"; the reason for it is that there will be a small hole at the junction of background and design, and by increasing or decreasing every row by one warp thread you will minimize this space. If you had a straight-up-and-down design, the line of demarcation would be pronounced and would weaken the fabric. You will do the whole piece in an over-one-under-one technique, working on the design first and then on the background. On each row, you will include the last warp thread of the design to anchor the background to the pattern.

Suppose you make a design of a white diamond set in a red background. Your pattern is ready, the loom is set up, you have all your yarn (or "thread") and a pair of scissors, and you are ready to begin. You can set the loom flat on the table, or you can hang it from a nail on the wall or from the branch of a tree.

First, weave in the design with white yarn. This will be done with a separate thread for each row, leaving about an inch on each end to float free on the back of the work. (If you wish to, you can knot these ends later.) Note the number of the warp thread on the graph, and start at the corresponding thread number on the loom. Weave across the design from right to left, cut the yarn, then weave the next row from left to right and cut that yarn. Continue doing this, back and forth, until the diamond motif is finished. (Figure 211.) Every few rows that are woven should be packed down firmly with the batten or with a wide-toothed comb and then tied to the sides of the loom to keep the piece straight; it will have a tendency to pull in tighter and tighter until it forms an hourglass shape, and these periodic anchorings will help the sides to stay even and avoid that problem.

Now you are ready to weave in the red background. Start at the right-hand selvage and weave across just to the first white thread of the design. Pass the shuttle over (or under) that first design thread, then weave back to the right-hand edge. Repeat this, weaving from the edge to the design and back to the edge again, filling in the background a few rows on the right, then a few on the left, to keep the tension even. Treat the three selvage rows on either side as one warp thread, to give the edges strength.

Because you have no way of knowing how many woof threads, or picks, the piece will take, it is a good idea to start in the middle and work toward

Figure 211

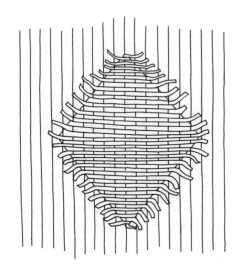

the top and bottom. In this way, you can add (or subtract) rows of weaving if necessary. It will depend on how tightly the rows have been combed down, how heavy the yarn is, and how loosely it has been spun; working this way will keep your design centered. It is always a good idea to have a few extra rows of tightly beaten heading at the top and bottom to give a strong edge to the piece.

When you are all finished, cut the warp threads off the loom, and knot them to make a self-fringe, or stitch a separate row of fringe or tassels to the ends, to complete the work. (Figure 212.) This type of tapestry weaving can be used for all manner of small pieces—table mats, wall hangings, handbags, or cushion covers. The loom can be set up easily, and it offers a wide choice of design not possible in other methods of hand weaving.

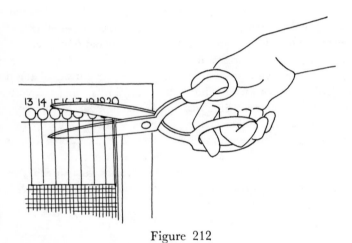

Figure 212

A small, lap loom can be made from a piece of firm cardboard—a shirt board or a piece of matboard—with notches cut into the ends for winding the warp. For instance, you could make place mats on a board about 14×18 inches. Cut notches about a quarter inch apart along the two 14-inch ends, and string a warp, back and forth, of carpet thread or fishing line, or gold or other colored wrapping twine. Weave the woof in heavy yarn or Swiss straw or a combination of artificial and/or natural fibers. Notches might be cut in groups to vary the warp sequence for interest, or warp threads might be skipped here and there at random, or knots made in the woof thread, or a border of wood beads woven in for a novelty. The shuttle can be made from a long, narrow strip of cardboard with a wide notch cut into each end to hold the wound woof thread.

Figure 213

NON-LOOM WEAVING

Non-loom weaving can be done wherever you happen to be, as long as you have a few simple necessities with you—strong warp thread, interesting woof thread, and a comb to act as a batten. Long strips for belts or ties or headbands can be made by knotting the warp threads together at one end, having them at least a yard longer than needed. Tie them to the leg of a table or to a tree or a rock, pull them taut, and knot the other end. Tie it around your waist, and you have created a backstrap loom. Using a smooth stick or a long upholsterer's needle, weave into the warp threads anything you wish for woof—natural grasses, thin twigs, string laced with beads or corks, raffia, odds and ends of yarn, or thin strips of cloth. (Figure 213.) Every so often, the rows should be beaten down with the comb, so that the piece will maintain some semblance of shape. If it is to be used for decorative purposes only, then the shape can be allowed to flow where it will, and even the basic rule of making a firm web need not hold. Designs can be worked in the same manner as in Indian needle weaving, and macramé can be worked into the warp by simply untying one end of the warp threads, working the knots in, pulling them taut again, and continuing with the weaving. Much ingenuity can be applied in this usually highly structured craft form, so that freedom of expression is possible as soon as you are no longer bound by the limitations of the loom.

Macramé wall hanging, 36×40 inches. It was made from orange and gold cords knotted in a symmetrical pattern. Contemporary. American. Abbe Sennett. Photo by B. F. Stein, Jr.

Macramé

Macramé is a form of non-loom weaving in which a set of cords are joined together by knotting them in such a way that they form a web of cloth. The knots are done in series, and they can be closely spaced or spread out thin. The whole piece can be made from one kind of knot or might be a sampler made from a variety of knots. It can be as little as a headband or as big as a hanging to cover an entire wall. It can be as simple as a fisherman's net or as elaborate as a ball gown.

Macramé is used by fisherfolk the world over. In the summertime they use it for mending the nets, and in the winter they work on elaborate pieces

Figure 214

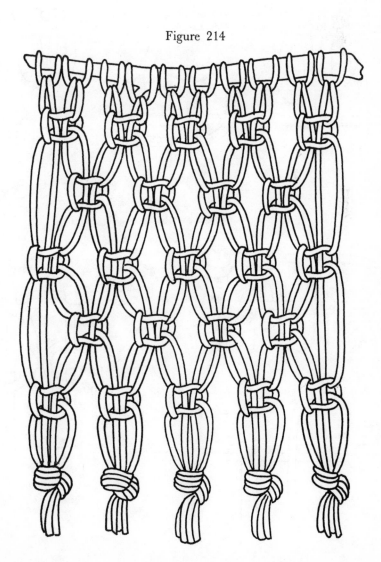

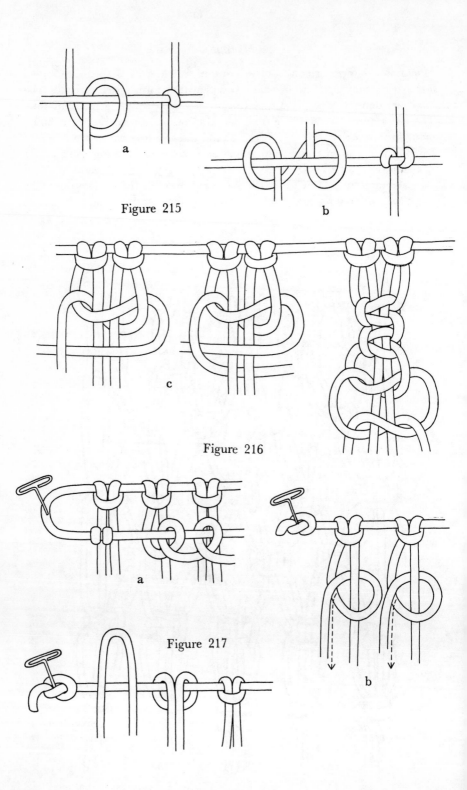

a

Figure 215

b

c

Figure 216

a

Figure 217

b

to while away the long months of the cold climates. A good way of learning
this craft is by browsing through the books on knots that can be found in
fishing- or boating-supply stores: here you will also find good selections of
cords as well as examples of macramé as used in nets and in covering floats.
Boating people are meticulously neat for safety's sake; some of the knottings
used in their day-to-day work are both intricate and beautiful and could
well be display pieces on a landlubber's wall. (Figure 214.)

In general, if the piece is to hang stiff, a tightly twisted twine such as
jute rope or plumb-line cord from the hardware store is satisfactory. But for
anything that needs a softer feel, flax or silk or any one of the numerous synthetics is best. In addition to the cord, all the equipment needed is a solid
support such as a cork or foam board to accommodate the width of your
work, and a package of furrier's T pins or long-shanked corsage pins.

With the exception of direct fringing, almost every macramé piece is
started by anchoring it to a holding cord, which is a length of cord attached
horizontally to the foam board with the T pins. This holding cord should be
as long as the width of your piece, plus a few inches for good measure.

The basic knots in macramé are the half hitch, the clove hitch, and the
square knot (Figure 215a, b, & c), and there are all kinds of variations on
these three themes. (Figure 216a & b.) The half hitch is the simple knotting
of a cord on itself, and in macramé it is often knotted around another cord
which is called a filler or carrier. The square knot, as you may remember from
your scouting days, is made with two strands: the left over the right, then the
right over the left—then left over right, and so on for as many times as you
wish.

You start the actual knotting by working back and forth so that you
form rows, just as in weaving. As the work progresses, put pins into the
finished knots to keep the piece taut against the board, to keep the tension
even, and to keep the width from going askew. The rows of knotting can be
placed as close together or as far apart as needed, depending on whether it is
to be a solidly built piece or an airy one.

If you take a length of cord, double it, and loop it over the holding
cord, then pass the two ends through the loop and pull them taut, you will
have made two half hitches; this is called a lark's head. (Figure 217.) The
beginning of a macramé piece is nearly always made by knotting as many of
these lark's heads onto the holding cord as is necessary for the width of the
piece. For instance, if you were using a heavy cable cord to make a belt
about one inch wide, you would require four cords, which, when made into
lark's heads, would give you eight working strands. If you were making a
handbag that was to be six inches wide, you would require twenty-four
cords. But if you were to use a thinner cord, such as silk or jute, you would
need many more lark's heads in order to make up the desired width. Each
cord should be about eight times longer than the finished length in order to
accommodate the knotting. After these are doubled over the holding cord

and formed into lark's heads, you can wind each strand into a little ball and secure it with a rubber band. Then, as your work progresses, you can unwind as much as you need—usually about twelve inches at a time. And as your piece grows, you would remove the first pins and shift the whole thing upward so that you always have space on the board for pinning your work to in order to keep it even.

Your belt or purse or wall hanging could be made by using any mixture of knots that you wish. You might use a simple square knot all across the cords for two or three rows, then you could give it some interest by grouping the cords into sets of four; still using the square knot, wrap the two outside strands of each group around the two inside ones. In order to form a continuous web, you could shift the sets over every row and re-form them, using two cords from one set and two from the next adjacent set. That way, each group would be anchored and would also be building a pattern if you continued it for a few rows.

The half hitch is used to make horizontal or diagonal bars. If a horizontal ridge is called for, you would lay the extreme right-hand cord on top of the others in a horizontal position, and tie each of the others to it in succession, with a half hitch, starting with the cord that is second to the right. If you want a diagonal bar, then you can lay the right-hand strand down at an angle instead of straight across, and tie the others to it; then you might lay the extreme-left-hand cord down and work across it to form an opposite angle, which would result in a zigzag design or a diamond shape, depending on where you started it. (Figure 218.)

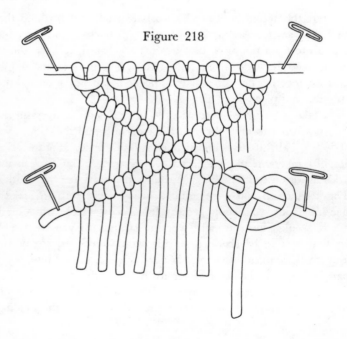

Figure 218

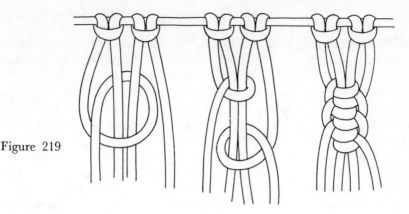

Figure 219

Sinnets

You can make a sinnet, which is a thick vertical rope, by using alternate right and left half hitches. (Figure 219.) You would divide the strands again into groups of four, knot the first cord over the second and third, which are the fillers, then knot the fourth cord over the two fillers, repeating this a few times. Then you could do the same thing with the next group of four, until you have used all the cords and formed sinnets all across the width of the piece. Or you could form these designs just on the edges of the work or just down the center if you wished, making the sinnets as long as you wanted.

There are intricate knots, such as the Josephine knot, or carrick bend, which, again, are versions of the square knot elaborately conceived. (Figure

Figure 220

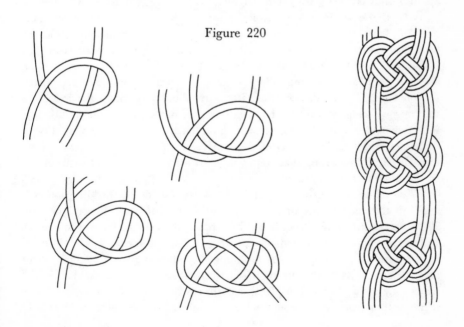

220a & b.) These may be done with two single strands, or two sets of multiple strands. They go over and around and in and out of each other's loops, and end up as highly decorative areas in the over-all macramé piece.

On the other hand, very simple knotting may be used to achieve an effect of weaving, and scenes or figures or flower motifs may be knotted in; beads or shells or driftwood could also be incorporated for any effect that you desire.

Macramé comes from the Arabic word *migramah,* which means "embroidered veil" or "fringed towel," and very often we see oriental rugs with macramé-fringed ends. This is done by knotting the excess lengths of the warp threads; the craftsman often does this to add an attractive touch to his weavings. It does seem a waste to cut off these dangling threads when they can be put to very good use. The macramé can be started by joining the first two threads on the right to the next two, with a square knot. Then the third pair can be joined to the fourth pair, the fifth to the sixth, and so on to the end of the row. For the next row of knotting, one thread from each pair is knotted together to form a new set of pairs, and then these new sets are joined all along the row in the same way.

The loose fringe on a rug should not be more than two inches long for safety's sake, but a wall hanging may be fringed to any length and perhaps finished off with a few beads or baubles incorporated into the knotting.

Fringing

Spanish shawls look elaborately fringed, but that effect is easily achieved by tying the knots in a given series. Suppose you were to edge a beautiful piece of batik with a three-section edging to make a handsome stole. In adding a macramé fringe to the fabric, you will choose a smooth cord that is not too heavy, because it has to be drawn through the edge of the material. A heavy silk embroidery or crochet cord is good. For the three-section edging, you will need pieces of yarn about four times the length of the finished fringe. So if the fringe is to be six inches long, you would start with twenty-four-inch lengths; if it is to be ten inches long, you would need forty-inch lengths. The beauty of a Spanish shawl is that the fringe is so long and silky and undulating that you could start off with yards and yards of the cord and knot it ad infinitum.

Thread an embroidery needle with three strands of the silk, doubled, and roll the edge of the material up into a ridge to form a hem. (Figure 221.) Starting at one corner, pull the strands through the fabric to exactly half their length, and knot them tightly up against the edge of the material with a lark's head. Repeat this all along the edge, spacing the cords about an inch apart. Each set consists of six strands—three strands doubled—and when they are all knotted in place, you are ready to start the macramé. Take three strands from the first set and three strands from the second set and tie

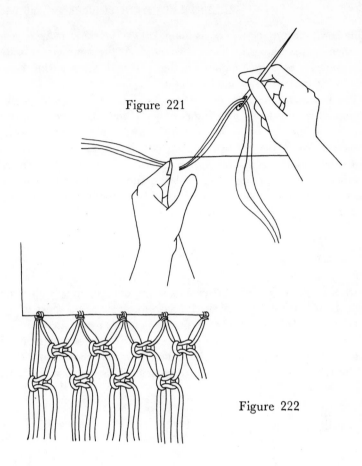

Figure 221

Figure 222

them together with a square knot. Then knot the remaining three of the second set to three of the third. Then tie the remaining three of the third set to three of the fourth, and so on all along the edge.

Now go back to the first of this new set of knots, and tie three strands of that set to three of the second set; and repeat the process again all along the line. This will form a diamond pattern, and the loose set of three strands on either end gets to be knotted every other row, so that the diamonds are continuous all along the edge. (Figure 222.) Do this again for a third row, and for as many rows as you wish; each row will line up to alternate the diamonds with the previous one.

For this type of Spanish edging there is always a long, loose fringe left dangling; take that into consideration both when you start with the lengths of cord and when you stop the knotting.

If you want to make a large piece of macramé, the simplest way to do it is to nail a piece of one-by-two to the wall and screw cup hooks in every foot or so. Place a piece of doweling or driftwood rod on the hooks to act as the holding cord and tie one end of as many balls of working cords to it as you wish; then start working the knots downward. As the piece grows, the whole one-by-two can be raised higher on the wall and the knotting continued downward as long as the strands hold out.

The craftsman likes to experiment, and he might build whole constructions from any kinds and colors of yarn, thread, twine, or string. He might use all sorts of boy-scout and fisherman's knots done in regular sequences, or knots placed in irregular sequences to form asymmetrical designs. He will use the macramé piece as an end in itself or in combination with other types of weaving or assemblages, and he might add beads, stones, corks, metal coins, or glass or plastic to add still more interest to the piece. It is an ancient, venerable craft turned modern, and anything goes.

BATIK

The art of batik, or wax-resist dyeing, is a very old technique that originated in Indonesia. It is a pattern-dyeing process using wax as a resist to the dye, and today it is used as a free art form, the designs being little related to the familiar exotic designs of yesteryear, which were taken mostly from nature. The technique, however, is still the same; the crude tool fashioned by the Javanese is still used and has hardly changed. This is called a tjanting. It

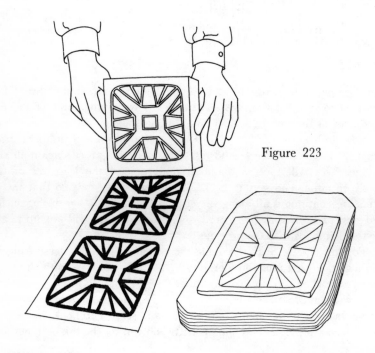

Figure 223

consists of a tiny oval cup made of thin copper, with a narrow, curved spout coming out near the bottom of the bowl; the cup is wired to a piece of bamboo, which becomes the handle. With this tool, the hot wax is dribbled onto the cloth to form the resist, which will in turn form the design.

The Javanese used a soft cotton cloth treated with coconut oil and then boiled and pounded to make it aged and mellow and receptive to the dye. Repeat designs were made with a tjap block, a small block of wood similar to a woodcut, the design being formed from thin brass strips fastened onto the block. (Figure 223.) The tjap was pressed on a flat, hot wax pad, and the wax was transferred to the cloth to make the resist to the dye. Strangely enough, while the women prepared the cloth and the dyes and did all the preliminary handwork, only the men worked on this process of repeating a design with the tjap block.

In batik dyeing, wherever the wax has blocked the pores of the fabric, the dye will not take. Colors are worked from light to dark, and a whole intricate design can be worked out with nothing but successively stronger and deeper shades of blue, for instance. Wax will be added to new areas before each dye bath, and these areas will remain the color they were before the new wax was applied. Everything left unwaxed will get darker with each dipping; if this operation is done five times, it could end up as an elaborate design made entirely of five shades of blue.

Batik dyeing today is done on silk, cotton, or linen. Synthetics are all right, but when you are working with so old and specific an art form, aesthetically the background should be a natural one to retain the proper feeling. The Javanese royal artisans, who were honored to spend years designing one piece of cloth, used the finest of natural materials, and it is pleasant to carry on this tradition. Scarves that are already hemmed are convenient to use, or white yard goods for a larger piece. The material must first be washed to remove any sizing that might interfere with the waxing, and for delicate designing it is sometimes desirable to use a very light starch to prevent the design from spreading and to give better control of the wax. The Javanese used a rinse of rice water for this purpose. (The Japanese used a heavy rice paste to act as the resist and, with this, a combination of stitch-resist and tie-resist, all of which allowed for very precise patterning.)

Suppose you were to make a batik of a large butterfly with pink circles on blue wings and a red body, on a dark-red background. Use a thin silk white kerchief, because it will dry quickly from having a fan played on it. The supplies you need are few but specific, and most of them can be purchased in a good hobby or art-supply store. You can use inexpensive Japanese water-color brushes, because they charge up well with the melted wax and will hold to a shape while you apply it. You can buy a tjanting inexpensively, or you can make one from a small piece of thin copper sheeting roughly formed into a bowl shape, with a very thin spout soldered onto one

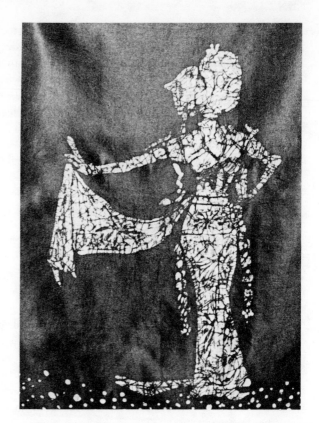

Batik panel in a
traditional design
done in a single color
on thin silk. The
crackle effect was
achieved by crushing
the hardened wax
before dipping.
Contemporary.
Javanese. Collection
of the author.

side near the bottom; nail a wood dowel to the bowl for a handle, and it
will serve adequately. The dye has to be of a type that does not have to be
boiled, because the heat of boiling would melt the wax and ruin the design.
The wax will be one part beeswax to one part paraffin, and the vessel used
for dyeing will be large enough so that the material has free movement in
the dye bath; it should be made of enamel or glass.

The only other things you need are a double boiler on a hot-plate to
melt the wax and keep it melted; rubber gloves to protect your hands from
the dye, and a stretcher of some sort to keep the material taut while waxing
it, because it must be free so that the wax will penetrate through to the
back. A picture frame, an embroidery frame, or even a shoe box will do.
You pin down the material on all four sides, and move it to wax it in sections if necessary. The waxing is always done on clean, dry material, and
you will apply the wax with the brush to large areas, and with the tjanting
to small areas such as lines and dots. Apply it wherever the original color is
to remain.

Now that you have all the equipment together, you are ready to begin.

Draw your design on a piece of white paper, lay the kerchief over it, and trace the design onto the silk with a soft pencil. Then stretch the fabric taut over the frame and pin it down securely. Place a chunk of paraffin in the double boiler, add an equal chunk of beeswax, and heat it to melting. *Never cook wax directly over the heat,* because it's very flammable.

There is no hurry between steps, and so you can do your waxing and prepare the dyes as you go along, one step at a time. You are using only two colors, red and blue, and you can start with the palest red, which is the pink on the wings. Block out with wax everything that is to be blue: successive dippings in red will produce the successively darker reds that you have planned. The wax should be allowed to cool and harden before the dyeing begins; the thin silk that you are using will require just a light film of the wax to penetrate it. Dip the tjanting in very hot water to warm it up, and fill the bowl with melted wax. Draw the tjanting over your sketch lines, allowing the spout to act as a pen point (Figure 224), and then with a brush wax in all the large areas that are to be blue. (Figure 225.) Mix a weak red

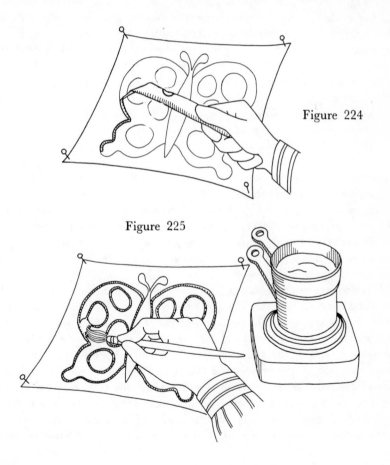

Figure 224

Figure 225

dye, which will show up as pink, and dip the piece into it, swishing it around a little. Then rinse it in cool water and dry it. When it is completely dry, wax out the next section, which will be the pink circles on the wings, which you want to remain in pink. Mix a stronger red dye and dip the kerchief once more, then insert it and dry it. Now wax in the body, which is to remain red, and dip the piece in a still stronger red solution for the background. Rinse it and dry it, and the piece is now ready for the blue dye bath.

All the pinks and reds have been dyed, and so everything except the blue areas must be waxed out to block the blue dye. The wax must be removed from the parts of the wings that are to be blue; you can do this with a Q-Tip and cleaning fluid or kerosene, which will dissolve out the wax just where you want it to. The wings and body are still waxed from the previous tintings, so you just brush melted wax onto the background to keep it red and then dip the piece into a blue dye bath. This is the last bath, and now the piece is all finished; it just remains to remove the wax. But at this point you might decide that some purple veining would be a nice addition to the background. Pick up sections of the background (which is red, remember) and crumple them gently between your fingers. Dip the whole thing into the blue bath again; the blue will penetrate where you have cracked the wax by crinkling it. Rinse the fabric, dry it, and remove the wax from it by ironing it between folds of paper toweling and newspaper. The newspaper is absorbent, but the ink might ruin your work, and so it is protected with the toweling or with brown wrapping paper. If the wax does not come out completely, a quick rinse in cleaning solution should do it. And then you are all finished.

Batik work is interesting for the uninitiated, because the results are unpredictable. For the experienced craftsman, there is much satisfaction in the control of the medium and in the working of a preconceived design to a predicted end. I once sat spellbound watching an Indonesian woman work with the tjanting on a delicate, intricate design covering some twenty yards of silk material. I don't think we have that much patience, but we appreciate batik for the demanding art that it is, and no other technique can give quite the same beautiful results.

Batik dyes are transparent, and any color on top of another will affect the final result; a two-color dye job can result in a three-color piece. If you wanted a design in red, orange, and yellow, for instance, you would block out all areas to be red, and dip the piece in a yellow dye bath. Then you would remove the wax from the areas that will show up red, apply wax to those that are to stay yellow, and dip it in a red dye bath. The red areas would dye red, the orange areas would appear where there is red dye over yellow, and the original yellow (having been waxed to resist) will remain yellow. And so, if a multicolor design is wanted, each area not to receive a particular color will be waxed out to resist that color, and areas previously blocked out will have the wax removed to receive the desired color. Therefore it is desirable that you work from a presketched plan, thinking out beforehand the procession of dyes and what they will do to each area and to each other.

Resist dyeing can be used for any fabric, whether it is to be useful or ornamental. Scarves and blouses might be made from lightweight materials, while cushion covers or draperies might be made from heavy linen or wool. Wall hangings can be made from batik work by hemming the sides of the fabric and weighting the top and bottom with bamboo or other decorative lightweight rods. They can be lighted from behind, much like stained glass, by hanging them in a window so that the light filters through. Any material receptive to dye can be used so long as it can be handled by the dipping method. When the material becomes too cumbersome to handle, it is best designed by other methods, such as silk-screen or wood-block printing, or even hand-painting with the dyes. Special batik dyes are available from India that are very intense and brilliant, and there are resists on the market that can be removed with cold water. But because synthetic resists are not always compatible with the old methods, the craftsman would be wise to plan his work through from beginning to end before investing in timesaving devices that might end up catastrophically.

TIE DYEING

Tying and dyeing of cloth is a craft that is ages old, probably one of the first decorative arts ever invented, because it is the simplest way that we know to embellish a fabric. In the process of dyeing a piece of cloth, the dye must reach all the fibers at the same time with the same intensity of color, if the dye job is to be even. In the dyeing, resists are put in the way in the form of ties or knots; the color takes hold in a programmed sequence, and the pattern is formed by the areas that have resisted the dye. (Figure 226.) The ties can be made by knotting the material itself, in which case there is practically no control over the pattern; or they can be made by gathering the cloth into florets and tying these little bunches with twine, so that presumably the dyeing will proceed in a predictable way.

Some fabrics do not lend themselves well to dyeing; natural materials are the best ones to use: cotton, silk, linen, and perhaps wool. Some rayons and some nylons will work out well, but the colors will not always come out true, and some of the man-made fibers will not accept the dye at all. In general, the synthetics are unpredictable, and any material that cannot be put into hot water should not be used.

The tying of the fabric is an art and a challenge. The beginning craftsman has no way of knowing how the piece will turn out, but the experienced designer can know fairly accurately just how and where the pattern

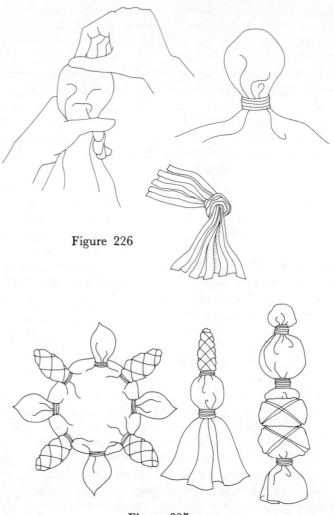

Figure 226

Figure 227

will appear. The number of ties made will affect the over-all pattern, and the manner in which the string is wrapped around the cloth will also be an influence. (Figure 227.) The resist occurs not only at the immediate site of the string but also to varying degrees in the folds of the material. If the material is gathered haphazardly it will give one effect; if it is pleated carefully it will give another. The kind and amount of wrapping cord will affect the penetration of the dye, as will the width of the wrap. The Indian peoples and the Japanese do incredibly fine work in this craft; the results they obtain are beyond imagination.

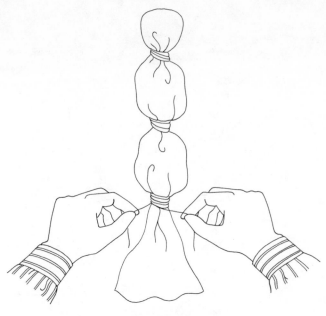

Figure 228

Suppose you try your hand at a small linen cushion cover with a large sunburst design in lavender edging out to blue. The equipment you need is simple: just two deep bowls for the dyeing, rubber gloves, and four 6-inch pieces of string. Use blue and red dyes from the supermarket. The linen square should be washed ahead of time to get rid of any sizing and then dried.

Lay the material flat on the table, and pinch up a little floret right in the center. Hold it between the thumb and forefinger, and about an inch down from the center wind a piece of string around and around, and knot it securely. (Figure 228.) About two inches down from that string, tie another string tightly around and around, and repeat this gathering and tying so that the cloth assumes a cylinder shape and is tied up in four places. Each section you have tied will resist the dye differently, because there are different amounts of material, and the more ties there are the more elaborate the design will be.

When the tying is complete, the material is ready to be dyed. In this method of decoration, you use a dry material, because then the resist of the string will be more pronounced and the dyeing will be less even and so more interesting. Mix about two quarts of each of the dyes in hot water, and pour each color into one of the bowls. Hold the cloth by the four corners, dip it into the red bowl to about half its length, and agitate it a little. (Figure 229.) Take it out, shake it a bit, and then immerse the material completely into the blue bath. Remove it and rinse it in several changes of cool water,

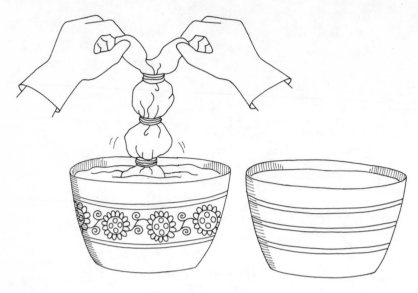

Figure 229

cut away the string, and spread the material out flat on a bed of paper toweling to dry. Press it with a hot iron while it is still a little damp, and you are all finished.

The bursts of design have remained in the original color of the linen—probably white—and the center is lavender, from the blue dye on top of the red. The edges are straight blue, and while you may not have a result that is to your liking, you have learned how a tie resist works, and what its limitations are, which are considerable. If you have the time and patience, you can rinse and dry the piece between colors, still keeping it wrapped. Also, you can add more strings before going into the second dye bath. That would mean that the first dye (red) would now be blocked to the blue in the tied areas, so that these areas would remain red, and a three-color job would result—red, blue, and a mixture of the two. Also, the material could be immersed into the red bath from the center halfway up, and then into the blue bath from the edges halfway down. This would come out with red in the center of the sunburst, purple at the overlap, and blue at the edges. The design itself will always be in the original color of the material, where, it is hoped, no dye has penetrated.

This sunburst is the simplest form of tie-dyed design. If you scatter little florets around, you will end up with a more complicated pattern, and if you use different materials for the tying, such as raffia, nylon, silk, rubber bands, or narrow strips of material, you can come up with a variety of results, some possibly good and some probably bad.

Another resist that can be used with tie dyeing is colored crayon. You might draw a circle on the material with a wax-based child's crayon, then tie up the floret inside or outside this circle. The material can then be dyed, and the wax removed with a hot iron. The ironing will be done between two pieces of brown paper, which will absorb the wax of the crayon, but the color will remain on the cloth as part of the design. Freehand painting can be done on fabric by this method, and it is possible to keep the dye from spreading by making a "cage," or cloison, of the wax. This, of course, is infringing on batik methods, but articles such as wall hangings can be made by using a combination of many techniques: stitchery on top of batik on top of tie dyeing, combined with loose weaving and/or macramé or rya knotting —beautiful and limitless, and there is no reason to be a purist. Tie dyeing is simple and lots of fun, and some gorgeous fabrics have evolved from an idle doodle in the dye bath.

TEXTILE DESIGN

The process of printing on textiles from rollers is very much like putting cloth through an old-fashioned clothes wringer with two rotating metal rollers. The design is engraved on one roller and then it is inked; another roller rotates with pressure on the engraved one, and as the material is fed through, the pattern becomes imprinted. With this method of printing, the design of the fabric is limited to the size of the roller, and the repeat of the pattern has to coincide with the circumference of the roller, as well as with its length. (Figure 230.) If, for instance, the roller is eighteen inches long,

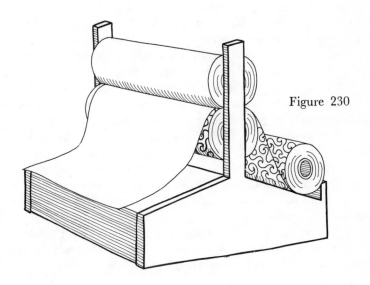

Figure 230

the design will have to repeat itself in the width of 36-inch material; if it is sixteen inches in circumference, then the repeat in length will occur every 16 inches. Rollers come in various sizes, and the designer in making his sketch has to know what size he is designing for, in order to plan it so that each repeat flows smoothly into the next one.

The technique of transferring designs onto textiles by silk-screening methods became popular in the 1950s, and as this means of printing developed, the designs became larger and freer, because they were no longer bound by the size of the roller. A commercial screen for printing can be as large as the building that houses it, and the problem of having to repeat a design because of size limitation became less of a factor; a whole wall of fabric could be printed today with never a repeat of pattern. While screen printing is a more expensive process than roller printing, the freedom of design offsets the cost: the design can be as wild and as colorful or as soft and ethereal as the artist wishes.

So, in planning a design for the printing of large quantities of material, whether it be cloth or paper, one must know what process of printing will be used for it. Where there will be no repeat in design, such as in a scenic panel on wallpaper or a dress with one panel of a motif from top to bottom, it is not necessary for the artist to sketch in the repeat, because each panel is an entity in itself, and does not have to reconcile with the next one.

However, before you can plan a design for the luxury trade, it is necessary that you know the mechanics of designing for roller printing. So let us make a floral design with a 12-inch repeat in the width and a 12-inch repeat in the length. Your design can come from anywhere—this is a field known for piracy—but one tries not to copy exactly, because original ideas are still premium. For the purpose of learning, however, study a section of a piece of material that you have around—a blouse or a tablecloth; this will give you an idea of the intricacies of textile design. Every mark on that cloth has been sketched there by the artist.

You will need large sheets of fair-quality white paper. A roll of paper is good, because much of the preliminary work is doodling, and rolls are much cheaper than quantities of sheet paper. This practice paper need not be of high quality but should be smooth and white. You will need, too, several large sheets of good water-color paper, some tracing paper, a 36-inch metal ruler, poster paints, inexpensive brushes, a gum eraser, and rubber cement; also, a large enough work area to spread out on.

Mark off a 12×12-inch section in the middle of a piece of paper, and on it draw the outlines of six different kinds of flowers—do them head on to simplify—and paint in the petals and other parts with your poster paints. You must not use too many colors, because each color is a separate printing, which adds to the cost. Now make eight tracings of each flower onto individual small pieces of tracing paper, and draw eight more 12-inch squares abutting each side of the original one, and one for each corner. (Figure

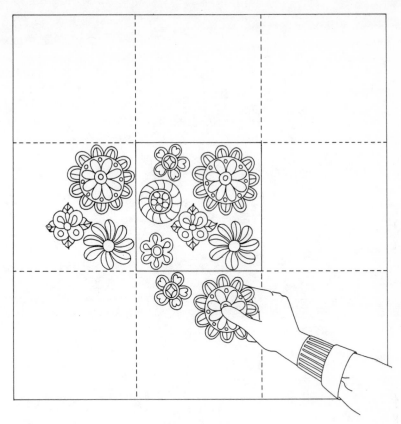

Figure 231

231.) Place the colored flower tracings in each new box in exactly the same position as they are in the original and stand away to look at it. Does the design flow smoothly in every direction? No? Surprised? The first try seldom works out right, so you must start all over again.

Cut out each original flower, and start with a new set of eight boxes. Scatter the flowers around in new positions by setting them in the center box and then putting the tracings into the adjacent boxes, again in identical positions to the center one. You will find that the edges of the center box are most crucial. The flowers nearest the right edge must live with those nearest the left edge in the adjacent box. And likewise top and bottom edges, and corners. So you must play around with these placements until you find that each set of the design follows right into the next set, which is identical. Remember that the roller is imprinted with the design of only one box, which it will be repeating over and over, and will print only exactly what the artist tells it to.

Figure 232

When you have decided that your design is properly placed so that it looks good from every angle, glue each flower down with rubber cement into the center box. The adjoining boxes need be filled in only where they join the center one, so that on completion you will have perhaps two inches filled in all around the original motif—roughly sixteen inches square of finished work. (Figure 232.)

Now all that remains to be done is to transfer this paste-up to the good water-color paper, and to do it in several different color schemes. Ordinarily, in the textile houses, copyists and colorists do these jobs, but, again, you must know how they are done. This is the work that you will be showing to the customer—whether it be a studio that will sell it for you or a factory that will actually use it, and you should have a perfect job, ready to go to the mill for engraving. For this you must use a good-quality paper, one that will not buckle under the wet poster paint and is not so absorbent that the lines will not remain defined.

Mark off the center 12-inch square lightly with pencil, and suggest the eight surrounding ones, then trace your finished design onto this paper, being sure that you transfer your design right side up. To do this, lay the tracing paper over the design and trace all the lines with a sharp pencil. Then turn the tracing paper over and go over the lines on this side with a soft pencil. Place it, reverse side down, on your clean sheet, tape it with Scotch tape so that it won't shift, and rub it all over with your thumbnail. The soft pencil marks will transfer nicely, and any smudges may be cleaned up with the gum eraser.

In the lower left-hand corner of the paper, mark off one-inch squares in a straight line from left to right. Each of these squares will be filled in with the same color you use in your design, and you need as many squares as you

Figure 233

Figure 234

have colors: these are the guides for the printer, so that he may mix his dyes to match. Now color in your design with the poster paints, filling in each sample square as you go along. It is wise to keep a scrap of paper under your wrist as you work, to minimize accidental smudging.

Each design is presented in three or four different color schemes. One is full scale, but the others can be smaller copies, done in the same way, but not necessarily technically correct except as to the colors. (Figure 233.) (You could, of course, make a direct tracing by using non-smudging erasable carbon paper.) Yard goods are almost always offered in a choice of color schemes, and someone had to think up these schemes, so who better than the artist?

Designing for silk-screen production is done in exactly the same way, because any all-over pattern must be designed with the repeat running smoothly. But the actual process of silk-screening allows more latitude, by virtue of the greater flexibility of the machine itself. Soft, splashy designs and halftone washes are easy to come by in a silk-screen process.

But there is a simple trick that is used in repeat printing to make a design look more elaborate than it really is; this is known as a half drop. If material is forty-eight inches wide and is being printed on a twelve-inch roller, then obviously the goods must be fed through the machine four times.

A half drop is accomplished by setting the roller one half turn ahead for each run-through, and in that way the design is stepped down by half its circumference for each successive printing. (Figure 234.) This makes the repeat look twice as large, and for still more trompe l'oeil, the roller can be set down a quarter drop for each run, so that the design would appear to be four times as wide as it really is. This maneuver can be accomplished in any method of repeat printing—simply by shifting the stencil or the wood block or the screen as work progresses.

This, then, is how textile designs are created. It is important for the craftsperson to understand how to plan a repeat, for it is used in many crafts. A repeat may be necessary in designing a bracelet or a round bowl, or in the block printing of fabrics or papers. Good planning is the basis of good design, and a well-planned repeat might be just what is needed for a flagging inspiration.

11

Sculpture

BUILDING AN ARMATURE

Complicated sculptures such as animals and human figures usually are built on a supporting core or skeleton. This core is called an armature, and it is formed to approximate the shape of the finished piece. In the building of a head, for example, the armature is simply an egg-shaped form that can be made of any material that will hold its shape—it could be chicken wire, or wadded newspaper, or a ball of Styrofoam. But a more complicated piece, with appendages, such as a full human figure, needs to have a more sophisticated base on which to build.

Suppose you make an armature for a half-size standing figure in a classic ballet pose, head erect, with arms extended and one leg bent at the knee. It will take the shape of a stick figure, and you will use one-inch threaded pipe attached to a plywood or formica base as the support, and heavy flexible lead or aluminum wire for the figure itself. The wire is free so that you can apply the clay all around it, and the stand will hold the figure rigid. Most of the supplies come from a plumbing-supply house, the rest from your art-supply dealer.

Buy about eight feet of 8-gauge wire, a piece of plywood about fifteen inches square, and two lengths of one-inch threaded pipe, one about eight inches long and one six inches. At the center of the back edge of the base, attach the eight-inch pipe with a plate fitting, so that it stands rigidly upright. This is the only place where the armature is supported, and so it must be securely screwed in. Now attach a right-angle elbow to the top of the pipe, and into it insert the six-inch pipe extending forward. To this, attach a small three-way coupling elbow; now the stand is ready to accept the wire "stick figure."

Since this is a half-size figure, it will stand about thirty-two inches high. Take a sixty-four-inches-plus length of the flexible wire, bend it in half, and insert it into the coupling elbow, looping the top open to form the head and separating it at the bottom to form the legs, one standing on the base and the other bent at the knee. The coupling is at about hip position; judge where the shoulders will come, and loop another piece of wire around the first one, to form the arms extended gracefully. (Figure 235.)

Now that the armature is built, the figure is ready to be sculptured. Plasticine is often used when one is working on an armature, because it is oil-based and never dries out, making it easy to put the work aside and pick it up again at will. It is used just like clay: small chunks are added, each being pressed on top of the last ones with the thumb. In this way, the whole figure will be built up. Because it is a half-size figure, all measurements will be half of reality: the thigh, for instance, being about twenty inches around in the human, will be ten inches around in the sculpture. (Figure 236.) The human head being twenty-two inches around, it will be eleven, and so on. Place the whole stand on a revolving base, and use calipers to check the measurements as you go along.

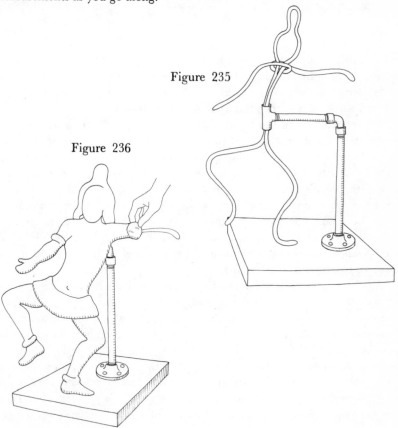

Figure 235

Figure 236

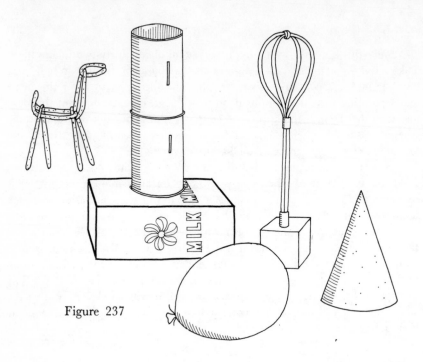

Figure 237

When the sculpture is finished, unscrew the plate fitting from the base: you now have a freestanding statue with an armature of lead. Obviously, this "skeleton" cannot be removed, and if you wish the statue to be permanent, you will send it to the foundry to be cast in bronze.

An armature stand can be used over and over for different positions by manipulating the couplings, and many materials other than plasticine can be used to form the figure: plaster of Paris, of course, and imitation stone or bronze, or waxes or clay. Papier mâché, or sand mixed in acrylic medium along with dry pigment, can be used to simulate terra cotta or stone or what-have-you. Gesso or modeling paste can be used, or a sculpturing "dough" can be made by boiling one cup each of salt and cornstarch with one cup of water; it will form a solid ball and can be kneaded like clay. Sand, sawdust, or oatmeal may be added to give surface interest, and it can be treated like plaster when hardened.

All these materials are for making figures and animals, but they can be used for other kinds of sculpture as well. There are many ways to make armatures and many materials available in the hobby shops and in the home for covering the armature once it is made. Tin cans can be glued together to form the "skeleton" for a modern sculpture. (Figure 237.) They can be draped with Fiberglas cloth impregnated with epoxy resin; they can be coated with concrete (three parts of sand to one part of cement) and made into outdoor planters or bird feeders; they can simply be sprayed with black paint to make a minimal sculpture. The rotor of an egg beater, a whole eggshell, an egg carton—any material or form at all—can serve as an armature.

Styrofoam makes a good support because it can be shaped with a warm knife. A great many things like radios and cameras come packed in Styrofoam, and if you heat a knife on the stove it will carve it easily. Styrofoam is not very strong but makes a good core and will be greatly strengthened if coated with powdered asbestos or vermiculite in polymer medium, acrylic paint, or Elmer's glue. It will still retain its lightness but will give a feeling of massiveness and solidity. A Mexican candelabra can be made from small plastic pill jars embedded in chicken wire and covered with papier mâché. Then it could be painted in bright colors and "varnished" with polymer medium or diluted Elmer's glue. The little jars serve as the candleholders.

Japanese dolls, which are very fragile-looking, are made by covering an armature of balsa wood with beautiful silks and brocades. So the possibilities for "sculpture" are unlimited, and ingenuity in devising an interesting armature can lead to all kinds of exciting new ideas. Lots of our throwaways can find a new life in an art form.

CERAMIC SCULPTURE

Sculpture in clay must be handled a little differently and a little more carefully than that of other additive materials. Building up a piece from plaster or from papier mâché is not too demanding, but because clay is fired to a very high temperature it is important that the piece be built up methodically and that there be no air bubbles trapped to cause trouble in the kiln. If the piece is intricate, such as a figure, it must have an armature to support it, and unless the armature can be removed, the piece cannot be fired. If it is a massive piece, such as a head, it must be hollowed out, because too large a mass of clay is almost sure to create a problem during firing.

Clay for sculpture is a little different from the clay that is used in ceramics. Sculpturing clay is coarser and heavier, usually red or brown, usually known as terra cotta, and usually mixed with grog. Grog is made from bisque-fired clay that is ground into small particles and added to a clay body to give it more strength without adding weight; it also adds an interesting, rough texture to the finished piece. As a rule, terra cotta is not glazed, and so compatibility in that area is not a factor for trouble.

Let us start by making a head (Figure 238), for which we can use either photographs or a live model if one is available. Sculpture of this sort is done on a revolving stand, because it is "in the round" and must be turned constantly while working to shape it correctly from all angles; if you are working from photographs, these should be views of the front, sides, and back, so that you will get all the proper proportions. A ten-inch square of

Aphrodite. Bronze. The epitome of grace and beauty, Aphrodite has been an inspiration for artists throughout history. Circa third century B.C. Greek. Courtesy the Trustees of the British Museum, London.

"The Dance." Henri Matisse. Bronze. 1911. One of this great artist's seemingly casual interpretations of classical beauty. He used this pose often in both painting and sculpture. Courtesy Nathan Cummings Collection. Photo by Malcolm Varon, New York. (left)

"Woman Standing." Alberto Giacometti. A bronze done in 1958. She stands nearly four feet tall, is exaggerated and drawn out, but nevertheless has a center of gravity and carries herself beautifully. Courtesy Nathan Cummings Collection. Photo by Malcolm Varon. (right)

"Phryné." Aristide Maillol. 1903. Terra cotta in a classical standing pose. This is a sophisticated sculpture in deceptively simple planes. Courtesy Nathan Cummings Collection. Photo by Malcolm Varon, New York.

Head of a girl. Terra cotta painted with natural earth colors. It was probably baked to hardness in the sun. Sixth century B.C. Roman. Courtesy the Trustees of the British Museum, London.

"The Teacher." A terra-cotta sculpture. Unglazed, but brought to a gloss by rubbing with seaweed. Contemporary. Israeli. Collection of the author.

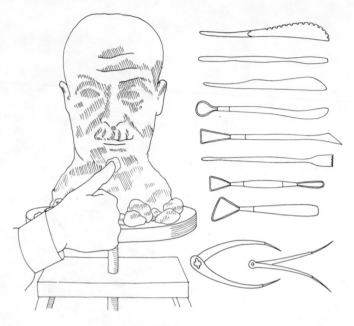

Figure 238

masonite makes a good surface to work on; this can be anchored with masking tape to a lazy Susan to make the revolving base. Other than that, you need a sculpturing tool—wood on one end for modeling and wire on the other end for scraping away; water and large cloths and a plastic for covering the piece to keep it from drying out between sittings, and about ten pounds of clay.

Heads and figures should be made less than life-size: a full-size statue tends to look enormous, and there is time enough when you are an expert to do a heroic piece. Working half-size is a good idea: all measurements will then be transposed to half the size they really are, which makes the calculations easy to manage. A starting piece should be realistic, and calipers are handy to this end for getting relative measurements. While you are working, look into a mirror from time to time and examine the muscle structure of your face. Every wedge of clay that you add on should form a plane made of muscle, and the closer you get to the true anatomy, the more lifelike the piece will be.

Start off the head by making a solid oval shape, from crumpled newspaper, wrapped around a foam cup or a piece of wood or any such form. This will be the armature, or core, of the piece. Attach this armature to the masonite base with masking tape, and then you are ready to begin sculpturing. Pinch off small chunks of clay—about the size of a walnut—and start building by adding these chunks all around the paper core. It is imperative that there be no air bubbles trapped; the pressure needed to add these chunks securely serves as a wedging operation and helps to expel any air that might be trapped. Continue adding clay in this manner until the head is roughly the size and shape that you wish. Then, with the modeling tool, start to mold the features by adding clay where needed and cutting away where there is too much. For the lips, form three small tubes roughly the shape of the lower lip and the two halves of the upper lip. Press them into place with your thumb, and then use the tool to do the fine modeling and to make contact with the clay at every point along their length. Use a moistened finger to get a final smooth effect. (To smooth large areas, use a moist sponge.) Form the nose, adding on for the nostrils, cutting away for the bridge. Then add on small pancakes for the forehead and cheekbones, press them firmly into place, and model them for the proper contours. For the eyes, cut away two hollows, roll two oval pieces the size of small olives, and press them into the sockets, modeling them into place with your modeling tool. For the eyelids, eyebrows, and ears, roll long, thin pieces and apply them in place: small pieces such as these should be fairly wet so that they will not crack. Hair may be added to shape the head and then modeled with a sharp little tool such as a hairpin or a toothpick.

If your work requires more than one sitting, cover it with a wet cloth, then with the plastic, to seal out the air. If you fasten the plastic to the masonite board with spring clothespins or hair clips, it should stay moist for weeks. (Figure 239.)

When the piece is completed, leave it for a day or two with just a damp cloth on it, and before it is really dry but hard enough to handle, turn it over and remove the newspaper core. Then scrape out the inside to leave a

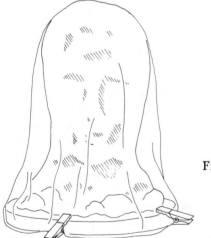

Figure 239

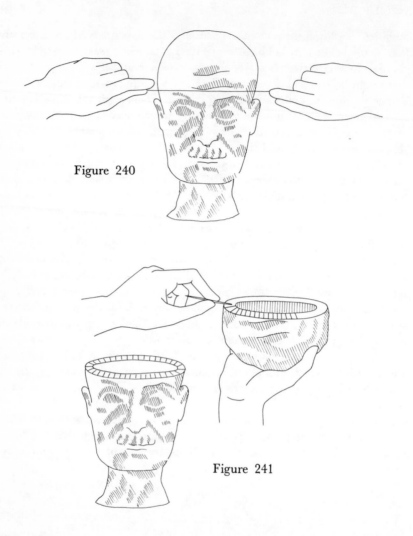

Figure 240

Figure 241

wall about half an inch thick all over. To do this, take a piece of piano wire, which is very thin and strong, and place it on the head at just about the eyebrows; pull it firmly with both hands through to the back, and now you have the head in two pieces. (Figure 240.) Scoop clay out of both halves with your modeling tool or a spoon or a small knife, and when the walls are scooped out to a fairly uniform thickness, you are ready to put the head back together again. Score the cut surfaces with a toothpick, mix a small amount of clay with water to make a paste, coat the two cut surfaces with this "slip," and put them back together again. (Figure 241.) Smooth the joint on the outside with a wet finger, model the hair back in place, and the head is as good as new. The slip that you have made acts as a glue, and the joint should be perfectly strong and secure. Sometimes, if you are not able to scoop out as much as you want to, you can make escape vents for trapped air by jabbing the clay here and there with a hatpin; air will seek out these little holes and come to the surface, where it can do no harm.

A small piece can dry in the air at room temperature. A large piece should be dried very slowly to avoid cracking: put it in a cool, closed cupboard—a drying cupboard—and you will slow down the drying process and prevent cracks. Thin areas such as the nose and ears will dry faster than thick ones, and for this reason it is sometimes advisable to put a damp cloth over these areas during the drying period, to slow them down and prevent them from pulling away. Some artists like to dry a large piece on a plaster of Paris batt, which draws the moisture out evenly. If cracks do appear, they can usually be repaired by moistening a large area and filling the crack with wet clay. The part adjoining the crack should be as wet as the new clay and should gradually blend with the dry areas so that there will be no strain. When the head is thoroughly dry, inside and out, it is ready for firing; it can be done right along with the other bisque pieces in your kiln.

An armature can be made from almost any material, but if it will not burn away and cannot be removed, then the piece must be cast to become permanent, or it can remain in its unfired state for as long as it will hold together, which might be for years. (And then again it might not; it's chancy.) The armature that you make can be of anything that will roughly assume the shape of the finished piece. If newspaper is used, it can be removed or left right in place to burn out during the firing, but any material that will not burn away cannot be put into the kiln. If it is not possible to remove the armature once the clay is added on, then it is best to use a different medium—plaster or self-hardening clay, or imitation sculpturing stone; all these are built up in the same way as clay but need not be fired. In making a figure with arms extended, for instance, it is possible to support the arms and body from the outside—improvising some sort of "crutches" to support the figure while it is drying. But there is only a fifty-fifty chance that such a figure could come through a kiln firing without cracking. Professional sculptors often use an armature of flexible lead wire and have their work cast in a permanent material such as bronze or, in these modern times, in plastic. Very often, plasticine is used when a piece is to be cast, or the newer modeling waxes that are put out by oil companies such as Mobil. They never dry or harden, and they can be worked over a long period of time and then cast in plaster.

For that matter, plaster can be used in much the same way as clay; in that case the armature is merely snipped off the stand with tin snips and the piece patinated to resemble bronze or terra cotta. In doing a plaster sculpture, mix small amounts of plaster at a time, because it hardens so quickly, and occasionally soak a small piece of cheesecloth in the plaster and lay it on to give strength to the piece. Surgical plaster dressings come already impregnated with plaster of Paris and need only be dipped in water to be ready for use. Never use plaster in clay that is to be fired; this would bring instant catastrophe in the kiln.

The finished piece may be rested on a pedestal or a plinth made from the same material as the sculpture, or on one made of wood that is cut or carved to set the piece off to best advantage. The plinth may be of common pine that is painted, or it may be of fine wood left in its natural state. The mounting of a piece of sculpture is very important, just as is the proper framing of a picture, and so if you have turned out a nice piece of work, try to do it justice in its presentation.

WOOD SCULPTURE

Wood sculpture is worked similarly to wood-block cutting; the tools used are more or less the same, but this is sculpture in the round, and the grain of the wood is an important factor in designing a piece. A smooth, sleek animal carved from ebony, which has practically no grain, will give a different feeling from one that is carved from rosewood or cedar, which is heavily marked, and the markings are usually significant in the finished work. The wood you use can come from faraway jungles or from the old apple tree in the back yard, but whatever the origin it should be studied well before you start work, so that the shape and grain can be employed to best advantage.

The wood must be well seasoned to avoid warpage later. Rare woods bought from a sculpture-supply house ordinarily are aged and ready to use; if you buy wood from a lumber-supply house, it should be kiln-dried when you get it, and if you pick up a stump or a log on a country walk, you will have to let it season slowly outdoors for at least six months.

Sugar pine is a good wood for the beginner, because it carves easily without chipping and is inexpensive and readily obtained. It is also quite uninteresting, in that it has no grain to speak of and doesn't take a good polish, because it is a little pulpy. The common woods for carving are mahogany and walnut, and I personally like teak: it can be carved in any direction, and having a natural oil it is nice to the touch.

The tools you need to start with are several gouges (chisels): a large and a small round gouge, a large and a small V gouge, and perhaps a straight chisel for roughing out. With these and a hardwood mallet, you knock out chips of wood until everything has been chipped away except the design. Files or rasps are then needed for smoothing, sandpapers and coarse terry toweling for polishing and waxing. (Figure 242.) The tools must be kept sharp while working, and for this you will need a fine carborundum stone with any kind of oil for lubrication, or an India stone, which can be used dry for light touch-ups because it has been impregnated with oil in the manufacture. You sharpen the concave side of the tool and remove the burr that forms on the convex side with a few quick strokes.

Hawk. A fierce totem of carved and painted wood.
Nineteenth century. Northwestern Indian. Courtesy
the Trustees of the British Museum, London.

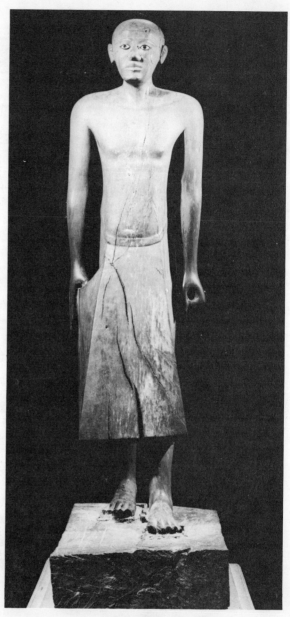

Portrait of Chancellor Nakht. In polychromed
wood, it is thought to be a true likeness. It is
remarkably detailed in its naïve lines. Circa
twentieth century B.C. Egyptian. Courtesy the
Louvre, Paris. Cliché des Musée Nationaux.

Burial mask. Modeled from shredded
hemp mixed with plaster, then painted
and gilded with gold dust. Probably this
was a death mask, attached to the
sarcophagus to ensure that the person
retained his identity in the afterlife. Circa
eighteenth century B.C. Egyptian. Courtesy
the Trustees of the British Museum,
London.

Girl's head. A portrait in ebony.
Contemporary. Haitian.
Collection of the author.

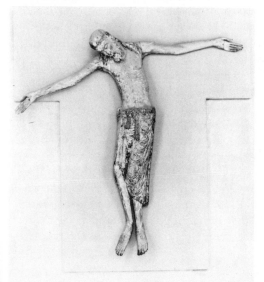

Christ on the Cross. Wood. Elongating
the figure was a device used to heighten
the mood of anguish. Twelfth century.
French. Courtesy the Louvre, Paris.
Cliché des Musées Nationaux.

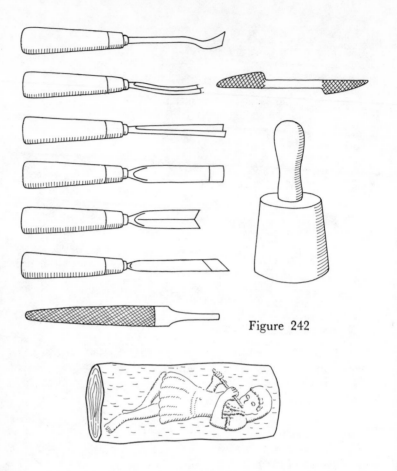

Figure 242

The block of wood should be securely anchored to a solid workbench by clamping it, nailing it, or fastening it down with angle irons. You should be able to work all around the table, but if you cannot do this by walking around it, you might drill a hole up through the bench and insert a huge screw right up into the block of wood. In this way it would be steady to work on and you may turn it on the screw to check all sides and angles.

Trace or draw the design with a felt-tipped pen. The sculpture can be in relief—that is, to be viewed from one side only—or in the round, in which case all planes must carry the same importance and must be worked with equal care. Start chipping away the background, working around the piece and turning it frequently to check other views. Start with large gouges and follow with ever smaller ones as you get down to detail. (Figure 243.) Mistakes can't be replaced, but usually a design can be altered so that mistakes can be incorporated. You can do anything you want to a sculptured figure, as long as it can "stand": that is, it can be caricatured as far as you want to take it, but as long as the center of gravity is right the figure is right. If the center of gravity is out of kilter, the sculpture is wrong and will never work.

After you have chiseled out your design with the mallet and gouges, use the rasp to do the final small work and the smoothing down. Then sand it, going to finer and finer grits, and oil or wax it. A good wax can be made by melting beeswax in a little turpentine in a double boiler. This mixture gives a soft, mellow, natural finish. Or it can be finished with boiled linseed oil, to which a little dry pigment may be added for a stain if you wish. A final burnishing with a small piece of hardwood gives a high luster, and your piece is ready to mount on a plinth or to hang on the wall if it is in relief. The plinth or pedestal is an important part of a piece of sculpture and should be chosen carefully. It can be an integral part of the piece, carved right along with the sculpture from the same block of wood, or it can be made separately, from similar or different material.

Sometimes cracks appear in wood from changes in temperature and humidity. A good filling for these spaces is softened beeswax; it is compatible with the wood and will still allow the crack to shrink and swell with the weather. The wood must breathe, and if you fill a space with a rigid material it will split somewhere else. Well-seasoned wood is less likely to crack than green wood.

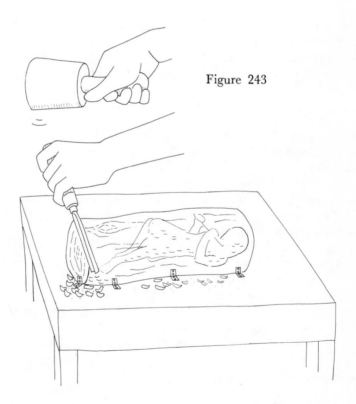

Figure 243

Yoritomo, governor of the Minamoto warrior clan. Made from blocks of wood laminated together, this 27-inch sculpture contributes in every line to the authority of this very important leader. Thirteenth century. Japanese. A National Treasure of Japan. Courtesy the Tokyo Museum.

Not all sculpture has to be done from a solid piece. Wood panels can be glued together with a good cabinetmaker's glue to form a block, and clamped overnight or longer. In this way, interesting effects combining end grain and cross grain can be gotten. Balsa wood and soap are good practice materials, as in Styrofoam; professional sculptors sometimes work a model piece from a block of plaster or wax before cutting into the wood.

Of course, if you have a good shop of electric tools, the whole job of sculpturing in wood can be very easy. You can do the roughing out with a jig saw or a band saw, gouge out large areas with a drill press, and with a small hand tool or flexible shaft do the final finishing and sanding.

Classic wood sculpture seldom has a finish on it other than something that will enhance the natural grain and color and preserve the wood. If you want a patina, it should be in subtle earth colors that are soft and compatible. If you want the wood gilded, you should do this gently, with bronze powders and a good grade of wax. Once you have put your heart and soul into a beautiful piece of wood, it should be able to stand on its own merits without trite embellishment.

STONE SCULPTURE

The carving of stone is a subtractive sculpture; that is, you start with a large mass, cut away parts of the material, and add nothing. Many kinds of stone can be used, the hardest being granite and the softest being limestone. The hard stones are most often brought to a high polish, but the soft ones are usually left natural, the roughness being part of the character. The highest grade of granite comes from the northern United States; limestones and soapstones are found almost everywhere. Marble is the most popular stone for sculpture, probably because of its natural veining and range of color, which makes it tempting to the artist who is always a little nonplused when faced with a blank surface. Marble is quarried just about everywhere in the world, but the very finest pure-black marble comes from Belgium.

A block of stone is seldom of a regular shape; one that is roughly a cubic foot in bulk will weigh in the neighborhood of a hundred and fifty pounds. Obviously, once it is set up for work it cannot be moved readily, and you should plan your work area and lighting ahead of time. The stand that you work on will have to be very sturdy, and the stone has to be set on it very firmly. This workbench should be freestanding so that you can walk around it to view your piece from all angles while chiseling. Roughing out can be done at regular table height, but finer detail is better seen from a higher point—at eye level.

Seal hunter. Carved and assembled from whalebone, walrus tusk, soapstone, leather, and rawhide. Contemporary. Canadian Eskimo. Collection of the author.

Sphinx of Tanis. This red-granite monument stands 7×12 feet, and today is in almost perfect condition. Circa twentieth century B.C. Egyptian. Courtesy the Louvre, Paris. Cliché des Musées Nationaux.

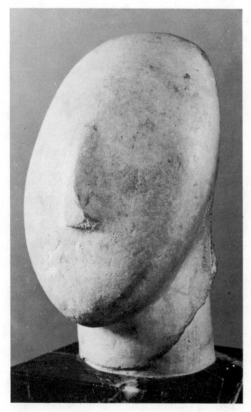

Head of a goddess. White marble. Perhaps
this was the beginning of abstract
sculpture. Circa twentieth century B.C.
Cycladic. Courtesy the Louvre, Paris.
Cliché des Musées Nationaux.

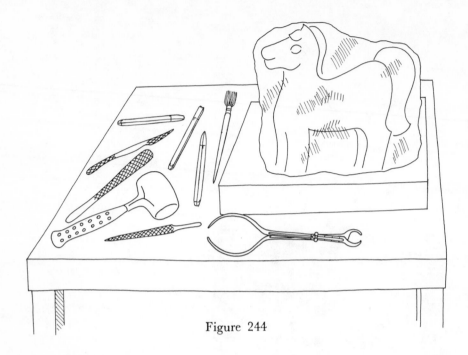

Figure 244

The tools needed to start are simple: several chisels similar to cold chisels—a short, stubby one called a pitcher, for roughing out the form, and a longer one called a point, for more detailed work; a claw bit, which is a toothed chisel; a heavy square-faced hammer; a rasp and some sanding papers; and a brush for dusting away particles as you work. (Figure 244.) The tools are highly tempered and should be sharpened frequently on a wet carborundum stone, because if you use a blunt tool you will do a lot of work with little result. Stone carving is a very dusty job, and a mask or a damp handkerchief should be worn over the nose and mouth; keeping wet newspaper on the floor helps to keep the dust down, but this craft is not recommended for anyone with respiratory troubles.

Soapstone and limestone can often be purchased in the local building-supply yard, and sometimes granite and marble too. You may visit a quarry and choose your blocks right there. The tools are adequate as purchased from the hardware store, or better yet, all your supplies can be had from a sculpture-supply house. Choosing your block is important, because the shape of the stone will give you ideas as to what to carve and how to go about carving it. Look for flaws, which sometimes can be incorporated to advantage into your design. Tap the stone with a piece of metal: a clear ring means the stone is solid, a dull thud means a hidden flaw. Veining in marble is natural and desirable, but all marble is soft and absorbent, and if you

pour water on it and dark "rivers" form, it means a softness that might be
disastrous to your work.

Look at your stone from all angles for a long time before starting to
chisel it, and then rough in your design with a grease pencil. When you are
sure you have sketched it to the best advantage, you might make a template
from zinc sheet or lead, but because you are bound to nick your fingers and
lead is toxic, the use of lead is unwise. The zinc "profile" will bend adequately around curves and help to keep you from glaring mistakes, but if
possible it is more pleasant to work free-form.

Hold the chisel in one hand and the mallet in the other. After a very
short working period you will begin to feel the strain of the pounding, and
so it is wise to stop and work gradually into longer periods. After a few days
of trying different positions, you will find the one that is most comfortable
for you, and at the same time you will fall into a rhythm, which is absolutely
necessary. Stone sculpturing is very hard work, and unevenness in stroke can
be extremely jarring to the arms and back.

Start off with the pitcher, to rough out your form. The first masses can
be cut away by cleavage, which is the breaking away of a large area of stone
at a given angle. To do this, file notches in the stone with the rasp, and then
insert the chisel into a notch, facing it away from the main body of the
block. Give it one sharp blow with the mallet, and the stone will split away
cleanly just where you have scored it.

Figure 245

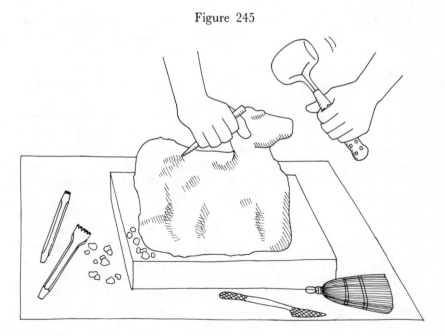

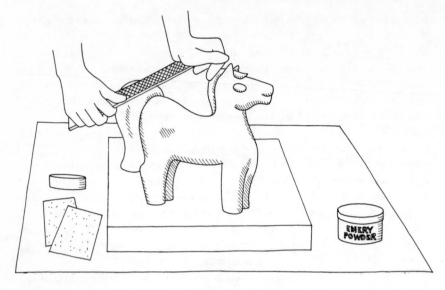

Figure 246

Continue roughing in the planes, working always in the round. Never allow yourself too much time in one area, because it is easy to overwork one spot and then find the whole aspect changed as you walk around it. (Figure 245.)

After your forms are pretty much as you want them, change to the claw bit and the point. Use them the same way, at an angle of about forty degrees, to carve away small pieces for finer detail. Where the piece looks pretty good, wet it down and polish it, first with the rasp, then with pumice stone and carborundum papers, and finally with emery powder formed into a pad with a nylon stocking. (Figure 246.)

It is not always necessary to do a piece fully in the round. A relief sculpture is one that appears to be coming out of the stone, the background left in the rough and the design polished so as to stand out. The hard, brittle stones will accept a high luster, but soft limestone and soapstone, which can almost be whittled with a penknife, are usually too granular to be smoothed off so that they're really shiny.

There are imitation stone-sculpturing materials, which may be cast or modeled into a rough shape and then chiseled and filed to give a hand finish just as in natural stone. These mixtures are usually made from cement and ground stone, and perhaps the same effect could be gotten by mixing sand with epoxy resin or acrylic medium. Some artists are using Styrofoam blocks —interesting, but not really the same thing as working a heavy stone with chisel and mallet. There is no substitute for the real thing.

METAL SCULPTURE

Sculpture made by welding metals at a heat high enough to melt them is extremely dangerous and must be done under controlled conditions. One must know how much oxygen and how much acetylene to use in oxyacetylene welding, and one must have knowledge of the process and precautions in-

"1973 2." A geometric sculpture of 11-gauge welded steel and copper. The organic shape of copper is brazed on and the center of gravity carefully calculated in order to balance on the tip. Naturally weathered patina of rust and oxidation. Forty-one inches high. Contemporary. American. Mark Eliot Schwabe. Photo by C. Lysogorski.

"Moon Head." Henry Moore. A bronze done in 1964. A highly stylized sculpture-in-the-round utilizing space as an integral part of the design. Courtesy Nathan Cummings Collection.

volved in arc welding. Both are high in fire hazard, producing temperatures of 6,000° to 7,000°. For that reason, these methods of handling metals should be learned at a shop or school where there is personal supervision to start.

Brazing, or bronze welding, however, is a simpler process. In this method of joining two metals, the parents are not actually fused: an alloy metal is used which has a relatively low melting point and which with a small amount of heat is sent by capillary action into the pores of the other metals. A small air-acetylene torch such as Prest-O-Lite, which has a premeasured supply of air and acetylene and only one gauge to worry about, is sufficient for brazing, and joining two unlike metals by this process is very simple. Practically any two metals can be joined, with the exception of aluminum, which is resistant to lead soldering too. There is a special brazing material for aluminum.

Sunburst. A high-relief sculpture made by brazing wire rods individually to a central core of wire. Five inches deep by sixteen inches in diameter. Contemporary. American. David Rose.

Sculpture made from any metal—steel or iron, for instance, which both rust—can be coated with bronze by brazing and will actually give the appearance of a bronze-cast piece. Brazing rods come in various alloys and give various results, so that one could "brass-coat" a piece in the same way by using a brass-colored rod.

No special cleaning need be done to the parent metals, but if they are very soiled or greasy, clean them with steel wool and vinegar or nail-polish remover—anything to cut the dirt—and the flux will do the rest. In the heat process, the two pieces are joined by butting or overlaying, then the torch is applied to bring them to faint red heat; they are fluxed, and the rod is applied to the heated area. The rod itself need not be flamed: the heat of the parents is enough to melt it. The joint hardens immediately, and so there are no problems of slipping or collapsing such as are met with in soldering.

Suppose you were to make a bug—a grasshopper—from found objects. The body could be a pair of pliers, the head a round top from a tin can; the legs might be two forks bent in half, and the feelers could be made from the brazing wire itself. When you have decided, either spontaneously or by presketching, just where each appendage should be, you are ready to begin construction.

With tin snips, cut the brazing wire into convenient lengths—one or two feet. Have a pair of tweezers handy, and for the novice perhaps an asbestos glove. Of course, your workbench and surrounding area are all protected with asbestos sheeting—fireproof roofing materials are good—and your plumbing-supply house will supply the brazing rods and the flux, along with all kinds of interesting junk for future purposes.

The flame on your torch need not be large. About a half inch is the most convenient to work with. Take the tin-can top and bend it in half to shape the head: a single fold, like a mantle, will do. With the torch, burn in a row of teeth along the jaw line by holding the flame to the edge of the tin for two or three seconds; it will melt right away. Now place the head on the pliers in such a position that the jaw of the pliers relates to the jaw you have just created. Hold it in place with the tweezers, and heat the pliers at the join. (Figure 247.) Dip the brazing rod into the flux, place it at the join, and apply the torch again, heating the heaviest part first and moving the torch gradually to the rod. In a few seconds, the "weld" will be made, and as soon as you remove the heat it will be hard. To cut the rod, simply apply heat to it and break it off.

The forks that are to form the legs will be attached in the same manner. Hold them in place with the tweezers, heat them, apply the rod, and make the join. For the antennae, simply touch the fluxed brazing rod to the spot where each feeler should be, and heat it for an instant; then break off the rod to the length desired.

The eyes can be two metal washers, or perhaps a piece of the rod, brazed on and cut. If you apply more heat to the stump, it will melt down

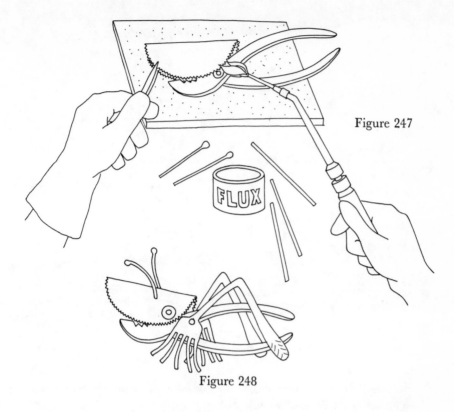

Figure 247

Figure 248

into a heap to form protuberances. And in no time at all, a sculpture has been created. (Figure 248.)

The piece may be polished with a wire brush or steel wool, or it may be painted with acrylic paints—all black, all white, or multicolored.

Tin cans can be cut and bent into flower forms, then the edges of the petals can be burned into interesting, jagged shapes. The flower can be brazed onto a rod for a stem, some leaves added, and the whole set into a flowerpot made from clay or cement or sheet metal. (Figure 249.) Interesting sculpture can be made from nuts and bolts, pins and spoons, anything. Actually, brazing is one of the simplest crafts because it involves nothing more than two metals, some brazing wires and imagination, and a steady hand.

Metal sculpture can be made with such simple equipment as some coat-hanger wire and a pair of pointy-nosed cutting pliers. Wire sculpture is no more than a three-dimensional extension of a line drawing, and doodling a drawing first is a big help in guiding the bending and twisting of the wire. As you get more proficient in making wire shapes, you can add sheet metals and solder or braze the joints to create solid sculpture.

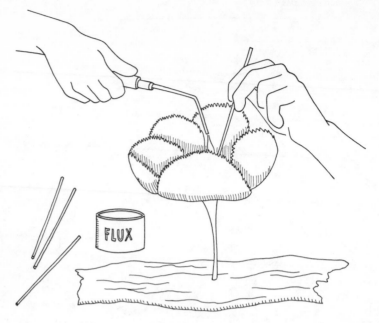

Figure 249

Soft soldering is another simple method of joining metals. Soft (lead) solder comes in coils, and because the melting point is so low, it is not necessary to use a torch; an electric soldering iron will do the job. The parent metals are cleaned and fluxed, and when the coil is applied to the heated joint it will flow onto the fluxed areas. The work can be done with a small propane hand torch with a low, cool flame, but it is easier to control with the iron. Solder is not really strong enough to join metals thicker than 18 gauge, because it remains flexible, and the weight of a sculpture might collapse it in time.

Soft solder can be used to coat another metal. For example, a stick man could be made from copper wire. While he is lying flat on a bed of asbestos, solder can be dribbled on him to give him shape and muscle. The original wire man is really an armature, and sheet metal can be cut and shaped or beaten, to be soldered onto him to form a solid sculpture. Abstract forms can easily be made with a combination of wire and sheet.

Sometimes, metals are not compatible with your method of "welding." The best solution for this problem is to visit your local welding shop where the men do auto repairs, and ask for advice. These men are always very helpful, and enthusiastic about meeting an artist. They will teach you lots of the tricks of their trade, and you only need translate them for your particular brand of studio work.

Tin-can Sculpture

Sculpturing from tin cans is a good introduction to this art, because the only equipment needed, besides a torch, is discarded tin cans, heavy gloves, tin snips, pointy-nosed pliers, and an ice pick; and for the serious tin artist, serrated snips, crimping shears, and soft solder.

The tops and bottoms of the cans are easily transformed into art works by a few well-placed cuts around the rim, and the body of the can might be used either in the round or flattened to form sheet for larger projects. The tin can is quite a sophisticated object—really a thin flash of tin on a base of another metal such as iron or zinc; usually the can is lacquered to protect the contents, and so it seldom rusts. The metal from tin cans is pliable, easily soldered or brazed, and takes paint well; holes for either decorative or useful purposes are easily punched with a nail and hammer or with an ice pick, and small sections can be bent to shape with a pair of tweezers if pliers are not handy.

Here are a few ideas for simple objects made from the round tops of cans of any size.

A base for a candleholder can be made from three can tops of different sizes held together by punching two holes in each center and then anchoring them together with a paper clip. The smaller, top circle can be snipped in five places (good design usually uses odd numbers) and the five petals bent up to support the candle. The larger, middle circle can be snipped into many sections, and each one curled with the pliers to make a frilly base—the smaller the section, the frillier it can become. Then the last circle, on the bottom, can be nicked in three places, and each section bent down at right angles to form legs, to keep the heat of the candle from marring the table.

A candelabra or a wreath can be made by anchoring many of these medallions to a form made from coat-hanger wire, then perhaps dabbing a little glitter on with Duco cement or Elmer's glue, or painting them with any water-based paint mixed with a little of the glue to make it adhere; and a string of tiny colored lights might be woven through for a festive, holiday decoration.

A hanging lantern can be made from the body of a can by removing the top, stuffing the body solid with rolled-up newspaper to make it rigid, and then punching a design all around the sides with an ice pick. Two larger holes at the top can be strung with wire for hanging, and a candle can be placed in it which when lit will show up the punched design. This makes for interesting outdoor lighting, because the high sides of the can will form a windbreak, and so it can be hung on a tree or a bush without too much worry.

A little decorative angel can be formed very simply from any can top by making four cuts about two thirds of the way in toward the center. Two opposing flaps are nicked with the snips to make feathery edges, then bent back

Figure 250

to form the wings. The bottom section stays in a straight wedge shape to form the long skirt, and the top section is curled forward with the pliers to become the bodice, with a little colored ball or glass marble or a gumdrop nestled in it to form the head. A little glue can be dabbed on here and there and braid or paper cutouts added to make her bright and cheerful.

Larger, more complicated constructions are made by soldering sections together that have been formed either from the flattened body of the can or from the round top, which has been fluted, crimped, or curlicued into elaborate designs. A crowing rooster might have a body made from several layers of flat tin sheet, serrated, soldered together in series to form feathers, then painted in bright colors, while a sweeping tail and full cockscomb can be added, preformed, the better to show its superiority. (Figure 250.)

A peacock with a grand, spreading tail is easily made by cutting several three-quarter rounds into many thin, feathery strips, curling them, painting them, and attaching them to a body made similarly to the angel's, with feet instead of a skirt and a small, pinched-in head made from a half top, held high and proud, with a beady eye repoussé with a nailhead.

Working with tin is great fun, a little like doodling with scissors and paper. Who knows what masterpiece will come from this doodling? Did not Picasso see in a discarded automobile radiator the world's most famous goat?

12

Casting

WAX MODELS FOR CASTING

The making of jewelry by casting methods is not always for the purpose of reproduction in quantity. Some designs are not possible to create directly in hard precious metal, and so they are formed from a soft, malleable material such as plasticine or wax, and then cast by any method that the craftsman sees fit to follow. And in any metal that he wishes. This forming of a preliminary model lends itself easily to all sorts of fantasies not otherwise possible. The professional modelmaker may use wood for his prototype, as soft as balsa or as hard as maple, or he may use a plastic or a soft white metal. But waxes are the most frequently used, and they come in many degrees of hardness, so that he can run the gamut of working them all the way from manipulating them by just the heat of his hand to carving them with an electric tool. His shop is set up with his flexible shaft always at hand, ready to use, and his waxes and carving tools ready to be heated in an alcohol lamp for incising a fleeting idea. (Figure 251.)

Intricate designs can be fashioned from wax in an instant. You can pass a piece of wax through the flame of a candle and form it into a soft, undulating shape that it would not be possible to make from a rigid material. You can warm a small dentist's probe on the kitchen stove and groove a length of wax rod in no time at all and with no scratch marks to cause trouble. You can make perforations in a ring blank with a hot pointed tool such as an ice pick, but you must blow these holes out immediately, so that the warm wax does not flow back in and close them up. You can attach appliqués of wax on wax with just a touch of a heated tool, and you can dribble little droplets of hot wax onto another wax surface to give the effect of granulation, which is a long, tedious process to do directly on metal. (Fig-

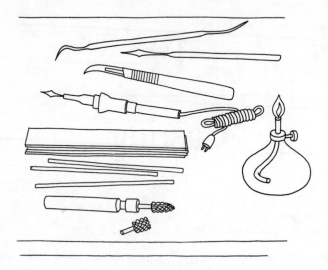

Figure 251

Figure 252

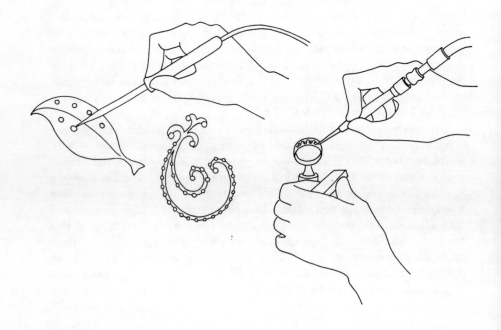

Sybil. A direct-wax study for a bronze casting. Made from oil-derived wax slabs Sixteen inches high. Contemporary. American. Stephen Werlick.

ure 252.) You can work a curled-up leaf, a fanciful little spiral, an intricate setting for an odd-shaped stone—any interesting shape can be achieved with a minimum of equipment, ready for casting.

The microcrystalline waxes that are used by the professional jeweler are the same as those used by your dentist. They are highly refined and come in small sheets, rods, sticks, and wires of standard gauge. Then, there are waxes available in good quantity too. These are put out by such large oil companies as Mobil; they're a by-product of the petroleum industry. They are sold in twelve-pound slabs, and they can be built up into full-scale models and then used in a lost-wax process of casting, perhaps in bronze, perhaps in plaster or a synthetic resin. The wax for a large sculpture is kept warm and malleable in a basin of water on a hot-plate, and is built up much like a ceramic sculpture—small chunks added to a central core. They harden quickly to an almost permanent state, and then can be carved with a heated tool for fine detail, if necessary.

Candle wax or household paraffin or beeswax is adequate for the beginner and can be worked to produce reasonably satisfactory results where fine detail and definition are not necessary. In cold weather they will keep their shape, but in hot weather it is well to keep them cool by plunging them into a basin of ice water now and again while working, so that the lines don't get blurry from the heat. Professional waxes are hard at room temperature and will retain their shape indefinitely; your craft-supply house has a variety to choose from. They also stock an assortment of wax models all ready to be cast.

CUTTLEBONE CASTING

Of the several ways to make cast jewelry from a model, the cuttlebone method is the simplest. While it cannot produce too detailed an object, it is quick and adequate for small jobs. The cuttlefish has a spongy inside and a hard shell outside; the cuttlebone is ready as it comes (by the pound from the craft-supply house) to receive the impression of the model. The only thing you have to do is to set up this already prepared mold to receive the model and then, later, the molten metal. Not much else is needed—some powdered graphite, borax, a crucible and a pair of tongs for holding it, and a propane torch for melting the metal. (Figure 253.) Your workbench, of course, is protected with asbestos sheet, and asbestos gloves are always handy when you are working with molten metals.

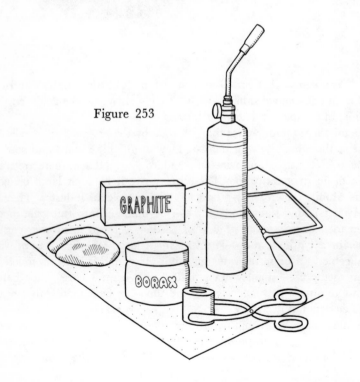

Figure 253

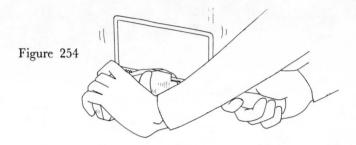

Figure 254

Take two cuttlebones and level off the spongy sides by rubbing them on a flat surface of sandpaper laid flat on the workbench. Place the spongy sides together and with a hacksaw trim the edges into a rectangular shape so that they can stand on end for pouring. (Figure 254.) It is not so important to straighten the sides, but the top and bottom ends should be level to avoid trouble later. This is all the preparation needed.

Suppose you want to match a favorite ring, or perhaps make a new model in hard wax. Lay the two "fishes" side by side, spongy side up, and press the ring flat into one fish until it is buried in the spongy surface to exactly half its width, palm (shank) side toward the top of the mold. Make three keys for aligning the mold by sharpening one-inch pieces of wooden matchsticks at both ends and inserting them into the fish, near the edge, at three places. (Figure 255.) They will remain in place throughout the operation to act as guides in reassembling the mold later for pouring. Place the second fish on top of the first, and press the two together as hard as you can with your bare hands. (Figure 256.) Open the mold carefully and remove the ring very carefully, and you will have made an exact impression of the ring in the two cuttlebones—half a ring to each fish. Now you must make a hole or a funnel-shaped opening into which you will pour the molten metal; with a sharp knife, cut a small cone shape out of each fish, leading from the top of the mold to the shank of the ring. (Figure 257.)

Figure 256

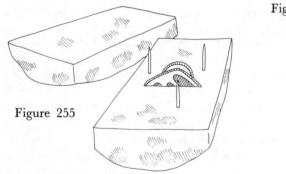

Figure 255

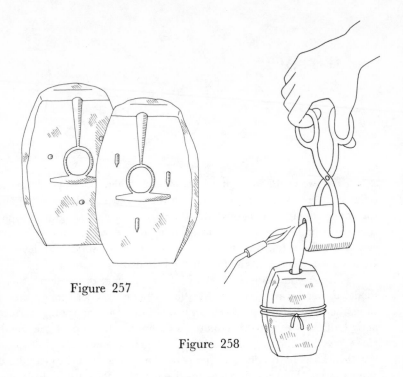

Figure 257

Figure 258

Gases will be trapped as you pour the hot metal into the mold, and so some means of escape must be planned or the mold will blow up. To make these vents, scratch several thin lines from the ring all the way outward to the edge of the mold. Then dust the whole mold with a feather, or blow on it, to remove any particles that may have settled in the impression, and you are ready to make the casting.

Put a little graphite on a square of thin cotton, close it up to form a bag, and dust a very light coating onto the surfaces of the fishes to protect them from the heat of the melted metal. Put the two halves of the mold together, lining them up accurately with the keys, and tie them together securely with strong string or binding wire. Stand the mold firmly upright with the cone-shaped sprue hole at the top.

The amount of metal needed to form the ring is estimated by water displacement. Set a full glass of water into a small pan, and drop the model into it. The amount of water that spills over into the pan is the amount of liquid that will be needed to replace the model; use one and a half to two times as much metal, to allow for the excess to fill up the sprue hole. Scrap silver may be used for this rather crude method of casting, providing it is clean—that is, has no solder on it, which would spoil the color. (Of course, precious metals such as silver and gold need not be used at all: less expensive metals are available, and alloys are interesting. But it would be very inadvisable to wear jewelry containing lead: it's toxic, and so it would be too easy to get lead poisoning.)

Dust the crucible with borax to avoid oxidation of the metal and apply heat with the torch. When the borax is glazed (melted)—and be sure to glaze the lip, where the metal will be poured out—place the silver in the crucible, sprinkle a little more borax on top of it, and apply the torch again. When the metal is melted (it will seem to be spinning) pour it into the sprue hole, keeping the torch on it so that it does not solidify while you are pouring. (Figure 258.) Fill it to the top of the hole, and allow it to sit for a few minutes to harden. Then break the mold open, and remove the cast ring. Put it into a cleaning solution of Sparex or 10 per cent sulphuric acid, then wash it in clear water. Saw off the "button," which is the excess metal that filled the sprue hole, file the edge smooth, polish it with a rough cloth, and you are all finished.

One precaution to be observed in cuttlebone casting is that there be no undercuts in the model, which would prevent removing it cleanly. And care must be taken in pouring the hot metal, because if air gets trapped in the impression it could cause the silver to spatter up. Goggles should be worn if possible, and in any case your *face should be out of range of danger.* It is wise to work over a basin of sand; in case the mold has a leak, the sand would act as a catch for the molten metal. Precautions must be taken, too, if you mix your own acid: *always add the acid to the water, never vice versa.* Use copper tongs when working with this cleaning solution, label it clearly, and keep it out of reach of children.

SAND CASTING

Sand castings as bas-relief wall sculptures are being used a great deal today. Old, reliable cement is coming back into fashion, to be hung on the walls of contemporary homes, and the new plastic media are very tempting for castings; they, as well as plaster and liquid metals, all take well to this simple technique.

No mold is needed for this method of reproduction. Instead, an impression is made in sand by any means possible, and any material in a molten state is poured over that impression. When the casting is hardened, it is removed and will be an exact mirror image of what went on in the sand. Not much is needed in the way of supplies: some sand, a form to contain it, some talcum powder, some glycerin from the drugstore, and a large dropcloth to keep the mess off the floor, and you are ready to begin.

The sand, which can be as fine or as coarse as you wish, is packed down in a wooden form or in a strong cardboard box—anything that can contain its weight. There should be a layer of sand about two inches thick, and the walls of the form should be at least five inches in depth; this will allow the

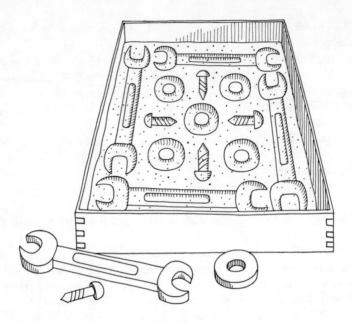

Figure 259

casting to be four inches deep. For a small casting, the walls need not be so high, because the sand need not be so deep, but for a large casting perhaps they will have to be even higher, and perhaps the sand bed will also need to be a little bit thicker.

Put one quart of water in a jar and add one tablespoonful of glycerin, which will help to keep the sand in place. Moisten the sand with this mixture, adding more of the liquid if necessary, pack it firmly into the form, level it off with a flat piece of wood—the edge of a ruler or tongue depressor—and dust it all over with talc.

For a relief sculpture, in which the design stands away from the background, you can impress your design with any instrument that comes to mind. As a rule, designing for sand casting is not too detailed, and a stick or a match or a pencil can be used for the drawing. Anything that will leave an impression in the sand—and anything will—can be pressed in to become part of the pattern. Marbles, tools, gears, pebbles, drinking straws, canapé cutters, buttons, coins, corrugated paper—any mark that is put into the sand now will become a raised area on the casting later. (Figure 259.) With some designs, you can go in deep and with others just scratch the surface for interest.

The design, of course, is reversed in the casting. If you press in a marble, for instance, and then remove it, the hole it has made will be filled with

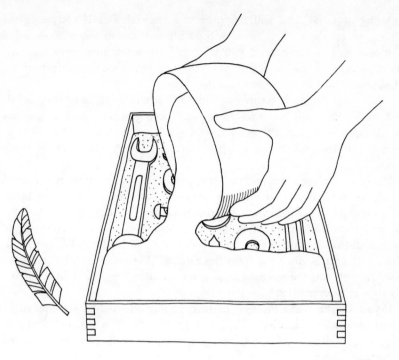

Figure 260

Figure 261

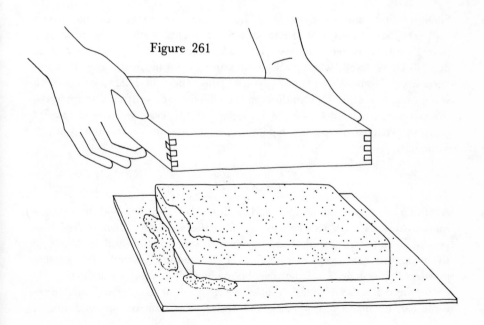

the casting material, and will reappear as a mound. But if you leave the marble in place, the casting liquid will go around it, and when hardened it will appear as a depression. If you wish to have something incised on the finished piece, then the object should be left in place on the surface of the sand, so that it will be impressed into the casting.

When your design is completed, dust the whole thing over very lightly with a feather or a soft brush to remove any loose grains of sand, and sprinkle it all again with talcum powder, which will act as a separator. Be sure the whole surface is covered with a thin layer of talc, and then you are ready to pour.

Mix your casting material according to directions, and pour it carefully, covering the sand slowly with a thin layer. (Figure 260.) Allow this to set for a minute or two, so that not too much weight is suddenly put onto the sand, and then pour the rest of it, to the thickness desired. Allow it to harden undisturbed, and then turn it over onto a dropcloth; lift the sandbox off, pulling it gently away from the casting. (Figure 261.) The sculpture is now finished, and the molding sand is retrieved and put back into its box, ready for the next casting.

If you wish to make multiple castings in any one design, you can make a model of wax or plasticine or putty or wood. Also, you can use that first casting as a model for all the others, just by pressing it into newly packed sand for each casting.

Small Castings

Small castings can be done in a shoe box or in an egg carton, which could reproduce twelve little flat-backed ornaments, each neatly in its own nest. Fine sand is generally used for small objects, but large pieces can be done in coarse sand, which will give texture to the finished piece. It is not necessary to use the binder of glycerin; the sand will hold together with water only. Sometimes, depending on the chemistry of your casting material, the talc might not work as a parting agent; in this case, you would have to find out what to use as the separator for the particular medium you are working with.

Candle Molds

Anything that can be poured and will harden can be used to make a sand casting. A wick can be inserted into the sand and then melted wax poured in to form a candle. And if you wish some of the sand to adhere to the wax, you can use a coating of acrylic medium instead of a parting powder. Papier-mâché castings can be made if the paper is shredded finely enough and the "soup" made dilute enough to pour. Plaster of Paris or cement can be made less weighty and easier to handle by the addition of aggregates of any inert material: shredded asbestos, vermiculite, plastic foam, cat litter! As a matter of fact, any of the inert materials can be mixed with acrylic or epoxy resins to form a casting on their own. The hobby shops have a wealth of ideas, but if you are working on a large scale, the building-supply house and the boat-building yard are good places to buy supplies in large quantities.

Two-piece Sand Molds

Objects in the round or small pieces of jewelry can be cast in sand by making the mold in two pieces, so that the castings can reproduce both sides.

This casting is done in a flask made up from two lengths of pipe or cardboard tubing stacked one on top of the other. The upper one is known as the cope and the lower one as the drag, and the two pieces together should be large enough to accommodate the model with at least an inch to spare all around. The keys for aligning the two parts consist of two or three pins attached to the edge of the cope, and matching ears hollowed out of the drag. The two parts of this "box" are packed tightly with sand, and the model is placed between them to make a solid impression.

Let us mold a coin or a double-faced medallion about an inch and a half in diameter, and later cast it in metal. You can purchase the flask all ready to use, or you can easily make one from two 3-inch lengths of 3-inch-diameter pipe. With epoxy cement, glue three small rods or nails or matchsticks onto the rim of the cope at irregular intervals, and three little hollow tubes or washers onto the rim of the drag to accept them. In this way, the flask can be assembled so that the two halves meet perfectly each time you use it. You need only a shallow flask to mold a flat coin, but if you make it deep you can use it later for little standing figures or pieces of jewelry: for large sculptures, the flask has to be at least two inches larger all around than the model. You will need fine sand known as French sand, a wire sieve or some window screening, some glycerin, a feather, and talcum powder to act as a parting powder. And you are ready to begin.

Sieve about a pint of sand into a small bowl and mix it with about half a cup of water and a tablespoonful of glycerin—enough to make it hold together firmly. Place the drag on a hard, flat surface such as masonite or plywood, pack it firmly to the brim with the sand, and level it off perfectly smooth with a table knife. Dust it lightly with talc, press the coin flat into the sand to half its depth, and then dust the whole surface with talc again. Place the empty cope on top of the drag and hold a pencil upright against the edge of the coin to act as the sprue gate. Pack the cope firmly with sand, holding the pencil in place so that it doesn't move around. Now the model lies between the cope and the drag and has made its impression on the sand in each half of the flask. The pencil will form the pouring hole.

Remove the pencil sprue pin carefully, separate the two halves, and remove the coin. You must make a few small vents in the cope to allow gases to escape during the casting process, and so, with a long needle or a piece of straight, stiff wire, pierce the sand from the edge of the impression to the surface of the cope, and the gases will seek these exits instead of exploding.

Dust the two meeting surfaces of the drag and cope with talc; now everything is ready to receive the molten metal for the casting. Put the two halves of the flask together, carefully lining up the pins with the ears and being sure that the sprue hole has not become blocked with drifting sand. Pour in the molten metal, and allow it to cool. Lift the cope off the drag, and you have made your first casting. Saw or nip off the sprue pin, and polish the piece as you wish. Smooth the sand in both halves of the flask so that it can be used over and over again for the same model or a different one.

A very simple casting flask can be made from tin cans, using powdered pumice from the hardware store instead of the specially sifted sand. Cut the top off one flat can (such as a tuna can) to make the drag; cut off the top and bottom of another to make the cope. Place them together and glue matchsticks to the side of the cope and plastic drinking straws to the drag to make the keys for assembling. (Figure 262.) Before you pour in your casting medium, be sure that you have made adequate air vents that come right to the surface of the packing material.

It is not always necessary to have a two-piece mold. If the piece has a flat back—perhaps an earring or a pin—then the impression can be taken only on the surface of the drag and the molten metal poured slowly into it. But if there are undercuts, or more than one surface to be reproduced, then a two-piece mold is necessary. More than two pieces are not feasible in sand casting.

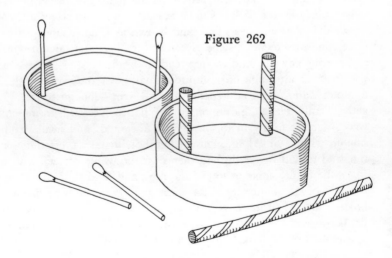

Figure 262

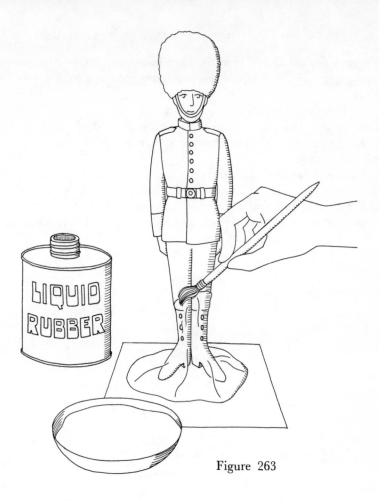

Figure 263

RUBBER MOLDS

Making a mold from rubber is a relatively easy method of reproducing. Liquid latex or one of the new synthetic-rubber molding compounds is used. The model can be made from clay, wax, or plasticine, or it might be a store-bought trinket: a whole battalion of palace guards could be made from one lone gendarme purchased in the five-and-dime. So let us go about making an array of palace guards.

Stand the model upright on a smooth surface such as formica, and coat it with soapy water to act as a separator. Pour a small amount of the liquid rubber into a saucer, and with a small brush paint on one layer, covering the gendarme completely, and extend the rubber at the base out onto the formica for about half an inch to form a flange all around. (Figure 263.) Let this coat dry for fifteen minutes, then paint on another coat, covering it completely again, and repeat this procedure until you have five or six thin coats.

Allow the rubber to cure overnight, and then peel it off the model like a rubber glove, turning it inside out. (Figure 264.) Wash it, dry it, and dust it with talcum powder. Then turn it back right side out, and it is ready for the first casting.

Place the mold upside down in a paper cup or a wide-mouthed jar, and start pouring in the casting material. (Figure 265.) Put in a small amount and jiggle it around to allow all the little crevices to be filled and to get rid of air bubbles, and then fill it up to the flanging lip. Let it stand until it is

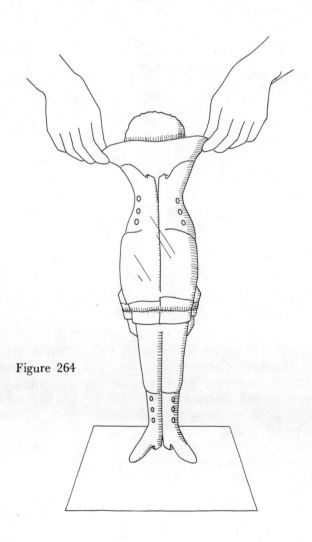

Figure 264

hard, and then peel off the rubber, again inside out; the first casting has been made. The talc has acted as the parting powder, making the casting easy to remove; you can make as many guards as you wish, just by repeating the casting process for each one.

If the mold is large, it may be necessary to make a casing to support it so that it will not stretch out of shape under the weight of the casting material. To do this, cover the rubber mold with soapy water or liquid detergent as a separator and then give it a rigid "overcoat" of papier mâché or plaster of Paris. Leave the model in place while you do this, or else stuff the mold with cotton or tissue paper so it will keep its shape while the casing is being made. Be sure the rubber is thoroughly dried and hardened before making

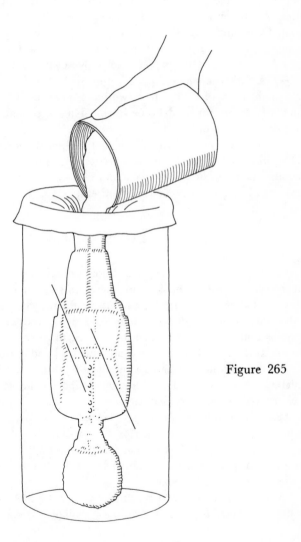

Figure 265

the casing. The overcoat should be made in two pieces so it can be opened easily; to do this, place a thin metal strip, or shim, down each side of the mold to keep the two halves separate. When this outside support is hardened, the rubber mold can be set into it each time a casting is poured, and you need not worry about the casting slumping when you pour the metal in.

Undercuts are allowed in a rubber mold. But if the model is very unwieldy, it might be necessary to make the mold in more than one piece. This breakaway mold is made similarly to a plaster mold, with very thin strips of tin or copper to make shims that go from the model to the last outside coat of rubber. Tape the shims on at right angles to the model, and coat the whole thing with the liquid rubber as before. When the rubber is cured and removed from the model, it will come away with as many seams as you have shims. When you are ready for pouring, you will have to put the mold together by sealing each seam completely, so the casting liquid cannot seep through; you can do this with masking tape or electrical tape. Then place the rubber mold in its papier-mâché overcoat (which is also in several pieces), and tie the whole thing together with string. It is advisable to apply six or eight coats of rubber to a two-piece mold, as stretching is not now so much a factor and it needs to be sturdy. Then it should be cured for two or three days before you use it.

Practically any liquid medium that will harden can be used to make a casting in a rubber mold, and it is particularly suited to the synthetic liquid "metals." Being so simple to make and to use, it is convenient for classroom work with young children or senior citizens.

PLASTER MOLDS

Plaster molds, which are used for slip-casting ceramics, are simple to make but messy. You will be up to your elbows in plaster, and so, once you start, you should allow uninterrupted time to see the project through to the end.

Molds can be made in as many pieces as necessary; a general rule to follow is that there must be one more piece to the mold than there are undercuts to the model. A simple mug with no handle, and wider at the top than at the bottom, can be cast in a one-piece mold, because there are no undercuts. Add a wide foot to the model, and you are creating an undercut, so your mold will have to be a two-piece one. Add a "sprigged-on" design to this base, and you have created another undercut, so your mold will have to be in three pieces. The reason for this is that the plaster must be pulled away from the clay, and as soon as this pulling away becomes impeded, then there has to be a separate section that can be freely lifted off with no impediment to catch and break.

Any simple object with no undercuts can be molded in one casting of plaster. However, a sphere, for instance, cannot be molded in one piece, because no matter how you turn it, half of it will be undercut. As soon as there are complications—an arm on a figure, or a heavily incised or excised design —the mold must be constructed in more than one piece. But a mug with a handle or a teapot with a spout and handle sometimes has the body cast separately, the handle and spout separate pieces that are welded on later.

An object that you wish to mold in one piece must be at least as wide at the top as at the bottom; otherwise, you will not be able to remove it from the mold. The pieces that you cast will be exact replicas of the original, and if you cannot remove the original from the plaster, then you will not be able to remove the castings either. If you were to encase a pyramid-shaped piece base down, you obviously could not remove it once the plaster had hardened, for the base would be too wide to pass through the narrower, tip end. But if you encased it tip down, it could be removed easily, once it was shrunken away from the plaster. This kind of mold is always used for ceramic castings, and the principle of slip casting is that the plaster absorbs moisture from the liquid clay, and as it does this the clay dries and then will drop away from the plaster wall.

Every plaster mold is made from a model. The model can be an original design that you have executed in plasticine or wax for the purpose of reproducing, or it can be any object that you care about and would like to make copies of.

Suppose you try your hand on a very simple object, a one-piece mold of a flowerpot saucer. The materials needed are five pounds of plaster of Paris from the hardware store, a dishpan, and several large bowls for rinsing your hands. You will need about two pounds of moist clay and a small jar of very soapy water to act as a separator; a small paintbrush, some strips of floor linoleum or rigid, heavy plastic about 8×24 inches, and several long strips of rag that will be used for tying around the mold for security.

The wall of the plaster mold must be about an inch thick in order for it to absorb the moisture from the clay properly—this, of course, being the purpose of the mold. So the form to hold the plaster must be two inches wider and an inch deeper than the saucer. The strip of linoleum or plastic is pliable and can be manipulated to take and to hold any shape you wish. This will form the outside wall that is needed to contain the plaster. It is absolutely necessary that there be no leaks in this form, but it is a good idea to set the whole thing in a dishpan anyway, so that if any leaks should develop, the plaster will run into the pan rather than onto the floor.

Make a flat bed of the moist clay an inch thick and two inches larger in diameter than the saucer. (This clay must be considered waste clay, because if you attempt to fire clay with any specks of plaster in it, there is a good chance that the piece will explode in the firing and ruin everything in the kiln.) Place the saucer face down on the bed and press it firmly into the clay. Now take the strip of linoleum and set it into the clay bed an inch from the edge, encircling the saucer and overlapping itself at the ends by at least an inch. Seal this overlap completely with moist clay and tie the form around with some rag strips to keep it from springing open. Press the form deep into the clay bed and seal it all around the bottom with more clay to be sure that no liquid plaster can seep out anywhere. Now the model is embedded securely, surrounded by a wall, and ready to be reproduced. Note that you are making a replica of the bottom, or outer, side of the saucer. The thickness of the slip in the castings will later form the inner side of the saucer shape.

Brush the whole inside of the form—wall, clay, and saucer—with soapy water as a separator, and be sure to cover everything. This will prevent the plaster from sticking anywhere so that it would be difficult to remove.

Now you are ready to pour the plaster. You can use plaster of Paris from the hardware store, but for finely detailed molds you might wish to obtain the finer, molding plaster from your ceramic-supply dealer. The proportion of water to plaster is two quarts of water to five pounds of plaster, approximately, and it is always advisable to have a little extra plaster on hand before you start mixing. The plaster will start to harden in about twenty minutes, so you must work quickly once you start to mix it.

Put about one quart of water into a large bowl. From the five-pound bag, start pouring the plaster over the spread fingers of one hand, which acts as a sifter. Stir it frequently with your hand as you are pouring, to get rid of lumps, and when the mixture is as thick as heavy molasses and quite free of lumps, pour it into the linoleum form slowly. When the saucer is covered, jiggle the form a little to get rid of air bubbles, and then fill the form to the top or to at least an inch higher than the saucer. Jiggle the form again and then allow the plaster to set; if you have any left, pour it into soaped pie tins to make plaster batts, which are useful to have for drying moist clay. The batts should be about half an inch thick, and it is a good idea always to have some on hand—you have to get rid of your extra plaster, and you should never wash it down the drain; it would clog it completely. Any excess after this should be allowed to dry slightly and should then be scraped up and thrown into the wastebasket. (Always rinse your hands in a bowl of water, for the same reason.)

Allow the mold to set for several hours to dry. First it will become hot, and then it will cool off. When it is cold and hard to the touch, peel off the linoleum form and turn the hardened plaster upside down—really right side up. Remove the clay bed and remove the saucer, and there you have a negative mold to make any number of positive saucers from. If there are any little air holes, leave them alone, because they will appear as bumps on your clay piece and can be removed easily. But, if there are any bumps, you should sand them down, because they will appear as holes in your clay piece. It will be about a week before it is ready to use, because it must lose all its own moisture before it can remove the moisture from the clay slip. As long as it is wet, it will feel cold to the touch; when it feels comfortably room temperature, it is dry enough to use, and you may pour your first piece.

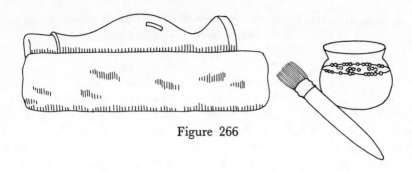

Figure 266

Two-piece Plaster Molds

Now that you have made a one-piece mold, which is the simplest to make, try doing a two-piece mold—this time, a vase with a foot. This, obviously, could not be extracted from the mold unless the mold could be opened to free the foot. You must construct it, therefore, so that it opens—by molding it in two halves. The preparation is the same: you will need the linoleum strips, the moist clay, soapy water, plaster, and the rest.

Fill the vase up completely with clay, level to the brim, packing it tightly so that there are no pockets for the plaster to run into; they would form undercuts, which would prevent your removing the mold intact. Now form a cylinder of clay about an inch in diameter and two inches long, and add it to the top center of this clay filling. Remember that, wherever the clay is, the plaster cannot go; therefore, this solid "stovepipe" will end up as empty space and will become the pouring hole later for the slip casting.

Prepare a bed of clay one inch thick, and lay the vase down on the bed on its side. Build the clay up to exactly the center line of the vase, and level it off with a knife. (Figure 266.) Make this clay bed rectangular and two inches larger than the widest part of the vase, and make it also come up to the center line of the stovepipe. The top of this pipe will butt against the linoleum wall, so that it will later be accessible from the outside. You have now bedded in clay exactly half of the vase.

Place the linoleum strip, which in this case should be about six inches wide, around the vase, sealing it in place as before with more clay. This mold is being made on its side, but later it will stand upright, so make the wall at the bottom of the vase as straight as possible, so that it will stand level later, during the slip casting. It is necessary to have guides for later putting the mold together accurately, and at this point you should make three "keys" to act as these guides. Roll three small cones of clay about half an inch high and place them on the bed at irregular intervals. Press them into place, being sure there are no undercuts and that they are wider at the base than at the top. These will come out as depressions in the plaster; the second half of the mold will have the protrusions to fit them.

Now brush everything that is inside the wall with soapy water and mix your plaster as before. If the vase is large, it will probably take three times as much as the saucer mold did, so start with three quarts of water and about fifteen pounds of plaster. Mix it as before, alternately sieving it and stirring it free of lumps, and then fill the linoleum form to the top, being sure that the vase is covered by at least an inch of plaster. Allow it to sit undisturbed for a few hours, until it has hardened, then turn the whole thing upside down, but do not disturb the linoleum wall. Dig out all the clay bed including the keys, but leave the vase and the stovepipe intact. The first half of your two-piece mold is now exposed, and you are ready to make the second half. Grease everything inside the wall with the soapy water, being sure not to skimp on the plaster surface and the depressions made by the keys. Mix a new batch of plaster and pour it to the top as before, covering everything within the linoleum wall.

When this half is hard, remove the linoleum and separate the two halves of plaster, prying them apart gently with a blunt knife if necessary. Remove the vase and the pouring-hole clay, and even off the outside bottom with a sharp knife so that the mold will stand level when upright; allow it to dry separated for about a week, when it will be ready for use. In the assembling of the mold for casting, the keys will always place it together accurately, and that is why they have been placed irregularly—perhaps two on one side and one on the other. When the two halves are together, the mold will appear as a solid piece of plaster, with a hole in the top for pouring slip.

Undercuts

Molds may be made in three, four, or more pieces, depending on the shape of the original. An object with many undercuts will have to be molded in many pieces, because each undercut requires a separate molding. The plaster is rigid and cannot be separated from the slip if there is a "hook" anywhere for it to catch on. With this in mind, the mold must be designed in as many pieces as necessary to avoid such a calamity. In making a mold of many pieces, mark off your original model with a grease pencil, outlining a section for each undercut. Then bed everything in clay except one section, and cast that. Leaving the plaster in place, in that section, remove the clay from the next section and cast that, and continue doing this until finally your original is bedded completely in plaster. Each section of the plaster mold must release easily from the original form, because your slip casting will be an exact replica of the original, only more fragile. If you are designing your original piece for the purpose of molding it, bear this in mind and try to avoid undercuts where possible. An original piece made only for casting need not be fired, and so it can be built solid from waste clay or plasticine or wax.

A well-made mold will keep indefinitely and be good for any number of

castings, and fine molding plaster will last longer than ordinary plaster of
Paris. But in due time it may become "dead"—that is, lose its power to absorb moisture—and when that happens, you have to discard it. But if necessary, you can always use one of the castings as a model for a new mold,
remembering that there has been a small amount of shrinkage as in any
casting process.

Any object, animate or inanimate, can be molded in just the same way.
If there are undercuts, the mold must be made in as many pieces as is necessary to accommodate them; if anything other than clay slip is used for the
casting, then a separating agent is necessary. Usually a grease works well,
but some of the casting materials might not harden properly on a grease
base, and so directions on packages should always be followed. Companies
put a great deal of money and research into their labels. Read them.

LIFE CASTS

It is quite possible to make an actual mask of a face from a plaster cast, provided the subject is willing and has confidence in the artist. The subject lies
down, comfortable and relaxed. (This is a messy job, so don't try it on the
living-room sofa.) You smear the face and neck generously with vaseline,
having protected the eyes, nostrils, and ears with pads of absorbent cotton.
The closed eyes should have a heavy coat of the vaseline to seal the cotton
and keep it in place. For breathing, the subject holds a large straw in his
mouth—or any large, hollow object that will project out at least two or
three inches.

Now the plaster must be prepared, and once that is done you must
work quickly to be finished before it starts to harden. It is always best to
have too much plaster ready, rather than too little, and any that is left over
should be allowed to harden and then be thrown out—never washed down
the drain.

Buy a five-pound bag of casting plaster from the hobby shop. (This is
less formidable than ordinary plaster of Paris.) Put one quart of water in a
basin or a large bowl, and slowly add plaster by pouring it over your spread
fingers, which act as a sieve. Every few seconds, mix the solution with your
hand to get rid of lumps, and continue alternately pouring and mixing until
it becomes about the consistency of cream.

Start applying the plaster by laying a thin coat over the whole face,
smoothing it on carefully with your fingers. (Figure 267.) Once the first
layer is on, covering the subject's face completely, apply more in thick globs,
working as quickly as possible. The part next to the face should be an accurate mold, but the outside coat needs no special attention, just as long as it is
at least an inch thick. Be sure not to interfere with the breathing apparatus,
because if any bits of plaster fall into the tube they can cause choking.

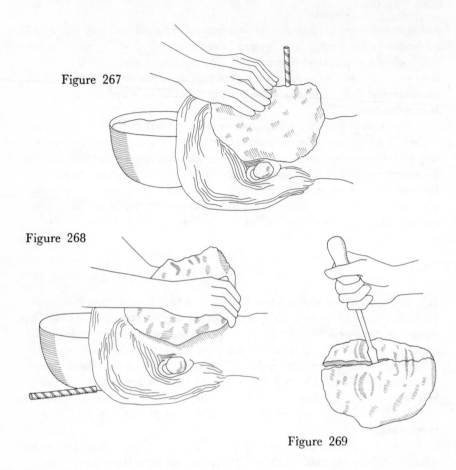

Figure 267

Figure 268

Figure 269

Apply the plaster just to the ear line and hairline, and down a little way under the chin; if the plaster goes into the ear or the hair, you will not be able to remove it.

Allow the plaster to dry sufficiently to be firm when you pull it off the face. (Figure 268.) The time will vary, but the plaster should be ready in twenty to twenty-five minutes. Remove it very slowly, easing it off from all sides, being careful not to touch the inside. Set it aside to dry for a day or two, and then it is ready for casting.

This of course is a negative, and from it the positives will be made. This may be made from clay, bronze, or plaster, from papier mâché or resin, or perhaps from one of the synthetic powdered stones that are mixed into a liquid for casting. Clay shrinks away from a plaster mold, and so it is easy to remove. The other materials, however, may be difficult to remove unless the mold can be opened. If you wish, you might "break" the mold as soon as it is removed from the face; this is a ticklish job. Make a score mark down the center of the outside with a screwdriver or a chisel, carefully force in a few wedges from forehead to chin, and gradually crack it apart. (Figure 269.) It is advisable not to have a clean, straight cut, because when the cast is dry, the unevenness will serve instead of keys for putting it together accurately. Once the break is made, do not handle it any more until it is dry, when the two halves should fit together perfectly.

In olden days, before photography was invented, death masks were made of loved ones in this manner. Today artists think nothing of molding not only a face mask but the whole figure. And the figure need not even be in repose, because an action figure can be made by casting various parts of the body and then putting them together. Made in this manner, store dummies need no longer be lifeless figures but might be reproductions of actual people.

LOST WAX

Lost wax, or cire perdue, is the commonest technique for casting an intricate piece of jewelry or sculpture. In this method, the original model is made from wax and is then encased in plaster. The wax is then melted out of the plaster investment and replaced with molten metal. Because the mold must be broken to retrieve the finished piece, it can be used only one time, and it is therefore known as a waste or a lost mold. This is the method that your dentist uses when he takes a wax impression of your teeth.

Suppose you make a silver casting of a key ring that you have modeled freely from beeswax into roughly the shape of a football. You will need plaster of Paris, a propane torch, a hot-plate (or the kitchen stove), and a crucible in which to melt the metal. In the case of gold and silver, which have high melting temperatures, this could be a graphite vessel which you coat with borax to avoid oxidation: but an alloy such as pewter, which melts at a much lower temperature and does not oxidize, can be heated in pyroceram (Corning Ware) or perhaps in an iron or steel frying pan.

Pyroceram, used for the nose cones of space rockets, undoubtedly could withstand high heat as well as the graphite does. The only other materials needed are a mixing bowl for the plaster and an empty cardboard container (perhaps a sawed-off milk carton), asbestos gloves, and an asbestos sheet on the workbench. With these you are ready to begin with the molding of the model.

Start with about three pounds of plaster and one pint of water. Put the water into a bowl and slowly add the plaster by sieving it through your spread fingers. Stir it frequently with your hand to break up lumps, and mix it until it has the consistency of molasses. Then pour it into the cardboard carton. Drop the wax model into the wet plaster, push it about an inch under the surface with your finger, and shake the box gently to remove air

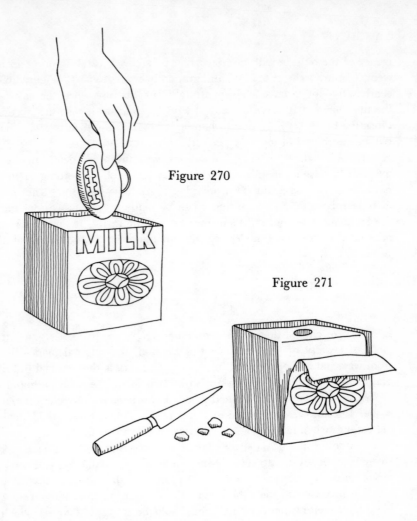

Figure 270

Figure 271

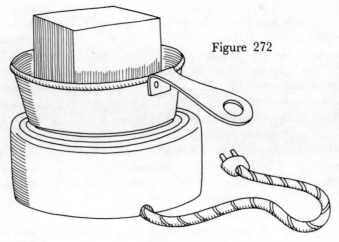

Figure 272

bubbles. (Figure 270.) When the plaster is set but still cold to the touch—
hard but still workable—use a small pointed knife to carefully dig out a
small funnel-shaped opening just to the surface of the wax football. It
should be about a quarter inch in diameter at the point of contact with the
model. This will be the sprue hole, through which the wax will be melted
out and into which the metal will be poured later. Now allow the plaster to
dry and harden thoroughly, which will take a few days, and then tear away
the paper carton. (Figure 271.)

Put a pan or a pot on the hot-plate on low heat and into it place the
plaster mold upside down. The heat will warm the plaster and melt the
wax, which will run out the sprue hole, leaving the mold empty, ready
to receive the liquid metal. (Figure 272.) Be sure that every last bit of wax
is allowed to run out, perhaps by inverting a pot over the mold briefly to be
sure it is receiving enough heat all the way through. When you are sure that
the mold is empty, stand it upright and put it aside to cool.

Now the space where the football was is empty, and you are ready to
fill it with silver. Dust the crucible with powdered borax, including the
pouring rim, and heat it with the torch until the borax is shiny and glazed.
Drop the silver in and continue heating it until it melts;
keep playing the torch all around the crucible to keep it
hot so that the metal remains liquid. Pour the molten
metal into the plaster through the sprue hole,
filling the mold right to the top, and
jiggle it a little to get out any air bubbles.
(Figure 273.)

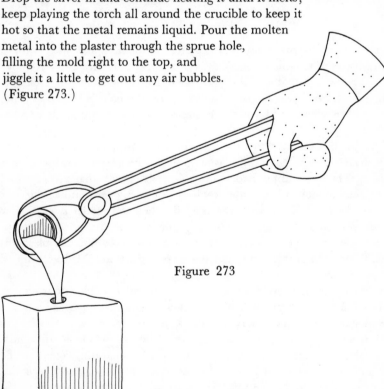

Figure 273

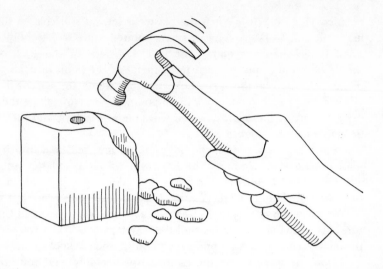

Figure 274

Let it stand twenty minutes or more, to solidify, and then with a few sharp blows of a hammer break the plaster open. (Figure 274.) Remove the silver football, with the metal that filled the sprue hole still attached. Saw off this "button" and file the rough edge on the ball; solder a loop on, hang it from a chain, and you have completed a one-of-a-kind, original work of art.

If the piece is involved, with extensions and depressions, it may be necessary to have some holes in the plaster to allow the gases to escape during the casting. These would be made from thin rods of wax that are attached to the original model with a heated tool—an ice pick or a spatula; the wax rods would melt out along with the model. When the model is cast, they would reappear as sprue pins (or buttons) and may be cut off with a snipping pliers and then filed smooth. (All the wax that goes into the plaster is removed during the burning out, and the empty spaces are filled with metal during the casting.)

The cast piece can be of gold, silver, or any other metal, or it can be made from one of the many new synthetics that keep appearing on the market. Epoxy resins or pure acrylics will harden satisfactorily, as well as the casting cements that resemble natural stone and are available from art-supply dealers. Certain materials may need special separating agents to be applied to the plaster mold before casting. It is always wise to check this with your supplier. And some materials will shrink in the process; if this is a critical matter, check with him on that too.

"Three Wise Men."
Lost-wax casting. The
forms were
individually cast in
18K gold and sterling
silver, then polished
and assembled on a
white marble base.
Mounted on a
rosewood plinth.
Eleven inches high.
Contemporary.
American. James
Schwabe.

Making a Hollow Mold

Another way to make a waste mold is to build a core from clay, cover it with a thin layer of wax, and model the wax into the final finished form. Then cover that completely with a thick layer of soft, moist clay, making the top of this clay coat flat. Allow it to dry for a week or so, then place it in the oven or in an open fire outdoors, where the wax will melt and run out. Turn it and shake it occasionally to be sure that all the wax has escaped.

Keep it in the heat while you melt the metal for the casting. Then turn the clay form upside down so that it rests on its flat top, and pour the molten metal into the channels where the wax used to be. Let it sit for an hour until the metal has cooled and hardened, and then chip away all the clay with a chisel or a sharp stone. You have now made a hollow casting, and the mold has been destroyed, making it a "waste mold."

As the wax model in cire perdue has been melted away forever and the mold is broken to remove the casting, duplicates can be made only by repeating the whole process. Obviously, there will never be an exact duplicate, human error being always with us.

In olden days, primitive peoples used materials at hand to sculpture unsophisticated heads and figures: clay from the earth, wax derived from the sap of trees, and the metal melted from scrap—perhaps from the spent cartridges on a battlefield. Today's ecology-minded craftspersons are going back to these ancient ways, with unusual and sometimes very interesting results.

CENTRIFUGAL CASTING

Centrifugal casting is the most accurate method of duplicating small objects. Any design, no matter how intricate, can be reproduced by this method, and, most important for the professional, multiple castings can be made all in one operation. These castings can all be of the same object, or they can be an assortment of different objects, even different sizes. A permanent mold can be made so that the artist can later make as many identical reproductions of each piece as desired.

The models are formed, and a rubber mold is made of each one individually. These molds are then cast in wax, and the waxes are all set into a single plaster investment. Then they are burned out of the investment, and the impressions left in the plaster are filled with molten metal. It is a lost-wax technique, but no other method of duplicating can produce such fine intricacies and delicate undercuts with as much accuracy, because the force of the centrifugal action sends the metal into every negative space in the plaster mold. While the principle is simple, the centrifuge, which whirls around at a tremendous rate of speed, *can be extremely dangerous*. The craftsperson must be very well organized and certain in the understanding of the principles involved before attempting an actual casting in molten metal.

The equipment needed is special, and the materials used must be of the finest, to withstand the pressures that will be put upon them. You will need sheets of unvulcanized rubber and a vulcanizing frame for molding the original model. You will need wax and plaster of special, jeweler's quality, and all your supplies should be purchased from the jewelry-supply house.

You should have a vulcanizer, a wax injector, a vibrator, an evacuator, a burnout oven, and of course the centrifuge and crucible. All these things are necessary, but some of them could be improvised by an ingenious craftsman for a home workshop.

You should have four C clamps, some talc, borax, benzene, and plasticine; a small flexible rubber mixing bowl and spatula, a debubblizer, tongs, a torch, some powdered borax, asbestos gloves, and a metal pail for water. Then you are ready to begin. (Figure 275.)

First off, you must have the model that you wish to duplicate. This can be a store-bought object, or you may design your own original. Try designing your own—say a little silver bird in flight, about an inch long, with every detail carved in, and perhaps carrying a sprig of olive branch for good luck.

The model, as in all methods of casting, can be made from soft "white metal" or from one of the synthetic waxes of varying degrees of hardness. You can carve it from a very hard wax requiring an electric tool, or you can model it by hand from a softer one. In any case, you must use a wax that has a melting point above 300° F, for that is the temperature it will reach in the vulcanizing process and you don't want it to melt prematurely. Make the model exactly as it will appear in its final form—the more accurate it is

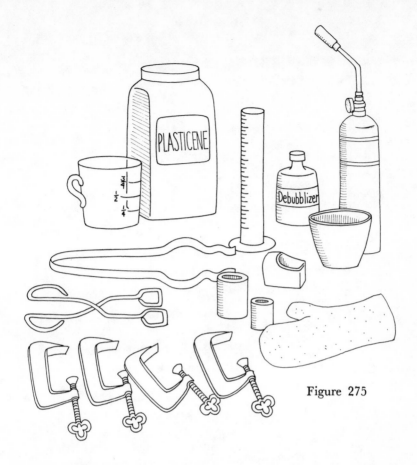

Figure 275

now, the less finishing work will be required at the end. Keep in mind, however, that the finished piece will be fractionally smaller than the original, because of shrinkage of the metal in the cooling-off period.

When the little bird model is finished, you have to devise a passage so
that you can get to it once it is transformed into wax. This passage—called
the "gate" or "sprue hole"—will be the opening through which the casting
wax, and later the final metal, will be forced in the different stages of the
casting process. Remember that everything that is solid now will become
empty space later, and so you will construct a solid "sprue pin," which will
form this gate. Make a wax pin in the form of a rod about a quarter of an
inch in diameter and an inch long, and attach it under the bird's wing or to
any inconspicuous place by touching both the tip and the spot with a heated
tool and welding them together.

Now the model is complete and ready to be cast into a rubber mold so
that you can duplicate it as many times as you wish. For this, you will use
thin sheets of unvulcanized rubber packed into a thick metal frame similar
to a picture frame. You will cure this in an electric vulcanizer or in the
kitchen oven.

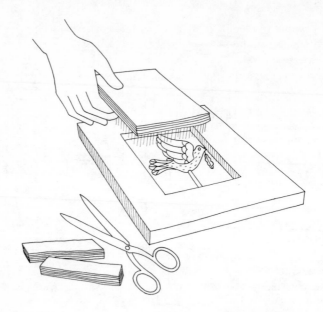

Figure 276

Figure 277

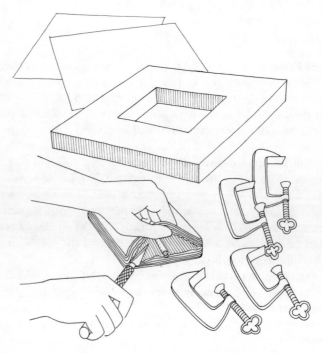

Before packing the mold, trim six rubber sheets to the exact size of the window of the metal frame and then clean them off with a little benzene to be sure they are free from grease. Place three sheets in the frame and lay the model on top, placing it so that the sprue pin extends to the edge of the rubber and hits right up against the metal of the frame. (Figure 276.) Now place three of the rubber sheets on top of the model, and sandwich the whole thing between two flat pieces of rigid metal such as aluminum or steel cookie sheets, and clamp it all tightly together with C clamps. The frames come in several thicknesses, and the thickness of the model will dictate how many sheets of rubber are needed: the frame should accommodate the model without any bulging or sagging and it must be packed level with the rubber. Sometimes two sheets are enough, sometimes more are needed.

Now the rubber mold is ready to be vulcanized into a solid mass. Set it into the oven at 300°; in about thirty-five minutes it should be welded together, or cured; remove it, and let it stand until it is cool enough to handle. Then remove it from the frame and slice it open, using a very sharp X-acto knife. Start slicing where the sprue pin shows, and cut carefully all around the rubber to separate it into two sheets. (Figure 277.) When the rubber is completely cut open, remove the model and set it aside. You now have a two-piece permanent mold that has an exact impression of the model plus sprue pin and can be used over and over to create as many little birds as you wish. The inside surfaces of the rubber will be jagged where you have cut into it, but this will in no way affect the wax casting. The next step is to inject a microcrystalline wax or a dental wax into the empty rubber mold. In cool weather a soft wax may be used, but in hot weather it should be a harder one, so that it will hold its shape. Dust the inside of the mold with a little talc held in a dabber made of stocking or a linen handkerchief; this will act as a parting powder, or separating agent, and make it easier to separate the mold later. Put the two halves of the mold together, lining up the edges accurately, and clamp it closed with several C clamps spaced around the edge. Now, the only opening in this rubber mold is the gate where the sprue pin was, and so it is necessary to use pressure to force the hot melted wax into this little sprue hole and send it into all the empty spaces that were left when the model was removed.

The machine for injecting the wax works by air pressure; it consists of two upright hollow tubes connected to a reservoir of wax. The tubes are heated with a torch, which melts the wax, and as air is pumped into one tube, the hot wax gushes up the other tube like a geyser. So, position the sprue hole on the tip of the hot tube and pump the melted wax into it. (Figure 278.) This is similar to pumping air into a tire (you could use a small bicycle pump for the source of pressure for injecting the wax).

The wax will harden almost immediately, and then the mold is opened and the wax model lifted out, with the sprue pin kept intact. Repeat the wax injections for as many castings as you wish; each casting must have its

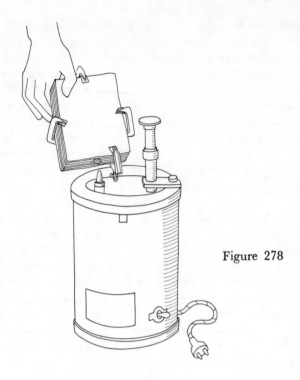

Figure 278

own wax impression, because from now on the process is a lost-wax method. The waxes are invested in a plaster form that will be heated to melt them out again, and the empty spaces will be filled with metal—gold or silver or perhaps bronze.

The waxes are now ready to be set into the plaster investment.

Each model has a sprue pin, and these, when melted out, will become the channels through which the molten metal will flow into the mold. But these are tiny, narrow channels, and so, to make the pouring easier, you construct a "sprue button," which will form a funnel or sprue gate leading into those channels. This sprue button can be formed from wax and later melted out, but it is easier to form it from plasticine and then remove it before putting the investment into the oven. To do this, form a little plasticine ball one inch in diameter and insert the waxes into this button by means of the sprue pins. You can fit quite a few waxes into it, by varying the lengths of the pins; of course, the smaller the models the more of them the sprue button will hold. They can be packed in close together just as long as they are free and don't touch one another.

Now that the waxes are set up, you are ready to mold them in plaster. The plaster used for the investment must be of dental or jeweler's quality, because it will be subjected to very high heat and also because you want a fine material that will mold the models with no loss of detail. The plaster must be contained in a form to prevent it from flowing free, the form in this case being called a "flask." This flask can be made from a length of steel pipe about three inches in diameter and three inches long. During the heating process the plaster will expand a little, and so the flask should be lined with a strip of asbestos cloth to absorb this expansion.

Center the prepared sprue button on a six-inch square of cardboard, then place the flask around it. There must be at least a half inch of space all around the models; if any of them are too high you will have to reposition them. (Figure 279.) (Larger objects of course would need a larger flask.) The flask should be at least a half inch higher than the tallest wax, so that the plaster will cover the waxes entirely, and this extra amount of space must be left all around the circumference of the waxes as well. When everything looks right inside the flask, seal the bottom edge to the cardboard base with plasticine to make it leakproof, and now you are ready to prepare the

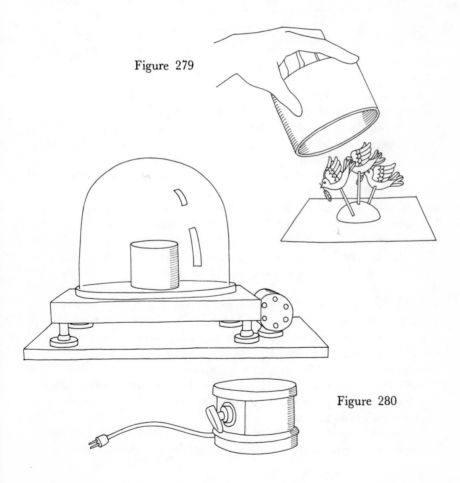

Figure 279

Figure 280

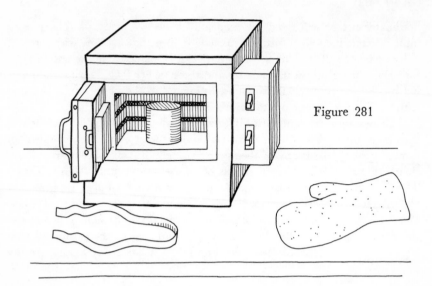

Figure 281

investment. Using the rubber bowl and the spatula, mix the plaster with water according to the directions on the package. Some investments call for 2 parts powder to 10 parts water, and some are in the ratio of 4 to 10, so you must follow the proper proportions for your particular material. When it is thoroughly mixed, place the bowl on the vibrator for a minute or two to get rid of any air bubbles. Now, to reduce the surface tension and so decrease the chance of new bubbles forming on the waxes, brush some debubblizer (12:1 mixture of strong soap and peroxide) over them, and then brush a little of the plaster on for further protection. Pour the plaster into the flask not quite to the top, and place the flask immediately into the evacuator. The vacuum created will cause the plaster to bubble up, thus freeing any air that has become trapped despite the precautions. (Figure 280.) Remove the flask from the evacuator and add as much more plaster as you need to fill it to the top again, then allow it to sit undisturbed until the plaster hardens—at least an hour. If you don't have an evacuator, you should try to expel as much air as you can by gently agitating the flask while filling it: it is important that as many of the air bubbles as possible be gotten out. (A handy craftsperson could make an evacuator using an old vacuum-cleaner or refrigerator motor.)

When the plaster investment is quite hard (when it is no longer cold to the touch), turn the flask upside down and remove the plasticine button, and leave everything else intact; the wax models now are embedded in the plaster contained in the flask.

The next step is to melt out the wax models, thereby leaving empty impressions in the plaster for the metal castings. This is done in the burnout oven, which is like a small kiln with a pyrometer. (Figure 281.) The wax must be burned away slowly so that it vaporizes instead of merely melting out. First it will turn to carbon, and as this carbon burns off, the investment goes from a sooty stage to pure white. If there is any soot remaining on the plaster, it means that the burnout was not complete.

Place the flask in the cold oven, sprue holes down, and slowly bring it to a temperature of 1,200°. This will take six to eight hours; at the end of that time the waxes should be completely burned out of the investment. Turn off the kiln but leave the flask in to keep it warm, because everything that is used in the actual casting of the metal must be hot enough to keep the metal flowing. But not so hot that it will destroy the plaster. In the case of your silver bird, you would maintain the flask at a temperature of 750°; if you were to cast it in gold, you would have to maintain it at 1,000°.

If you look at the bottom of the flask (tongs are a necessity from now on), you will see the concave sprue gate with as many little holes—sprue holes—as there were models invested, and each of these holes is the gate to its own impression. Each was a wax sprue pin leading to its wax model, which has now been melted away. The crucible holding the hot metal is shaped like a little Dutch shoe, with a hole in the toe that will fit into this concave sprue gate to send the molten metal into each impression.

At this point you are ready for the actual casting, and things must be very well organized, because once the metal is melted it must be poured as soon as possible, to avoid a breakdown of the molecules. The plaster mold is kept at the proper temperature to receive the molten metal: if too hot it will damage the metal by keeping it liquid too long; if too cold it will solidify it too suddenly; neither is desirable.

The centrifuge used for casting is the same as that used by dentists for making inlays. (Figure 282.) (In fact this method of duplicating a wax im-

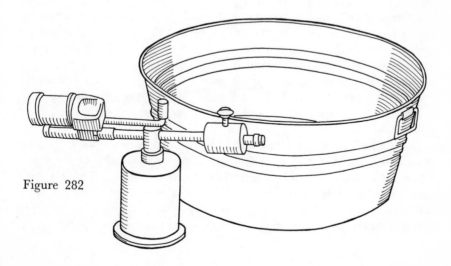

Figure 282

pression was invented by a dentist; he found it almost as painful to himself as it was to the patient when he had to pour molten gold into a cavity.) The centrifuge is a very simple machine. It consists of a horizontal arm on a strong spring, which is wound up. When the spring is released, the arm will swing around in a circle. The flask with the plaster impressions in it is placed in a receptacle on the very end of the arm, and the molten metal is placed in a crucible just in front of it with the toe nested in the sprue gate. The centrifugal force of the turning arm throws the hot metal into all the empty spaces in the plaster, and all the wax models will now be cast in silver.

Wind up the centrifuge so that it will be set when you need it. To do this, grasp the end of the arm and turn it two full turns clockwise. Pull up the pin that is set into the base, and it will act as the stop to hold the arm at this tension.

Caution must be observed at all times; it is a good idea to practice winding the centrifuge, a little at a time, until you get used to the action and understand it perfectly. Once you release the holding pin, you cannot stop it. If the arm is filled with hot molten metal and everything is not perfectly synchronized, the metal could spatter, causing serious injury. Observe its action first with nothing on the arm, then gradually work up to a full load. Get a demonstration when you buy the equipment, and practice under supervision until you feel confident. Your centrifuge should be set into a round metal washtub, and both should be anchored to the workbench firmly with long screws. In this way, the tub would serve as protection in case of any accident that could cause spattering.

With everything in order, you are ready to start the actual casting.

The silver may be melted right in the crucible on the arm: a good method because it saves having to heat the crucible separately. Everything that the metal will touch must be hot enough so that it will not cause it to solidify too soon. The amount of silver needed is measured by the water displacement of each model, and one and a half to two times as much metal should be used so as to fill up the sprue gates and the button. This is really a precaution to be sure that there will be enough metal to fill all the impressions completely, and the amount of excess that you need will have to be learned from experience. It depends on the size of the models and on the number that are being cast. The excess of "waste" metal is quite all right to use in future casting in a proportion of one to three with new, unused metal.

Put a little powdered borax into a bag made of nylon stocking, and dust the whole crucible with it. This will help to prevent oxidation of the metal. Cover the crucible entirely, not forgetting the toe area. Heat it with a torch until the borax melts, and then put the needed amount of silver in. Apply the torch to the crucible, bringing both it and the metal up to temperature slowly. (Figure 283.) As soon as the metal is molten, remove the hot invest-

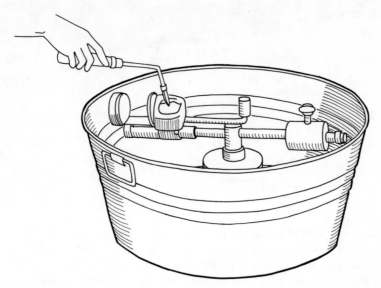

Figure 283

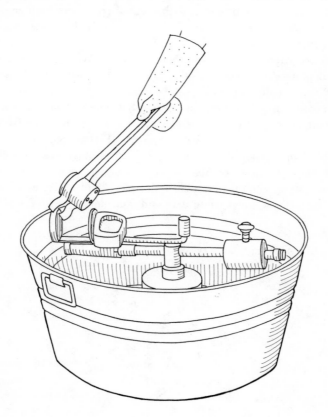

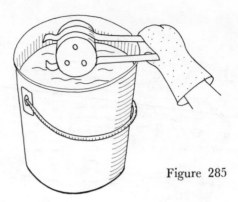

Figure 285

ment flask from the kiln and place it on the end of the arm of the centrifuge, the concave side with the holes facing in toward the center. Place it directly behind the crucible, meshing the open toe into the sprue gate. (Figure 284.) Hold the centrifuge arm firmly with the right hand, release the pin with the left, and then jump out of the way as quickly as possible. The centrifuge will start spinning, and the centrifugal action will force the hot metal through the toe of the crucible and through the sprue gates into the impressions.

The centrifuge will spin for about a minute. When it stops, remove the flask and plunge it into a pail of cold water. (Figure 285.) It is very hot, and will cause boiling up, so, again, be quick to get out of the way. The hot plaster investment will dissolve immediately in the water, and if any bits of plaster remain on the castings they can be scraped out later with a sharp tool. The process of casting is now completed. (Figure 286.)

Nip off the sprue pins and place the casting in a pickling solution—10 per cent sulphuric acid, or Sparex—for about an hour. Then you can file any rough spots smooth and polish the piece with a series of abrasives: tripoli, the coarsest; then white diamond, and finally rouge for a high-gloss finish.

Figure 286

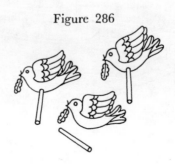

Where quantity is not a factor, that is, if you are making a one-of-a-kind piece, it is not necessary to make a rubber mold of the object. The model would be cast directly into the plaster investment and would in itself become the lost wax, being later burned out of the investment. The steps would be these: wax model to plaster to burnout oven to centrifuge and finis. The purpose of the rubber mold is to have a permanent impression of the model, to be used for as many more reproductions as you wish.

Carving sculptural models is a specialized craft, but very interesting pieces can be made by using wax rods, beads, wires, and preformed blanks that need only a touch-up from a heated tool to make them unique.

Waxes of ring settings can be bought, and both prong and bezel settings are available, ready to be cast, to fit standard-size stones. Beads, pendants, chess sets, figurines, an earring—anything can be duplicated by centrifugal casting. And the best thing about it is that convolutions and involutions are not the problem that they are in most other methods of reproduction. Centrifugal casting is almost foolproof.

"Head of a Man." Jean Dubuffet. Mixed media. 1946. Made from tar, cement, white lead, plaster, and glue. This was the period of experimentation with new media, and the artist went on to create monumental sculptures in plastic resin. Courtesy Nathan Cummings Collection. Photo by Malcolm Varon, New York.

13

Plastics

The first synthetic plastic that we know of was celluloid, and the first use for celluloid that we know of was for billiard balls. We have come a long way since that first billiard ball, and today the list of possibilities for the use of plastics is long indeed. As science moves forward, the artist finds more and more choices among these industrial compounds with which to work, and it sometimes is difficult to decide which one to use. Synthetic molecules called monomers are made to join together to form more complex molecules called polymers; and it is this polymerization that produces the plastic resins.

The three most popular resins used by the artist-craftsperson today are acrylic, epoxy, and polyester. Liquid plastics are toxic in the hardening stage, but acrylic is the least noxious of the liquid resins. Even so, *the studio should always have adequate ventilation,* and sometimes it is advisable to take further precautions by using gloves, masks, or goggles if any discomfort becomes evident.

In general, the synthetic polymer resins fall into two categories: the thermoplastics, which can be softened by heat and re-formed any number of times; and the thermosetting types, which, once hardened, will never deform. Some harden by themselves, some need a catalyst to initiate the chemical changes that take place in the process of setting, or curing.

Acrylic, which is a thermoplastic, can be heated and re-formed many times over, like wax. It comes in the form of clear resin; acrylic medium and gel, which dry clear and colorless; and the pigmented paints, which dry opaque, or if diluted heavily with water, will dry translucent.

Acrylic is used just as it comes from the can or jar or tube. It hardens on exposure to air. Acrylic is also available formed into sheets under such trade names as Lucite and Plexiglas, and in rods, cubes, and scraps—which are leftovers from manufacturing processes.

When pouring liquid resin, you usually need a form to contain it and a separator to keep it from adhering to the base (and the sides). These can all be bought from your supplier, or you can construct a form from wood, clay, or plasticine, and use oil or grease or Saran or Mylar for the separating agents.

Every resin has its own cement, but many of the resins are themselves adhesive and will bond to any surface they come in contact with. A separator is always used, unless bonding is desired. Liquid acrylic will cement two pieces of acrylic together. Liquid catalyzed epoxy will cement two pieces of epoxy, but some resins should not be intermingled, for they might react chemically (and this could be very dangerous). Always get the information on glues from your supplier.

THERMOPLASTICS

First, suppose you make yourself a plastic sheet from clear liquid acrylic. You will need the resin and two identical pieces of glass from the hardware store. Coat the glass with a thin film of oil of any kind, and then tape them together all along three edges with strong masking tape. Insert the handle of a tablespoon into the fourth side, and pour clear acrylic into this glass sandwich, using the spoon as a funnel so that the liquid flows down without spilling. (Figure 287.) Leave the piece undisturbed for a few hours to allow the plastic to harden, then remove the glass casing and you will have a nice smooth sheet of clear acrylic. Another way to do this would be to pour a little of the liquid resin into a sheet of Saran Wrap or a pan that is coated with Teflon. It won't stick to these surfaces, and if you immediately swish the liquid around you can form a film that will harden very quickly as it is exposed to the air.

It is possible to color the sheet by using a small amount of transparent pigment in a mixture of three parts acetone to two parts water. The acetone acts as a penetrant, and it must be washed off quickly, so as not to ruin the surface of the hard, glossy sheet. Or you could make your sheet a patterned one by impregnating a drawing or a painting that has been done on thin absorbent paper or cloth. To do this, brush or pour a thin film of resin onto a sheet of Saran, and lay the drawing carefully down in it. Brush it over with another thin coat to cover it, and lay another sheet of Saran on top of that. Press this down by stroking it from the center outward to the edges, using a brayer or a glass to roll over it to remove any bubbles. Allow it to harden, then remove the Saran, and your painting or drawing will be sealed in. You could add some surface interest by removing the top piece of Saran after a few minutes and lightly drawing a design in the tacky gel with a toothpick. When it hardens, the design will be visible on the clear surface.

You can achieve the effect of stained glass by applying pools of colored resin to a sheet of clear, rigid plastic. Mix some sand with resin, and apply it to the backing sheet in a design of enclosed areas, to simulate the leading. Mix small quantities of clear resin with transparent organic colors (from your plastics supplier), and pour these colored resins into the cloisons that have been formed by the sand ridges. Allow the piece to dry flat, and when it is dry and hard, you can hang it in a window to catch the sunlight.

As your panel has been made from thermoplastic acrylic, you might shape it by manipulating it in a warm oven, perhaps draping it over an oven-proof mold such as a Pyrex bowl. Or you might try to slump it into the mold, which would be more difficult, and too much time in the heat could cause it to break down chemically. If you were to make several of these shaped pieces, you could join them together with a compatible bonding agent, or touch them lightly at point of contact with a heated tool, causing them to fuse instantly. The join could then be sanded and painted with resin to smooth it over, or with acrylic paint to add color. (But the opaque paint, of course, would affect the crystal-clear transparency.)

In Byzantine days, artists scribed a thin sheet of pure gold with a design and then laminated it between two pieces of glass by fusing it all together in

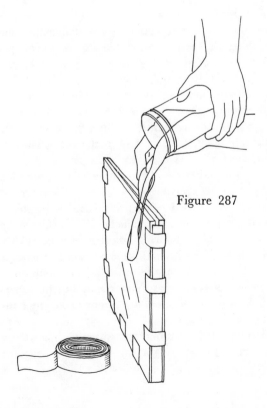

Figure 287

a furnace. You can do the same thing by scribing a design on gold leaf, then putting it between two sheets of the acrylic and fusing it in the kitchen oven at 275°. You could manipulate this laminate into an undulating free form by wearing heavy oven mitts and maneuvering it while it is hot and flexible; but as soon as the desired shape is reached, you would have to remove it from the oven to prevent it from slumping. Once it cools, it will hold its shape; but you can reshape it if ever you want to by simply reheating it.

Figure 288

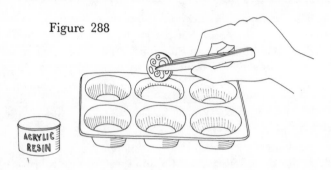

Embedding in Resin

Objects can be embedded in plastic very easily by using a mold such as a small milk carton or a paper cup or some shaped aluminum foil or a caster cup—anything that will contain the liquid as you pour it. If you wanted to mount a special coin, for instance, you could set it into clear acrylic resin and it would be visible from all angles. Coat the inside of the container with a separating agent, which could be wax or grease, and fill it halfway with the liquid resin. (Figure 288.) Let it harden to a loose gel, which will take ten to twenty minutes. Then brush some acrylic over the coin to minimize air bubbles, drop it onto the tacky plastic, and pour in more resin to fill the form. Let it set for a day or so to harden completely, then remove the form and you will have made an acrylic block. You could make a drawer pull or a paperweight by molding the resin in a small coffee measure, and you could embed some translucent object such as a painted Venetian bead or a slice of Italian millefiori glass. Or you could make a whole bowlful of baubles by pouring colored resin mixed with sequins or glitter of any sort into glass Christmas-tree ornaments, using a funnel made from waxed freezer paper. When the resin has set, break away the molds to expose the hardened plastic forms. You might do the same thing with a child's rubber ball as the mold, and you might make the balls multicolored by layering various colors of the resin.

You could follow this bedding procedure with anything you wanted to display or preserve, just so long as your mold was large enough to contain the object.

Resin Films

Acrylic hardens very quickly when exposed to air, and if you were to make a circular loop out of thin wire and dip it into the liquid resin it would form a film that would harden almost immediately. You could dangle some films from the arms of a mobile and hang them indoors or out to catch the light as they move in the breeze. Or you could glue several of them together to form the petals of a blossom. They can be colored by using acrylic paints or organic colorants, to be either opaque or transparent. Little light objects such as feathers or glass chips or snips of colored paper could be impressed into the films before they harden, and holes for stringing could be punched in later by piercing them with a hot needle. Swizzle sticks are sometimes made from thermoplastics, and if you heat the ends of two of these rods in the flame of a candle, you can weld them together, and they could be built up to form a stabile, or freestanding sculpture. (Figure 289.)

Plastic resins for use in sculpture have been a boon to the artist-craftsperson. Most of the resins that we use are clear, and aggregates of various kinds can be added to achieve various effects. They can be used to add interest or to supply bulk or perhaps to decrease weight. There are many things to experiment with: vermiculite, shredded asbestos or mica, marble dust, glass chips, plaster, talc, or even coffee grounds. Plastics impregnated with imitation stone and bronze powders can be cast in a mold to look just like bronze sculpture when finished. Artist's acrylic medium (which is a resin) can be mixed with sand and will look just like cement and be just as strong, if not stronger, when hardened. It can be used as the glue in papier

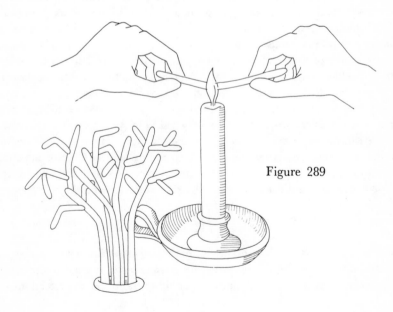

Figure 289

mâché, which could be modeled like clay while moist or chiseled like stone when dry.

If you wanted to layer objects or create an interesting optical effect, you could do it by molding successive pourings of the resin. A translucent color construction, for instance, could be obtained by layering various colors of transparent acetate papers. Pour a layer of acrylic into the mold and let it gel a little; then coat an acetate with the resin and lay it carefully on the slightly gelled surface; pour another layer of acrylic, let it harden slightly, add another acetate, and continue doing this as many times as you wish, allowing each layer of the resin to gel a little and ending with a sealing layer of the acrylic. Then let it harden and remove it from the mold. You might try this with metal foils or chunks of colored glass or faceted transparent "jewels" to make some very interesting refractive effects in the clear plastic.

Relief Sculpture

A high-relief sculpture could be made in much the same way. It could be built up by layering the resin so that thicker areas would gel by stages and the setting would go on at an even rate, to avoid cracking or crazing due to uneven curing. You could also make a relief sculpture by coating a piece of masonite or plywood with a thick layer of acrylic modeling paste. Let it harden a little, then dribble a design on, using a cone of waxed freezer paper to funnel the paste to the areas where you want it. After a short drying period, you could carve more design into it, and then, when the surface has fully hardened, give it a coat of clear acrylic for protection.

Another simple way to make a bas-relief is to fill up a flat container with resin, and when it has gelled to a fairly stiff consistency, partially embed small objects to give it a surface interest. These could be transparent objects such as glass rods or chips or plastic beads, or they could be opaque —watch parts or nuts and bolts, or designs cut from a plastic foam drinking cup or packaging material or from screening. Hang these on the wall or use them as printing blocks, just as you would use wood or linoleum blocks.

The self-hardening, relatively nontoxic acrylic polymer can be used in many ways by adventurous artists and craftspeople. While other liquid resins are used in the same manner, acrylic is the most popular, because it doesn't require a catalyst and is reasonably safe to use as long as there is adequate ventilation in the studio. With supervision, it can be handled by youngsters and by oldsters, and it dries to a clear, hard, and durable finish.

THERMOSETTING PLASTICS

Polyester and epoxy resins both require the use of a catalyst to make the transformation from liquid to solid. This hardening or curing process takes place by chemical interaction, and it is very important that the directions for each resin be followed explicitly. When you are ready to pour these liquids, add the catalyst; too much or too little of this agent will interfere with the hardening of the resin, and it is most important that you know what type of plastic you are dealing with and that you read all instructions carefully.

The volatile chemicals formed during the curing stage of epoxy are very dangerous, and good ventilation is an absolute necessity. Polyester is less toxic and therefore is most often recommended for studio work, but good ventilation is still a necessity, and, as the catalyst used to make it harden can cause eye irritation, it might also be advisable to wear goggles.

Epoxy and polyester resins are thermosetting. That is, once cured they can never be re-formed and are not affected by heat. A reinforced thermosetting resin is perhaps the most permanent, impermeable, strong material known. The reinforcing material is often Fiberglas cloth, which is made from glass threads; it is very strong, and being transparent, it is widely used with epoxy when large areas are involved. By strengthening the resin with the woven cloth, you obtain a crystal-clear, hard, almost indestructible finish. The term Fiberglas as applied to boats usually means that the surface of the hull has been given a coating of the glass cloth embedded in epoxy resin; the hull will be practically impervious to the ravages of sun and salt water.

You can use this unbeatable combination for making "soft" or "hard" constructions in which an armature is used. The "armature" could be Fiberglas cloth (or mat, which is a heavier, nonwoven material), and it could just be draped on itself to a pleasing sculptural composition, or it could be laid on a formed base, in either case frozen into position forever by the application of epoxy resin.

RESIN LAMINATES

You can make a rigid decorative panel by laminating a painting with a Fiberglas cloth in polyester or epoxy resin. Cut the cloth to the same size as the painting, and cut a piece of Saran several inches larger. Lay the painting face down on the wrap (which acts as the release agent), and brush on a thin coat of catalyzed resin. Let it stand until it gels slightly—about fifteen minutes—then carefully lay the piece of Fiberglas cloth on the tacky surface. (Figure 290.) Dab on another thin coat of liquid resin, brushing from the center outward to remove any air bubbles. When it has gelled again, apply another coat and let it dry undisturbed until it is quite hard. Then turn the whole thing over and brush several coats of resin onto this side in the same way, letting each thin coat dry to a gel; for that matter, let them dry completely. You could build up as many coats as you wanted, to get a desired thickness, and you could imbed another piece of Fiberglas cloth on either side if you needed the added strength. When it has hardened completely, you will have made a glassy, stiff, flat Fiberglas laminate.

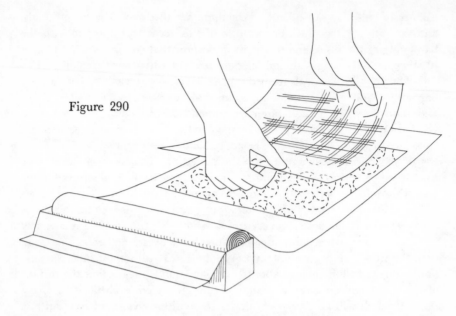

Figure 290

DRAPE MOLDS

If you wanted to do the same thing in a curved shape, you would spray the outside of a bowl or a can or a box with a separating agent and drape the Fiberglas cloth over it, so that it acts as a drape mold. Apply several coats of resin, and when it is cured, it will have assumed the shape of the form beneath it. The edges can be straightened by trimming them with a sharp knife or hacksaw before it sets completely; but once it has set, it requires an electric cutter or a vigorous filing and sanding. Unlike other casting materials, such as metal or plaster, plastics show practically no shrinkage. Humid weather might affect the drying, and polyester has a tendency to turn cloudy if moisture forms during the curing stage.

Plastics can be used to form delicate jewelry by the use of a thermoplastic resin, or mammoth sculptures by the use of a reinforced thermosetting resin, perhaps built on an armature of expanded foam. Large sculptures and constructions are made in exactly the same way as small studio pieces. They can be cast in liquid resin, or they can be assembled from sheets or blocks or rods or scrap pieces available from the supply houses. Separate modules can be anchored together with transparent or opaque fasteners, with polymer glue, or sometimes with heat. They can be reinforced with a colorless additive such as chopped Fiberglas or opaque ones such as powdered gypsum or shredded asbestos. They can be bulked out with batting or foam or extruded down by being forced through a mesh screen to form thin filaments. They can be engraved, etched, sandblasted, or faceted. They can be painted, sprayed, or left unadorned, in their own high luster.

FOAMING PLASTICS

Foaming plastics are made by mixing two chemicals together at room temperature (about 70°). They expand to ten to fifteen times their original bulk, and when directed into a form or mold, they will quickly and readily assume its shape. They must be poured as soon as they are mixed, because the foaming action starts almost immediately. If they are not contained, they could foam you right out of the room, and the higher the temperature of the room the more they will expand. Molds of any kind may be used, but the foam is highly adhesive and so the parting agent is very important. Polyvinyl alcohol is often used as a separator, and so is Saran, another vinyl, but they

"The Hussar." An extended-palette painting. Semi-bas-relief in synthetic media. Made with plastic foam, liquid metals, polymer paints, acrylic and epoxy resins, all man-made. Contemporary. American. A. Raymond Katz. Courtesy Barney Weinger Gallery, New York.

Figure 291

are by no means universal and you must always check instructions carefully for proper use.

Plastic foams are extremely toxic in their volatile form. Ventilating precautions must be strictly observed, and as some are strong eye irritants, goggles and perhaps gloves and masks should be worn.

Foaming plastics are light in weight and will reach into any empty space, but how forceful the expansion is will have to be determined *in situ.* In a commercial plant, for instance, a polyurethane foam used in molded furniture is mixed by machine and injected by spraying from a gun. Its expansion rate might be anywhere from four to forty times its original bulk, and the manufacturer can regulate the density and therefore the strength that is needed in the finished piece.

Liquid resins are often used in combination with foams, but sometimes they will melt the foam, and so an isolating layer—perhaps plaster of Paris —is advisable. After that, the combinations are limitless.

In the 1960s the pop artist worked in whimsical ways with this new toy. He sewed up a canvas shape on a sewing machine and then draped it and propped it until it fell into the position he wanted. Then he injected into it a foaming plastic and retained the canvas mold as an integral part of the sculpture. In the same manner, he could have used any flexible or inflexible material as the container.

Plastic foam can be used in casting in a lost-wax technique. You could carve a Styrofoam sculpture, using an electric knife and heated ice pick as your tools. Then you could mold the sculpture with liquid latex, melt away the Styrofoam over low heat (with ventilation!), and fill the latex form with clear acrylic, polyester, or any plastic resin (Duco cement, Elmer's glue, even acrylic paints are all resins and will harden in a few hours).

This new synthetic medium has opened whole new horizons for the craftsperson. Stage designers use ever newer polymers for mock-ups and for flats and scrims. Scientists use plastic for mounting and preserving specimens. Architects and decorators use it for buildings, both outside and in. Engineers use it for prototypes, and experimenters have built houses of expanded plastics and have actually lived in them quite comfortably. (Figure 291.)

When you consider that Thomas Edison made his first incandescent-lamp filament from cotton string coated with lampblack, it stretches the mind to think what he might have come up with in this new era of synthetics.

The impact of plastics on our daily life is everywhere. We see it in plastic bags made from polyethylene, flexible bottles made from polyvinyl, rigid chairs and soft pillows made from urethane foam, typewriters molded from polyester, packaging made from polystyrene. In Texas, the Astrodome is covered in acrylic; in Mexico City, for the 1968 Olympics, the floor of the stadium was made from poured plastic; in Montreal, for the 1976 Olympics, the facilities were built almost totally from man-made synthetics. Today playing fields, racetracks, ski slopes, and tennis courts are being so constructed, always to be in prime condition regardless of the weather. Artists and sculptors as well as craftspeople are constantly exploring new avenues for this medium, which is but an infant, with a long way to go.

Glossary

A

ACRYLIC   A thermoplastic synthetic resin

ADDITIVE SCULPTURE   Sculpture made by adding to a core

AGGREGATE   An inert material added to a sculpturing material for strength
   or texture

ALLA PRIMA   A final effect achieved in the first application of paint

ANNEAL   To remove inner stress by heat

AQUARELLE   True, transparent water color

AQUATINT   An etching made by working on a soft, crackled ground

ARBOR   A shaft on which cutting and polishing tools are mounted

ARM   The part of a mobile that supports the hanging device

ARMATURE   A framework on which a sculpture is built

ART GLAZE   An unusually striking ceramic glaze

ARTIST'S PROOF   The first print, which the artist uses to check for errors

ART NOUVEAU   Curvilinear motifs popular in the late-nineteenth century

ASSEMBLAGE   A sculpture made from a collection of articles

B

BACK-BAND   A wood molding milled in an L shape which can serve as
   framing for a stretched canvas

BACKSTRAP LOOM   A loom made taut by anchoring the loose ends of the
   warp to a strap slung across the back of the weaver

BALL PEEN   A hammer with a round head

BAREN   A small, flat pad of woven bamboo leaves used for impressing a print from a wood block

BAS-RELIEF/LOW RELIEF   Wall sculpture that is raised only slightly from the background

BASSE-TAILLE   Transparent enameling on engraved metal; also known as French enameling

BATIK   A wax-resist method of textile printing

BATT (ALSO BAT)   A hardened circle of plaster of Paris used to extract moisture from clay

BATTEN   A flat stick used to pack the woof threads into place

BEAT   To pulp

BEATEN   Woven

BEATING   Pressing the rows of weaving together with a batten or a comb

BEND   A pyrometric cone bends over to one side when it melts

BEVEL   An edge cut obliquely

BEZEL   A thin wall or rim of metal that anchors a gem stone in place

BISQUE   A ceramic piece that is fired but not glazed; also called biscuit ware

BITTEN IN   Etched with acid

BLEED   A color that does not set but affects subsequent overlays

BLOCKOUT   A resist

BLOCK-RESIST PRINT   A print made by clamping cloth between two mirror-image relief blocks (the design acts as a barrier to the dye)

BONE DRY   Said of an unfired ceramic piece that is air dry

BORAX   Used to prevent oxidation during heating

BOULE   A synthetic gem formed by a build-up of chemical crystals

BRAD   A thin nail with a very small head

BRAYER   A small rubber roller with a handle

BRAZE   To join two metals without using excessive heat

BRAZING ROD   A rod of copper and zinc that will fuse to other metals with heat and flux

BREAK THE MOLD   To open a mold very carefully

BRIDGE   A support for the hand to keep it off work in progress

BRILLIANT CUT   The classic faceting of a gem, which enhances its brilliance with the least loss of weight

BRITTLE   Said of clay that fragments easily

BROWN COAT   The structural masonry of a wall

BURIN   An engraving tool with a small, angled point like a lozenge

BURL   A knot in wood used ornamentally

BURR   A rough edge raised in tooling metal or in sharpening tools

BUTT JOINT   A right angle made by joining two pieces of wood, broad edge to narrow edge, without mitering

BUTTON   The plasticine that holds the waxes for casting. The excess metal in the sprue hole

C

CABOCHON   A gem stone polished to a smooth convex shape, not faceted; cab

CALLIGRAPHY   Ornamental, expressive penmanship

CAME   A grooved lead bar that supports the individual design pieces in leaded glass

CANING   Weaving strips of rattan to form the seat or back of a chair

CARAT   A unit of weight for gem stones (one carat is one fifth of a gram)

CARBON BLOCK   A small brick that is resistant to heat

CARBORUNDUM   A fine grinding stone

CARDING   Combing fibers between two brushes to prepare them for spinning

CARRIER   A cord used to support knots in macramé

CARTOON   A preliminary sketch drawn exactly to size

CASEIN   A binder of milk glue used for opaque water-color paints

CAST   A reproduction made from a mold; a casting

CATALYST   A chemical agent that initiates polymerization

CAUSTIC   A corrosive substance

CENTER OF GRAVITY   The point of rest or balance

CHALCEDONY   A semiopaque gem stone

CHAMFER   A bevel at a bottom edge of a stone, usually at a 45° angle

CHAMPLEVÉ   An etched area on metal that is filled with enamel

CLEAVAGE   The breaking of a stone in such a way as to be harmonious with the crystalline structure

CLEAVE   To split or divide

CLOISON   An enclosure made of thin wire

CLOISONNÉ   Enamels fused inside a wire enclosure

CLOVE HITCH   A double knot used in macramé

COEFFICIENT OF EXPANSION   The degree of change in size caused by heat

COIL   A rope of clay used in hand building

COLD-PRESSED PAPER   A smooth water-color paper

COLLAGRAPH   A print made from a low-relief collage

COLLARING   Forming a narrow neck on a wheel-thrown clay pot

CONE   A small pyramid made of chemicals that will melt at a certain known temperature

COPE   The upper half of a sand-casting flask

CORRUGATED FASTENERS   Thin, wavy metal strips used to strengthen butt joints

COUCH   To lay flat

CRACK THE KILN   To open the door very slightly and very cautiously

CRAZING   The forming of minute cracks

CROWN   The part of a polished gem stone that is above the girdle. The decorative flange at the top of a lampshade

CRUCIBLE   A highly refractory heating vessel

CURE   To harden to a final form; to mature

D

DABBER   A soft pad holding the wax ground used in etching

DAPPING BLOCK   A concave form used for shaping metal

DEBUBBLIZER   A chemical brushed on wax models to prevent bubbles from forming during casting

DECKLE   The upper frame that encloses the wet pulp in papermaking

DEFORM   To distort or change form

DENTS   The notches in the reed on a loom

DISK   A flat, circular piece of metal

DISTRESSED WOOD   Wood having nicks and scratches and scars from age

DOP STICK   The tool used to hold a gem while grinding it

DOUBLET   A jewel made by laminating two stones together for increased depth

DOWEL, DOWELING   A length of round wood

DRAG   The lower half of a sand-casting flask

DRAPE MOLD   A mold in which the outside shape is utilized

DRY MOUNT   Plastic film applied in a pressing machine with heat

DRY POINT   An intaglio printing process in which a burr is left on the plate by the pointed needle that directly inscribes the line

E

EAR   A depression that receives the pin for aligning the pieces in a two-piece mold

EGG-OIL EMULSION   A painting medium

EGG TEMPERA   A water-color technique used for permanent, fine works

ELECTROFORMING   Constructing a design by electroplating metal

EMERALD CUT   A stepped-up faceting of a gem stone that is rectangular in shape

ENGOBE   Colored slip used for decorating pottery

ENGRAVING   An etching that is made with very fine lines

EPOXY   A thermosetting synthetic resin

ETCH   To incise

ETCHING   An intaglio print made from an acid-incised plate

F

FACETING   The grinding and polishing of a gem stone into small, flat refractive planes

FAIENCE   Earthenware decorated with colorful, opaque glazes

FELTING   Twisting fibers together before feeding them into the spinning wheel

FELTS   Absorbent pads used to dry the sheets in papermaking

FERRULE   The ring used to anchor the bristles of a brush

FETTLE   To remove mold marks on a ceramic piece

FETTLING KNIFE   A thin, flexible knife

FIBERGLAS   Filaments of glass woven into cloth

FILIGREE   Lacy patterns formed with fine wire

FILLER   A carrying cord used in macramé

FIN   A hanging device on a mobile

FINDINGS   Accessories used for completing jewelry

FINE SILVER   Silver that assays at 99.9 per cent pure; has a higher melting point than sterling

FIREBRICK   A brick made of clay that withstands high temperature

FIRE SCALE   A heavy oxidation

FIRING   Bringing a ceramic or enameled object to a high temperature in a kiln in order to mature it

FLASK   The container used for making a mold

FLORET   A small cluster used in tie-dye

FLOW   To melt

FLUX   A chemical used to remove oxides from metals to be joined by soldering: it combines with the impurities to remove them

FOOT   A supporting base on a bowl

FOURCHETTES   Strips that are sewn between the fingers of a glove

FRENCH ENAMEL   Engraved metal overlaid with transparent enamel; also known as basse-taille

FRESCO   A painting done on moist plaster

FULCRUM   A prop or support for a lever

FURNITURE   Anything that goes into a kiln to aid in stacking the pieces for firing

FUSE   To melt; also, to join

G

GATHER   The glob of molten glass collected on the end of a hollow rod for blowing

GAUGE   A standardized unit of measure

GEM   A precious or semiprecious stone used for decoration or in industry; a jewel

GEODE   A hollow stone with a crystalline formation under the skin

GESSO   A plasterlike paste made of whiting and animal-hide glue

GILDING   Applying gold leaf

GIORNATA   A day's work

GIRDLE   The widest part of a cut gem, separating the upper facets from the lower ones

GLASSINE   A thin, transparent plastic sheet

GLAZE   A vitreous powder that fuses to coat and seal a ceramic piece; a thin, transparent final layer on a painting

GOLD LEAF   Very thin foil made of gold

GOUACHE   An opaque water color

GOUCH   The opening of a glove trank into which the thumbpiece fits

GOUGE   A beveled chisel

GRANULATION   Droplets of metal fused to a parent metal without using solder

GRAPHITE   A highly refractory carbon compound

GREENWARE   A clay piece that is finished but not yet fired

GREEN WOOD   Lumber that is not fully dried

GRISAILLE   Crushed glass and earth colors used in early stained-glass work. Also, monochrome painting executed in gray tones

GRIT   A disk or band with abrasive particles impregnated

GROG   Clay fired and then crushed and added as an aggregate to sculpturing clay

GROGGY   Coarse clay containing a high percentage of grog

GROUND   An acid-resistant compound through which a design is drawn in etching

GROUT   A light mortar used to fill crevices

GUM TRAGACANTH   A gummy extract used as a light adhesive

GUSSET   A wedge of material used to give width to a handbag

H

HALF DROP   Lowering a printing roller or block by half its diameter or length for each run-through

HALF HITCH   A simple knot, used in macramé

HANK   A skein of yarn not yet formed into a ball

HARNESSES   The frames on which the heddles are hung to guide the pattern in weaving

HEDDLES   Vertical wires on a loom that keep the warp threads in sequence

HEISHI   Tiny beads made from stone or shell cylinders

HIGH RELIEF   Wall sculpture that extends far out from the background

HOLDING CORD   The bar on which macramé lace is started

HOOKER   A hooked needle used for rugmaking

I

IMITATION JEWEL   A simulated stone resembling a gem stone

INDIA STONE   An aluminum-oxide grit that is impregnated with oil

INTAGLIO   A process in which a design is incised into a plate, so that an impression can be made on a softer surface

IN THE ROUND   To be viewed from all sides; freestanding

INTONACO The final layer of plaster on which a fresco is painted

INVESTMENT Moist plaster applied to a model to form a mold when hardened

J

JAPAN COLOR A fast-drying opaque matte paint

JEWELER'S-BENCH PIN A small rectangle of wood with a V-shaped cut-out on the front end

JUMP RING A link

K

KEEPER A small bar of metal or leather used to keep the tip of a belt in place

KEWPIE CATCH A slip-on catch that grips a stickpin to anchor it securely

KEYS Extensions in a mold used for aligning; also, triangles of wood used to stretch canvas fully

KILN A small furnace or oven, made of firebrick, that can be brought up to very high temperature. Used for firing ceramic wares and sculpture and for fusing enamels onto metal surfaces

KILN WASH A mixture of china clay and flint used to keep a kiln clean by preventing glaze from adhering

L

LACQUER A resin obtained from crushed insects. Sap of certain trees. A smooth paint.

LAMINATE To bond together two or more layers for increased thickness or strength

LAP A rotating abrasive disk

LAPIDARY The art of polishing precious stones; also, the craftsperson who works with them

LARK'S HEAD The knot that anchors the working cords in macramé

LATTICE STRIPS Long, thin strips of wood about one inch wide

LAY SHEET Paper put between waterleaves to keep them from sticking together in papermaking

LEADING Outlining a stained-glass design with lead strips. Cames.

LEAF Extremely thin sheets of gold or silver

LEATHER HARD The stage at which ceramic greenware is firm but not yet bone dry

LEG A small piece of wood that props a screen up off the workbench

LEHR The annealing oven used in commercial glassblowing

LIGHT TABLE   A work surface of glass with a light under it

LINOCUT   A linoleum block for making prints

LINSEED OIL   A drying oil, usually boiled to make it faster drying

LITHOGRAPH   A planographic print made from a stone

LUSTER   A high-gloss finish with iridescent colors

M

MACRAMÉ   Long cords knotted to form a pattern

MANDREL   A shaft or spindle

MARQUISE CUT   A many-faceted cutting of an oval gem stone

MARRIED METALS   A design formed from varied metals by soldering them
together like a jigsaw puzzle

MASK OUT   To block areas so they will remain in the background color

MASTIC   An adhesive or sealing agent

MAT   An inner framing for a picture, used under glass

MATRIX   A gem stone in which foreign crystals have become embedded

MATTE   Having no gloss

MATURE   To bring a clay or glaze to a high enough temperature so that it
becomes a finished object

MATURING POINT   The temperature at which all moisture is driven out of
clay; the temperature at which powdered glaze or enamel fuses

MEDIUM   The material or technique with which the artist works; in acrylic
painting, the term refers to the vehicle

MESH   The size of the holes in a screen or sieve; also, to strain through a
sieve

MEZZOTINT   An etching made by burnishing a roughened plate

MICA   A thin leaf of silicate mineral, usually colorless

MICROCRYSTALLINE   Synthesized from minute crystals

MILLEFIORI   The crosswise cuts of multicolored glass rods embedded in
clear glass canes

MINERAL SPIRITS   A petroleum distillate used as a paint thinner

MITER   To cut two pieces of wood at 45° so that they align perfectly at
right angles

MOBILE   An active sculpture having balanced units that move independently

MODEL   The original object from which a reproduction is to be made

MOHS' SCALE   A system of scaling the hardness of gem stones on a curve,
with diamonds at the top with a rating of 10

MOLD   A hollow form into which molten or plastic material is put to make
a casting. See also Mould

MOLD RELEASE   A surface coating that prevents a casting from sticking to
the mold; a separator or parting agent

MONOMER   A simple molecule

MORDANT   A biting agent that helps to set dye into the fibers; also, the acid used in etching

MOSAIC   A design made from small pieces of glass or ceramic set in a mortar

MOTIF   The central theme of a design

MOULD   The lower screen that holds the pulp in papermaking. In this sense, never spelled "mold"

N

NEEDLE FILE   A thin-pointed jeweler's file

NICHROME   A nickel-based alloy able to withstand high temperatures

NIELLO   A black design, made from metallic sulphides, fused to a silver base in jewelry

O

OAKTAG   A piece of stiff cardboard, such as a manila folder, that retains a hard edge when cut

OFFSET   A print made by transferring the design to a roller and then to the paper

ORANGE PEEL   The pebbly appearance of an underfired enamel

ORANGEWOOD STICK   A hard, fine-grained wooden instrument used in manicuring

OVERGLAZE   A decoration applied to a ceramic piece after glazing

OXIDATION   Tarnish—a discoloration of metal

OXIDATION FIRING   A glazing technique in which additional oxygen is introduced into a hot kiln

P

PAPIER MÂCHÉ   Layers of paper pressed together with a glue binder to form an object

PATINA   An enhancing film on an *objet d'art,* caused by oxidation and denoting age; may be artificially produced

PAVILION   The part of a polished gem stone that is below the girdle

PICK   One woof row in weaving

PICKLE   An acid cleaning solution for metals

PICTURE AGATE   An agate matrix that depicts a scene when slabbed open

PIN   A protrusion that fits into a depression to align a mold accurately

PLANISH   To smooth metal

PLANOGRAPH   A print made from a flat surface

PLASTIC   A synthetic resin; clay that is malleable

PLINTH   A block of wood or stone sometimes placed between a sculpture and its pedestal

PLIQUE-À-JOUR   Fusing transparent enamels to pierced metal with no backing, producing stained-glass effect

POLYCHROME   Many-colored

POLYMER   A chemical compound made by grouping molecules to form synthetic resins

PONTIL   An iron rod used to gather molten glass for blowing; a punty

POT   A handmade clay bowl or vase

PRECIOUS   A class of gem stones of high quality and intrinsic value

PRIME   To cover a surface with a coating that is receptive to paint

PROFILE   The contours of a picture-frame molding

PROOF   The first print that the artist studies for corrections on the plate

PYROMETRIC CONE   A small pyramid of refractory material that melts at a given temperature

Q

QUARTZ   A transparent gem stone; also powdered silica

R

RABBET   A groove along the window edge on the back of a picture frame

RAISING   Forming a bowl shape by hammering metal on the outside over a form

RAKU   Porous low-fired ceramic ware characterized by deep, subtly changing colors

REAM   Five hundred sheets of paper

REDUCTION FIRING   A method of producing depth of color on a clay body by reducing oxygen during firing

REED   A notched bar that keeps the warp threads aligned while weaving

REFRACTORY   Highly heat-resistant

RELIEF   A print made from a raised surface

REPEAT   A recurring design

REPOUSSÉ   A thin sheet of metal worked by raising a design from the back

RESIN   A natural gum obtained from trees; also, a synthetic plastic

RESIST   A substance applied to a surface to prevent ink or dye from penetrating that area

RET   To soak in water to aid in weakening fibrous material

RIVER   A soft vein in marble

ROCK   A rough, uncut gem stone

ROCK-HOUNDING   The hobby of searching for rough stones that might be transformed into gems

ROPE   A coil of clay used in hand building

ROSIN   A hard natural resin used in printmaking

ROTTENSTONE   Decomposed limestone

RUN   One series of a print; crack in glass

RUSHES   Long grasses or fibers that are twisted to form a thick cord

RUTILE   A common natural mineral, titanium dioxide

RYA   A type of knotting used in Scandinavian rugmaking

S

SALT GLAZE   A pitted glaze achieved by throwing salt into a hot ceramic kiln

SANDBLASTING   A method of etching away a design on a hard surface

SCOTCH STONE   A fine abrasive used for wet polishing

SCRIMSHAW   Engraved or carved ivory

SEAM   The point at which two *giornate* join in fresco

SEPARATOR   A substance that prevents adhesion

SGRAFFITO   The technique of scratching through a surface layer to expose the ground color

SHAG   The cut loops of a rug

SHED   The group of warp threads that are raised to allow the woof threads to interlace in weaving

SHELF   A firebrick platform used in a kiln

SHELLAC   A mixture of lac, sealing wax, and beeswax used in lapidary to anchor a stone to the dop stick

SHIM   A thin piece of metal used to keep two pieces of a mold from adhering to each other while hardening

SHORT   Not holding together well—said of clay

SHUTTLE   The needle used to carry the woof threads in weaving

SILK-SCREEN   A resist method of printing through a silk mesh

SILVER LEAF   Very thin foil made of silver

SINKING   Forming a bowl shape by hammering metal from the inside

SINNET   Vertically knotted cords, used in macramé

SIZE   A clear, thin adhesive used in applying gold leaf; any glutinous material used to give raw canvas a working surface; also, to make a pattern to exact dimensions

SKIN   The rough, outer layer of a rock; also, an uncut piece of leather

SKIVE   To thin leather by scraping layers from the back

SLIP   Liquid clay

SLIP CASTING   Making a ceramic object by pouring slip into a plaster-of-Paris mold

SLIPSTONE   A small grinding or polishing stone

SLUMP MOLD   One in which the inside shape is utilized

SLURRY   A thin abrasive mixture of grit suspended in a vehicle of oil or water. A thin slip

SLUSH   Enamels suspended in liquid for trailing

SOLDER   An alloy used to assist the fusing of two metal pieces

SPIDER   A heat-resistant metal-mesh support

SPIN   To turn a metal bowl on a lathe

SPINEL   A synthetic gem that has the molecular structure of a sapphire

SPOKES   The straight, stiff reeds that form the warp in basket weaving

SPRIGGED ON   Applied with slip to ceramic greenware—said of decoration

SPRING RING   A jump ring that can be opened easily; used as a catch in jewelry

SPRUE GATE   The opening in a mold that leads from the outside to the impression of the model

SPRUE PIN   A rod of wax, placed in a mold, that will be melted out later to leave an empty space

SQUARE   A right-angled ruler

STENCILING   A decoration painted on furniture, notably on Hitchcock chairs.

STERLING   An alloy of 925 parts silver and 75 parts copper

STILT   A minimum-contact support for a glazed ceramic piece during firing

STIPPLING BRUSH   A stiff, short-haired artist's brush

STITCH RESIST   A series of small running stitches that resist dyeing

STONEWARE   A dense, durable, nonabsorbent ceramic ware

STOP-OUT   A varnish used to protect some areas of the metal plate from corrosion in etching

STRETCH   To make fabric or paper taut for painting

STRETCHER   A wooden framework on which the canvas for an oil painting is stretched

SUBTRACTIVE SCULPTURE   Sculpture made by chipping away from a block

SUMI   The black ink used in Japanese monochromatic painting

SUMI-E   The black-and-white painting done with sumi

SUPPORT   A firebrick post used to support a shelf in the kiln; also, the material on which a picture is painted

SUZURI   A stone dish used for liquefying the ink stick in sumi painting

SWORD NEEDLE   A sharply pointed triangular needle used to sew leather

SYNTHETIC GEM   A man-made gem stone having the same properties as a natural one

T

TABBY WEAVE   A simple over-one-under-one pattern in weaving

TABLE   The flat top of a faceted stone

TAPA   Bark of the paper mulberry tree

TARLATAN   A stiff, loosely woven cloth used for wiping a printing plate

TEMPERED   Toughened, usually by heat

TEMPLATE   A pattern made of thin wood or metal outlining the contours of an object

TERRA COTTA   A coarse, red-brown earthenware usually left unglazed

TESSERAE   The small pieces of glass or ceramic used in mosaics

THERMOPLASTIC   Softens whenever heat is applied—said of resin

THERMOSETTING   Hardens permanently once cured—said of resin

THREAD   Anything used to weave a web of fabric

THROWING   Turning clay on a potter's wheel to form a ceramic pot

TIE-DYE   A method of dyeing with tie-resist patterns

TJANTING   A penlike tool that holds the melted wax in batik printing

TJAP   A small printing block used in batik for repeat design

TOLEWARE   Painted and decorated metalware

TOOL   To impress a design in leather with a pointed, rounded instrument

TOOLING LEATHER   A hide specially treated to retain impressions

TOOTH   The rough texture of water-color paper

TRANK   The main body of a glove pattern

TREADLES   Pedals used to raise the harnesses to change the shed in weaving

TUMBLED STONES   Rocks that have been polished by friction in a revolving drum, or tumbler

TUMBLING   A method of polishing gem stones by having them rub against each other in a gritty solution

TURNING   Forming a circular wood object on a lathe

TURQUOISE MATRIX   A turquoise gem with the impurity of other, darker minerals embedded

TUSCHE   A greasy substance receptive to printer's ink

U

UNDERCUT   A groove in a model that would impede the removal of the mold

UNDERGLAZE   Ceramic painting done before glazing

UNIVERSAL PERSPECTIVE   Having no set viewpoint, as if seen from all angles at once

UTILITY KNIFE   A metal handle that holds changeable razor blades

V

VEHICLE   The liquid with which pigment is mixed for painting

VENEER   A thin layer of wood used for facing

VENETIAN BEADS   Glass beads elaborately painted

VERMEIL   Sterling silver with a finish of 24-carat gold

VULCANIZE   To harden or cure rubber

W

WARP   The lengthwise threads on a loom, with which the woof is interlaced in weaving

WASH   A thin, transparent color used as a background in a painting

WASTE MOLD   A mold that is destroyed in the first casting

WATERGLASS   Clear glass rods used in glass sculpturing

WATERLEAF   A sheet of paper just removed from the mould and still water-laden

WAX EMULSION   A homogenized wax-and-oil painting medium

WAX ENCAUSTIC   A painting technique using wax and pigment

WAXES   Wax models ready for casting

WAX-RESIST   A method of painting by immunizing some areas with wax

WEAVERS   Flexible fibers that form the woof in basket weaving

WEB   A cloth formed by weaving or interlacing or knotting

WEDGE   To knead clay to remove all air bubbles

WELD   To fuse two pieces of metal by heat; to join two pieces of clay with slip

WHITE METAL   A soft alloy of no intrinsic value

WINDOW   The open portion bounded by the four sides of a picture frame or mat

WOODCUT   A relief print made from a wood block by cutting away the background

WOOF   The horizontal threads that are woven across the warp; the weft

Z

ZINC PLATE   A plate used for etching (instead of the traditional copper)

Index